# The Basque Series

DONALD T. GARATE

# Juan Bautista de Anza

*Basque Explorer in the New World*

University of Nevada Press   Reno   Las Vegas

The Basque Series
Series Editor: William A. Douglass

This book was funded in part by a grant from the Program for Cultural Cooperation Between Spain's Ministry of Education and Culture and United States Universities.

University of Nevada Press,
Reno, Nevada 89557 USA
Copyright © 2003 by
University of Nevada Press
All rights reserved
Manufactured in the United States
of America

Cover design by Erin Kirk New

The paper used in this book meets the requirements of American National Standard for Information Sciences—Permanence of Paper for Printed Library Materials, ANSI z.48-1984. Binding materials were selected for strength and durability.

University of Nevada Press
Paperback Edition, 2005

*This book has been reproduced as a digital reprint.*

[*Frontispiece:*] Map of eighteenth-century Northwest New Spain

Library of Congress
Cataloging-in-Publication Data

Garate, Donald T., 1950–
Juan Bautista de Anza : Basque explorer in the New World / Donald T. Garate.
p. cm.—(The Basque Series)
Includes bibliographical references and index.
ISBN 978-0-87417-505-9 (hardcover : alk. paper)
ISBN 978-0-87417-626-1 (paperback : alk. paper)
1. Anza, Juan Bautista de, 1693–1740.
2. Basques—Southwest, New—Biography. 3. Explorers—Southwest, New—Biography. 4. Explorers—Spain—Biography. 5. Southwest, New—Discovery and exploration—Basque. 6. Frontier and pioneer life—Southwest, New.
7. Southwest, New—History—To 1848.
8. Southwest, New—Biography.
I. Title. II. Series.
F799.a74  2003
979'.01'092—dc21                    2002155365

*In memory of the late*

*Doctor James E. Officer*

*Born July 28, 1924, Boulder, Colorado*

*Died May 27, 1996, Tucson, Arizona*

# Table of Contents

List of Illustrations — xi

Preface — xiii

Acknowledgments — xxi

**Chapter One**

Anza in Antiquity — 1

**Chapter Two**

Life in Hernani — 19

**Chapter Three**

The New World — 54

**Chapter Four**

The Cavalry of the Frontier — 82

**Chapter Five**

Apaches, Livestock, Politics, and Jesuits — 115

**Chapter Six**

The Final Years — 157

Appendix — 211

Notes — 227

Glossary — 289

Bibliography — 297

Index — 303

# *Illustrations*

### CHART
Anza family tree     33

### MAPS
Eighteenth-century-Northwest New Spain *frontispiece*     iv
Hernani     36

### DOCUMENTS
*(following page 114)*
Prescription written by Dr. Agustín Zabala, Hernani, 1699
Anza's letter to Father Oro, 1729
Anza's last page of letter to Father Nieto, 1729
Captain Anza's certification of receipt of "Arizona" silver, 1736
Fronteras Presidio, drawing by José de Urrutia, 1766
Janos Presidio, drawing by José de Urrutia, 1766

### SIGNATURES
| | |
|---|---:|
| Antonio de Anssa | 25 |
| Agustín de Zavala | 28 |
| María Estevan de Anssa | 38 |
| Juan Phelipe de Ansa | 39 |
| Miguel de Mendiguren | 69 |
| Joseph de Zubiate | 74 |
| Antonio Bezerra Nieto | 82 |
| Pedro Phelipe de Ansa | 85 |
| Gregorio Álvarez Tuñón | 87 |
| Nicolás de Oro | 93 |
| Pedro de Rivera | 111 |
| Phelippe Segesser | 122 |
| Agustín de Campos | 137 |
| Luis María Marciano | 140 |
| Joseph Toral | 145 |
| Carlos de Roxas | 152 |
| Juan Antonio de Rivera | 160 |
| Santiago Ruiz de Ael | 163 |

| | |
|---|---:|
| Francisco Xavier Moraga | 195 |
| Benito Crespo | 199 |
| Martín de Elizacoechea | 201 |
| Pedro de Echenique | 202 |
| Joseph Manuel Diaz del Carpio | 207 |
| Juan Bautista de Anza | 217 |
| Juan de Echagoyen | 217 |
| Francisco de Garduño | 218 |
| Tomás de Garnica | 218 |
| Domingo de Gomendio Urrutia | 219 |
| José de Gorraez | 219 |
| Blas de Gortazar | 219 |
| Juan Domingo de Guraya | 219 |
| Francisco de Longoria | 220 |
| Luis de Mendivil | 220 |
| Francisco Xavier de Miranda | 220 |
| Antonio Bautista de Morueta | 221 |
| Martín de Murrieta | 221 |
| José de Olave | 221 |
| José de Osorio | 221 |
| Gabriel Prudhom Bulrón Mújca | 222 |
| Claudio Antonio de Segura | 222 |
| Francisco Pérez Serrano | 222 |
| Juan de Sesma | 222 |
| Pedro Regala de Urias | 223 |
| Bernardo de Urrea | 223 |
| José de Usarraga | 223 |
| José Joaquín de Usarraga | 223 |
| Lorenzo de Velasco | 224 |
| Agustín de Vildósola | 224 |
| Juan Antonio de Vizarrón | 225 |
| Juan José de Zarasua | 225 |
| Andrés de Padilla | 225 |
| José Romero | 225 |
| Manuel José de Sosa | 226 |

### TABLES

| | |
|---|---:|
| Table 1. Muster Roll of the Janos Presidio, April 10, 1723 | 211 |
| Table 2. Silver Impounded by Juan Bautista de Anza, 1736 | 214 |

# Preface

The story of Juan Bautista de Anza, whether one is speaking of the father or of the son with the same name, is long overdue in the telling. The senior Juan Bautista de Anza, the subject of this volume, arrived in the New World in 1712 at the age of nineteen from the Basque village of Hernani in the Province of Gipuzkoa, Spain. He probably spoke only rudimentary Spanish when he arrived in Culiacán at the home of his mother's people, the Sasoetas. His skills in speaking and understanding the Spanish language undoubtedly improved quickly, however, as he found himself in one of the biggest melting pots in the New World. Culiacán had been a Spanish city for nearly two hundred years at that time. It was located on the coast of the Gulf of California in the Province of Sinaloa, Nueva España, or New Spain. Although Nueva España would become Mexico, that political entity, as we know it, did not exist in those years. It came into being only after independence was gained from Spain, after Juan Bautista de Anza and his youngest son with the same name had both been dead for decades. What was called "México" in their era was what we today know as "Mexico City." The senior Anza traveled through México on his way north. As far as we know, he was there on only one other occasion—when he delivered some important papers to the viceroy in the spring of 1722.

His life in the New World was destined to be played out hundreds of miles north of that great capital city, on the far northern frontier of Nueva España—partially in what would become the American Southwest. There, he quickly became involved in mining, ranching, soldiering, and politics. Although he was certainly not the first Basque among hundreds to arrive in Nueva Vizcaya, he was one of the first in the northernmost parts of what are today the Mexican provinces of Sonora and Chihuahua. As far as can be determined, he started the first three livestock ranches in what is today southern Arizona—the Guevavi, the San Mateo, and the Sópori. A fourth, the Sicurisuta Ranch, was also probably mostly, if not totally, located in Arizona. And he did all of it slightly less than two hundred years before the territory known as Arizona became a state. In fact, although he was one of the earliest European pioneers in the area, long before the United States of America became a political entity, it can be said that he was responsible, in part at least, for the naming of the forty-eighth state. As *justicia mayor*, or "chief justice," of Sonora in 1736, his handling of a remarkable, though controversial, silver discovery brought the name of an obscure ranch called "Arizona" into prominence. The legend that built up around the discovery in the years that followed inspired the naming of the state. That name, familiar to Anza and his Basque contemporaries, lost its meaning as the Basque language gradually ceased to be used during the great *mestisaje,* or "mixing," of cultures that created the Mexican race.

Having achieved success on all fronts—his mining interests booming, his cattle and sheep ranches flourishing, government and church officials in quasi-harmony after years of squabbling, and the dreaded Apaches more or less held at bay—Juan Bautista de Anza may have gone on to even greater accomplishments. Certainly he had many enterprising intentions—the discovery of a land route between Sonora and California not the least of them. A *cédula real,* or "royal decree," commending him for his outstanding work on the frontier was in the works. Things had probably never looked better. Unfortunately, that is when a small band of Apaches struck, leaving him to die on the hot desert ground. The great works that he had planned would now be held back for many years, until his three-year-old son of the same name could grow to maturity and take over where the father had left off. That son would rise to greater heights than his father had probably ever imagined, accomplishing acts so important to the history of the United States and Mexico that the name Juan Bautista de Anza should be on the tongue of every student who has ever completed a fourth-grade history class. Every United States citizen whose ancestors trekked west across the Great Plains and every person of northwestern Mexican ancestry should hold the name of Juan Bautista de Anza in the highest esteem.

Unfortunately, however, that is generally not the case. Seldom have two such dynamic individuals been so routinely ignored in the pages of history. These two men named Juan Bautista de Anza are almost unheard of in the three principal nations that should remember them—Spain, Mexico, and the United States. I suppose it is understandable that Spain has forgotten them: it was so long ago that the senior Juan Bautista de Anza left there seeking his fortune in the New World. It is also understandable, though reprehensible, that the United States should have forgotten them. After all, they were working for the wrong government well before the United States had its beginning. As for Mexico, Mexican historians have tended to prefer writing the history of Mexico after her independence. Thus, it is natural that they should have forgotten the senior Juan Bautista de Anza. However, his son and namesake was a Sonoran, born and raised in Sonora, Mexico, and although he died before Mexican independence, one would think he would be one of Mexico's great all-time heroes. Sadly, that is not the case.

While it is true that many Sonorans, especially those in Arizpe, remember the junior Juan Bautista de Anza and hold him in the highest regard as a soldier, explorer, colonizer, and even a distant relative, the majority do not. Nor do most of the old-time families on the Sonora River know that they are descended from the senior Juan Bautista de Anza. Many Californians, especially those descended from the Anza Expedition of 1776, revere the younger Anza almost to the point of worship. Yet, again, by far the majority of Californians have never heard of anyone by that name.

One reason that both Anzas are little known is that very little has been written about them in the secondary literature. Hubert Howe Bancroft,[1] writing in the late nineteenth century, was one of the first to bring the name Juan Bautista de Anza to light. Herbert Eugene Bolton,[2] in the 1920s and 1930s, almost succeeded in making the junior Anza's expeditions to California a household topic, in the Bay Area at least. Alfred Barnaby Thomas,[3] also writing in the 1930s, brought the Anza expeditions of New Mexico and Colorado to light after one hundred fifty years. None of the three, however, gave much, if any, personal or biographical information about their subject, and all touched only lightly on the life of either of the Anzas. Since their day, few authors have consulted primary documentation for further information concerning either Juan Bautista de Anza, but have simply retold, reiterated, and reinterpreted what the aforementioned scholars wrote so many years ago.

This has led to much confusion and misinterpretation over the years. Although the subject of this volume is the first Juan Bautista de Anza, we must here examine the two together in order to understand and dispel the many erroneous notions extant today. One example, which is easily traced, begins with the statement made by Bolton that Juan Bautista de Anza (the son) was a third-generation presidial captain.[4] Although this statement is technically correct, Bolton failed to point out that the first-generation presidial captain was the junior Anza's maternal grandfather. Not understanding that, the next generation of authors began to say that he was the third-generation frontier presidial captain with the surname of Anza.[5] The final misinterpretation came as authors began to write that there were three presidial captains on the northern Spanish frontier with the same name—Juan Bautista de Anza I, II, and III.[6] In an evident attempt to correct this misconception, one author makes the assumption that Pedro Felipe de Anza was the frontier military captain who was the father and the grandfather of our subjects.[7] As will be seen in chapters 2, 4, and 5, Pedro Felipe de Anza was a first cousin to the senior Juan Bautista de Anza, the godfather of his son, and in no way connected with the military. In reality, the senior Anza's father and father-in-law were both named Antonio.[8] His father was a pharmacist who never left the Basque country or set foot in the Americas.

Many other factors have caused confusion about the Anzas over the years:
- The extreme difficulty in reading and translating old seventeenth- and eighteenth-century Spanish documents[9]
- Variations in spelling of the eighteenth-century Spanish[10]
- The writing or the telling of their history by individuals who have not understood their language, times, or culture[11]

- The fact that there were two individuals in different generations with the same name[12]
- Unsubstantiated traditions,[13] family stories,[14] lack of proper footnoting,[15] present-day popular thinking,[16] speculation,[17] and local legend[18]

The intent of this life story, then, is twofold: (1) to dispel as much of the aforementioned misinformation as possible, and (2) to bring to light the voluminous known material that exists about the Anzas in a full and complete biography, thus allowing readers to determine for themselves the relative importance of these two individuals. This first volume, then, examines the life of the first Juan Bautista de Anza. Two more volumes are projected to cover the life of his son and namesake.

Two important side benefits emerged during the research for the present biography: (1) close ties between the families and generations of the *gachupín* (born on the Spanish peninsula) father and his *criollo* (born on this continent) children have been made, something that has seldom even been attempted in the history of the Southwest, and (2) a firm carryover of Basque cultural, language, and ethnic awareness between the Old and the New World has been established.

The ethnicity of so-called Spaniards of the eighteenth century who inhabited northern Mexico still requires extensive research before it will be understood. Such research will enable a refreshing, alternative viewpoint to the idea that "a Spaniard is a Spaniard is a Spaniard." However, it also poses challenges for the writer. The Basque language was then, and is now, a language of trade and commerce.[19] In that era it was almost exclusively a spoken language. Few, if any, writers of the eighteenth century ever made any serious attempt to write it. The official written language of the day was Spanish. Although we know that the Anzas and others of the Basque community on the northern frontier spoke their native tongue, Spanish was the language of government written by all servants of the king who were literate. So, the question arises when writing such a history, should modern Basque spelling be used to reflect the cultural and ethnic setting, or should modern Spanish rules apply even though they did not in the Anzas' day? Should Basque words, which would only have been spoken in their day, be used in a modern written work when they do not reflect the Spanish writing of the era? Depending on the situation, in this volume a combination of both Basque and Spanish has been used and footnoted with further explanation.

A word needs to be said as well about the author's translations of Anza's writings. Although Anza's handwriting and other evidence point to an adequate education, Spanish was a learned language for him. Consequently, he spoke—and wrote—a broken Spanish. Numerous letters that carry his signature were written by somebody else, such as the scribe, Manuel José de Sosa. Whether physically written by Anza himself or Sosa, the letters are from the mind of Juan Bautista de Anza, as evidenced by his affirming signature. Sosa's Spanish, however, is flawless and easily translates into flawless English, whereas Anza's own disjointed writing requires more imagination. Since any translation is merely an attempt to convey the meaning of the original author from one language to another, the translator could convert what he thinks, or even feels certain, Anza was trying to say into perfect English. In doing so, however, the feeling for how difficult the Spanish language was for Anza would be lost. Therefore, I have not attempted to create proper grammar and word choice in English when they are not there in the original Spanish.

Research for this project has taken ten years and could easily have run another ten years. However, at some point it becomes necessary to stop searching and start writing. Every detail about the life of Juan Bautista de Anza will never be known. Indeed, there are areas of his life about which little or nothing is known at this time. It is the author's firm belief that because of the scrupulous record keeping of colonial Spaniards, much of that information can, and probably will, come to light. And certainly, it is my hope that this work will not become the last word on the subject. I also hope that the meticulous footnoting of this work will facilitate the work of other authors in correcting and adding to what is written here.

It was not my original intent to write a biography of either of the men known as Juan Bautista de Anza. I first began work as historian at Tumacácori National Historical Park in 1990 with a vague knowledge that the junior Juan Bautista de Anza had led a group of colonists to San Francisco in 1776, and little else. However, three weeks prior to my arrival at Tumacácori, the U.S. Congress established the Juan Bautista de Anza National Historic Trail. Since the old mission at Tumacácori is an integral part of the trail, it became imperative that I know something about the man for whom it was named. Indeed, I was asked several questions about him and the expedition my first day on the job. Therefore, I began researching who he was and why he was deemed important enough to have a national historic trail named after him. That fall I attended the annual Anza Days[20] in Tubac, Arizona. Following that three-day celebration, I confronted the assistant manager with the fact that I had not heard the name "Anza" mentioned once in the three days of festivities. The result of the ensuing conversation was that I agreed to develop a living history presentation of the younger Juan Bautista de Anza and present it at Anza Days the following year.

Over the course of the next year, I read everything I could find in the secondary literature about both Juan Bautista de Anzas and started exploring primary sources to learn more. In doing so, I began to realize the tremendous impact these two individuals had on the history of the southwestern United States and northwestern Mexico—an impact and history that has gone largely unnoted. Furthermore, it soon became apparent that much of what was recorded was more legend than fact. As I prepared for the living history presentation about the younger Anza, I began to see the great injustice done these men by the fact that no one had ever written a biography of either of them.

Having published a number of local histories and biographies, I knew the monumental effort that would be required to write a biography of such dynamic individuals. I contacted various historians and scholars associated with universities and offered to help with the research if one of them would write the biography. They, too, evidently knew the immense amount of time and effort that would be required, because I found no takers. Dr. Jim Officer did agree to work with me after he had completed some other projects he was working on. Unfortunately, however, Dr. Officer passed away before that partnership could take effect.

Even so, by the time the Anza living history presentation had made its debut, I had committed so much time to research that I felt a major piece of my life would be wasted if what I had learned was not recorded and published. So, knowing full well that I would have to become obsessed with the project, I recommitted to completing the three-part biography of the two Anzas that Dr. Officer and I had outlined, whatever effort was required. Because of that commitment, I have been accused of being an Anzaholic,[21] of having an excessive interest in the Anzas because they were Basque, as am I,[22] and of having tunnel vision, with an interest in nothing else—to all of which I plead guilty. However, following in the Anzas' footsteps has provided some of the most memorable experiences of my life.

It has led me to Anza sites in four countries on two continents. I have marveled at the beauty of the countryside around Zisa, Benafarroa, France, where the Anza name had its origins. I have stood at the baptismal font in the ancient San Juan Bautista Church in Hernani, Gipuzkoa, Spain, where the senior Anza was baptized in 1693. I also felt history come to life a few hundred yards away in the *sala principal* of the town hall of Hernani, where his first known signatures were executed in 1709 and 1710.

In that very room in 1996 I had the opportunity of introducing some twenty descendants of the Anza Expedition of 1775–76 to nearly thirty Anza family members from the town of Hernani and the surrounding area. There, for the first time in over two hundred years, the Anzas learned of their illustrious *pariente* (relative) who went to America. A few days later, I had the unique privilege of introducing those same Californianos to another large group of descendants of Gregoria Anza, the daughter of the subject of this volume, at the beautiful Vildósola Estate in Elejabeitia, Bizkaia, Spain. What a privilege it was to exchange information about the Anza and Vildósola families with those beautiful people after a separation of over two hundred years. Probably the most emotional gathering came when we were able to bring some of the Anzas from Spain to meet their cousins from California, Arizona, and Sonora at the second annual Anza World Conference held in Arizpe, Sonora in 1997. After lunch on the closing day of the conference as we were all leaving for home, in the beautiful Cajón de Jiósari, those of us who knew the words sang "Agur Jaunak" ("Good-bye Gentleman"). There was not a dry eye in the crowd.

Across Spain, Mexico, and the United States, attics and archives, from tiny to enormous, have produced ancient documents relevant to the Anza history. Following Juan Bautista de Anza to the New World, I have stood at family mines and ranches at Aguaje, Tetuachi, San Mateo, Guevavi, Sicurisuta, and many other places in Sinaloa, Sonora, Chihuahua, and Arizona. The presidio sites of Janos, Chihuahua, and Fronteras, Sonora, where Anza was stationed, have inspired understanding of his story. Apache and Seri battlefields in Arizona's Chiricahuas, the Cerro Prieto of Sonora, and Tiburón Island in the Gulf of California have also been an inspiration.

It is not the purpose of this work to examine and critique the effectiveness of the Apache policies of Juan Bautista de Anza and his father-in-law, Antonio Bezerra Nieto, in comparison to French Indian policies in Canada—or to examine any other such technical subject, even though such things are totally relevant. The purpose of this work is to tell the story, plain and simple. With such extensive and important material, even that has proven to be a monumental task. The story is a spellbinding, gripping glimpse of the harsh, northern frontier of Nueva España, and what it took to get there from Europe and then survive. That alone, for those interested in a good, true narrative, should be sufficient.

The reader needs to be aware that this biography is written in a "story" form, which some critics will think contains excessive embellishment. Any writing of history and what constitutes "historical fact" is a controversial matter. We need all be aware that there is very little historical fact in any recorded history. Most of it is someone's interpretation of an event, and any event has as many interpretations as it has participants. Furthermore, as time passes we begin to see interpretations of interpretations of events, until we sometimes arrive at a representation quite different from the original happening. Thus, the never-ending search for primary materials.

Landscape can often tell us how an affair had to have transpired—what pass an attacking band of Apaches came through, for example. Weather patterns can provide an idea of the mechanics of such an occurrence and how it probably happened. Through mathematics, we can determine the phase of the moon on any particular night in history. However, even after determining that there was a full moon on a particular night, and knowing from weather patterns that there was an extremely small chance of storm, there is no guarantee that a cloud did not pass in front of the moon at 11:30 P.M. Nor can it be certain that at that late-night hour someone did not crawl out of his bedroll and build up a fire that had nearly died down. The only probable facts in all of this are that the Apaches did attack and a certain number of people were killed.

However, in such a scenario, limiting the narrative to the two above-mentioned facts, the only part of the story that is 100 percent known information, makes for such dull reading that the average person would never examine the story. And, even if the writer did limit the story to that, readers would visualize in their own minds how the occurrence transpired, without the benefit of the other mentioned supporting evidence. Thus, I have tried to examine every fact, record, probability, and possibility and then tell the "most likely" way that the event, or series of events, took place. On the other hand, this work is extensively footnoted for those who might wish to do further research or to critique it. Hopefully, the biography will do justice, in some small way, to the sensational story it attempts to record. I entertain one other hope, and that is that the reader might gain some portion of the immense pleasure that I personally found in researching and telling this story.

# Acknowledgments

On Saturday, May 25, 1996, we were informed of Jim Officer's serious condition and that he would not be able to join us as planned at the First Annual Anza World Conference held in Arizpe, Sonora, Mexico, to present his paper entitled "Anza in Arizona."

At eight o'clock on Sunday morning, May 26, 1996, we attended a special Mass held in his behalf in Nuestra Señora de la Asunción Cathedral in Arizpe. Five pages of notes and signatures were collected from all in attendance at the symposium, wishing him a speedy and full recovery.

At four o'clock that afternoon at Fronteras, Sonora, during the final session of the conference, we were informed that he was then able to talk and that the day before he had remembered and told his wife, Roberta, that he was supposed to be in Arizpe the next day. All in attendance cheered and applauded and our hopes were raised.

However, as we traveled home late that night our friend and colleague passed from this life. May he rest in peace and may his family and all who loved him find solace in the tremendous legacy that he left us and in the memory of a true giant among humankind. His knowledge of historic families of the United States' Hispanic Southwest, and Mexico's Gran Noroeste, including the Anzas, was unexcelled, and his passing has left an immense void in the research and understanding of the peoples and cultures of ancient times in this great region.

Without his support, encouragement, enthusiasm, and counsel, this volume would have never been started, let alone completed.

*Juan Bautista de Anza*

# Chapter One

## Anza in Antiquity

### *Nafarroa, Sobrarbe, and Gipuzkoa*

*en estas montaynas se alzaron muyt pocas gentes, et diéronse á pié faciendo cavalgadas, et prisiéronse á cavayllos, et partiéronse los bienes á los más esforzados ata que fueron en estas montaynas de Aynsa et de Sobrarbe mas de* CCC.<sup>os</sup> *á cavayllo* . . . in these mountains a very few people rose up, and they took to foot making raids and capturing horses, and they divided the spoils among the strongest until there were more than three hundred men mounted on horseback in these mountains of Ainsa and Sobrarbe.[1]

The name *Anza* is variegated. It is charged with meaning. It is unique. It is ancient. At the start of a history or biography of anyone of that name, the reader should understand these characteristics.

The variable nature of *anza* is seen mostly in its dialectal pronunciions and in its spelling. It is Basque in origin, and since the Basque language has historically been spoken in a number of dialects, the word has been pronounced with some variation. *Anza*, regardless of spelling variations, which will be taken into consideration later, is pronounced "än-sa," with the accent on the first syllable. The second syllable is pronounced "sah" rather than "zah." Typically, that is how it was pronounced in northern Nafarroa, Gipuzkoa, and Bizkaia.[2] However, in southern Nafarroa and Aragón, the word, and name, has traditionally been *ainsa*, pronounced "īn-sa," again with the accent on the first syllable. Other dialectal variations include *anda, ando, andu, anso, anzo, inda, indo, insa, inso,* and *gainza*. Although *anza* is not used as a word in conversational Basque today,[3] its current use in several hundred Basque names is evidence of its past usage and meaning.[4]

Used to describe certain areas within the present-day Basque Country of Spain and France, the meaning of *anza* is far-reaching. It would take a number of descriptive words in any other language to depict and illustrate what is meant by *anza*. Its root meaning is "pastures" or "pasturelands," even an abundance of the same.[5] However, an anza is not just any grassland or hay meadow. One of the most common of all Basque names, Aguirre, describes meadowland,[6] but the word *anza* describes a specific kind of pastureland in the rugged foothills of the Pyrenees Mountains. Beneath the lofty crags of these majestic peaks are mountain valleys whose beauty defies description. Abundant water in their streams and rivulets flows southward to the Ebro River or north to the Bay of Biscay, leaving their pastures green and lush. Hills and ridge tops are green as well. Even the rocky outcroppings and ancient stone structures, built by men, spring forth in a brilliant display of green foliage. These pastures offer some of the finest summer grazing in the world. It has always been thus.

It is not just succulent grasses and ferns that make up this radiant green color. The higher ridges are cloaked in forests of oak, pine, poplar, ash, chestnut, and beech trees, to name but a few. Except where humans have cleared or cultivated, there is also a great variety of shrubbery. Blackberry bushes, ferns, and laurel are nearly ubiquitous. One shrub seen in nearly every panorama is the elderberry. These so-called dwarf elders are found everywhere in the Basque Country. They have always been there and, in fact, are another source of the word *anza*, and especially *ainsa*.

It is possibly one of these pastures, nestled beneath the mountain peaks but elevated well above the plains and large valley floors, that the word *anza* describes—a pasture among, or sprinkled with, elderberry shrubs. Whether *anza* or *ainsa* or any of the other variations, it is just such a scene that this lone word describes. The pluralization of any word in Basque is accomplished by simply adding a *k* or *ak*. Thus, more than one such pasture would be *anzak*. However, proper/place names are generally pluralized by the suffixes *eta* or *aga*. Therefore, the name Anzeta *(anza-eta)* has its origin in more than one *anza*. If it was in the vicinity of such a pasture, the name became, for example, Ainciondo *(ainsa-ondo)* or a "near ainsa." If it was a place or area in which that type of pasture was found, the name became Anzuategui *(anza-tegi);* if a person lived on such a pasture that was large, the name that described his home would be Ansoandia *(anza-andia);* and if the pasture was located at the top of the mountain the name became Aintziburu *(anza-buru).* And so on.[7]

Then there is the spelling of the name. The majority of people who have the surname today spell it *Ansa*, as did a majority of those people who were literate in the seventeenth and eighteenth centuries.[8] Indeed, the only two people by that name who spelled it with a *z*, of whom the author is aware, were the junior Juan Bautista de Anza and his niece, María Rosa.[9] With very few exceptions, in the earliest records of the fifteenth and sixteenth centuries the name was spelled with an *s*, although a few scribes spelled it with a cedilla (the modern-day equivalent of a *z*), as in *Ança*. Roughly beginning in the late seventeenth century and continuing through the first quarter of the eighteenth century, most writers developed a habit of using double consonants, such as in *Anttonio* and *Anssa*. In fact, every known signature of the senior Juan Bautista de Anza, who lived and died in that basic time frame, was executed "Juan Baup.<sup>ta</sup> de Anssa," followed by a rather elaborate rubric.

Although the name is usually seen spelled *Ansa*, or *Anssa* during the aforementioned time period, it begins to appear periodically as *Anza* from the middle to the end of the eighteenth century. Of course, since the junior Juan Bautista de Anza, the most famous person of that name, spelled it *Anza*, people who are familiar with any part of his story expect to see it spelled that way. Anciently there were no rules, just as there are none today, stating that the name had to be spelled in some specific fashion. Therefore, since the best-known form among English-speaking North Americans is *Anza*, that is the spelling that has been adopted for this work.

Of course, the foregoing is modern history in comparison with the antiquity of the name. The name Anza is inseparably connected to the Basque culture, and the Basques have been associated with Spain since time immemorial, albeit often reluctantly. Thus, the history of this name parallels the history of Spain, and that history is ancient. It begins, as far as the Basque ancestors of the Anzas are concerned, with the arrival of the Romans on the Iberian Peninsula in 218 B.C., although it was not until some seventy-five years before the birth of Christ that Roman influence was felt in the northern Basque regions. Any era prior to that time would have to be considered prehistory, and any discussion of it could only be based in speculation and conjecture.[10]

The arrival of the Romans brought a unity to the Iberian Peninsula never before known. Even though the borders were not precise as we of the modern age would want, the entire peninsula was under the rule of one government, and "Spain" was used to refer to its several provinces. The homeland of the Anzas, high up in the northern mountains, was part of that entity. When the Romans were defeated by the Goths in the fifth century A.D., the Iberian Peninsula was again divided into various political units. It would not be united under one flag again for another thousand years.

In the meantime, however, there was minimal Roman control, or even apparent interest, in the mountains of the north. Nonetheless, the Romans slowly brought change to the Basque country in the form of outside cultural and religious influence. Although the Anza ancestors and others resisted that change, the change still came. Over the course of the next couple of centuries even the Romans themselves were being converted to Christianity. Paul, that stalwart apostle of the new faith, himself a Roman citizen, may have been the first missionary to bring the message to Spain sometime prior to A.D. 65. At least, that was his intention as evidenced by his own words in a letter to the Romans: "When I have finished my task and have safely handed over this contribution to them, I shall set out for Spain, passing through your midst on the way."[11]

Paul's statement of intent is documented, but there is a much more enduring legend about Saint James (Santiago), another apostle of Christ. He is said to have preached in Spain sometime about A.D. 40. Later, after his death in A.D. 44, his body, it is said, was brought to the northwest coast of Spain and buried. It was eight hundred years later that the grave was miraculously rediscovered. A shrine was soon built and pilgrims began to wend their way from all over Europe to the sacred site, which became known as Compostela, or Santiago de Compostela.[12] More will be said about this later, since the ancestors of the Anzas lived at key points along three of the pilgrimage roads to Santiago de Compostela.

It is doubtful that either Saint Paul or Saint James reached the Basque country, but Christianity did. In fact, the new religion may have been present as early as the third century A.D.[13] The Basques certainly did not convert as quickly as the Romans, for it took nearly eight hundred years,[14] but convert they did, and the Basque country eventually became one of the bastions of Catholicism in Europe. A strict adherence to the new faith dictated many actions of the early Anzas as Spain and the Basque country emerged from the Dark Ages, and provided a legacy that would be carried forward to the New World by their descendants.

Although Roman pressure of any kind on the Basques, especially in the mountains, seems to have been slight during their 600-year rule over Spain, their presence left its mark in other ways besides Christianization. It was during the Roman rule that the general term *Vascones* was first applied to one of the Basque tribes, eventually leading to the establishment of the Dukedom of Vasconia.[15] Later, it would become a universal term applied to all speakers of Euskara, or the Basque language, and evolved into the Spanish word *vascos* and the English word Basques. However, the Romans recognized six Basque tribes, the Vascones being only one of them.[16] The Gascones later occupied the territory that is today the Basque country of France on the north slope of the Pyrenees. The Vascones lived on the southern slopes in what is today Nafarroa, Zaragoza, and Huesca, Spain. In the western corner of present-day Spain and France, bordering the ocean, was another tribe called the Caristios. This tribe inhabited what is today the Provinces of Gipuzkoa and Araba in northern Spain. It was from these primitive tribes that the Anza ancestors sprang.

Some of them probably came down from the mountains like others of their countrymen to join with the Roman legions to fight in distant lands. They probably fought alongside the Romans in defending their lands from the Germanic Goths. As Rome withdrew from the Iberian Peninsula, however, the Anza ancestors found themselves sandwiched between the Franks on the north and the Goths on the south. Like Basques everywhere, they found themselves involved, one way or another, in a continuous jockeying for power by nations and forces bigger than themselves. There was no need to defend their home cities. There were none in the mountains, only small and scattered villages, and the larger powers had little need for those. The ancestors of the Anzas likely joined in the military alliances of their fellow mountain tribesmen and went off and fought as mercenaries in whatever cause seemed appropriate at the time.[17]

In time the Arabs, or Moors as they were known, invaded the peninsula and overran the lowlands. This constituted an insufferable blow to a land that had either converted, or was in the process of converting, to Christianity. The Moorish conquest did not extend into the mountains, although the cities in the lowlands, like Zaragoza and Pamplona, fell. In the words of Douglass and Bilbao, "The Arab armies, like previous invaders, preferred to sack cities rather than control forests." Thus, the early Anzas may have never felt the oppressive thrust of the Arab conquest, even though the occupation lasted nearly eight hundred years. Although the Basques seem to have gotten on well with the Moors, for a time at least,[18] it was from their mountain stronghold, and that of their neighbors, that the forces were eventually organized that drove the Arabs off the peninsula.

As can be imagined, however, with an 800-year span, the process was slow and painful. Almost overnight the Moors had conquered much of Spain, bringing a new culture, a new language, and the Muslim religion. The conquered territory had become known in its entirety as "El Andalus." Insignificant in size, the unconquered portion was a thin strip of sparsely populated mountain country in the north, made up of the Pyrenees, Cantabria, Asturias, and Galicia.

In response to the invasion from the south, the very first nations that can be considered true Spanish kingdoms arose from this unconquered area. Don Pelayo established the Kingdom of Asturias in A.D. 718 on the western side of that strip of land. Just under a century later the Kingdom of Nafarroa came into being. Located in the center of the Basque country, it was established by Iñigo Arista[19] in the year 800. Cataluña, on the eastern end of the strip, followed suit in 874, under the leadership of Wifredo I. Aragón came into being in 1035 under Ramiro I, the son of King Sancho Garcés III, the eighth king of Nafarroa. The Kingdom of León grew out of Asturias and eventually united with Castilla to form one large kingdom. The three Basque areas of Bizkaia, Araba, and Gipuzkoa also eventually came under the jurisdiction of "León y Castilla." Early on, Gipuzkoa had been divided between the Kingdoms of Asturias and Nafarroa. However, in 1076 it was granted the title of *terra* and came under the jurisdiction of the king of Castilla. In 1109 it voluntarily reverted back to Nafarroa and continued that way until 1200 when it again was incorporated into Castilla, this time permanently.[20]

Each of these kingdoms and political jurisdictions established what were known as *fueros* (Basque, *forua*), or compilations of laws by which that particular entity governed itself.[21] It is in the Fuero of Nafarroa, written about 1200, that the name Ainsa makes one of its first appearances in primary documentation. The Mountains of Ainsa and Sobrarbe are mentioned specifically. Sobrarbe was an elusive political jurisdiction that was first part of the Kingdom of Nafarroa. Later, when the Kingdom of Aragón was established, Sobrarbe was incorporated into it. There was even a fuero established for the jurisdiction of Sobrarbe, though it was never its own kingdom.

It was within the poorly defined boundaries of Sobrarbe that the Mountains of

Ainsa were located.[22] By the eleventh century A.D. there was also a village and/or region of Sobrarbe in Aragón that was known as "Ainsa." In the last will and testament of Sancho el Mayor (Sancho Garcés III), written sometime prior to 1035, in which he divided his kingdom among his three sons,[23] the village of Matidero in Aragón is mentioned as being "no lejos de Ainsa"—"not far from Ainsa."[24] Today, the village of Ainsa is located in the municipality of Boltana in the Province of Huesca. It was in this area that the name Ainsa first began to be used. As with all such names it is impossible to tell which came first, the surname or the village name. Regardless, by the eleventh century both were in existence.[25]

To the northwest of Ainsa and on the same southern slopes of the Pyrenees, near the village of Jaca and spanning the present-day border between Nafarroa and Aragón, was another early geographic region called "Anso." It came under the political jurisdiction of the kings of Nafarroa.[26] However, further to the northwest and on the opposite slope of the Pyrenees, near a mountain pass called Zisa, is where the people known as "Anza" lived.[27] Anciently, that general area was firmly set in the Kingdom of Nafarroa but today is in the French Basque province of Benafarroa. The area around Zisa, from whence the name Anza sprang, and Ainsa, as well as Anso, were all located within fifty miles of one another.

Although that fifty miles was across rugged mountain terrain, the people who lived there and called themselves by these same names were rugged mountain people. They moved about swiftly and over long distances, so it would be safe to assume that the names Anza, Ainsa, and Anso did not arise totally independent of each other. Yet, regional differences in pronunciation and spelling of the written word, over time, would guarantee variation. It is also safe to assume that there was a certain amount of evolution and change in the spelling of each of these three names, and others of the same root word, over the generations. Change was inevitable as the various families moved down out of the higher mountains into Gipuzkoa and Aragón and took up residence there. Regardless of spelling, however, the name denoted pride in a beloved mountain home.

These ancestors of the Anzas, then, are the ones spoken of in the prologue to the Fuero of Nafarroa, who rose up and elected a king to lead them in the defense of their mountain homeland against the Moors.[28] They took back the great city of Pamplona, and it is likely that Anza ancestors were involved in the massacre of some forty thousand of Charlemagne's rear guard at the Battle of Roncesvalles on the opposite side of the mountain from Zisa in 778.[29] These were the fierce mountain warriors known as *etxeko jaunak*, or "lords of their homes," who guarded their mountain passes against invading Franks, Goths, Moors, and all others who dared to set foot in their homeland. Fleet of foot and dressed mostly in animal skins, they were expert archers and lancers. Darting out of the shadows on the heavily forested ridge tops, they could fire their arrows and disappear before the enemy ever saw them, and then reappear momentarily to fire again from an entirely new vantage point.³⁰ Their abilities as guerrilla warriors were passed down from generation to generation. It was something that would serve their descendants well a thousand years later in America.

The population of their mountain wilderness was small, indeed, but they came down to the valleys and raided Arab settlements. They fought their guerrilla war against the non-Christians, dividing up the spoils equally until, as the ancient document says, "there were more than three hundred men mounted on horseback," the beginnings of a fierce mountain cavalry.³¹ That some, if not many of them, were known to their contemporaries by the name Anza, or some derivative thereof, seems unquestionable. The extreme ruggedness of their mountain wilderness was surpassed only by the great beauty of its verdant and lush pastures. It is little wonder that as people began to inhabit the area, they chose for themselves the same name that they had given their home—Anza.

## Zisa, Irun, and Hernani

*En la tierra de los vascos, en el camino de Santiago hay un monte altísimo que se llama puerto cisereo o porque allí están los confines de España o porque es cosa necesaria para pasar de una tierra a otra, cuya subida es de ocho millas y de ocho semejantemente la bajada . . .* In the land of the Basques on the road to Santiago, there is an extremely high mountain that is called the Pass of Zisa, perhaps because there lies the border with Spain, or because it is the only route by which one can pass from one country to the other. It is an eight-mile ascent and, by the same token, requires eight miles to descend.³²

Aimery Picaud, a cleric from southwestern France and pilgrim on the main road to Compostela in the year A.D. 1120, probably wrote the *Guía del viaje a Santiago*, or *Guide for the Trip to Santiago*.³³ He apparently went into culture shock on entering Nafarroa and voiced an extremely low opinion of the Basques he met along the way. His obvious fear of the unknown and willingness to listen to rumor about it make him a questionable source of knowledge about Basque character of that era. However, his descriptions of what he saw along the way are enlightening and colorful, if somewhat exaggerated. It would be hard to find a more accurate description of what one feels when crossing the high mountain pass at Zisa than his, as quoted above. "It is so high," he said, "that whoever climbs it, feels as though he can touch the heavens. From its summit one can see the British Ocean and the Western Sea, and the lands of three regions, that is to say: Castilla and Aragón and France."³⁴

In reality, the summit, as well as the present-day French/Spanish border, is situated just five miles from the village of Zisa. The ancient stopover on the road to Compostela called Garazi³⁵ borders the village of Zisa. However, the community is much older than that. Records from the Roman era tell of the building of a fort in the year 55 B.C., the ruins of which still stand today.[36] The scenery is breathtaking. Lofty mountains abound on all sides. Thickly forested ridges with narrow and winding *bidezidor,* or "footpaths," create a sense of remoteness that travelers on the road to Compostela must have felt when the forests were more ubiquitous and the human population was minimal. The setting is rural, the inhabitants are pastoral, and the "barbaric" language that so disgusted Picaud is still spoken there today. Authorities agree that this is where the people named Anza, at least the branch with which this story is concerned, had its beginnings.[37]

By the time of the establishment of the Kingdom of Nafarroa in 800 the names Arista, Abarzuza, Ezcaurre, Alsasua, and Leyre were in use.[38] It is likely that the name Anza also came into being sometime in that period. In spite of his obvious prejudices, Picaud's writings give a colorful description of what those first Anzas may have been like:

> [They] wear garments that are black and short and come only to the knee, like the Scottish wear. Their shoes, of hairless, untanned leather, which they call *abarcas,*[39] are tied on with leather straps near the ankle, but only cover the soles of the feet. Their legs are bare, but they wear dark woolen cloaks that they called *saias,* the sleeves of which reach to the elbow and are fringed like those of the *penule.* They are base in their dress and vile in their eating and drinking habits. Indeed, the entire family in the Navarrese home—the servant as well as the Lord, and the domestic, like the Lady of the house—are accustomed to eating together in the same room and from the same pot, without spoons. Rather, they use their hands and they all drink from the same cup.[40]

It is doubtful that Picaud, with his obvious dislike for the Basques, ever sat down at the table to eat with any of them. Furthermore, he describes a dining scene that was universal throughout Europe, with the exception of the heads of households eating with their servants.[41] This was normal in Zisa, however. The Anzas and their countrymen had adopted a system of universal nobility early on.[42] The servant was as good as his master. Such principles were unwritten at first, but eventually, as time passed and the fuero of the Kingdom of Nafarroa became more clearly defined, towns and villages were granted their own fueros guaranteeing such individual rights and privileges.[43] It is doubtful that any such laws were in place during Picaud's day, however. Such conventions were just a customary and accepted way of life.

The Anzas and their kinsmen at Zisa and other communities in the Valley Garazi were mostly farmers and herders, making their living from the soils and the abundant pastures in the surrounding mountainsides. Apples, cider, livestock, and milk were found in abundance. Some residents in the valley were elders who, through their councils, ruled the communities. Others were warlords who led on the hunt or in the plundering of other tribal territories. Generally, women were responsible for the farming activities of the family, and it was through their line that lands were inherited.[44] At least one branch of the Anza family built and maintained a castle at the "foot of the pass" during this era.[45] Some of the Anzas may even have been part of the cadre of "evil toll collectors" bewailed by Picaud.

If one takes Picaud at his word, these toll collectors were everywhere to be encountered, jumping out of the bushes and waylaying unsuspecting pilgrims. They would extract the "unjust tribute" at the point of the lances they carried. Should some poor wayfarer be fool enough to refuse to pay the money, they would "wound him with their lances."[46] It is doubtful that the situation could have been as serious as he portrays, however. Had it been, pilgrims would have started taking another route to bypass this danger. On the other hand, a certain amount of this type of activity likely took place.

The main route on the way to Compostela de Santiago—and there were many routes—passed directly through Zisa. On leaving the village, an alternate route could be taken to avoid going over the mountain. It was actually a shorter route, but the heavy undergrowth in the canyon and the treacherous river bottom probably made it even more dangerous than the mountain trail. If all travelers on the road to Santiago heard the same rumors and had the same fears as Picaud, they might have opted to take the alternate route. However, it was on the peak that the pilgrim got his or her first breathtaking view in the direction of Compostela, and it was on the peak that the first prayer to Santiago was traditionally offered. For it was here that the soldiers of Charlemagne, on their way into Spain, had hacked and chiseled through the rocky crags and timber to reach the summit. Charlemagne had said the first prayer on this site. Now it was tradition for other pilgrims to do the same.

With thousands of pilgrims traveling the dimly lit and tortuous trail through this dense mountain forest to reach the summit every year, it only stands to reason that some enterprising but unscrupulous persons would set themselves up as spurious tax collectors.[47] Again, if one believes Picaud, the robberies were much worse going over the mountain before the Navarrese and the Basques became converted, but by this time the Anzas, and everyone else in the vicinity of Zisa, were Christians.[48] Still, it is possible that even Picaud himself was accosted on the mountain. And it would go against logic to think that there were no Anzas involved as "tax collectors" over the several centuries that this type of activity took place.

It would seem that the Anzas learned business techniques in Zisa that served them well, whether gained through spurious "toll collections" or through legitimate trade negotiations with travelers on the road to Compostela. They carried those techniques and talents with them to other areas of the Basque country, and eventually to the New World. Just when it was that the extended family became too large, or their sons began to develop a wanderlust and leave the little communities around Zisa, is unknown. It may have occurred in 1335 when García López de Lazcano, a war chief from Gipuzkoa, invaded Nafarroa. There he and his forces stormed the Anza castle, overthrew its defenders, and claimed the Anza lands for themselves.[49] It could be that this was when some of the Anzas left for a safer haven, or it may have been even earlier that two of the known Anzas moved away and started new branches of the family elsewhere. One moved to Aragón, and there we find his descendants in the service of the king. Martín de Anza was the custodian of the armory for King Alfonso V of Aragón in 1440. His son, Miguel de Anza, continued in the same service for King Don Juan II in 1472. Another descendant, Gerónimo, served in the Aragonese Cortes as an *hidalgo* in 1528.

The other Anza who started a new family lineage, and with whom we are concerned here, moved down out of the mountains to the coast and established a *casa solar*, or "house of nobility," in the village of Irun.[50] Always referred to as the Universidad de Irun, or "Community of Irun," in ancient times,[51] it is today situated in Spain on its frontier with France. Then, as now, the village lay within the boundaries of Gipuzkoa. Probably by the time the first Anzas arrived on the scene, Gipuzkoa was a satellite of the Kingdom of Castilla. By moving to Irun the Anzas left the patronage of Nafarroa and became citizens of Gipuzkoa. Many of the family remain so even today.

One of the oldest coastal communities in the Basque country, Irun was established as part of a chain of churches built along the seaboard from the Basque frontier to Galicia for the convenience of pilgrims traveling the coastal road to Santiago de Compostela. The discovery of the apostle James's remains at Compostela brought about an intense Christian fervor in, and the evangelization of, these provinces. By 814 the event had caused such a sweeping sensation in Europe that it brought on a virtual stampede of pilgrims rushing to see the site. The pilgrimage was to last throughout the entirety of the Middle Ages. The most direct and most traveled route went out across the Pyrenees at Zisa, through Pamplona, Logroño, Nájera, and Burgos, or from Pamplona through the plains of Araba to Burgos. However, for those timid pilgrims afraid to cross the mountains, a coastal road was established. The churches that sprang up like a rosary of sacred sanctuaries, beginning at what is today Hendaia, Lapurdi, France, were generally named in honor of the ancient apostle. Thus, Santiago de Irun came into being in the earliest years of the ninth century.[52]

The ancient rock casa solar called "Anza" still stands there today, a reminder of what was once the hub of the extended Anza family. Those who established themselves in Irun seem to have been more involved in business than in farming and quickly began to fan out into the other small, rural communities of the area. Again, as in Zisa, they occupied themselves in business negotiations with both the locals and other traders from the region, as well as travelers on the road to Compostela.

Various Anza business establishments were soon to be found in Oiartzun, Urnieta, Andoain, and especially Hernani.

Hernani, too, was a vital stopover on another of the roads to Compostela. Actually, there were two spurs from the coastal route that converged on Hernani. This was because the northern path to Compostela was treacherous in that it followed the jagged Basque coastline where the rocky mountain ridges fell off into the sea and where many heavily wooded canyons and fast-flowing rivers had to be crossed. So, the cautious wayfarer had the option of leaving the coastal road at either Oiartzun or Donostia and traveling up the Urumea River to Hernani and out across the somewhat less treacherous mountains via Tolosa to the plains of Araba.[53]

It was during the beginning invasions of Sancho el Mayor, king of Nafarroa, into Gipuzkoa in the early years of the eleventh century that the name Hernani was first recorded. There, in 1014, he captured the monastery of San Sebastián de Hernani and granted it to the monastery of San Salvador de Leire in Nafarroa. The captured monastery was in the jurisdiction of the village of Hernani but was said to be "on the borders by the sea." In time, San Sebastian, or Donostia as it is known to the Basques, would become the capital of modern-day Gipuzkoa.[54]

In 1141 King García Ramirez IV granted the title "Lastaola"[55] to a family in Hernani, in another of the earliest written documents that make reference to the village. Hernani already held an oral title of *villa*, or "town with special privileges." Exactly when the town's *villa* status was ratified is unknown,[56] but the written charter was probably executed in 1256 when the other Gipuzkoan towns of Tolosa and Segura were granted theirs by King Alfonso X of León y Castilla. The king granted a number of charters to various towns, both inland and coastal, at this time to create a net of communication between Castilla and the coast.[57]

This gave Hernani its own fuero, and its citizens, including any Anzas who may have been living there, were guaranteed various privileges. One of these was universal *hidalguía*, or the right to own land and live wherever they desired within Gipuzkoa.[58] *Hijos dalgo*, literally "sons of something," were of the middle nobility,[59] and everyone in the Basque region of the Kingdom of Castilla was guaranteed that privilege by the reaffirmation in 1272 of the Fuero Viejo,[60] a vague and mostly oral canon of laws that had been passed down since time immemorial. This granted the title Muy Noble y Muy Leal, or "Very Noble and Very Loyal," to Gipuzkoa and many of her towns, including Hernani.[61] This status was reaffirmed by most of the kings of Castilla and later, beginning with the Catholic monarchs, Fernando and Isabel, by the rulers of a united Spain.[62]

From the early 1400s forward, all Basques, including the Anzas, would have a Spanish "de" inserted before their surname in any official or legal documents to indicate the family name on which their hidalguía was based.[63] Those who learned to write would henceforth always include the "de" in their signature. A signature thus executed constituted a title of nobility and guaranteed certain privileges that the signer fully understood but never confused with his or her Basque name. A majority of people in the Middle Ages never learned to read and write and, thus, never knew the "de" was recorded with their name. Nor did they use it in any way when speaking their native tongue. The written tradition, however, continued in all the provinces of the Basque country of Spain at least until the time of the Carlist wars in the nineteenth century, and in most cases until the end of the Spanish Civil War in the twentieth century.

The patriotism, customs, and character of these hijos dalgo, Hernani's native sons, have been immortalized by the soldier Captain Juan de Urbieta. At the beginning of the sixteenth century, France and Spain were in a nearly constant state of war. The French army under Louis XII had burned Hernani to the ground in 1512. Three years later when Louis' cousin, Francis I, succeeded to the French throne, he invaded Italy in an attempt to recover the French position there. When Carlos I of Spain was victorious in 1519 over Francis in the election for emperor of the Holy Roman Empire, and assumed the title of Charles V, animosity between the two countries intensified. It was at this time that Juan de Urbieta of Hernani rode off in the service of his king to fight the French in Italy. There in 1525 he was commander of the company of Spanish troops that captured the French king at Pavia, south of Milan, and brought him back prisoner to Madrid.[64] Anzas were present when Urbieta rode triumphantly back to Hernani. Anza children heard the story of this great soldier and local hero repeated from generation to generation, and how the king had granted him a new coat of arms and knighted him in the order of the Knights of Santiago.[65] His tomb beneath the floor of the nave was a source of inspiration to many Anza children who grew up attending Mass in the immense San Juan Bautista Church.[66]

This massive stone church was constructed between 1548 and 1595 on the point of a hill overlooking the Urumea River, when the parish was moved from its old location on the north side of town to its present location at the town plaza.[67] The *udaletxe,* or "town hall," was built abutting the church on its southwest corner.[68] The two buildings form one corner of the main plaza. Running in a sweeping arc from the udaletxe around the point of the hill, on the side of town above the river, is a block of stone buildings, tightly fitted one against another, that form the southeast wall of the village. The northwest wall is formed by another row of buildings that attach to the opposite corner of the church from the udaletxe. Between the two outer rows of buildings is another double row of stone structures that begin on the opposite side of the plaza from the udaletxe. Kale Nagusia, or "Main Street," runs between the northwest facing houses in this center row and the houses of the outer northwest wall. Kale Kardaberaz, or "Kardaberaz Street," lies between the center houses and those of the southeast wall.

These buildings that form the nucleus of the ancient village were all built of cut stone, three and four stories high. Constructed to tightly adjoin each other, they form an impenetrable wall that completely encircles the town. Gun portals in the exterior walls of the buildings and the two narrow streets that are barely wide enough for ox carts give an eerie feeling of the Middle Ages even today. An archway beneath the udaletxe and one at the end of each street at the point where it enters town form gateways leading into the heart of the village. There is also one cross street that cuts both Kale Nagusia and Kale Kardaberaz into two blocks. It, too, had an archway and a heavy, closeable oak gate at each end where it entered the village. These, of course, could be closed during times of siege or attack.

The main entranceway beneath the udaletxe was looked upon disdainfully by the *baserritarrak*, or "farmers," who lived outside of town. They called it *ifernura atea*, or "the gate to Hell," because of the shameful behavior of the townspeople. Caught up in the liberality of modern Europe, the people who lived in town would dance holding each other during festivities in the town plaza. No self-respecting *baserritar* would ever dance in such a fashion![69] Of course, the farmers were not the only ones who were scandalized over dancing in Hernani. Since at least 1539 the Church had been trying to stamp out the pagan Basque dances throughout Gipuzkoa. The inhabitants of Hernani, however, performed and continue to perform their ancient dances. There, as would also happen in the New World, the Church finally gave up trying to abolish "idolatrous and ungodly" dances; instead it attempted to adapt them into Church ceremony and turn their original meaning into one of Christian doctrine.[70] Maybe it was an inborn heritage from this era that would cause the junior Juan Bautista de Anza to be so tolerant of the Indian dancing and customs of Sonora and New Mexico a few centuries later.

Regardless of their views concerning the townspeople, farmers entered daily through the devil's gate to trade with people living inside the village walls. Arriving shortly after daylight, each would leave his *asto*, or "donkey," tethered outside while he set up his station for display of his produce on the plaza. After selling his fresh milk and vegetables, or whatever products he had that day, to the villagers, he would gather up his donkey and return to his *baserri*, or "farm," to accomplish his day's work. The baserritar often had to travel several miles to display his wares. So, if he was not selling milk or some other product that might last for just one day, he would possibly come only for the big weekly market that took place every Saturday on the town plaza.

Farm workers were easily the largest social class in Gipuzkoa from the late Middle Ages through the nineteenth century, but were often looked down upon and abused by the *aberatsak*, or "upper nobility," in the towns. Yet, they needed each other.[71] In the greater community of Hernani, the farmers needed the market that a few hundred people[72] living within the town supplied, and certainly, the townspeople needed the products supplied by the *baserritarrak*. A number of the villagers actually owned outlying *baserriak* and hired the farmers who ran them. Over the years, from the late 1400s to the present, the Anzas maintained themselves as merchants in Hernani, keeping close ties with the farmers.

## The Anzas of Hernani

*Sepan quantos q la carta depago Estando quitami en que verame p. Ju⁰s de ansa Vecino de esta cuatro dias del mes de junio de myle c$^{uo}$ c$^{os}$ setenta y un años — Fran$^{co}$ de Olaçabal* . . . Know all men that the amount for settling the debt is being released in my presence by Juanes de Anza, resident of this town, fourth day of the month of June, 1471—Francisco de Olazabal.[73]

We will probably never know when the first person calling himself Anza arrived in Hernani or set up business there. Very few written records of a personal nature were kept during the Middle Ages—one of the reasons being that very few people could write. It was left to people of the so-called modern age to start keeping the records of the average person. In medieval times there was no such thing as civil documentation, and even the Church generally did not start keeping vital records until after the Council of Trent (1545–63). In an attempt to stem the flow of the Protestant revolt, it was mandated that every parish keep baptismal, marriage, and death records.[74] However, it took time for parishes everywhere to implement the mandate and even longer to become seasoned at record keeping. It was not until 1584 that the first parish recordings in Hernani began.[75]

It is not surprising, therefore, that the first known written document of a member of the Anza family living in Hernani was executed toward the end of the Middle Ages (1450), yet it was over a hundred years before the first parish entry was recorded. The handwriting on the document, like all fifteenth-century writing, is extremely difficult to read, a problem that is magnified tenfold with this particular record because the ink from the opposite side of the paper has soaked through the page, making the writing on both sides nearly illegible. Just the same, this remarkable document provides a starting point in lieu of any other known record. It is a receipt for payment in full on a promissory note provided to one Juanes de Anza by a Francisco de Olazabal on June 4, 1471.

Olazabal was Hernani's municipal *escribano de número*, or "notary public," and Anza owned a store in the village. It is unclear what he sold in the store, or for what purpose he borrowed the money, or how much he borrowed, or even from whom he borrowed it. What is abundantly clear, however, is that he paid it back in full on that day in "hard cash," with the assurance that it would "no longer obligate his person, either presently or in the future." He further demanded that "a public reading be made of the above-mentioned receipt, that no person might return to ask or demand payment of me in full or in part at any other time or in any other manner."

It appears from the above wording that this transaction was something more extensive than a mere agreement between two locals. It is also evident that there were several reasons why Juanes borrowed the money in the first place. One appears to be the "sale of wool."[76] If that is the case, he may have been involved in some of the early shipping of wool through the Port of Donostia. Not only was Hernani a crossroads on the route to Santiago de Compostela, but it became a thoroughfare for wool being transported from Spain's interior to the northern coast for export. Navarrese wool from the Pyrenees and other fine Merino wools shipped via Pamplona or the banking and trading hub at Burgos came through Hernani on pack animals and in ox carts.[77] It may very well have been that Juanes de Anza was involved in buying and selling in his corner of the Spanish wool market.

As a storeowner and merchant in Hernani, another business venture that Juanes may have been involved in, aside from the typical supplying of goods to craftsmen and farmers, was the iron industry. Beyond stock raising and farming, the production of iron in Gipuzkoa was a major factor in its economy. Iron forging in the region assuredly predated the Roman occupation. Processing methods required large amounts of charcoal from the forests in the mountains around Hernani, and in the early days the foundries were also located in the mountains close to the source of the iron. However, prior to Juanes's time, several foundries had moved down to the Urumea River to make use of hydraulic power for greater production.[78] The iron industry began in Hernani in the thirteenth century and was a highly developed enterprise by 1471.[79] It is possible that Juanes de Anza was involved in supply and marketing for some stage of the production.

Nothing else is known of this man—from where he came, how long he was in Hernani, who his family was, and so on. As the earliest known Anza to live in Hernani, however, it is likely that he was an ancestor or, at the very least, a relative of those who came later. It is significant that he was a local storekeeper and merchant, because other Anzas followed in his footsteps over the next few centuries and plied similar trades.

It is also obvious that the name Juan (Joan, Joanes, Juanes), in whatever form or spelling, was a family tradition among the Anzas of Hernani. Very few families had children without giving that name to least one of them. Sometimes, the name would skip a generation but would be picked up again with the grandchildren. In two hundred years of parish records there are only three instances of the name Juan Bautista, our subject and two of his distant cousins, one of whom died shortly after birth. However, the name Juan, or Juanes, with or without other middle names, is a common occurrence. Although the Hernani parish records began in 1584, it was not until after the turn of the century that anyone with the surname of Anza appeared. During the period from 1616 to 1628, however, there were four different families with children in which the father's name was Juanes de Anza.[80]

## Juanes de Anza and Elena de Bula

*En ocho de decienbre del ano de mil seiscientos y sesenta y quatro secassaron joanes de anssa y Elena de Bula presidiendo los tres proclamasiones que dispone y manda el S.*<sup>to</sup> *Concilio de trento Siendo testigos Don Simon de artozqui y Don Alonsso de Erinozu y Domingo de Zuaznavar en facie eclesizecta — Don Agustin de larramendi (rúbrica)* . . . On December eighth in the year 1664, Juanes de Anza and Elena de Bula were married in church ceremony, the three proclamations ordered and mandated by the Holy Council of Trent having preceded [the marriage]. Witnesses were Don Simón de Artozqui, Don Alonso de Ereñozu, and Domingo de Zuaznabar.—Don Agustín de Larramendi (rubric).[81]

At present not a lot is known about Juanes de Anza, grandfather of the senior Juan Bautista de Anza. In a document written thirty-three years after Juanes's death we are told that his parents were Martín de Anza and Gracia de Elgorriaga.[82] However, this information is probably erroneous. Gracia de Elgorriaga was apparently Martín's second wife, whom he married after his children were already born. Of the five aging witnesses who testified concerning the parentage of Juanes de Anza, none had known Martín and only one, Juan de Galardi, claimed to have known Gracia de Elgorriaga.[83] Having seen her in the home of Juanes de Anza when he was a small child, he, naturally, would have thought she was his natural mother.

However, it is more likely that Juanes's mother was actually Agustina de Alzega, as recorded in the Hernani parish register, who married Martín de Anza at the altar of the beautiful San Juan Bautista Church on February 5, 1629. Nearly everyone in town turned out for the event, while Father Juan de Araeta, the village priest of nearly twenty years, performed the ceremony.[84]

The newlyweds moved into their home on Kale Nagusia across the plaza and just a few hundred yards from the church. Just eight months and eleven days after their marriage, Martín and Agustina's first child was born on October 16, 1629. The family stood around the imposing baptismal font at the northeastern end of the church and watched while Father Araeta baptized the new baby boy. Juanes de Anza, probably the boy's uncle, and his wife, stood as godparents for the occasion. Unfortunately, the wife's name was not recorded in the baptismal record and, as mentioned previously, since there were at least four Juanes de Anzas living in Hernani at this time, she could have been any one of the four wives.[85]

Later that evening, by the light of a candle, the good padre went to the sacristy and opened the leatherbound book of baptisms, which by this date was beginning to run out of blank pages, and recorded the child's name as Juanes de Ansa. Some years later another priest, writing the names of the baptized in the margin beside the baptismal entries, recorded the name as Juan de Anssa.[86]

It was nearly three years before Martín and Agustina's next child, Ignacio, was born, and he died shortly after birth. In February of 1633, however, another son was born, and he, too, was given the name Ignacio. Over the next ten years, Juanes would get two more brothers, Felipe and José, and a sister, Josefa.[87] The children would grow up exploring and playing down by the river and in the town plaza. Considering the size of the community and the culture they were raised in, they knew everyone in town and everyone knew them. It was as though they and the other children of Hernani were the community property of all the villagers. If they needed correcting, whoever was nearby took care of it. On the other hand, if they needed to be cleaned up and have tears wiped away after a fall, and be given a tender hug, whoever was nearby also took care of that.[88]

During this generation there were at least two, and possibly four, boys named Juanes de Anza who were growing up together. The oldest Juanes was actually Martín's younger brother and, thus, an uncle to our Juanes. His first wife died and he possibly remarried, either once or twice. If he remarried twice, there were only two Juanes de Anzas in Hernani during this generation. If he remarried only once there were probably three. And if he did not remarry at all, there were probably four young men by the name of Juanes de Anza.[89]

Our Juanes de Anza did not get married until he was thirty-five years old. It is unknown what he was doing for a living at that time, but he was still living in the family home on Kale Nagusia. Both of his parents were now dead, and it appears that he was living with his stepmother, Gracia de Elgorriaga. He chose for his bride a young lady from the neighboring town of Usurbil named Elena de Bula.[90] Even less is known about her, but she and Juanes were married at the same altar in Hernani's parish church as Juanes's father and mother. Again the whole town came out to witness the marriage and celebrate in the grand festivities in the town plaza afterward. Father Araeta was long since dead, so it was now Father Agustín de Larramendi, in his long, flowing priest's robes, who performed the solemn ceremony.[91]

Following in the footsteps of the previous generation, the newlyweds set up housekeeping in the already old family home on Kale Nagusia, across the main plaza and just a few hundred yards northeast of the front doors of San Juan Bautista. It was a three-story stone building that faced west across Kale Nagusia. The building shared its back wall with another house just like it facing east onto Kale Kardaberaz. There were no windows or doors on the three interior walls. The only windows in all three stories looked out on Kale Nagusia. Clean laundry was carried up the hill from the *garbileku*, or "washing place," at Leoka Spring and hung out from the upper-story windows to dry. The cooking and living area of the house was on the second story, and the bedrooms were on the third.[92]

Juanes and Elena lived their entire married lives in this house, and Elena lived in it thirty-one years as a widow. Their six children, two sons and four daughters, were born and raised here. The daughters, María, Francisca, Josefa, and Clara, all younger than the two sons, eventually grew up, married, and moved away. The second son, Felipe, grew up and moved to Donostia (San Sebastián). But the eldest son, Antonio, born January 17, 1666, lived his entire life and raised his family in this same home.[93]

## Chapter Two

## Life in Hernani

### *Antonio de Anza and Lucia Sasoeta*

*Dijo el dho Antº de Anssa que se alla exsaminado de Voticario con intento de poner publica Votica, empleandolas en cossas necess<sup>as</sup> para ello dhos ochenta ducados y que desde aora para quando llevarse efecto lo referido hipoteca de los votes, drogas, y demas adherente a dha Votica. En la noble y leal Villa de Hernani a Veinte y siete dias del mes de Mayo del ano de mill y seiss<sup>os</sup> y ochenta y nuebe — Antonio de Anssa (rúbrica)* . . . First, the said Antonio de Anza says that he has been examined as a druggist with the intent of establishing a public pharmacy and will spend the said eighty ducats on things necessary for the same, and that from henceforth, the said mortgage of the canisters, drugs, and other things pertaining to the said pharmacy shall be in effect. In the noble and loyal village of Hernani on the twenty-seventh day of the month of May in the year 1689 — Antonio de Anssa (rubric).[1]

Saturday, January 3, 1693, probably dawned chilly and overcast. Like every Saturday morning in Hernani, the streets were jammed with oxcarts and pack-laden donkeys bringing supplies and produce for sale, both in the open market on the plaza and to the stores lining Kale Nagusia and Kale Kardaberaz. The light that did manage to filter down past the tall buildings lining both sides of the narrow streets was dim indeed. As the cold mist changed into a slight drizzle, people scurried to complete their business and get back inside by their warm fires. Lucia Sasoeta, a slight woman of thirty-five years,[2] bundled against the cold with her shawl tightly pulled close around her face, hurried back from the open market on the plaza with a small cloth bag that carried a few items of merchandise. She opened the door on one of the north-facing houses about halfway down Kale Nagusia and disappeared inside.

The dark, age-blackened stone of the front of the three-story building gave little indication of what lay through its door. To the casual passerby there was no difference between this building and the many others that lined both sides of the street. For the few people who could read, there was a small, painted, wooden sign on the door advertising the proprietor's business. It stated simply, "Antonio de Anssa,

Boticario." A glance through the window that faced the street presented a view of walls lined with shelves, bins, and hoppers. On the shelves were what seemed to be hundreds of small metal canisters and glass and ceramic bottles and boxes. Again, if one could read, there was writing on the containers.

As one passed through the outside door to enter the large front room, a strong but pleasant odor of herbs met the senses. A closer look at the labels on the containers on the shelves revealed such exotic names as *piedra alumbre rudo* (coarse rock alum), *bejuquillo* (root of the Brazillian plant ipecacuanha), *trosisco de mirra* (myrrh lozenges), *goma de limón* (lemon gum), *infusión de rosas alejandrina* (Alexandrian rose tea), and *serpentaria virginiana* (Virginia snake root). There was *theriacta magna*, or syriac from opium, used for tertian fever; *mirabolano sitrinos*, a lemon-colored, prunelike, dried astringent fruit from India, used as a cathartic; *alquen quenges*, or Barbados winter cherry, used as a diuretic; and *tormentilla*, or septfoil, a slender, trailing, Old World herb, the root of which was a powerful astringent used for diarrhea. Less exotic, but still part of the inventory on the shelves, were such things as *conserva de rosas rubias* (dried red rose), *hunguento de plomo* (lead ointment), *tartaro emético* (emetic tarter), and *agua de flor de sauco* (elder flower water).

Toward the back of the room was a heavy oak table on which were positioned a number of tools of the trade. There was a large brass mortar with its iron pestle. Beside it sat a small glass mortar and pestle, alongside of which was a medium-sized rock mortar that also had an iron pestle. Next to it was a heavy copper distilling flask, a box of candles, a small balance scale, and a box of measuring spoons and other devices. On the back wall of the room hung a cupboard with a number of leatherbound books and several stacks of paper.[3] Seated at a table beside the cupboard was Lucia's husband, Antonio de Anza.

Stacked in front of him in a pile on the table were a number of small scraps of paper of various sizes. Handwritten in Latin on each one of them was a prescription for one of several drugs or herbs in different mixtures and combinations. He was dipping a quill pen into an inkwell in front of him, writing a notation on each of the prescriptions,[4] and placing them in another pile as Lucia entered the room. Her entrance into the room reminded him of the time and that they had an appointment to meet with Antonio de Ayerdi, an old friend of them both and presently the town's official escribano de número.

Lucia hurried past her husband into the next room, which housed the kitchen, and placed her bag of articles on another table there. As she removed her shawl and busied herself putting away the articles she had brought home, she spoke to her twelve-and fourteen-year-old sisters-in-law who were preparing the *tortilla*[5] for the family's breakfast. Lucia's aging mother-in-law, Elena de Bula, was seated by the fire, cradling Lucia's and Antonio's small baby daughter. In three more days little María Estevan would be one year old. Presently, Lucia was three months pregnant with their second child.[6] Married for almost two years now,[7] Antonio and Lucia were struggling to make a start in the world.

At twenty-seven, Antonio was eight years younger than Lucia.[8] A licensed *boticario*, or pharmacist, he had been building his impressive inventory for nearly four years. Although his business was growing faster than expected and a profit was being shown every year, he had his aging mother and two younger sisters to care for, plus a wife and growing family. Besides, he was in debt and struggling to reach solvency. Although his loan of eighty *ducados de vellón*[9] required a yearly payment of only four ducados to his friend Juan de Galardi, it had to be paid promptly at Juan's house at the end of every year.[10] As Antonio put away his papers and writing materials and prepared to walk up to the udaletxe with his wife for their meeting with Ayerdi, he had cause to hope that after today there would be a faster and more timely paying off of that debt.

Indeed, that loan had been the only way Antonio could start his *botica*, or "pharmacy," and realize his lifelong dream of becoming a boticario. In his day, Hernani had not had public school teachers, so he had received instruction in reading, writing, and ciphering from the local priest.[11] He also learned to speak *castellano*, the Spanish language, a necessity for learning to write. Then his father, Juanes de Anza, had made arrangements for him to serve an apprenticeship under Dr. Agustín de Zabala. There he began learning about medicines and cures as he followed Dr. Zabala on his rounds to the hospital and to patients' homes. He also worked as an apprentice at the public hospital where he could see the effects of the various cures. He learned the art of weighing, mixing, and dispensing drugs from Francisco de Herauso,[12] the only maestro boticario in town at the time.[13] Francisco, who was overworked and anxious to have help, had shown a keen interest in the young Antonio's education. Unfortunately, however, Antonio's father died when he was only nineteen years old and his education had barely begun.

At the funeral Mass on a blustery Tuesday, March 6, 1685, Antonio and his brother, Felipe, had assisted and comforted their mother and four younger sisters. The youngest sister, Clara, was not yet four years old. After the Mass the boys had led their family and the procession of mourners behind the coffin as it was borne on the shoulders of six strong men, Juanes's closest friends, from San Juan Bautista to the cemetery west of town. Nearly all of the townspeople attended the funeral, and the procession was so long that the last of the mourners were just leaving the church when the coffin arrived in the cemetery. When everyone was there, Juanes's body was lowered into the ground to join his ancestors and relatives of many generations before.[14]

Back at their home in Kale Nagusia, the family had to decide what to do next. Juanes had left them a small inheritance, but it would be gone quickly without an outside source of income. Antonio was being paid a small wage as part of his apprenticeship. It was decided that Felipe would move to Donostia and find work there at the docks. Elena and her older daughters would find work washing and cleaning and sewing. Everyone would help and the family would get by.

As time passed, Felipe did well in Donostia and was soon in business for himself.[15] The older girls left home as soon as they could support themselves. Antonio struggled to complete his studies. Part of the time, when needed for his schooling, he boarded with Dr. Zabala and his wife, Catalina de Sasoeta, or pharmacist Herauso and his wife, Josefa de Araeta. Both Zabala and Herauso helped him in his study of Latin, a necessary skill for reading prescriptions.

Over time, Antonio became very close with Dr. Zabala and his wife. It was through them that he also became interested in Catalina's cousin, Lucia. She was the middle child and only daughter of Juanes de Sasoeta and Josefa de Barcaiztegui.[16] There had been other children, but life was not easy in the seventeenth century. One little girl had died. Two daughters, Francisca and María Josefa, and possibly the son, Juanes, had emigrated to America.[17] Lucia, whose father died when she was only nine years old,[18] had been raised by her mother and older brother, Domingo, who was nine years her senior.[19] She also had a brother, Nicolás, who was nine years younger than her and only two months old when their father died. Nicolás Sasoeta and Antonio Anza had grown up together and were close friends. They were only a year apart in age,[20] whereas there were eight years between Antonio and Lucia. That, however, did not seem to matter much in those years, and the Sasoetas were anxious to see Lucia married to a man of ambition and character. In fact, they were probably anxious just to see her married. After all, she was already past thirty and seemingly on the road to spinsterhood. It was agreed by all that once Antonio had established his botica, the two would marry.[21]

Antonio completed his schooling in the spring of 1689 and immediately set to work to procure a loan for use in the purchase of necessary equipment and supplies to establish a botica.[22] He remodeled the front room of the already ancient Anza house on Kale Nagusia to receive the merchandise that he would sell through the store. Having appeared before a panel of medical people, including Dr. Zabala, boticario Herauso, and master surgeon Santiago de Amitesarobe,[23] he had been pronounced fully trained and ready to open and operate a public botica. A license for the same had been issued by the *sindico procurador general* (attorney general) of Hernani. All that remained to do was obtain the money and make the necessary purchases to get started in business.

So, one Friday afternoon in May,[24] Antonio Anza, Dr. Zabala, and Juan de Galardi met at the udaletxe to finalize an agreement whereby Anza would be loaned the money he needed by Galardi. There to formally record everything on paper and see that all the proper signatures were made was the escribano de número, Antonio de Ayerdi. The four men sat down at the enormous oak table in the *gela andi*, or "main room," of the udaletxe where Ayerdi witnessed everything that was said and dutifully recorded it with quill pen and ink.

Anza swore that he was fully ready and eager to start into business as a boticario. He agreed to mortgage all the "containers, drugs, and other items" that he would purchase for his botica as part of the agreement. Dr. Zabala agreed to act as security for the money that Anza would receive and mortgaged two houses that he owned in Hernani. One was on Kale Nagusia, down several houses from Anza's, and between the houses of Licenciado Antonio de Miner and that of Don José de Leizaur. The other house put up for mortgage was on the road that led down to the river from the udaletxe. It stood between the Widow Mariana Herauso's house and the retaining wall above Leoka spring where the garbileku for the town was located. Dr. Zabala gave evidence that the rent he collected from these two houses far exceeded the four ducados de vellón that Anza would have to pay against the loan yearly. Even beyond the two houses, however, Dr. Zabala further agreed to mortgage a farm that his wife, Catalina, had inherited called Agerregi, and which they also rented out to tenants.

Juan de Galardi listened closely as the escribano de número read back what he had written in the agreement. When he nodded his satisfaction with the instrument, Antonio and Dr. Zabala both signed it. Galardi counted out the eighty copper coins and pushed them across the table to Anza. Ayerdi wrote out a receipt to which Anza affixed his signature and then gave it to Galardi. Anza put the coins in a pouch that he carried around his neck beneath his shirt. The four men all shook hands and, walking downstairs, each put on his *txapela* (hat or beret) before stepping outside and walking across the plaza in a group to the nearest *edaritegi*. In the tavern they sat down at a table and ordered a glass of wine to consummate the agreement.

Nothing had been recorded concerning the amount of interest that Anza would have to pay. Nor was anything set down in writing that indicated the amount of time necessary to settle the debt. Without interest, at four ducados per year, it would have taken twenty years. With interest it probably would have taken thirty. That is the very process, however, that Antonio and Lucia hoped to speed up on this chilly January day nearly four years later. Antonio had already made four payments at the end of each year beginning in 1689. Now, through the kindness of Lucia's older brother, Domingo, they had come into some money that they hoped would help them get out of debt sooner, even though an interesting obligation came with it.

The young couple wrapped themselves against the cold and dampness outside and, leaving little María Estevan with her grandmother and aunts, hurried up the street to the udaletxe where they sat down at the same oak table at which Antonio's original loan papers had been signed. Seated at the table this morning with them were Martín de Lecuona, Francisco de Soroa, Juan Bautista de Zuaznabar, and of course the escribano de número, Ayerdi. The former three sat as witnesses and as parties to the transaction, although there was little to be done other than for Antonio and Lucia to agree to the contract.

Lucia's older brother, Domingo, was the vicar of the local San Juan Bautista

Parish, a duty he had performed for exactly a year, having been appointed to the same by Bishop Juan Grande Santos de San Pedro of Pamplona on December 31, 1691.[25] His presence was not needed at the meeting this morning. He and the other three gentlemen seated at the table with Antonio and Lucia had previously made all the necessary arrangements. Now all that was left was for Antonio and Lucia to sign the papers saying they accepted the transfer. Father Sasoeta was a very busy man, and it is possible that he simply couldn't find time to meet with the others. On the other hand, considering the fact that all he had to do was walk a few hundred feet from his offices in the church to the udaletxe, it is doubtful that being preoccupied was the excuse. The cold and rainy day might have deterred him, but in reality it was probably out of piousness that he did not come to the meeting. By old-country custom, when there were family secrets as shameful as this one, it was best that any negotiations be carried out quickly and quietly and that as few people as possible should know about it. Truly, it would be best if the local parish priest were not seen as being involved with it.[26]

The problem had all started over ten years earlier when a thirteen-year-old cousin of Domingo and Lucia, Ana María de Larramendi,[27] had been found to be pregnant. It had been no secret who the father was. His name was Estevan de Zuaznabar. Although little is known about him, he must have been involved with the military, as he was always referred to as *capitán*. Although the Sasoetas were one of the larger, more affluent families in Hernani, they were probably surpassed in such things by the Zuaznabars.[28] The fact that others of the influential Zuaznabar family always seemed to get involved after one of Estevan's intrigues leads one to believe that he was just one of the family, albeit a black sheep.[29]

Estevan and Ana María's child, Teodoro de Zuaznabar was born in 1682.[30] Then, to make things even worse for the already disgraced family, Estevan and Ana María produced a second child. Miguel Antonio Zuaznabar was born in 1685.[31] Estevan died or disappeared sometime after that. Since Ana María was still only a few months past her fifteenth birthday in 1685, she continued to live at home. The two boys, however, were made wards of a farm family in the country. How Martín de Miranda and his wife, Feliciana de Soroa, were or were not related to the boys is unknown. They took them in, however, and a stipend of seventy ducados in silver was awarded, probably provided by some of the Zuaznabars. Of the total amount, 200 silver reales were to be paid each year for the boys' maintenance, and three ducados de vellón were to be provided for their education annually.

It was not until after this arrangement was worked out that Hernani got its first public school teacher. Therefore, Domingo de Sasoeta, as a parish priest and first cousin of the boys, one generation removed, was appointed their *curador y tutor*, or "guardian and tutor," and they became his "pupils." It was the three ducados, paid to him annually, that Domingo was proposing to transfer to Antonio and Lucia as a belated donation to Lucia's dowry that had been promised for the day of her wedding.³² This little gift would nicely offset three-quarters of Antonio's yearly payment against his loan on the botica. The remainder of the seventy ducados would also be paid to Antonio and Lucia in the annual 200-real installments. They would deserve that sum many times over by bringing the two little boys into their home and raising them as their own sons.

As at any such conference in the seventeenth century, Lucia was at the meeting this morning with "license and express consent asked for, obtained, and possessed of her husband." From henceforth, although they would be collecting Father Sasoeta's three ducados de vellón and the other 200-real payment annually, Antonio would also be in charge of administering the seventy *ducados de plata*. He and Lucia evidently felt, however, that the money received would outweigh the obligation. On the other hand, family ties ran strong among the Basques, and although the two little boys were only their children's second cousins, they felt a deep sense of responsibility to them and might have taken them in even without the money. Antonio de Ayerdi read the agreement out loud as he had written it at the request of Vicar Sasoeta. All in attendance nodded their understanding of the same. Anza dipped a quill into the inkwell on the table and signed his name "Antonio de Anssa," followed by his conservative rubric. As required by law, Ayerdi then offered Lucia the opportunity to sign. When she refused, stating her inability to write, Juan Bautista de Zuaznabar³³ signed his name in her stead and it was so noted in the document. The document was written and signed in duplicate, one copy staying at the udaletxe and the other being carried home by Antonio and Lucia.

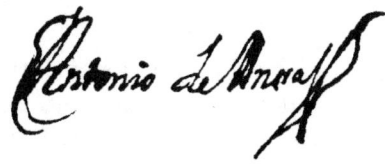

Things had gone well for the young couple over the past year and ten months since their wedding. As they scurried home through the drizzling rain, they now had cause to hope that this added income would make things even better in the future. Antonio was doing what he had always wanted to do—operate his own botica—and the business was doing well. The couple had a beautiful daughter who would be one year old in just a few days, and Lucia would give birth the coming summer to their second child. They would pick up the two Zuaznabar boys that afternoon out at the baserri. They could look to the future with anticipation, but reflecting back to the day when it had all begun was not unpleasant either.

The wedding ceremony had been one of the grandest ever seen in Hernani. As things got under way that day, people were wedged into the church, milling in the doorways, and visiting on the plaza. Four couples were to be married that morning at the altar of San Juan Bautista. They were popular young people of the town, known by everyone in the village and on the surrounding baserriak. People from as far away as Donostia and Irun, and several from villages in Nafarroa, had either come the night before or had left home early that morning so they could be in attendance. The mood was festive and everyone was dressed in their finest attire. Cleanly shaven and handsomely dressed old men were seated on benches around the plaza, smoking and visiting, their *makilas,* or "walking sticks," in hand. Old women could be seen standing in groups and talking in hushed voices. Young people were also gathered in groups, and little children were underfoot everywhere. All of them were related to each other in one way or another. It was like a grand family reunion.

Early morning Mass was long since over. The clock on the church tower said it was nearly ten in the morning. A crisp and beautiful morning it was, too. According to the Gregorian calendar, which had been in use in Spain almost from the day of its approval by Pope Gregory XIII in 1582, this particular Sunday was the eighteenth day of February, 1691.[34] Old Father Sebastián de Amitesarobe, the vicar of the parish, had been preparing himself for weeks. Several altar boys and assistants had helped him with his robes that morning so he might look his finest. As the bells in the church tower tolled the hour, everyone who was not already inside filed in and seated themselves in preparation for the Mass—at least those who could find a seat did. Probably half of the congregation was standing, tightly packed against the walls and in the doorways. The prospective brides and grooms, along with their families and those who had been asked to be witnesses, were seated in the front nearest the altar.

The future brides were crisp and beautiful in their long sweeping dresses of camlet and Rouen linen imported from northern France. Flowing white veils were draped over their heads and cascaded down their backs and over their shoulders. The grooms were dressed in their finest black suits transported from either Segovia or Tarazona, and each man held a fine, black, dress txapela in his hands. Their white silk shirts were starched and shining, and each man had a colorful cravat tied fashionably around his neck. Each also wore an overcoat or a nearly floor-length cape.[35] José Egino and his wife, Josefa Goicoechea, owners of Hernani's main clothing store, and Domingo Zuaznabar, the village tailor, had been busy over the last few weeks outfitting everyone for the occasion.[36]

The four men who were to be married had grown up together. They were the closest of friends and were nearly the same age, between twenty-four and twenty-six. The ladies, as was customary in seventeenth-century Hernani, were a little older than their future husbands. The eldest of the four was Lucia Sasoeta at thirty-two years of age. The youngest was Josefa Irigoien at twenty-six.[37] They, too, had known each other all of their lives.

When the Mass was over, Father Amitesarobe invited each of the couples simultaneously to come forward with their witnesses. He asked each couple in turn if they desired to wed each other and, upon hearing their affirmative answers, pronounced the words that sealed their marriages according to the dictates of the "Holy Council of Trent." Starting at his left he performed the ceremony first for Nicolás de Orcolaga and Dorotea de Olloquiegui.

Next in line were Lucia's brother, Nicolás de Sasoeta, and Josefa de Irigoien. Although they were the youngest of the four couples, Nicolás was already well established in the mercantile business. His store, located on Kale Kardaberaz, had most things that people needed, and he made regular trips to Donostia and other large towns to keep it supplied. The future certainly looked bright for this couple.

Next to be married by Father Amitesarobe were Antonio de Anza and Lucia de Sasoeta. As they pronounced their vows, everyone's eyes were on Lucia. She wore an exquisite camlet dress. Its satiny fabric of tightly woven silk and wool was brightly dyed and embroidered. Her younger brother, Nicolás, had imported it from the Orient and presented it to her as a pre-wedding gift, a part of her dowry.[38]

The last couple to be married was Miguel de Lubelza and Josefa de Isasa. One of their witnesses was Alonso de Ereñozu, *sargento mayor* of the militia troops of Gipuzkoa and son of the deceased and famous captain of the same name.[39] His nephew, Francisco de Beroiz, stood as witness for both the Orcolaga and the Sasoeta marriages.

Francisco was one of the most prominent individuals in attendance that day. His father, Miguel de Beroiz, before his death many years earlier, had also held the position of sargento mayor of Gipuzkoa's militia. He and Francisco's mother, Mariana de Ereñozu, were owners of farms, foundries, and mills up and down the Urumea Valley. Francisco had inherited it all.[40] He was married to Nicolás and Lucia's cousin, Margarita de Larramendi.[41] His mother, although aged and decrepit and requiring help from her family, was also in attendance.

Second to none in notoriety among the witnesses was Juan Bautista de Araeta, who also served as a witness for the Orcolaga wedding. A very dear friend of Francisco de Beroiz and his wife, he was well known as a trader and businessman throughout the region. Most people held him in high esteem, although some looked upon him as a "wheeler and dealer."[42]

Others in the lineup of witnesses represented the most influential and affluent businessmen and professionals in the town of Hernani. When the weddings were over, however, everyone in the group mingled with everyone else, rich or poor. It was all one big family. There was singing and dancing on the plaza. Family groups gathered in the several *edaritegiak* (taverns) around town for eating and drinking and, of course, singing and dancing. It was an incredible day.

It was probably good that the four happy couples could not see into the future, because just two years down the road their fortunes had varied considerably. Miguel de Lubelza and Josefa de Isasa moved away and contact was quickly lost between them and their old friends. The most tragic of the four stories involved the first couple married that day. Dorotea de Olloquiegui died on December 2, 1692, due to complications from pregnancy.[43] In the seventeenth century, of course, offspring, and preferably many of them, were every newly married couple's greatest hope. Nicolás de Orcolaga would later remarry, but would not see his first child until 1697. Two years after their marriage, Nicolás de Sasoeta and Josefa de Irigoien were starting to be concerned that children were not forthcoming in their marriage. Sadly, they remained childless for the rest of their lives. By the beginning of 1693, however, Antonio de Anza and Lucia de Sasoeta had a baby daughter and a second child on the way.

Over the years, Antonio became involved in just about everything that had to do with business and politics in the village of Hernani. In the early days after his father's death, it quickly became obvious to the townspeople that he was a youth of many talents and abilities. A young man did not reach the legal age of majority until he turned twenty-five, however, so it was six years after his father's death before Antonio was able to enter into contracts, file petitions with the town authorities, or vote.[44] It appears that Dr. Agustín de Zabala was his curador, since all existing papers of that period that were signed by Antonio were also cosigned by Dr. Zabala. The first known contract that he signed after turning twenty-five in January of 1691 was the marriage contract signed with Lucia's family on February 3 of that year.[45] Because Antonio reached the age of "competency" that year, he also voted for the first time in the yearly village elections.

It would be another four years before he was elected to a town office, but that election began a lifelong tradition of service to the community. Antonio was elected to the office of *regidor*, "alderman" or "town councilman," three different times, in 1695, 1715, and 1721. He was chosen *mayordomo y juez ordinario*, "city manager and ordinary judge," in 1713, and *mayordomo tesorero de haber y rentas*, or "administrative treasurer of property and revenue," in 1699 and 1701.[46] Beyond his business as a boticario he seems to have had an influence in one way or another on much of what took place in Hernani. He was involved in everything from borrowing and loaning money to administering estates and representing people in court.[47] He was curador for a number of minors over the years.[48] He administered various town contracts for such things as cutting firewood in the mountains around Hernani.[49] As an alderman in 1713 he was even responsible for obtaining and administering a contract between the town of Hernani and the whaling fleets of Donostia for the purchase of whale oil for the village lamps.[50]

To understand Antonio's many years of service in the town government of Hernani and how that heritage of public conscience and duty was passed down to his children, it is necessary to first have a rudimentary understanding of the Basque form of government. Even though the Basque lordships were under the jurisdiction of Castilla, they had all been guaranteed autonomy by the Spanish government in keeping with their ancient fueros. Elections of officers in the villages, valleys, and provinces were considered to be a God-given right and privilege by Basques everywhere. Voting was a yearly activity that had been taking place since before anyone could remember. Beyond being privileges, however, voting and public service were looked upon as important obligations. If one had the time and the means, since civic jobs required true service in which the officeholder was unpaid for his efforts, one would never refuse a year of service when elected by one's fellow citizens. It was considered such an honor to be an alcalde or regidor of one's village or region that almost annually men who had gone to other areas in Spain or America were elected to honorary offices, while their countrymen who had stayed home were elected to the real offices and did the work.

There were generally two kinds of elections: one in which men were chosen to serve their town or municipality, and one in which they were chosen to meet in regional or provincial congresses, called yearly for the purpose of establishing laws. Although conducted differently, the best known of such congresses was held yearly in Gernika, Bizkaia, where participants met under the now-famous oak tree.[51] There appears to be no evidence that Antonio Anza ever served outside of Hernani in any of the provincial meetings in Tolosa, Gipuzkoa. However, his active service in his local municipality is a statement of his loyalty to his countrymen and the two majesties, God and King. This legacy of service was passed on to his children and grandchildren, especially the two men known as Juan Bautista de Anza.

The elections were similar throughout the Basque country but were handled in different ways, depending on the location and situation of the people involved. As mentioned, lawmakers of Bizkaia met beneath the Tree of Gernika, but the elections that sent them there were held in various places and at various times throughout the lordship. In Elejabeitia elections were held in an udaletxe[52] similar to that in Hernani. Voting in the valley of Ayala was done in a meadow on an open mesa called Saraube on the first of January every year.[53] In Zeanuri elections were held in the cemetery of the Santa María Parish.[54] In Hernani, however, the yearly election of the alcalde, regidores, and sindico procurador general took place at the udaletxe at three o'clock on the afternoon of the feast day of San Miguel.[55]

Every eligible voter, unless deathly ill, was expected to be there. On the afternoon of September 29 one would be in the udaletxe to exercise one's right and obligation to vote and to participate in the village government. Eligibility was not universal as those of the modern age might understand it. Yet, in its own way, suffrage in Hernani was universal. As in most places throughout the Basque country, the rule was simple. It stated "one fire [fireplace], one vote." The head of the family, be it husband and father of the household or widow with minor children, was the only one who actually voted, but his or her vote, in theory at least, was cast for the well-being of the entire family. Single children in a family could not vote. Usually the eldest son, upon getting married, became the head of the family. At that time the father lost his eligibility and the son voted in the elections from then on.[56]

There were forty-five such heads of households, or eligible voters, when Antonio Anza was first elected to the office of regidor in 1695. By now his botica was well established and worth at least 1,000 ducados,[57] quite a growth from the mere 80 ducados he had borrowed to start it. He was one of several noteworthy young businessmen who were quickly becoming leaders in the town. His young family was growing rapidly. He had both a daughter and a son, María Estevan and Juan Bautista, and Lucia was due to give birth to their third child in just one month. Like the other men of the town, he dressed in his best suit of clothes to attend to this most important duty that Thursday afternoon. Like most of the others, he was already in his seat in the assembly room of the udaletxe when the bells in the church tower rang loud and long, declaring that the annual *congreso general* of Hernani was now in session. Voting was about to begin.

As everyone took up their positions in the gela andi, outgoing alcalde Francisco de Herauso instructed that a roll call be taken. As the name of each man on the list was read and answered with "Hemen naiz," "I'm here," escribano de número Antonio de Ayerdi recorded their names in the town book of elections. It was determined that there were only two men absent, but they were both away on legitimate business. Therefore, the instructions they had left concerning how they desired their votes to be cast were considered and approved. After the role was taken, the first item of business was to elect an honorary alcalde. The name of Captain Don Juan Martinez de Alzega, a native son living in the city of Sevilla in southern Spain, was suggested. The suggestion passed with a unanimous vote of the assembly and Ayerdi was instructed to notify him of his election to this honorary position.

Now it was time to choose electors. It was customary to choose five from among the assembly. This afternoon only five were nominated. Had there been more nominated, it would have been necessary to choose five from among the total. The five, who were elected unanimously, were San Juan de Miner, the outgoing sindico procurador general, Domingo de Ugalde, Juan de Galardi, Alonso de Ollo, and Dr. Agustín de Zabala. These men would do the actual nominating of alcalde, regidores, and sindico procurador general. They arose and went with escribano Ayerdi into an adjoining room. He explained procedure to them, and each nominated one person for the office of alcalde. As each of electors proposed a name, Ayerdi dutifully wrote it on a slip of paper. Then all went back out into the assembly room and returned to their seats.

Ayerdi read the names of the five men who had been nominated. Each, in turn, stated that he would be able to serve if elected. Then each slip of paper containing one of the nominees' names was placed into a silver *bolilla*, a thimble-like object with matching lid that resembled a tea ball. When the lids were secured on the bolillas, all five were placed in a silver drumlike object called a *cántaro*.[58] It was about eight inches in diameter and rotated by means of a small crank. Once the bolillas were in the cantaro and its lid was closed, Ayerdi rotated it several times and then invited a small boy, who was brought to the meeting by his father for this express purpose, to step forward and draw out one of the bolillas. The first name to be read was that of outgoing sindico procurador general San Juan de Miner, making him the new mayor. Each of the next four names was also read as the boy drew them from the cantaro. Each man in turn became the next in line to be alcalde should something happen to Miner.

Next, following the same procedure, the five electors nominated five men of the assembly to be regidores. Antonio de Anza was nominated by elector Domingo de Ugalde. Afterward, when the cántaro was rotated and the first name drawn out, it was Anza's name. The second drawing produced the name of Lorenzo de Aguirre, concluding the second phase of the election, since only two regidores were chosen each year. The alcalde and either one of these regidores made up a quorum for business purposes.[59]

Five men were then nominated for the office of the sindico procurador general, and escribano Antonio de Ayerdi was elected following the same procedure. Then nominees were chosen for the office of *veedor de cuentas,* or "administrator of accounts," and four of the five were elected in a like manner. Finally, Sebastián de Araeta and Andres de Izagirre were elected as *guardamontes,* or "forest rangers." At that point, outgoing alcalde Sebastián de Miner turned over the Vara Real de Justicia, "the Royal Staff of Justice," to alcalde elect San Juan de Miner. The new mayor and the two new regidores, Lorenzo de Aguirre and Antonio de Anza, each signed the book of elections in their new official positions, and all in attendance went downstairs to join the festivities of the feast day of San Miguel on the town plaza.

## The Children

*Por el mes de Maio del ano demil y setecientos Tenia a hazer Viaje a Endaia Lugar de francia por algunas mercadurias en casa de Juan de Buti mercader — Nicolas de Sassoeta (rúbrica)* . . . In the month of May in the year 1700, I had to make a trip to Hendaia, a village in France, for some merchandise at the house of the merchant, Juan de Buti—Nicolás de Sasoeta (rubric).[60]

The birth of Juan Bautista de Anza came in the wee hours of Monday morning, June 29, 1693. The event took place in one of the upper rooms of the Anza house on Kale Nagusia. It is not known who Lucia's midwife was, but there is a good chance her mother, Josefa Barcaiztegui, was present, and certainly Antonio's mother was there. Although the baby's two young aunts, Josefa and Clara Anza, were probably not present at the birth, they most likely were awake and knew what was happening, and may even have assisted in some way. It is likely they were responsible for spreading the word around town as soon as people started to wake up in the morning. It is even more likely that little Juan Bautista's eight- and ten-year-old cousins, Miguel Antonio and Teodoro Zuaznabar, slept through the entire event.

Before daylight one of the aunts hurried over to the priest's quarters beside the church to notify the vicar, the new baby's uncle, Domingo de Sasoeta. She carried a candle because the tiny sliver of the waning moon provided almost no light to the darkened streets of Hernani. A few words were exchanged between her and the priest, enough for him to learn that the baby and mother were healthy. In that case, it was not necessary for the priest to visit the home; rather, the family could come to the church later that morning to take care of the baptism and naming of the child. A short time later the huge bells high up in the church's tower tolled the breaking of day. Immediately after the daily ringing in of the dawn, the heaviest bell tolled three times in slow succession, announcing the birth of a baby boy during the night.[61] Everyone in town now knew that a birth had taken place the previous night, but since everyone also knew that Lucia Sasoeta and Ana María Zabala were both nearing their time of delivery, the question circulating rapidly around town must have been "who was it?" Within a short time the question became immaterial. The massive bell in the tower again rang three times, announcing the birth of Ana María's baby.[62] Now it was known by all within the sound of the deep, booming church bell that both women had successfully delivered baby boys.

And so it was that later in the day the Anza family arrived at the church. The new baby was wrapped warmly against the outside air and tucked snugly into a hand-held basket with a bright ribbon tied around its handle. The ribbon announced to all who saw the procession that the little person inside was a boy.[63] Antonio, with young cousins Teodoro and Miguel Antonio Zuaznabar in tow, helped Lucia through the heavy oak door and into the dimly lit nave of the church. Nicolás de Sasoeta and his wife, Josefa Irigoien, were at their side. Josefa had been designated godmother of the new child, and therefore, as custom dictated, she was carrying young Juan Bautista in his woven cradle.[64] Following closely behind them were Antonio's two younger sisters and the two grandmothers, one of whom was carrying little María Estevan. Father Sasoeta and a number of well-wishers and other family

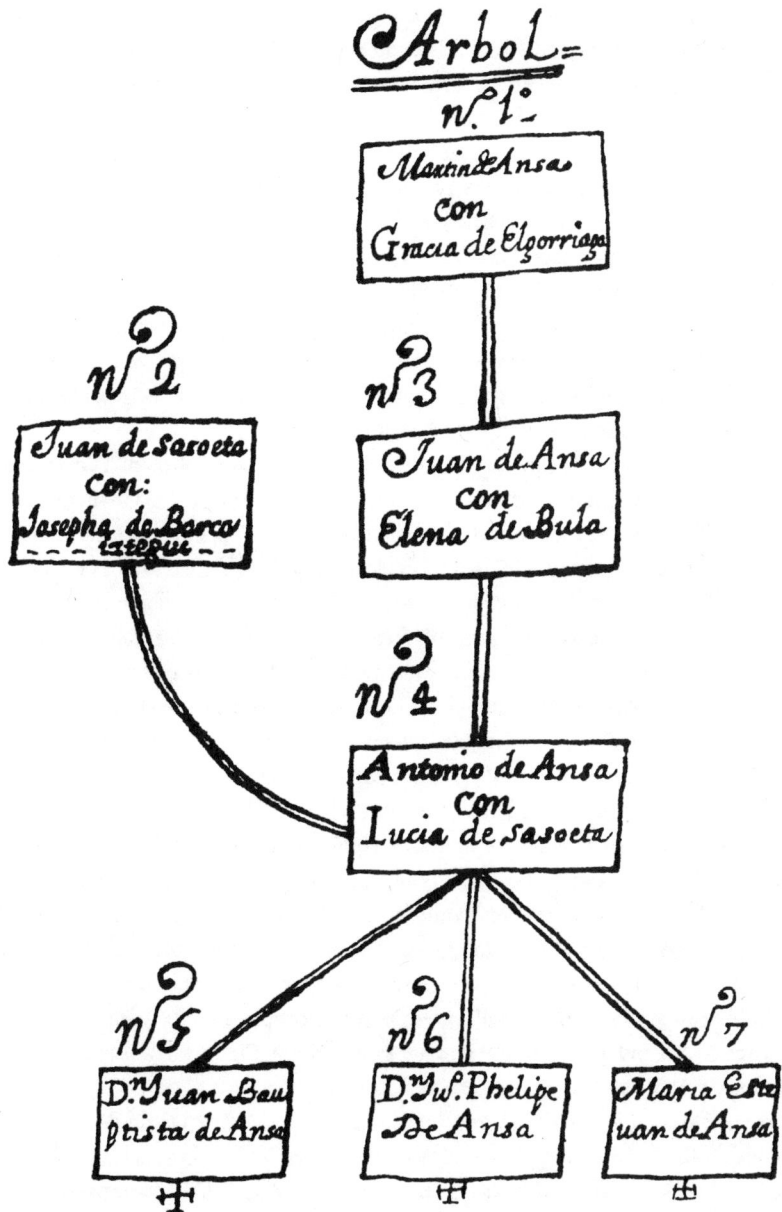

*Family Tree ("Arbol") of Juan Bautista de Anza* GAO, SS212, exp. 2, Demanda de filiazion por Antonio de Ansa como padre y administrador de Don Juan Bauptista y Don Juan Phelipe sus hijos y ausentes en Yndias; Hernani, Gipuzkoa, Spain; 1718; frontispiece.

members were there to greet them. It is doubtful, however, that Antonio's brother, Felipe, would have arrived from Donostia on such short notice. After the initial greetings, everyone paused to admire the new baby. Then the group moved quickly to the back of the nave and entered the baptistry, where they gathered around its massive baptismal font. The beautiful font probably weighed close to a ton and had been carved out of stone nearly 130 years before by the master stone cutter Juan de Ayerdi.[65] When everyone was in position, Father Sasoeta performed the baptism that he would later record in the church's third vellum-bound volume of such ceremonies: "On the twenty-ninth of June in the year one thousand, six hundred and ninety-three, I baptized Juan Baptista de Anssa, the legitimate son of Antonio de Anssa and Lucia de Sassoeta. The godparents were Don Theodoro de Zuaznabar and Josepha de Irigoyen, whom I have advised of their spiritual relationship and obligation—Domingo de Sassoeta (rubric)."[66]

It was fitting that the new baby should be named Juan Bautista. The weeklong fiesta centered around the Día de San Juan, honoring John the Baptist, the patron saint of the parish, had just ended the Saturday before.[67] A more appropriate name for the first son of the family would have been difficult to find.[68] Why he later adopted San Antonio de Padua as his patron saint[69] is not as obvious; regardless, from this day forth he would honorably bear the name of the great John, the Baptist.

What an honor it must have been on the day of the baptism for the new baby's cousin, the ten-and-a-half-year-old Teodoro, to be given the privilege of being the godfather. He must have felt the love and concern that Antonio and Lucia, the vicar, and other members of the family had for him as Father Sasoeta explained his obligations. As the family moved out of the church after the baptism, Antonio slipped a few *maravedís*, or *txanponak* as the Basques generally called them, "small denomination copper coins," into the boy's hand. This was for a traditional Basque ceremony in which the godfather would scatter a few coins around the plaza. The young "orphan" boy had to have known that he was accepted as part of the family. He must have felt the great tribute being paid to him as the one who would scatter the coins randomly across the plaza while other people, mostly young boys of his own age, raced and grappled to try to get one of them. On this day, Teodoro was the prominent figure in this age-old custom.[70]

As time passed and Teodoro and Juan Bautista grew, they would develop a close friendship based on their spiritual relationship as godfather and godson. What they perceived their blood relationship to be is another matter. They were actually second cousins, but they may not have known it. Timeworn tradition says that they were most likely raised as brothers, even though they had different last names. Children did not ask questions about such family matters, and it is doubtful that they ever did. Although Teodoro likely visited his mother often as a boy, he was probably told that she was an aunt, and Ana María would never have told him anything different.[71] As they grew to manhood, both Teodoro and Juan may have thought about it and wondered, but even that is doubtful. As Juan grew to manhood he would have never questioned Teodoro's legitimacy. Although he would one day question other men's illegitimate births in court, they were different. They were not vizcaínos (Basques). They were not family.

Surely Juan Bautista de Anza's earliest memories were of family and places near at hand. Probably the first things that made an impression on him were the trips that he made with his mother as a toddler to the garbileku just outside the town walls. The women of the town went there daily to wash clothes. Juan would go there with his mother and older sister. There was water to play in and other adventures for a boy of two or three years of age. There were always other children, who had come with their mothers, with whom he could play.

Walking down the road from the udaletxe to the garbileku, you could never see who was there until you turned onto the short trail that led from the road and down the bank to the front opening of the facility. You had to first pass the Widow Herauso's house. She had died just four months after the wedding of Juan's parents,[72] but everyone still called it the "widow's house." Between her home and the retaining wall was Dr. Zabala's house.[73] The back wall of his house and the upper retaining wall of the garbileku were one and the same. Then one had to go past the retaining wall between the road and the garbileku itself. A tile roof extended from this retaining wall to the south wall of the spring house, a heavy rock structure darkened by age and dripping water, with heavy green moss growing out of its cracks. Beneath the roof were troughs that were built into a large U shape. Water was piped from the spring house to these troughs, by which the women would kneel to do their washing. Behind them on three walls of the garbileku little wooden shelves had been built where they could place the clean clothing.[74] None of this activity could be seen until one walked through the open front of the structure. For a small boy it must have been a fine surprise to see who else was there.

As small boys got together there was great adventure in searching for worms and frogs and other creepy things in the two open ditches that carried the water away from the troughs on each side of the washing station. It was here that Juan began to make his first acquaintances beyond that of his sister and two Zuaznabar cousins. The two Sebastiáns—Herauso and Miner, Miguel Egino, José Orcolaga, Jacinto Vizarrón, and José and Manuel Zuaznabar were all Juan's age[75] and came with their mothers to play at the garbileku while the women worked and visited. Sometimes there were only one or two, and sometimes they all were there.

As the boys became better acquainted and grew to be more adventurous, they would meet on the town plaza to play on the ruins of the old fort wall. It had once protected the city before the parish church and udaletxe were built surrounding the *plaza nagusia*, or "main plaza," and took its place.[76] They could spend hours protecting the old rock wall from invasions that were mounted from the udaletxe, the

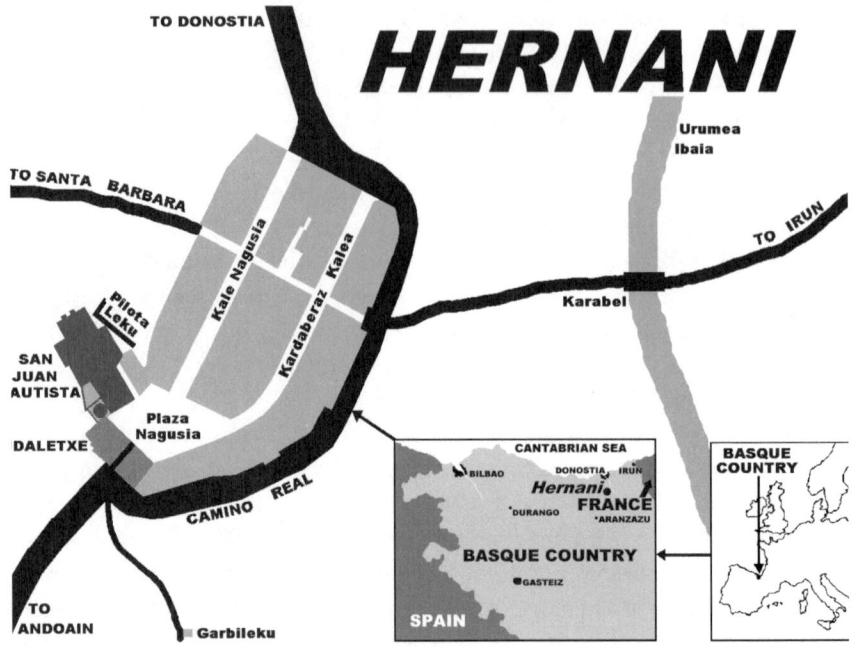

women's prison, or the slaughterhouse and butcher shop on the other side of the plaza.[77] Or they could ride off gallantly from the fort like Juan de Urbieta of old, whose tomb beneath the floor of the parish church they had all admired. That campaign was always followed by a triumphant reentry at the fortress with the captured French king.

On sunny days when Juan and the other boys tired of their various games, there were always other people on the plaza with whom they could visit, especially the old men who came to sit in the sun on the benches around the plaza. Juan de Lizarraga, the aged stone cutter with the scar on his face that he got in a knife fight,[78] was often there and never tired of telling the boys about rock quarrying and how he had built many of the structures around town. He loved to tell of the difficulties and trials of transporting the heavy dressed stones by oxcart from the quarry on the mountain down to the village. Antonio de Miner, although not as old, was another one whose stories fascinated the boys. He was a semiretired state attorney with the Real Chancillería in faraway Valladolid.[79] Actually, the High Court was not even two hundred miles away, but it might as well have been on the other side of the world as far as the children of Hernani were concerned. In his association with the Chancillería, Antonio had personally been all over Spain and had dealt with litigation that came to the court from northern Spaniards everywhere in the New World. His knowledge of faraway and exotic places, whether real or imagined, kept the boys spellbound. He may have been the first to plant the seed of foreign adventure in young Juan Bautista de Anza's mind.

After Juan was older and had learned to swim, his and the other children's adventures took them to the river on hot summer days. There they would play in the water and jump from the ancient wooden Karabel Bridge.[80] Also, it was always fascinating to visit the *convento* of San Agustín north of town. This ancient structure with its looming bell tower had once been the original parish church of Hernani before San Juan Bautista had been constructed in the sixteenth century.[81] It was so old as to stagger the imagination. The greatest adventure of all, however, was to go west of town across the cemetery and climb Santa Barbara Ridge. There, on top of the mesa, stood a majestic old stone fort. It was ancient and long since abandoned, but its ten-foot-high walls were fully intact. Moss grew in the shady corners of the little windows where its weapons had once protruded. The great door that had guarded its entryway was gone, but the massive oak jamb that supported the wall above the door was still flawless. The stone walkways beneath the gun ports were as solid as they had been centuries before when the fort was built.[82] Here, extended boyhood games of attack and siege could be, and were, played. Little could the young Juan Bautista de Anza have imagined, as he and the other youth of Hernani played in that great and ghostly fort on Santa Barbara Hill, that he would one day be fighting a much more serious and deadly game of war on the faraway Apache frontier of North America.

Schooling was important in a young village boy's life. It was especially important if he was to grow up to become a businessman, and that is what many young men of Hernani became—businessmen. Young boys from the baserri seldom had the opportunity to receive an education, and many who lived in town were denied it also. The village priest had always tried to teach as many of the young people as possible to read and write, but he had scores of other duties to attend to, and besides, there was money involved, something that not every family could provide. Eventually itinerant schoolteachers began to appear throughout Europe, including in the Basque country.

Although such schools were in place in some Basque cities a century earlier, Hernani got its first such *maisu*, or "schoolteacher," in the person of Juan Bautista de Vizarrón sometime in the latter part of the 1680s. He came down from the mountain village of Ituren in Nafarroa.[83] Where he got his education or why he chose Hernani as a place to teach is unknown, but once he came, he never left. He lived the rest of his life in Hernani. In fact, he married his wife, Mariana de Zuaznabar, a local Hernani girl, exactly one week after the big four-couple wedding in which Antonio Anza and Lucia Sasoeta were married.[84] Over the course of the next twenty years Vizarrón and his wife produced eight children, many of whose ages corresponded with those of Antonio and Lucia's children. Indeed, María Bautista Vizarrón was just three weeks younger than María Estevan Anza, and Jacinto Ignacio Vizarrón was born exactly four days after Juan Bautista Anza.[85]

During his first years in Hernani, Vizarrón earned his living by charging the parents of the children whom he was educating. It was not until 1718 that the village government became involved and began to pay him to educate the town's children.[86] Although Antonio and Lucia were not rich in comparison with many of the other families in town who sent their children to *irakasle* (schoolteacher) Vizarrón for his services, it is to their credit that they could see the value of education clearly enough that they were willing to pay the price to send all of their children to him, at least part of the time. María Estevan learned to read and write[87] when most girls of the day never had that opportunity. It was generally only the young men of the town who could be seen entering and leaving the classroom.

*María Estevan de Anssa*

The boys would gather at Vizarrón's house in the morning. There they would go through grueling exercises in learning the Spanish language, both written and oral. They practiced reading daily, both out loud and to themselves. They learned arithmetic and spent hour after hour working with quills and ink to perfect their writing styles. None developed a more beautiful hand than did Juan Bautista de Anza but, like the others, he would always speak castellano with a heavy Basque accent. The school day was long, but there were always a couple of hours in the middle of the day for the children to go home and eat lunch. After the midday meal, the students generally found time for another diversion before meeting back at the irakasle's house. They would congregate on the *pilota leku*, or "handball court," on the back side of the church and outside the north town wall.[88] There they would play a fast game or two of *pilota*[89] as their ancestors had done at the very same place for over a hundred years, ever since the new church had been completed in 1595. Sometimes the irakasle or even the *apez*, "priest," would come out and play with them. Almost all Basque boys became skilled at this fast-moving game. Juan Bautista de Anza and his friends were no exception.

When school let out, the scholars would sometimes play more pilota. If not, they might visit the workmen who were redesigning the mills at Zeago, or those who were repairing the town clock set high up in the church's bell tower.[90] The scaffolding was recklessly high beneath the clock, and the boys would have loved to climb up to the clock had it not been fervently forbidden by the workmen. There was little wonder that the clock was in need of repairs. It had been in use on the village plaza even before the church was built. In fact, the Royal Grant of 1540 gave permission for the church to be moved to the village plaza where the clock was located.[91] Regardless, everything about its overhaul and repair was intriguing to the boys. Sometimes they would visit the workers inside the church who were whitewashing the walls, also high up on scaffolding. One day when no one was around, the scaffolding fell, breaking an altar dedicated to the "Mystery of the Sorrows of the Mother of God." Although it was never proven what caused the expensive accident, certain rambunctious young boys were suspect.[92]

Although they played hard, they also worked hard under the supervision of Juan Bautista de Vizarrón. The boys admired and respected him, and he them. Associations were developed and a budding network established, both with the other boys of the village and this outstanding teacher, that would multiply and magnify the accomplishments of Juan Bautista de Anza and the generation that followed him.

Like any child, Juan experienced times that were agonizing and sad. He was just eight and a half years old when his beloved old grandmother, Josefa, died on January 2, 1702.[93] He may not have been as close to her as he was to his father's mother, because she did not live in the same house with them like Amona (Grandmother) Elena. Yet his mother went to see her own mother every day, and at that age Juan usually went with her. Although Juan never knew either of his grandfathers, he developed a close relationship with both of his grandmothers. Now his maternal grandmother had died. Hers was probably the first funeral Mass he ever attended.

Yet the young Anza probably never experienced a more distressing death than that of his brother, José, eight years later. In 1710 there were five children in the Anza family. María Estevan was a beautiful eighteen-year-old girl whom, more than likely, most of the boys in Hernani had their eye on. It would be nearly another twenty years before one would take her to the altar, however, and he would be an outsider from the mountains.[94] Juan Bautista, of course, was seventeen years old that year, a hardworking, likable young man known by everyone for miles around. Born on October 23, 1695, José was another bright and upcoming young man who had celebrated his fourteenth birthday just four months before his death.[95] Juan Felipe, the next brother, born on September 5, 1698, was not yet twelve,[96] and the last of the Anza children, little Nicolás, born November 30, 1700, had not yet seen his tenth birthday.[97]

By this time there was no one but the immediate family living in the Anza household. Antonio's two sisters, whom his older children had known as part of the family, had also moved on and started their own households. Amona Elena, Antonio's aging mother, who was nearing ninety, still lived with the family at the time of

José's death. His death (the cause of which is unknown) came as a dreadful shock to all of them, but it must have been especially painful to the old grandmother who had seen so many years of trials and death and had outlived everyone of her own generation.

Sadly for the parents, in a short time, two more of the boys would also be gone just as permanently as if they had died. Two years in the future, Juan Bautista would be in the Americas on the other side of the world. Four years after that Juan Felipe would be in Sevilla on the opposite side of Spain. Although both boys would marry and raise families, Antonio and Lucia would never see the grandchildren that resulted. They would never know their daughters-in-law, nor would they ever see their sons again. Their youngest son, Nicolás, would enter the priesthood and become a parish priest of San Juan Bautista of Hernani.[98] Although that undoubtedly brought pride to the hearts of his aging parents, they once again saw no grandchildren from this son. Fortunately, María Estevan married in time for her parents to know their son-in-law, Juan Domingo de Larreta. Antonio and Lucia were fortunate to be associated with all four of his and María Estevan's children, a son and three daughters, before their own deaths.[99] Nevertheless, there would be times of sadness on both sides of the world when the Anza family members thought of those they had lost.

How close a relationship Juan and his father had is unknown. It is obvious, however, that much of Juan's understanding of business and Spanish law was gained from his father. It is also known that his father involved him in the family business early on and that he was present with his father at numerous investigations and court hearings to which Antonio had been assigned by the town government. Going with the elder Anza took young Juan to places outside of town such as various baserriak, apple orchards, cider distilleries, flour mills, and iron foundries. It took him to the mountains where firewood was being cut for use in the town and charcoal was being made for use in the foundries.[100] He even worked several summers on Agerregi Baserria, a farm owned by his mother's cousin Catalina de Sasoeta.[101] There he learned to milk cows, load turnips and corn onto a donkey for transport to the big stone farmhouse, work for hours driving two heavy cows while the tenant managed a plow or a harrow behind them, and pick apples for hours on end in the cool fall weather.

He never understood the situation between the cousin, Catalina, and Dr. Zabala. Actually, no one else did either. He just knew that Catalina's three children, who were several years older than him, were also Dr. Zabala's children. He had been too young to remember when Dr. Zabala had abandoned his family. Catalina's brother, one of the parish priests, had taken care of her and the children until she could get her feet under her and make her own way.[102] Dr. Zabala had remarried,[103] and he and his second wife, Ana María de Kardaberaz, had three children in the early 1700s.[104]

Dr. Zabala died in February of 1708,[105] but prior to that Juan had seen him and been associated with him often through his own father. Sometimes Antonio would have to take some mixture of drugs or herbs to the hospital,[106] and Juan would tag along with him. Many were the times that they met Dr. Zabala there. It was also not unusual for Dr. Zabala to send a message over to the Anza botica that he needed some specific drug for a patient he was treating.[107] Often, it was Juan who was sent to deliver the prescription. The doctor was always friendly and treated him cordially. There also seemed to be nothing out of the ordinary in the relationship between Antonio and the doctor. Like all such ignominious situations, however, everyone was tight-lipped about it. Even Catalina, who was most likely bitter about the situation, never spoke a word about it in front of Juan. Children were not told about such things and they knew better than to ask.

Juan maintained the silence, and his experience on the baserri was a good one. He learned farming techniques there, especially in the cultivation of wheat and the care and handling of livestock, that would help him immensely later in life in a far distant land and a vastly different environment. An awareness of the stagnant situation of the *baserritarrak* had begun to develop in his mind, however. They had always been there, and their ancestors before them, and they always would be, doing the same hard, backbreaking work, year in and year out. Things were no different back in town. People slaved away there at the same old drudgery day after day, too. How could one ever break away and improve his lot in life? America seemed to be the only answer.

There was a *camino real*,[108] or "royal road," that ran from Donostia through Hernani to Andoain and on to Tolosa. Every morning while working on the baserri, Juan would leave his house on Kale Nagusia and walk down past the Leoka garbileku. There, he would connect with this camino real and follow it up the hill away from the river for nearly a mile before turning off to walk up the mountain to the baserri. Traffic was heavy on the main road, some of it traveling to and from markets in Hernani and other towns, and much of it heading toward or returning from the docks at Donostia.

The traffic was extremely varied in its content. There were those who were just walking to or from work in town or out on the farms. There were always donkeys laden with vegetables and other produce to be sold in town. Sometimes a donkey, and once in a while even a horse or mule, would be pulling a wooden wheeled cart, loaded with similar merchandise. Heavier, ox-drawn carts plied the road daily. They would be loaded with firewood, charcoal, building stone, or other heavy and cumbersome commodities. Dozens of these carts would be seen daily in the spring and early summer moving enormous sacks of wool that were being transported from the shearing pens of Nafarroa to the shipping docks of Donostia.[109] In the fall and early winter, the road would be filled with the same carts carrying heavy casks of *sagardoa,* or "apple cider," for which the Basque country was famous in those years. Sometimes the carts would be loaded with the *sagarrak* themselves, from which the cider was made.

The young boy spoke to the others on the road and learned of their trades and professions—the ox drivers and those leading pack-laden donkeys, the day workers and itinerant laborers, the carpenters, woodcutters, and rock masons, millers and foundry workers—all the many travelers on the camino real. None were of more interest to him, however, than the occasional nobleman, dressed smartly and mounted on horseback, or those riding in the daily horse-drawn coaches that funneled through Hernani on their way between Iruñea (Pamplona) or Gasteiz (Vitoria) and Donostia (San Sebastián). Those travelers on horseback or in the coaches were not just coming from Nafarroa and Araba. Many were coming from locations all over Spain and often Europe. Each time he stood at the edge of the camino real in the dust of a passing coach, a decision that he had made when he was not yet seven was probably confirmed again in his mind. He would one day own a horse and see the world for himself.

His excitement had been nearly uncontainable one evening back in the early part of May in the year 1700. His uncle, Nicolás Sasoeta, had come to the Anza home. Over a glass of wine he and Juan Bautista's father had discussed various business matters. His uncle had mentioned that he had to make a trip to Endaia in France to obtain various items of merchandise that he needed for his store on Kale Kardaberaz.[110] He had asked Juan's *aita* (father) if Juan might go with him. Osaba (Uncle) Nicolás and Izeba (Aunt) Josefa did not have any children of their own. Osaba could greatly use the help of a young boy on the trip. Juan was ecstatic—his father had agreed! Think of it—he was going to have the opportunity to go all the way to Francia!

A week later they left the house before daylight. When Osaba arrived, Juan was already up and dressed and nervously waiting. His *ama,* or "mother," had prepared him a lunch of bread and cheese, which she had wrapped and tied in a piece of cloth. Osaba also had a cloth sack with his lunch, some paper and writing materials, an account book, and his *txanponzorro,* or "coin purse." Slung over his shoulder was the omnipresent goatskin wine bag, or *zato,* filled with bitter local wine called *txakolin.*

Juan and his uncle said a quick goodbye and headed down Kale Nagusia to the cross street and through the east arch leading out of town. They crossed the Karabel Bridge, and on the other side of the river, just as a dim light was beginning to show in the east, they stopped at a baserri where Osaba had made arrangements for the rental of three *astoak,* or "donkeys," for packing. With lamp in hand, the baserritar led them around to the main entrance of the house where the donkeys were tied. There they loaded the pack baskets onto the sleepy animals. Taking leave of the baserritar, Juan led one of the donkeys and Osaba led two of them as they continued on their way northeast toward Astigarraga.

Young Anza may have gone over the ridge as far as Astigarraga previously with his father. However, when he and Osaba left that village and turned east toward Oiartzun, they were traveling through country he had never seen. Compared to the camino real that ran by Hernani, this was hardly a road, but rather a *bidezidor,* or "footpath." It wound up and down over ridges and through canyons. The trees and undergrowth were so thick all along the trail that they sometimes formed a canopy overhead blocking out the sun's light almost entirely. It was cool and beautiful in the forest. The three astoak plodded along gently behind the lad and his uncle. It was a tremendous experience for a young boy of nearly seven as he and Osaba walked along visiting, man to man.

They probably crossed through Oiartzun well before noon as they took the road down to Irun. The road was a little more well traveled between those two towns, and they may have had company as they stopped along the way for lunch. The bread and cheese, washed down by gulps of txakolin, tasted wonderful after the long walk. Juan was amazed at the number of people they met along the way who actually knew his osaba. He was also astonished at the size of Irun when they arrived at that city. Even there, however, his uncle seemed to know a number of people, and they stopped at several enterprises in town for Osaba to do business. Juan would wait outside and hold the astoak while his uncle negotiated with the proprietor.

It was fairly late in the afternoon before they left Irun, but it was only a short walk of a couple miles down a swale and there they were—in Hendaia—in Francia! It was nearly dark and the twenty-mile hike had been strenuous. Although Juan was happy to think he was actually now in France, he was even happier to lay down a blanket on the floor in the upper story of Osaba's friend's house and fall asleep after a quick supper. It had been a long day for a little boy.

The next morning Juan and Nicolás were up early and, after breakfast, they retrieved the three donkeys from where they had been tethered and fed overnight. From there they went down several blocks and across town to the store of Juan de Buti. He was French, and he and Osaba had to resort to communicating with each other in Spanish. Although Juan had been studying castellano under the tutelage of Juan Bautista de Vizarrón, he was new to it and found it hard to follow what Osaba and the storeowner were saying. The value of being able to speak Spanish, however, was impressed upon his young mind. Juan de Buti seemed to have just about everything in his store, and what he did not have that Osaba needed he sent a runner across town to find. Soon large stacks of merchandise began to pile up on tables and on the floor. Juan wondered if they would be able to get it all on the three little donkeys.

The new suit of clothes that Osaba purchased for Juan's *lehengusutipi*[111] (male second cousin), Francisco Antonio de Beroiz, brought Juan the greatest thrill. Juan and Francisco Antonio were related in exactly the same way that Juan and Teodoro de Zuaznabar were related. Teodoro's mother, Ana María de Larramendi, and Francisco's mother, Margarita de Larramendi, were sisters. Both ladies were first cousins to Juan's mother and Osaba Nicolás. Whether Juan actually knew that, at least at this age, is questionable. His cousin Teodoro was like an orphan passed from family to family. Teodoro's mother, these many years after her liaisons with Captain Zuaznabar, was now respectably married to Estevan de Arrasain,[112] and Juan knew that she was his cousin. It is doubtful, however, that either he or Teodoro knew that she was Teodoro's mother.

Francisco Antonio, on the other hand, was heir to one of the largest fortunes in Hernani. His father, Francisco de Beroiz, had died, and Francisco Antonio and his sisters would one day own the entire estate that had been passed down from their grandfather and grandmother, Miguel de Beroiz and Mariana de Ereñozu. An old friend of the family, Juan Bautista de Araeta, probably the most ostentatious entrepreneur in Hernani, was administering the estate for Margarita and the children. He and the children's mother had decided it would be in Francisco Antonio's best interest to send him to Madrid to school.[113] Therefore, when Margarita had heard that her cousin, Nicolás, was going to Hendaia on a supply trip, she gave him six *doblones de a dos*[114] in gold to purchase Francisco Antonio a new suit of clothes, and to buy some clothes for the other children as well. José de Egino and Josefa de Goicoechea had a fine clothing store in Hernani, but evidently Margarita wanted something a cut above what they could provide for her only son's trip to Madrid.

Young Juan Bautista was impressed with the beautiful black suit of drugget woolen cloth that Osaba picked out for Francisco Antonio. It was soft and velvety and there were elegant silk stockings and a hat to go with it. Rouen linen breaches and white silk gloves were also befitting a madrileño scholar.[115] However, the blue cape that Osaba chose to go with the suit was the most spectacular of all. It was set off in a trim of fine gold thread. Juan could imagine what a majestic figure his older cousin[116] would make as he boarded the coach in Hernani to begin his journey to Madrid, home of His Majesty. Although Juan might one day have a desire to see Madrid, for the present he was in France and that was probably enough excitement for one small boy.

Once all of the purchases were made at Jauna Buti's store, and several trips had been completed by various runners around town to find articles that the storeowner did not have in stock, it had gotten far too late in the day to try to return home to Hernani. So another night was spent at the home of Osaba's friend. Early the next morning the merchandise was loaded onto the three pack donkeys, and, after a long exhausting walk, the uncle and the young boy arrived home late the next afternoon. Although Juan was tired when he entered his door on Kale Nagusia and greeted his mother, a sense of fulfillment burned brightly deep within him. He had been to

France. He would go again. And he would go other places and do other things far greater.

## Invitation to Wanderlust

| | |
|---|---|
| *Agur nere biotzeko* | Good-bye beloved mother |
| *amatxo maitea,* | the dearest of my heart |
| *laxter etorriko naiz* | I'll come soon to comfort you, |
| *konsola zaitea* | but now my journey starts. |
| *Jaungoikoak nai ba du* | For the call to cross the oceans |
| *ni urez joatea—* | comes from God on High— |
| *Ama, zertarako da* | Mother, oh dear Mother |
| *negar egitea?* | Why is it that you cry?[117] |

The lure of the outside world was strong everywhere in the Basque country of the seventeenth century. Her young men and, to some extent, her young women felt the allure of distant lands and exotic places. The young people of Hernani were no exception. Young Juan Bautista de Anza may have been enticed even more strongly than others. Because of his father's business and position in the town, he often had opportunities to go places and see and do things that other children, especially the farm youth, never enjoyed. The trip to Hendaia had been only a beginning.

By the time Juan was in his teens he had traveled extensively to neighboring towns carrying messages, making deliveries, and transporting merchandise for his father, his Osaba Nicolás, and others. He had been to many businesses throughout the area and had become acquainted with the proprietors. He had been inside the Urruzuno iron foundry between Hernani and Donostia,[118] and had visited his cousins' foundry, the ferrerías (ironworks) de Ereñozu,[119] on numerous occasions. In Usurbil he had visited the royal shipyards[120] and may even have met old Blasio de Echeveste, who had been the master shipbuilder there many years before.

He had been in Donostia, the town that Spanish speakers called San Sebastián, numerous times. He went there to visit his uncle and aunt, Felipe de Anza and Antonia de Oiza. Their oldest son, Pedro Felipe, who was five years younger than Juan Bautista, looked up to Juan and idolized him.[121] The other children were progressively younger than Juan, the youngest, María Nicolasa, being born just a few months prior to his departure for America.[122]

Juan also went to Donostia with the *cargador* (freighter) Mateo de Aiarragaray on various occasions to help with the loading of incoming freight or for transporting iron from the foundries to be shipped out at the docks. In most of these instances, Mateo was in the service of the master buyer and seller Juan Bautista de Araeta, and

Anza had merely been helping him. Aiarragaray would pick up iron at the Ereñozu or some other foundry, and transport it by means of his team of heavy oxen and his unwieldy wooden *carreta* to the wharves to be shipped out to America.[123]

On the docks, the youthful Anza got a close-up look at all the many fishing boats and whaling vessels whose owners called Donostia their home port. He saw merchant sailing vessels that plied the Atlantic, traveling to such faraway ports as Ireland, England, the Mediterranean, Africa, and the Americas. At different times, he had even seen all four of the great war *galeones* that had been constructed by the famous shipbuilders Ignacio de Soroa and Blasio de Echeveste and constituted the Escuadra de Cantábria.[124] Probably more influential in shaping the young man's desire to leave his homeland and travel to some distant shore, however, were the men who sailed the ships and others that he met along the way.

There were those who were content with their lot in life and would continue to struggle to make a living, the best they could, in and around Hernani. For instance, Mateo de Aiarragaray would continue freighting until he died.[125] Ramón de Arbelaiz was content with his life as a *carbonero*, and would continue the dirty, backbreaking work of manufacturing charcoal and transporting it to the iron foundries.[126] José de Isasa would continue work as a founder in the ferrerías de Ereñozu,[127] and José de Iribarren and Juan de Arrasain would go on slaving away as seasonal and day workers on the baserriak around Hernani, never owning anything.[128] In town, others like Domingo de Zuaznabar, the tailor,[129] and Pedro de Recarte, the butcher,[130] were also content with their simple life and could not have imagined trading it for anything else. Although the young Anza was good friends with these men, he had already begun to formulate a plan to escape the doldrums of the village, and even the Basque country.

For the teenage boy there were those who seemed to have risen above the ordinary and whose occupations and life pursuits appeared worthy of emulation. Juan Beltran de Portu, *alcalde de sacas* for all of Gipuzkoa,[131] was one such individual. He was in control of wool shipments, and his association with the wool trade had taken him all over Spain. Old Antonio de Miner, of course, was the same. Even though he had kept his home and headquarters in Hernani, his work with the Chancillería in Valladolid had sent him to many places in Spain and France, and the opportunity had been there to travel to America if he had so desired.

Juan's lehengusutipi Francisco Antonio de Beroiz was also an inspiration. Only seven years older than Juan, he had been educated in Madrid and had seen other exotic places that most of the other local boys had little hope of ever seeing. However, he had little reason to be interested in America. He was heir to a vast estate, something of which Juan had no hope. The botica was a great little business, but far beneath Juan's sights.

Although it may have been a disappointment to Antonio, Juan had no desire to follow in his footsteps as a boticario. Rather, he wanted to do something similar to

Francisco Antonio's uncle, Francisco de Larramendi. He was *capitán de mar y guerra*, "captain of sea and war." He sailed with the Escuadra de Cantábria, going wherever the king sent him.[132]

No one could have been more impressive to the young boy than the pretentious Juan Bautista de Araeta. A native of Nafarroa, he had lived in Hernani as long as Juan could remember. He and his wife, Josefa de Roteta, had eight children, all close to Juan's age.[133] They lived well, but Araeta himself was seldom home. He was involved in buying and selling everything from firewood to apple cider,[134] but his main business was iron. In his negotiations with the foundries and the iron industry he had often traveled as far south as Cádiz and had even been to the Americas.[135] The youthful Anza desired to be like him.

Little could Juan have known that his association with Beroiz and Araeta, coupled with helping his father in his many financial and legal pursuits, would give him a background in law and judicial procedure that would help him attain that goal. He could never have imagined that just a few years hence he would be in an unusual land that was virtually lawless. What he was learning today would be a great benefit to him tomorrow.

During the years at the turn of the century the rains did not come like normal.[136] Livestock feed and farm crops were stunted, and the Urumea River was running low. Worse than the drought, Francisco de Beroiz had died, leaving his wife, Margarita de Larramendi, with little Francisco Antonio and his five[137] sisters to care for. Beyond that, Margarita was sickly. Although she was under the care of Dr. Zabala, and Antonio Anza was supplying her with the medicines the doctor prescribed, she continued to decline in health. In delivering the drugs, Juan Bautista had the opportunity for close association with his older cousins, especially Francisco Antonio until he went away to Madrid.

Because of her poor health and the tremendous responsibility of caring for so many small children and the family farms, mills, and foundries, Margarita had asked Juan Bautista de Araeta to manage the family businesses for her. Operated by tenants and renters, most of the businesses were fairly self-sufficient. The flour mill called Errotaberri, in operation since at least 1418,[138] was one business owned by the Beroiz heirs. It was operating smoothly under the expert care of its renter, *maestro molinero* José de Iparragire. Basterrola, Errotaburu, Beroqui, and other baserriak under Margarita's management and run by longtime renters, also required little, if any, supervision.[139]

The *molinos* ("mills") de Zeago were a different story. Located across the river and a little south of Hernani, they also had been in operation since at least 1418. They were being seriously affected by the drought. The *acequia*, or "irrigation canal," that brought the water from the river to the mill had become clogged with mud and leaves because of the shortage of rains. By 1700 it was becoming increasingly difficult to get the water from the low-flowing river to the ditch. Maestro molinero Antonio de Amitesarobe had rented the mills for a number of years. It had been customary for him to pay one and one-half *fanegas* of wheat flour and three *cuartales* of cornmeal in weekly rent from the grain that he ground. What he was able to pay had fallen off to half that amount in the fall and nothing in the winter and spring.

Margarita had tried to make a land exchange with the baserri above the mills so that the acequia could be extended and thereby raised in elevation. Unsuccessful in her negotiations, she had at that time resorted to asking Araeta, a longtime friend of her deceased husband, to help. On March 5, 1700, they signed a formal agreement whereby he rented the mills for eight years from January 1, 1700, at the rate of five cuartales of wheat and three of corn. Araeta attacked the problem with resolve. First, he hired as a consultant one Juan El Sordo ("the deaf man"), a maestro molinero of great fame who operated the mills at Loyola. Two men with a team of oxen were employed to clean the acequia and repair the holding pond at its head. A team of carpenters was brought in to repair the *orza*, the Basque term for the "weir" that diverted water from the acequia to the *anteparas*, the canals that then carried the water to the heavy *ruedas*, or "mill wheels."

Of course, the cleaning and repair of the acequia and anteparas decreased the elevation of the water coming to the ruedas, such that it was below the tops of the wheels. El Sordo and Araeta devised a complicated plan whereby cranes were set up in front of the ruedas to lift the water up to them by means of wooden casks, called *upelak* in Basque. Although the system worked and increased the weekly output of the mills, it was labor-intensive and extremely costly.

Construction of the complete system ran throughout the entire year of 1700 and well into 1701. Juan Bautista de Anza and the other boys from town spent many of their midday breaks from school and other times watching the heavy construction and visiting with the maestros *carpinteros* (carpenters) and *canteros* (stone cutters). Just a few years in the future, it would be to the benefit of Juan and his father that he had spent so much time watching the construction.

The Beroiz *mayorazgo*, or "family estate," was vast and included numerous baserriak, the ferrerías, and both the well-known molinos of Hernani. The rights of succession were especially complex. Miguel de Beroiz had died in the mid-1600s, leaving his widow, Mariana de Ereñozu, with the entire burden. Known as a "vigorous rent collector," she managed the entire operation efficiently. Upon her death on June 28, 1689,[140] it fell to her son, Francisco de Beroiz, to manage the estate for himself and his two sisters. Unfortunately, he died less than six years later on February 16, 1695,[141] and his frail wife, Margarita de Larramendi, as curadora of their six children, inherited the entire mayorazgo. She, too, lived barely six years after her husband's death, dying on May 13, 1701.[142] The day before her death, escribano de número José de Ugalde recorded her last will and testament in which she named

Antonio de Miner curador of her children. He was married to her husband's sister, Gertrudis de Beroiz.

Beyond all this, over a year before her death, Margarita had named Juan Bautista de Araeta manager of her affairs and had rented him the molinos de Zeago for eight years. He died just five years after Margarita on July 1, 1706,[143] leaving his wife, Josefa de Roteta, with his own vast and complicated estate. Furthermore, Nicolás de Lecuna, tenant at Baserri Basterrola, had also died, leaving his poor, illiterate widow, María de Lecumberri, with all the problems of managing that farm.

Francisco Antonio de Beroiz, the only son of Francisco and Margarita and designated male heir of the mayorazgo, even though he was still a minor, was away at school in Madrid and did not arrive back in Hernani until 1707. By that time, the estate was in complete chaos. Nobody knew for sure how much money was owed to or should be collected from anybody else. Antonio de Miner, attorney for the Chancillería in Valladolid and guardian of the Beroiz children, was married to the children's aunt, Gertrudis de Beroiz. Because she was named as an heir in the estate, he could not prosecute any litigation due to conflict of interest. Therefore, on April 1, 1707, he and the Beroiz children appointed Antonio de Anza curador ad litem to settle the estate through the court system.[144] That process was to drag on for the next several years. It took all of Antonio's spare time and involved his son, Juan Bautista, as a messenger, investigator, interrogator, and witness.

Juan was especially involved in the ensuing court case brought about to settle matters between the estate and Juan Bautista de Araeta's wife and children over the matter of the molinos de Zeago. He was closely acquainted with almost everyone that had been or was involved. It seemed as if everyone had spent a lot of money and no one was collecting anything. Furthermore, the mill was still not working like it should. When Araeta's lease ran out, Antonio de Amitesarobe again rented it for three years. Amitesarobe was unable to pay his rent. As Juan listened to court testimony and watched his father and the attorneys, judges, and others involved in the system, he began to understand the workings of Castilian law and the Basque fuero. The first known signature of Juan Bautista de Anza, at sixteen of years of age, was executed as a witness to a sworn statement of Antonio de Amitesarobe.[145] On the very same day, September 28, 1709, in another and different hearing, he attested to the truthfulness of a statement made by his older cousin:

> In consideration of these decrees and by way of defeasance, and attentive to what Don Francisco Antonio de Beroiz has said in the declaration on folio sixteen, in which he declared there are other heirs of Doña Mariana de Ereñozu, his grandmother, who left three children, to wit: Don Francisco de Beroiz, his father, and Doña Gertrudis and Doña Ana María de Beroiz, her daughters, and that the principal heir[146] of his father is Doña María Josefa, Don Francisco Antonio's sister. He, therefore, petitions to have the above-mentioned successors

and heirs cited in the documentation in case of his death, because after three days it is anyone's right to convene through summons and proceed by his absence and default. By this, whether it is concurred or not, he delivers up these decrees that justice might be served on advice of his legal counsel and the Lord Mayor Sebastián de Kardaberaz in the village of Hernani on September 28, 1709.

Sebastián de Cardaveraz (rubric)
Licenciado Don Miguel de Artaxcos (rubric)
Witness Joseph de Torres (rubric)
Witness Domingo de Ansorena (rubric)
Witness Juan Bauptista de Anssa (rubric)[147]

His third and only other known signature written in Hernani and still in existence today was also executed at the udaletxe on a warm Monday morning the following summer. He had gone there specifically to participate in a court hearing considering the Widow Lecumberri's inability to pay her rent at Basterrola. Juan had already heard testimony of witnesses called by his father on behalf of Francisco Antonio, in which evidence was given of the poor management of the widow's deceased husband and of her own inconsistent payment of the rent. Today he would hear three men, whom he knew well, testify about the struggles brought on by the drought and other problems at Basterrola. They would tell of circumstances that would show the rent was too high. The aging widow, whom he also knew well and respected highly, was there as well that morning:

Beneath the porticos of the town hall of this Very Noble and Very Loyal Town of Hernani, when the clock on the tower said it was nine o'clock in the morning, today, Monday, June 2, 1710, María de Lecumberri, widow of Nicolás de Lecuna and resident of this village, appeared as a witness before me, the undersigned notary. By way of proof and investigation of what is contained in her interrogatories on the preceding page, she presented for witnesses José de Isasa, José de Iribarren, and Juan de Arrasain, residents of this town. By virtue of the commission given me, the said notary, by the writ of proof in the said interrogatories, I received the oath from each of them by the sign of the Holy Cross in the required form, to tell the truth in whatever they might be asked. That they did as required by the oath and as promised to tell the truth in their presentation and interrogation was witnessed by Juan Francisco de Zuaznabar and Juan Bautista de Anza.

Before me, Joseph de Ugalde (rubric)
Witness Juan Francisco de Zuaznavar (rubric)
Witness Juan Bauptista de Anssa (rubric)[148]

Over the next couple of years Juan Bautista de Anza learned the power of the court system. He saw both success and failure on the part of his father as he attempted to obtain the best for the Beroiz children. He heard witnesses, including Osaba Nicolás, tell how Juan Bautista de Araeta was an honest and good man. He listened as other witnesses, especially maestros molineros, expressed their opinions that the repairs made at Zeago by Araeta and the famed El Sordo caused more harm than good. He was in the udaletxe the day a decision was finally handed down in the Zeago case. The court had determined that the estate should pay the Widow Roteta 970 reales de plata of the 1,463 reales she had demanded in consequence of the many expenses her husband had incurred in his attempts to repair the mills.

Both sides agreed that it was a fair judgment, but since the mills were operating at a loss, something drastic had to be done. The mill had been put up for sale a number of times but had never received even one bidder. Amitesarobe claimed that he had taken the lease at a price no one else would consider and that his expenses far outweighed his income. Therefore, he requested a reduction in rent. Because Amitesarobe was unable to meet the rent agreement he had made with Antonio de Miner, Antonio de Anza moved unsuccessfully to have Amitesarobe's three-year contract terminated and the mills closed.

This time, even the King of Spain, Felipe V, got involved. Because of the importance of both Zeago and Errotaberri to the economy of the area, he dispatched a *real cédula*, or "royal decree," in Amitesarobe's favor, forbidding the closing of Zeago.[149] It was the first and probably only cédula that Juan would ever see. Thirty years later the same Bourbon monarch would issue a real cédula honoring Juan Bautista de Anza for his service to the king. It would arrive too late on the far northern frontier of Nueva España for him to see it, however. He would already be dead, a victim of marauding Apaches.

For the present, Juan knew nothing of the Apaches and had only the vaguest knowledge of Nueva España. Had he known about them, however, he probably would have still taken the same course of action he was about to follow. In 1712, at the age of nineteen, he made his decision. He was going to America.[150] The desire for adventure burned bright within him. In the faraway Indias there were fortunes to be made, lands to be owned, fame and honor to be achieved. There were military victories to be won among untold numbers of enemies of the king. For long enough now he had walked across the tomb of Hernani's famous soldier, Juan de Urbieta, every time he attended Mass. The village and local community had become much too restrictive. It was time for him to leave home and make his own name for himself. Yes, America was where he belonged!

Juan had heard many stories from people who had family members in America.[151] José de Torres, who had signed the two documents with him at the court hearings back in September of 1709, had a brother living there. He had often told Juan Bautista of the letters he had received from his own brother, Juan, living in Nueva España in the great city México.[152] Nicolás de Lecuna, son of the Widow Lecumberri and her deceased husband Nicolás,[153] had left for the New World when Juan Bautista was a new baby. Although Juan could not remember this son, he had often heard the widow speak of him and knew he, too, was living in Mexico City.

A number of boys from the town who were several years older than Juan had already left for the Americas. Asencio de Egino, six years older than Anza and a brother to one of his best friends, Miguel Antonio de Egino,[154] was already living in America. The family had received several letters from him describing its virtues in glowing terms. Francisco Herauso was seven years older than Juan, but like Asencio he was an older brother of one of Juan's best friends. Ignacio Herauso and Juan were the same age,[155] and the two boys had often made plans about how they would travel to America as Francisco had done. Ignacio Antonio de Zuaznabar,[156] the older brother of José de Zuaznabar, another of Anza's close friends, had recently left Hernani to join others of the family in Argentina.

Records have not been found that tell of Juan Bautista's emigration, but a number of things are probable. It is likely that he did not leave Hernani alone. There were several boys his own age that migrated to America, and there is a good chance that two or three of them left together. There is always security in numbers, and when embarking on such a new and adventurous undertaking it is always good to have company. Sebastián Manuel de Herauso, José de Zuaznabar, and Sebastián de Miner had all grown up with Anza and were within just a few months of the same age. That any combination of the four, or all of the group, left together is entirely plausible. Although Anza went to Nueva España and Zuaznabar went to Argentina, it would not have been unusual for them to have left Hernani together, only to part company at the proper time in Cádiz, in Spain, or in Vera Cruz, on the east coast of Nueva España. Nicolás de Miner was a year and half younger than Juan but may have left at the same time. If that was the case, since he also went to Nueva España, he and Anza would probably have traveled together at least as far as Mexico City.

There were many routes leading to the New World. Juan Bautista de Anza could have gone overland to Cádiz, but given his connections in Donostia, the chances are greater that he set sail from there. If he left from Donostia, his immediate family were probably not the only ones there to see him off. Juan's osaba Felipe de Anza and his family would also have been there. It would only be a few years before Felipe's son, Pedro, would follow suit and join Juan Bautista on the far north frontier.

Juan's family could take heart that he was not disappearing into a black abyss of unknown regions and unseen dangers. He was going to live with family in a large Spanish city. Culiacán in the Province of Sinaloa had been established nearly two hundred years before, in 1531.[157] His two aunts, Francisca and María Josefa, sisters of his mother, were both there, as was Lucia's cousin, Alonso de Sasoeta. Others of the extended Sasoeta family also lived in Culiacán.[158] Although Juan's mother could take heart in those facts, she probably sensed that he would not stay in the city, among family, for long. The pull of adventure and wanderlust was too great in her oldest son for him to settle for something so ordinary.

Possibly until such time as the Pasajeros de Indias (Spanish immigration) records become more readily available, the exact time and route of Juan's journey will never be known. Although it is uncertain whether he left by sea from Donostia or by land from Hernani, and where the family stood as they watched him depart, there is one thing that is sure—it happened with every young adventurer departing for the Americas. Juan Bautista's beloved mother, Lucia de Sasoeta, cried as she waved good-bye to her oldest son, knowing full well she would never see him again. Another thing is almost as certain. He, a nineteen-year-old boy, departing on the greatest adventure of his life, could not understand why.

# Chapter Three

## The New World

### *Aguaje*

*Por apoiar la virtud religion y jun$^a$ de los R$^s$ P$^{es}$ enestos therritorios y aunque Jamas educaecido enestto siendo entodas parttes plausor delo que tan justa$^{te}$ venero entodos los religiosos de la Comp$^a$ de Jh$^s$ mi madre—Juan Baup$^{ta}$ de Anssa (rúbrica)* . . . Although I have not been educated in this sentiment, I feel in every case I must praise my mother[1] for how I justly respect all the religious of the Company of Jesus and [for my desire] to protect the virtue, religion, and organization of the reverend fathers in these territories—Juan Bautista de Anza (rubric).[2]

Nuestra Señora de Guadalupe de Aguaje[3] was probably the wildest, most lawless royal silver mining camp in all of Nueva España, and, with the exception of Álamos to the south, it was the largest current mining operation in Sonora. A true boomtown, it had been in operation for only a few years.[4] In every way it was the antithesis of anything Juan Bautista de Anza had ever known. He may have been involved in its founding, or he might have arrived shortly after it was started. Regardless, his mother's apprehensions had been right. He had stayed with the family in Culiacán barely long enough to get acquainted. Drawn by the lure of fast wealth, he had moved north quickly, following the mining industry, and had probably arrived at Aguaje via Álamos, the most famous of all of Sonora's mining districts at the time. His history in the New World up to this point is as sketchy as that of this *real de minas*, or "royal mining camp," where we first encounter him in the New World in 1718.

What is certain is that Anza found himself in an environment totally different than anything he had ever known. The relative serenity of faraway Hernani, with its gentle people and familiar customs, had been replaced by previously unknown mixtures of humanity and the harsh, raucous life of a primitive, frontier mining camp. There was money to be made, however—big money—and for a young man in his early twenties, the enticement of wealth, coupled with the sheer adventure of being at the farthest point out on such an untamed frontier, was irresistible.

There were no other settlements of any kind for distances that were incomprehensible to the mind of a person coming from northern Spain. The closest was a *ranchería* made up of eighteen families of Pimas Bajos, or "Lower Pima Indians." Known as La Santísima Trinidad del Pitic,[5] it was located some twenty-five miles north of Aguaje. There was one hardy Spanish citizen, Diego Moraga, who lived in that vicinity and operated a small ranch and mining claim.[6] Just a few miles above Pitic, at San Francisco Xavier de Tucuaba (later known simply as "San Francisco") on the San Miguel River, was another small settlement of Lower Pimas.[7] A couple of lone Spaniards, the brothers Antonio and Blas Nuñez, lived near their village, prospecting and operating small livestock farms.[8] About forty miles to the southwest, on the other side of the impenetrable Cerro Prieto mountain range and along the coast of the Gulf of California, were various settlements of the Guaymas Indians. The only other Spanish settlement within a fifty-mile radius was situated barely within that limit. It lay to the east over some extremely rugged and inhospitable country. It, too, was a frontier mining camp, known as Nuestra Señora de la Purificación del Aigame.[9] Although smaller than Aguaje, Aigame had been in existence since about the turn of the century.[10]

There were other mining camps and several missions and *visitas*, or visiting stations, farther to the north in the Sonora and San Miguel River valleys. The missions were operated by la Compañía de Jesús, the "Company of Jesus," or the "Jesuits," as they were commonly called. The closest mission, however, at well over fifty miles distance, was San Miguel de Ures on the Sonora River. Although there was a modest adobe church at Ures at this time, there seems to have been no resident priest there.[11] The mission was evidently being visited occasionally by a Jesuit missionary from one of their establishments father north along the Sonora River. There were some fifty-five Lower Pima families living at Ures.[12] Going north along the San Miguel River in the next valley west of Ures, there were several *visitas*, but it was over a hundred miles travel before one reached the first *cabecera*, or "headquarters," where a Jesuit priest lived.[13] That was at Los Santos Reyes Magos de Cucurpe, a mission to both the Opata and the Lower Pima Indians.[14] Just a little north and the west of Cucurpe, Father Luis Xavier de Velarde was presently stationed at Los Dolores, the southernmost mission to the Upper Pimas.[15]

Northwest of Cucurpe and in the next river valley, called Santa Magdalena, was a lone priest stationed at San Ignacio de Cabórica, some one hundred fifty miles north of Aguaje.[16] Most of the time Father José Agustín de Campos was trying to serve the entire Pimería Alta, or "land of the Upper Pimas," by himself. If he and Juan Bautista de Anza knew each other at this point, it was probably only through written correspondence. It was from the missions that the mines purchased much of their food, such as corn, beans, wheat, and dried meat.[17] On the other hand, since the Indian population of Sonora was small and the Spanish population was even smaller, it is possible the two had met in person. Regardless, over the course of the next several years they would become well acquainted.

For now, neither man came in contact with many representatives of his own race and culture. Father Campos, of course, was completely by himself among the Pima Indians. Anza did have a few Basque and a number of Spanish neighbors in the lively boomtown where he lived. The majority of the population, however, was made up of Africans, Indians, and various mixed bloods that the Spaniards called *mestizos, mulatos, coyotes,* and *lobos,* or "wolves," among other things.

The Indian population was made up of several different tribes, including Lower Pima, Opata, and Yaqui. There were numerous Guaymas and Seri Indians in the vicinity, but whether any of them worked the mines is unknown. Everyone in the old country, of course, had heard of the indigenous people of America that were called *indios,* or "Indians," but Juan had had no idea of the great number of tribes, cultures, and languages represented by that designation. Since owning and operating a mine at Aguaje, he had come to know of some of the differences. He and the other miners hired Yaquis to work their mines and to prospect for other possible veins of silver or gold. Anza had found them to be excellent workers, though possibly somewhat more independent and volatile than the sedentary Lower Pima and Opata, whom he also hired. These latter two tribes were farming peoples and, although they were excellent workers, the mines virtually shut down when planting season came during the summer rains.[18]

The Pimas and Opatas also seemed receptive to Anza's much loved Catholic religion. The Yaquis also generally were receptive to Catholicism, but they tended to incorporate it into their culture after their own fashion. At Aguaje, Juan had also come in contact with the Seri, Guaymas, and other coastal Indians. These groups, especially the Seri, seemed less interested in Catholicism and the Spaniards' way of life. For the present, all of the tribes got along with the Spaniards. However, they tended to fight among themselves, especially the Seris and the Lower Pimas, raiding each other's villages and causing death and destruction.[19] That, of course, would change in time as more and more animosity would be directed toward the Spaniards. Already, there was news of the viciousness and barbarity of a northern tribe of Indians known as the Apache.

A *presidio,* or "garrison of soldiers," had been established only a few years before on the far northern limits of the territory to curb the hostilities. Instituted as a *compañía volante,* a "mobile company," La Caballería de las Fronteras, or "The Cavalry of the Frontier," was located 200 miles to the north in the Opata country at a place called Santa Rosa de Corodéguachi.[20] Although the company was originally established as a mobile unit, it had increasingly made its home base at Corodéguachi, until it was known as the Presidio of Corodéguachi. That, also, was changing. Since it was the "Cavalry of the Frontier," it was becoming known more and more as the "Presidio of Fronteras." Over the next few years, the growing differences between the Spanish community and the indigenous tribes would become so acute, and Spanish politics on the semilawless frontier would become so corrupt, that the tiny garrison of fifty soldiers would find their job nearly overwhelming and virtually impossible.

Presently, however, an even greater contrast for Anza than the people was the physical environment. He had been raised in a moist, cool climate with soft, green foliage everywhere, shaded by massive pine and oak trees. The only shade to be found at Aguaje was in the depths of one of the mines, inside one of the crude dwellings made of mud, grass, and sticks, or in or beside one of the small grass-roofed, adobe stores that made up the village.[21] Nowhere was there a stone building to be seen, and there was certainly no structure of more than one story. Even in the meager shade provided by one of the tiny mud cottages, a feeling of "cool" was seldom experienced. Hot—extremely hot—was a much more likely description of the temperature on any given day. It was also dry—extremely dry. Never before had Juan experienced the cracking of his lips and the dry feeling of his skin and hair like he did in this arid climate.

Aguaje was in the heart of the basin and range country of the Sonoran Desert. The fault block mountains that lined the valleys, with craggy fault lines facing west, were extremely rugged and, in some ways, resembled the rocky, jagged, higher elevations in the Basque country. Their color and makeup were different, however. The mountains around the mining camp were gray and brown, and their rock cliffs were generally more crumbly and fragile. Nowhere to be seen was the vibrant green of his homeland. Gone were the meadows of velvety green ferns and grasses, sprinkled with elderberry and other lush shrubbery. Replacing them in this new environment were sparse bunch grasses with an occasional cat claw, white thorn, or creosote bush. It was here that he had first seen the strangely shaped senita, organ pipe, and cardón cacti. Nothing was friendly. All the plants had huge thorns and stickers, especially the cholla cactus that dotted the hillsides. The mesquite, paloverde, and ironwood trees that were plentiful in the upper elevations resembled bushes more than they did the trees to which Anza was accustomed. Although the old-growth mesquites were gigantic, it was hard to find a straight limb that would provide poles or timbers of any great length. On the other hand, these trees were some of the hardest wood in the world and made the finest charcoal he had ever seen. Although there were no iron foundries here that utilized charcoal, the silver smelters servicing the mines consumed huge quantities of it.

Animals were different here, too. Many were as unfriendly as the plants and even more dangerous. Anza had never seen anything like the Gila monsters that lumbered awkwardly around the hillsides, and certainly there was no *suge*, or *víbora* as was said in Spanish, in the entire Basque country that resembled the western rattlesnake in ugliness or deadly venom. The eerie buzz of its rattles left one's heart pounding and adrenaline flowing even if one was not bitten. Scorpions crawled out from under rocks and delivered extremely painful and infectious stings, and even spiders here could be deadly. Most young men think themselves immortal, however, and this was all part of the adventure of a new life in a faraway land.

The mountain ranges and basins of the Sonoran Desert run on a north-south plane. Nuestra Señora de Guadalupe de Aguaje was located at the southern tip of a group of mountains today called the Sierra Santa Teresa. To the southwest across a basin and today's La Poza Creek is another mountain range, the imposing Cerro Prieto. Aguaje lay at the upper limits of a box canyon beneath the peak of a ragged butte known even today as Cerro El Aguaje. The camp was at an elevation of about 1,000 feet, and the peak rose to 1,500 feet above sea level. The valley floor and the headwaters of La Poza Creek lay well below and to the south. *Recuas*, or "mule trains," carrying mining tools, clothing, and other items from Mexico City via Parral, Chihuahua, came over the mountains in the east and turned north up the canyon to bring much-needed supplies to the busy mining camp. Recuas bringing food from the northern missions came south along the arroyo via Ures and Pitic, skirted the southern tip of Cerro El Aguaje, and also turned north up the canyon.

A cluster of adobe huts, tents, and makeshift lean-tos, scattered about in seeming chaos, constituted the camp. Something that resembled a street ran up the canyon through the middle of the buildings. There was also a town square in the middle of it all. Ten supply stores, one of which was owned by Juan Bautista de Anza, lined the street and the plaza. These stores were housed in small, grass-roofed, adobe structures. At this time there appears to have been no church, chapel, or public building of any other kind in Aguaje. There was the mandatory archive of mine records, required by Spanish law, but it seems to have been housed in someone's private dwelling, most likely that of Manuel de Acuña, the town's *teniente de justicia mayor*, or "deputy justice," under Sonora's chief justice.

On the talus slopes that rose toward the rim of the canyon on both sides of town were several telltale rubble or tailing heaps and various ore dumps that indicated where the mines were located. Each of the ones being worked had a vertical shaft, known as the *boca*, or "mouth," with a *xacal* above its opening. More of a *ramada*, or open "arbor," than an actual walled shed or hut, the xacal housed the mining tools and protected the workers, who had to climb up and down the ladders, from the weather.[22] On the slope west of town were five such working mines. There were two on the east slope, one of which was owned by Juan Bautista de Anza. There were also numerous *arrastres*,[23] mule-powered devices for crushing ore, located near the mouths of all the mines. At the lower end of town were three *haciendas de sacar plata*.[24] These crude beehive-shaped adobe and rock kilns, aerated by sheepskin bellows[25] and operated around the clock, required great stocks of firewood and charcoal, piles of which could be seen all around town.

All the silver mines at Aguaje were owned by three old-country Basques. On the west side of town Martín de Ibarburu owned the mine called La Soledad. It was the largest of the seven in operation. Actually, La Soledad was two separate mining operations. Ibarburu's mining claim was divided into twelve *barras,* or "shares," of which he had leased half to Juan Gonzalez de Mercado.[26] The main, and most productive, shaft was operated by Ibarburu. Gonzalez de Mercado was attempting to operate the other shaft where the *panino*[27] was good but the rock was crumbly and decomposed. It kept caving in, requiring the use of shoring timbers throughout its full depth and length.

Martín de Ibarburu had been around this part of Sonora for a long time. In fact, it is likely that he or one of his hired men actually discovered the silver lode at Aguaje. Known to his close associates as El Anciano de la Soledad,[28] "the old-timer of Soledad," he was getting to be an old man. Conversely, the other two mine owners in town were young men. Juan Bautista de Anza was twenty-five years old in 1718. Francisco de Aldamiz was twenty-seven. A native of Gautegiz de Arteaga in Bizkaia,[29] Aldamiz owned and operated the other three mines on the west side of town. They were named the San Antonio, the San Vicente, and the Nuestra Señora de la Bien Aparecida. All were operating at full production.

On the other side of the canyon above the eastern edge of town, Ibarburu owned La California Mine, and Anza owned and operated the San Antonio, named for his patron saint, San Antonio de Padua. Beneath its xacal, the open shaft of San Antonio was about twelve feet across *(cuatro varas)*[30] and between thirty and forty feet deep *(seis estados).*[31] Its *plano,* or "floor," followed the vein in a drift eastward into the mountain, lighted by candles purchased from the Jesuit missions to the north.[32] The *escalera,*[33] one lone timber, cut from the lodgepole pine in the higher elevations of the Sierra Madre far to the east and dragged in by mule team, served as a ladder to facilitate entrance and exit in the vertical shaft. Yaqui *barreteros*[34] descended its deeply notched steps at the beginning of the each shift, carrying their heavy iron implements, to begin their work of pounding and chiseling the solid rock face into manageable chunks and pieces.

This was probably the way the youthful Juan Bautista had gotten his start in the mining industry—and it was probably in the colossal mines at Álamos, far to the south. In addition to his daily wage, a barretero was paid a *partido,*[35] or "percentage," of the ore he extracted beyond the daily *tequio,*[36] the amount he was required to extract for his employer, depending upon the hardness of the ground. If he was willing to work hard, and if the mine had rich ore, a barretero could get ahead expeditiously. Some barreteros even worked in two different mines, or during two different shifts in the same mine, to double their wage and partido.[37] If the circumstances were right, and they appear to have been for Anza, a barretero could soon own his own mine.

The work of hammering and pounding chunks of rock out of a sheer rock face was extremely grueling, especially considering the fact that the miners of Sonora had not, as yet, developed the technique of extracting ore by using black powder.[38] It was also dangerous work. Small slivers of rock, embedded in the eye, could blind a barretero. Larger pieces of rock, slipping or falling in the wrong direction, could break bones or cause internal injuries and even death. The work required using heavy iron crowbars and sledgehammers and driving iron wedges into cracks to flake off blocks of stone. However, Anza's foreman, a man by the name of Ignacio de Ocampo, and his team of Yaqui barreteros, could readily keep up with the larger group of *tanateros*. These were the workers who carried the heavy *tanates*, or "baskets," made of rawhide or agave strips and loaded with chunks of rock, up the escalera to the arrastres.[39] Like the labor of the barreteros, this was backbreaking and extremely dangerous work. At the arrastres, the big chunks of rock were dumped out of the tanates to be pulverized into smaller pieces that could be smelted, and the tanatero went back down inside the mine for another load.

The tanateros were generally always Indians, Africans, or mixed bloods, as were most of the other workers involved in such mining activity. The tanatero's job, however, was at the bottom of the scale. His was the lowest wage paid for the most strenuous, backbreaking, unfulfilling job in the mines. Only the lowest-class citizen worked as a tanatero. The *repartimiento* system was still in effect in Sonora, whereby 4 percent of the mission Indians could be worked in the mines at a minimum wage for two weeks. These conscripted Indian work crews, or *tapisques*, as they were called, were escorted to and from the work site by a trusted mission Indian known as a *topil*.[40] Had things worked the way the law was set up, an exchange would have taken place every two weeks. However, there was much room for abuse within the system, and many of the mine owners exploited it to its fullest, shaving the already paltry wage and working the Indians well beyond the two-week limit.

The Jesuit missionaries were adamantly opposed to the repartimiento system, largely because of such excesses. Consequently, it is doubtful that tapisques were ever used at Aguaje. If they were, the mine owners were most likely careful in abiding by the letter of the law. It is a known fact that Juan Bautista de Anza and Martín de Ibarburu were avid supporters of the Jesuits[41] and the missions, as were most Basques.[42] Since Francisco de Aldamiz was also an old-country Basque, and there were no other mine owners in this particular real de minas, the Jesuit sentiment probably prevailed, and free workers, or those who came of their own accord, made up the workforce at Aguaje. Besides, the repartimiento system, which could not draw from missions or visitas with fewer than 100 adults, was already overtaxed in its effort to supply workers for the northern mines at Bacanuchi, Basochuca, and Nacozari.[43]

Indeed, the workforce at Aguaje necessary to keep seven mines, three smelters, and ten supply stores in operation was enormous. Exactly how many is impossible to say, but there were hundreds of workmen. Like mines everywhere in Sonora, those at Aguaje operated on a twenty-four-hour basis.[44] Just the workforce of barreteros, tanateros, and the *ademadores*, the men who constructed the shoring within the mineshafts, went well over a hundred. And that number does not even take into consideration the many blacksmiths sharpening tools, carpenters cutting and hewing *ademes*, or "shoring timbers," and the numerous arrastre and hacienda workers. There were crews for cutting firewood and carboneros for making charcoal. There were *arrieros*, or "mule packers," who came and went, transporting food and other supplies into the camp. Certainly there was also a great need for *vaqueros* to care for the mining camp's cattle and other livestock. In all, the numbers were staggering for a community that had been in existence such a short time.

Juan Bautista de Anza was only one person in a veritable anthill of human activity. Everything considered, however, he was one of the few at the top of the heap.

## The Visita General

*En el R$^l$ y Minas de Nûra Señora de Guadalupe en veinte y un dias del mes de hen$^o$ de mill setez$^{oz}$ y diez y ocho años Ante mi el cap$^n$ D$^n$ Antt$^o$ Bezerranieto Juez Viss$^{or}$ grâl en esta prov$^a$ de Sonora esttando de visita en la Mina nombrada S$^n$ Antonio que es de D$^n$ Ju$^o$ Baup$^{ta}$ de Anssa, Man$^l$ de Acuña y Mig$^l$ de Arriola beedores nombradas p$^a$ este efecto Dixeron antemi haver bisto y rreconoz$^{do}$ la dha Mina y sus lavores y q esta todo mui conforme a lo dispuesto por R$^l$ hordenanzas — Antt$^o$ Bezerra Juez R$^l$ (rúbrica)* . . . In the Royal Mining Camp of Our Lady of Guadalupe on day twenty-one of the month of January of 1718, Manuel de Acuña and Miguel de Arriola, appointed inspectors, appeared before me, Captain Don Antonio Bezerra Nieto, general visiting judge of this Province of Sonora, while on an official visit of the mine named San Antonio that belongs to Don Juan Bautista de Anza. They testified before me that they had seen and examined the said mine and its workings and that everything is in total conformance with what is mandated by the royal ordinances — Antonio Bezerra, Royal Judge (rubric).[45]

Because of the huge numbers of people at Aguaje, progress was made. Silver bullion was being shipped out over the Sierra Madre to Parral by mule train on a regular basis.[46] Money, in the form of pesos, reales, and other coins, was rolling in. Men were becoming wealthy overnight. The mines were all about six estados deep. The veins here were closer to the surface than they were in some of the older, more well-established reales de minas of Sonora. For instance, far to the northeast at Nuestra Señora del Rosario de Nacozari, the silver ore was located at least twice as deep, at twelve to fifteen estados.[47] The ancient mines at San Juan Bautista, the first capital of Sonora, had gone down so deep that they had become flooded with water and were virtually inoperable at this time.[48] At the mining camp called San José de

Basochuca, west of Nacozari in the mountains above the Sonora River, the veins closer to the surface had begun to play out. The original miners, including José de Zubiate,[49] his son-in-law José de Aguirre,[50] and Gregorio Álvarez Tuñón y Quirós,[51] had moved on to other more productive lodes, considering the cost of driving the shafts deeper at Basochuca to be too expensive. Here at Aguaje, however, the silver ore was still fairly close to the surface and abundant. Mine owners and workers alike were making money. Without the benefit of law enforcement, so were the corrupt and the depraved.

Boomtowns have always been the same, regardless of the era, place, or political climate. Raucous and riotous, they have always attracted every element of human society, especially the lawless. The mining camps of the mother load during the California gold rush, nearly one hundred fifty years later, might well have taken a lesson from the real de minas at Aguaje. Francisco Xavier de Gamboa, a famous criollo Basque mining jurist of the Real Audiencia in Mexico City and a contemporary of Juan Bautista de Anza's children, might well have been describing Aguaje when he penned a treatise on such mining camps a generation later:

> There are no undertakings better attended than the mines and reduction works when a bonanza has been discovered. The fame of the discovery spreads through the whole kingdom, and the odor of its richness brings crowds from the most remote parts to the newly discovered district. What was before a waste, becomes, on a sudden, an inhabited neighborhood. But the object which attracts this influx of persons, leading them to defy the length and ruggedness of their journeys, is not their daily pay. That they can procure anywhere. But it is the share of ore usually allowed to the barmen, and the opportunities they find of theft and pilfering, both in regard to the ores (for which purpose they will often conceal and pillage the vein), and to the iron, powder, and other requisites for the work entrusted to them. They often carelessly throw the ores among the heaps of rubbish. They conceal each other's thefts. And, as the work proceeds day and night in these excavations, no vigilance can detect their cunning and cautious frauds. They are more like lords and masters than servants or day laborers.[52]

Even in lawless boomtowns, however, there are always those who respect law and order. There are those who are willing to risk their own safety to bring lawlessness under control. There are also those who respect authority and who appreciate honesty in other men. Juan Bautista de Anza and Antonio Bezerra Nieto were two such men who were about to meet for the first time at Nuestra Señora de Guadalupe de Aguaje.

Nicolás was a large, imposing black man. Just his size commanded attention, but his booming voice, his ability to read, and his flawless use of the Spanish language caught everyone's attention as soon as he started to speak. Besides that, he had positioned himself in such a way that those attending the early morning Mass that Sunday had to pass by him as they turned to leave. It was January 16, 1718. Everyone in town already knew that Captain Bezerra's inspection party had camped down the canyon just below town the evening before. They knew that he was here to inspect the mines and the supply stores. In fact, they had most likely known he was coming for several days or even a week before he got there. Although Sonora was sparsely populated by Indian and Spaniard alike, word of such things as this spread rapidly. Bezerra Nieto had begun his official general inspection of the ranches and mines of the province back in the latter part of December at the ancient real de minas called San Juan Bautista de Sonora. Even though that village was only a hundred miles to the north, it had been a full three weeks since the examination had started—plenty of time for the news to reach Aguaje.

The inspection had actually begun after Mass at San Juan Bautista on Christmas day, 1717, with Nicolás telling everyone to listen closely, just as he was doing here.[53] The only difference was, San Juan Bautista had a church, whereas Mass at Aguaje had been held on the town's open plaza. At San Juan Bautista, Antonio Bezerra Nieto had already traveled all the way from Janos, Chihuahua, bringing with him a fairly sizable party of soldiers, workers, and political appointees, but other officials had also been appointed there. They, too, had been traveling with the party ever since. Felipe Bezerra, a resident of San Juan Bautista and possibly Antonio's son, had been selected as alguacil mayor for the expedition. Diego Laines, Tomás de la Cruz, and Miguel de Mendiguren, also of San Juan Bautista, were appointed as the captain's *asistencia*, or assisting staff, and Juan de Dios Barrios was chosen to be the expedition interpreter for some of the native languages that would be encountered along the way.[54] In all, the captain's party was probably made up of between thirty and forty men. With all their horses, pack animals, and gear, they made up a very noticeable party of travelers. Even if someone had not known that the inspection party was coming prior to its arrival, there was no one in town who did not know it after they got there. This was a big occurrence on such a remote frontier, even for a rowdy boomtown.

Had anyone wondered what was going to take place, they quickly found out the next morning after Mass. The big Negro *ladino* informed everyone that he had an edict from the governor of Nueva Vizcaya that he was going to read and that no one, at that time or during the reading, could leave the site. No one did. Alone, Nicolás was imposing enough, but with the several soldiers who were standing with him, he had everyone's undivided attention as he read from the piece of paper. They were informed that the governor had ordered an official government inspection of all the mines, ranches, and supply stores in all of Sonora to determine if they were operating honestly with their fellow Spaniards and if they were paying their full share of fees and taxes. They were advised that no one, under penalty of prosecution by the law, was to leave town until the inspection was completed, and all were to make an effort to inform those who were not at Mass that morning.

The order of procedure was outlined so that everyone clearly understood. Tomorrow, Monday, the captain would inspect all of the supply stores in town. All workers in the stores were to be present at their respective establishments the first thing in the morning, and were to wait there until the examining party had completed its inspection. The storekeepers were to have all of their scales, measures, and balances, together with their books and accounts, out and available for inspection. The following day, all mine owners, lessees, engineers, foremen, and other officials were to make themselves available for a meeting with Bezerra Nieto and his party, so that a couple of mine inspectors might be chosen from among them. The inspectors were to begin their audit of the mines on Wednesday the nineteenth. Once the audit was completed, the inspection of all the haciendas de sacar plata was to begin. The captain expected all workers, whatever their station, status, or race, to be present at both the mines and the haciendas while the inquiry was being conducted at their particular place of employment. That way, they would be able to tell him of any grievances or complaints and show him anything that was not in compliance with the mining regulations.

When Nicolás had completed his announcement, most people turned to go home to complete their day of Sabbath rest, however they chose to spend it. Most of the mine owners and other officials gathered around Bezerra Nieto and his several assistants. This may well have been the very first time that Juan Bautista de Anza and Antonio Bezerra Nieto met. Regardless of when that meeting first took place, however, the two were immediately drawn to each other. Bezerra Nieto was old enough to be Anza's father, but age differences aside, they had everything in common. Both were devout Catholics. Both had a deep and abiding respect for what the Jesuit missionaries were attempting to accomplish in the missions of northern Nueva España. As a boy, Anza had dreamed of being a soldier. Bezerra Nieto was one, and had been for nearly thirty years, having joined the military at Janos, Chihuahua in the spring of 1688.[55] Now, he was *capitán vitalicio*, or "lifetime captain," of the Royal Presidio of San Felipe y Santiago de Janos, a position he had held for almost five years.[56]

It cannot be said with any certainty that Bezerra Nieto was Basque, like Anza, but it is possible. Bezerra is a name used by both Spaniards and Basques, and thus ethnicity cannot be determined just from the name. Judging by the large numbers of Basques that he seemed to associate with and those he had in his asistencia, one has to wonder if he was not of that heritage himself.

As outlined by Nicolás after Mass on Sunday, a general inspection of Aguaje's supply stores started on Monday morning. The officials began at the southern end of town, closest to Bezerra Nieto's camp, although most of the stores were located around the town plaza. Of the total number of stores, at least half were owned by Basques: José de Amasola, Miguel de Gomiziaga, Martín de Ibarburu, Francisco de

Aldamiz, and Juan Bautista de Anza. The ethnic backgrounds of the owners of the other five are unknown. While José de Campo was probably Basque, Francisco Salmón, Jorge Rodríguez, Francisco Vásquez Sotuyo, and Rosa de Sierra were probably not.

Rosa de Sierra was the lone female proprietor among the other nine owners. This brings up an interesting question concerning women in such lawless frontier mining camps. The fact that Rosa was there, operating a store, indicates that women did inhabit such places. Nothing in the record indicates whether she was the wife of one of the miners, a widow, or just what her status might have been. There is nothing in the record that indicates there were children at Aguaje. However, numerous records in Spanish colonial archives indicate that the miners brought their wives and children with them once mining camps were established. So, it is safe to assume that the population of Aguaje was made up of both sexes, all ages, many races, and people of every status. Nor is the work status of women at Aguaje clear, but again, judging from other records it is safe to assume that they worked as cooks, gardeners, cleaning ladies, and obviously storekeepers.

At every store in town, as the inspection progressed, Felipe Bezerra, the expedition's alguacil mayor, checked the establishment's weights, scales, and balances to determine that they were accurate and that fraud was not being committed. While he was doing that, Bezerra Nieto and his asistencia were going over the proprietor's books. At the end of the day it had been determined that all ten stores were operating according to law, and there was no indication of fraud on the part of any of the owners. Juan Bautista de Anza's store was no exception.

As Bezerra Nieto and Anza visited in his store, they were drawn to each other. Bezerra Nieto liked the young man, and sometime during the week he invited Anza to join his staff. For now it was agreed that the mine owners and managers would meet at Anza's store the following day to determine who would be the official mine inspectors for Bezerra Nieto's investigation of the mines.

On Tuesday morning it was decided that Manuel de Acuña, a mining engineer working with Juan Gonzalez de Mercado in an attempt to get his mine shored up and usable, would be one of the official inspectors for all of the mines. Juan Bautista de Anza's foreman and manager, Ignacio de Ocampo, was selected as an inspector for the mines on the west side where he would not be in conflict of interest. Similarly, one of Francisco de Aldamiz's foremen, Miguel de Arriola, was chosen for the east side. Each of the three men was sworn to uphold his duty and the laws of the king by making the sign of the cross.

The inspection of mines that got under way at Aguaje on the morning of January 19 was the very first during this expedition. Even though the inspection trip began at San Juan Bautista, the capital of the province and at one time the most productive silver-producing mining camp in all of Sonora, all of the old mine shafts had flooded with water and none were operable. Now it was just a ranching community.

Bezerra Nieto examined the land deeds and branding iron registries of eleven ranches while he was there.[57] As the expedition continued, it stopped mostly at missions and Indian rancherías. Rather than conducting official inspections of those sites, Bezerra Nieto had held *tlatoles*,[58] or "conferences," with the Indians, asking them through interpreters if they were happy with their missionary, with their way of life, and if there was anything that the Spanish officials could do for them.

At the mines of Aguaje, everything got very formal. The first inspections started at Ibarburu's La Soledad mine and continued through those of Gonzalez de Mercado and Aldamiz. The two inspectors, Acuña and Ocampo, carefully climbed down each shaft and, by candlelight, followed each drift to the extent of its excavation. They kept conference with Felipe Bezerra who dutifully took all the measurements, and then they all reported back to Bezerra Nieto at the mouth of the mine, where he had been discussing work conditions with the mineworkers. As everyone reported their findings, Bezerra Nieto's scribe hurriedly jotted down notes.

The only mine found not to be in compliance with royal regulations was that of Gonzalez de Mercado. It was not because he was doing anything wrong, but rather because the ground where the mine was located was so unstable as to cause danger to the workers. Regardless, Bezerra Nieto ordered all of Mercado's mining operations to cease until all shafts could be properly shored up. This, of course, would mean a great expense in manufacturing and hauling timbers from the mountains. The record is silent as to what took place afterward, but the finding may have meant abandonment of the mine—at least until all inspectors were out of sight.

The only other problem that the captain's scribe made note of was the fact that several other open pits dotted the hillside, but no one was working them. Furthermore, most of the mines were not staffed with a full complement of workers and were not operating to their full capacity.

The next day, Thursday the twentieth, all inspections stopped while the scribe caught up with recording everything that had taken place the day before. The captain, his staff, and the two official mine inspectors proofread each document he wrote and then signed it. On Friday, Anza's San Antonio mine and Ibarburu's La California, on the east side of town, were inspected. Like those inspected on Wednesday, they were found to be in compliance with the royal regulations. Then, on Saturday morning, Bezerra Nieto's group visited the three haciendas de sacar plata that were refining all silver that was mined. The smelters belonged to Ibarburu, Aldamiz, and Gonzalez de Mercado.

Once again, everything was found to be in order. There were no serious complaints from any of the workers about their work conditions or wages; so that afternoon the officials retired to Bezerra Nieto's tent in the camp below town to compile and organize all the official papers of the inspection. This time there was a new official in the group—the newest member of the captain's asistencia—Juan Bautista de Anza. Bezerra Nieto had been hearing complaints daily over the last week about the lawlessness of this boomtown—the robberies, the injuries, and the assaults on its upstanding citizens. He had determined to issue an edict against such behavior with provisions for severe punishment if it did not cease. Anza had readily agreed to sign it with him. So, the two men, with others of the captain's staff, sat down to compose the decree.

Bezerra Nieto had already determined to have it read by Nicolás right after High Mass the next morning. However, it was already late in the afternoon. The sun would be down before six o'clock and there would be no moonlight. As it got too dark for the scribe to write, someone was sent out for candles and the work continued until well into the night.

Finally, it was finished. The next morning, as on the Sunday before, Nicolás placed himself in a strategic position and, when the Mass was over, announced in his booming voice that a proclamation from the royal visiting judge was to be read and all were to comply with its contents. Everyone was also obligated to pass the word on to those who were not in attendance that morning. Then he began to read clearly and slowly, his powerful voice echoing across the plaza:

Captain Don Antonio Bezerra Nieto, presently of the Royal Presidio of San Felipe y Santiago de Janos, alcalde mayor of the jurisdiction of San Antonio de Casas Grandes, and general visiting judge in this Province of Sonora for His Majesty our sovereign:

While engaged in the general inspection ordered by my superiors in the government of this Province of Sonora[59] in this mining district of Our Lady of Guadalupe, its environs and adjuncts, it has been reported to me that a number of miners have several different mines without the people to excavate and work them for the better part of the year and that taking workers from some to work the others benefits neither the ones nor the others.

For this reason and that of wishing to support all of them at once so that none could claim to be cheated, production has been cut, to the detriment of His Majesty's Royal Fifth,[60] whereas it could be increased if each mine were worked continuously. This benefit could be achieved by concentrating the work in some mines, while the rest could be worked by persons who have discontinued doing so, either from disregard or ignorance of the applicable royal orders in this particular. Thus, this threat to the common good is added to the other things that look to me for necessary remedy.

For that reason I said I should order, and I do hereby order, that those miners must comply with ordinance number thirty-seven,[61] and punctually and promptly populate their mines with at least four persons to work them. It is to be understood by those unable to provide the competent number of diggers to work and improve their mines as asked, they must forfeit them so that the royal income may be augmented. On the contrary, violation of the said law under pretext is not justified by the Royal Will. I made it clear to all that any person could freely denounce the said mines,[62] and nobody could impede him or unjustly prevent a hearing. Such action shall carry a penalty of 500 pesos to be levied, which, from this time forth, shall be divided, half to go to the Royal Treasury of His Majesty and half to the local court[63] for the expenses of restitution.

The latter is because some of the residents are vexed that some persons, without license or consent, drive off their mules and horses. These persons steal and kill their cattle with impunity, and others carry knives. The use of this weapon has led to disturbances that resulted in serious wounds. For this reason and due to the present mood, I have decreed that from now on no one of whatever class, quality, or condition, be they Spaniards, Mulatos, Negroes, Coyotes, Mestizos, Indians—all present inhabitants of this mining camp and its environs—will be allowed to carry knives or machetes,[64] either displayed or concealed, on pain of losing said arms, and that any minister of His Majesty may disarm them and proceed against the recalcitrant individuals and transgressors in this manner: For Spaniards, for the first offense, they shall lose the said weapon and pay ten pesos toward the Most Holy Sacrament. For the second offense, twenty pesos in silver, as it is said, and for the third offense fifty pesos toward building a public jail in this mining camp, seeing there is fitting need for its completion. For Mulatos, Negroes, Mestizos, and Indians, whether slave or free, the first time his weapon shall be confiscated and he shall spend fifteen days with his head in stocks. For the second offense, the weapon shall be hung about his neck while he is given fifty blows with a cane. For the third offense, six months in the Presidio of Corodéguachi[65] of this province without any salary, serving His Majesty for the said time. And a Spaniard, if caught with a stolen beast or a stolen and slaughtered beef in the state of being half-eaten, as proven by an investigation of the Real Justicia,[66] shall be condemned to three months in said presidio. Others who are not Spaniards shall be sentenced to six months in the said presidio in order to cut down on such offenses. At the same time I am ordering that all the present residents of this mining camp appear together before me on the twenty-fourth of the present month to pass muster with their arms and ammunition in order to see whether they comply with the orders given by the superior government.[67] This edict that serves as decree and proclamation is published in this mining camp and brought to the notice of the public as they depart from High Mass on the twenty-third so that the news will pass from those in attendance to those who did not come, to ensure the observance and compliance of this mandate of the teniente justicia mayor[68] of this mining camp, as is fitting in the service of His Majesty, and this I affirm and authorize as visiting judge with two witnesses of my staff, since there is no escribano público in this Royal Mining Camp of Our Lady of Guadalupe this twenty-second day of January of 1718.

Antonio Bezerranieto, Visiting Judge (rubric)
Witness Juan Bauptista de Anssa (rubric)
Witness Miguel de Mendiguren (rubric)[69]

Anza's signature here, as a member of the captain's asistencia, with fellow Basque Miguel de Mendiguren, is his first known signature in the New World. Exactly what his job with Bezerra Nieto entailed at this point is unclear, because when the captain left to continue the inspection, Anza stayed behind. It probably meant that Bezerra Nieto had signed him up as a corporal or sergeant in the militia. Eventually, it would mean an appointment as lieutenant of the Sonora militia,[70] and probably various other duties until such time as he would be commissioned an *alférez* in the frontier presidial cavalry at Janos, Chihuahua.

That was all in the future, but it appears that both men had plans for Anza's future career. Both were aware that Juan would eventually need papers proving his noble status and clean bloodlines. Even though he was Basque and, therefore, guaranteed the privileges of hidalguía, he was unknown in the New World and on this far northern frontier. Someone was bound to contest his right to hold such jobs or to own land, especially here where people were fiercely independent and often held little respect for the law. The captain may well have suggested to him that he start the process necessary for obtaining such a *prueba,* or proof, but if he did, the young Anza was a step ahead of him. He had already written home to Hernani, several months before, asking his father to start that very process.

By extraordinary coincidence, probably ten or twelve hours before Bezerra Nieto and Anza signed the decree banning knives and machetes in Aguaje, on the very same Saturday, nearly halfway around the world, Antonio de Anza walked into the udaletxe of Hernani and presented a written petition to the alcalde, stating that "my children, Don Juan Bautista, Don Juan Felipe and María Estevan de Anza, through their parents and paternal and maternal grandparents and their other legitimate ancestors are well-known descendants of this Very Noble and Very Loyal Province of Guipuzcoa and in it, of the widely proclaimed houses of nobility of noblemen named Anza, located in the community of Irun." And asking that "they be admitted to all honorable occupations and offices, in peace and in war, and that they be placed on the list with all other noble caballeros and hijos dalgos by blood."[71]

Antonio paid the necessary fees that same day. Alcalde Miguel de Ogillurreta started the process the following Wednesday with an official decree instructing the town government to do the necessary research and complete the required interrogatories. His mandate came just within the three days required by law for the process to be implemented after the petitioner had filed his declaration of intent. With the alcalde's proclamation in hand, Hernani's sindico procurador general—none other than Juan's old teacher, Juan Bautista de Vizarrón—began the laborious process of getting certified documents and oral statements and recording them. It would take another eight months to complete all the paperwork. Witnesses would have to be interrogated, certified copies of baptismal and marriage certificates would have to be obtained, the fact that Juan's ancestors had served in the local government would have to be certified, and the local *justicias*, *abogados* (attorneys), and escribanos de número would all have to get involved. Once the document was completed, it would be at least six more months before it reached Anza in such a far corner of the world.

The important thing, however, was that the process was under way.

## Tetuachi

*Siendo mi primera obligazion dar quenta a VS. deel estado deesta Provincia, me ôbliga a poner en su notizia en el miserable estado que la tienen zinco Sujetos deella, y principalmente Un muchacho depoco mas de Veinte y zinco años llamado Juan Bapp<sup>ta</sup> de Ansa — Gregorio Albarez Tuñon y quiroz (rúbrica) . . .*
It being my first obligation to report the state of this Province to Your Honor, I am obligated to notify you of its miserable condition caused by five of its subjects, and especially a boy of little more than twenty-five years called Juan Bautista de Anza—Gregorio Ávarez Tuñón y Quirós (rubric).[72]

Tetuachi was, without a doubt, an Indian name—most likely Opata. Exactly what the term meant is open to debate. Exactly where it was located is unknown today, although below Arizpe on the Sonora River, bounded on the north and east by beautiful crimson cliffs, is an enchanting little valley and *rancho* known as Tetuachi. The only thing known for certain is that somewhere up the rugged canyon intersecting the river from the east—"muchos años pasados"—"many years ago," there was a real de minas known as Nuestra Señora de Aránzazu de Tetuachi. For more than half of a century silver was mined and refined there, and it was transported out by mule train.

Located in the Opata country of the upper Sonora River, this real de minas, unlike Aguaje, had a number of populated Spanish settlements, Jesuit missions, and other reales de minas fairly close by. Arizpe to the north and Aconchi to the south were both old, well-established Spanish mission communities. Other nearby visitas and missions included Sinoquipe, Banámichi, Huepac, and Baviácora to the south, Chinapa, Bacanuchi, Bacoachi, and Guepavérachi to the north.

East and slightly north of Tetuachi, in the Sierra del Carmen, are two peaks rising some six thousand feet in elevation called Los Crestones. A *crestón* is the crest of a soldier's helmet where the feathers are placed, and certainly these two massive peaks resemble such. However, *crestón* also means an outcropping of an ore vein, and this could be the source of the name. During the early years of the 1700s, at least five reales de minas operated on the western slopes of Los Crestones: Tetuachi, Bavicanora, San José de Basochuca, Santa Rosalia del Oro, and Santa Barbara del Cajón. Nuestra Señora del Rosario de Nacozari, of course, was on the eastern slopes of this great mountain range. Across the Sierra San Antonio range, west of Tetuachi, was the ancient real de minas called San Juan Bautista de Saracachi. Bacanuchi was north and slightly west near the headwaters of the Bacanuchi River and beneath the jagged Picacho de Bacoachi. San Antonio de Motepore was to the south, on the west side of the Sonora River.

Even the Presidio of Fronteras was no more than fifty miles away from Tetuachi, although it was across a rugged and difficult distance. Southwest of Fronteras was the massive mountain range called La Púrica, at nearly eight thousand feet in elevation. The lower-lying foothills between La Púrica and Los Crestones formed a pass over which traffic flowed between the Sonora River valley on the west and Fronteras, Nacozari, and the northernmost mission to the Opata Indians, San Ignacio de Cuquiárachi, on the east. The terrain was extremely broken and craggy. Cholla, ocotillo, mesquite, prickly pear, organ pipe cactus, yucca, and desert broom were ubiquitous. There were juniper, manzanita, and oak in the higher elevations of the pass and actual pine forests in the upper reaches of La Púrica and Los Crestones.

Tetuachi was also different than Aguaje in that it was well up off the desert floor in these extensive and wild mountains above the Sonora River. Mining operations differed little there, however, as compared to Aguaje. One improvement was that since it was in the mountains, it was closer to timber for shoring. The water supply was probably better, and the weather was moderately cooler, making working conditions somewhat more pleasant at Tetuachi. It was also, of course, not as far off the beaten path as was Aguaje. Mule trains carrying silver bullion from the mines at Tetuachi simply dropped down the canyon to the Sonora River, headed north beyond Arizpe, crossed over the pass south of La Púrica, and continued on into Nacozari. From that central station they joined other mule trains carrying silver to Parral in Chihuahua, and eventually to Mexico City. The Tetuachi mining camp was established sometime in 1719. It is not known who discovered the silver deposits at

Tetuachi—possibly a Yaqui or Opata Indian working for some Spanish citizen. Nor is it known who gave it the saint's name "Aránzazu." Without question, however, the name-giver was someone of Basque descent.

Wherever and whenever the name Aránzazu is seen, it is guaranteed that a Basque applied the name. The name comes from one of the most important Basque shrines, which came into being in 1447 with the appearance of the Most Holy Virgin to a Basque goatherd, Rodrigo de Baltzategui. The Virgin made her appearance in a thornbush high in the mountains south of Oñati in present-day Gipuzkoa. Indeed, Aránzazu means "are you in the thornbush?" The name is known and revered by Basques throughout the world.[73]

The earliest miners at Nuestra Señora de Aránzazu de Tetuachi were Basque—Juan Bautista de Anza, Francisco Xavier de Barcelón,[74] José de Goicoechea,[75] Antonio de Miranda,[76] and Juan Domingo de Berroeta.[77] Shortly behind them, if he did not arrive at the same time, was Francisco Pérez Serrano, another Basque.[78] Prior to the silver discovery at Tetuachi, the only one of the six who can be said with all certainty to have been involved directly and completely in the mining industry was Juan Bautista de Anza. Barcelón was known to have been involved in the cavalry at Fronteras. Berroeta may have previously been involved in mining, either directly or indirectly, but this comes only from the circumstantial evidence that he operated a supply store at the real de minas of Bavicanora a couple of years after the establishment of Tetuachi.[79]

Therefore, it seems plausible that Juan Bautista de Anza, because of his interests in mining, even though he was living many miles away at Aguaje, may have had a hand in the discovery of the Tetuachi mines, whether personally or through one of his hired men. He may also have had an influence on the naming of the new mining camp, or may even have been the person who named it. Born and raised just thirty-five miles down the mountain from the original Aránzazu, he knew of the shrine and may have visited it before leaving the old country.[80] Considering his great love for the Church, it would not be at all surprising if he were the one who applied the saint's name to the area referred to by the Opatas as Tetuachi.

After the discovery of silver at Tetuachi, Anza took up residence there, leaving his workers at Aguaje to manage those mines. It stands to reason that he would have brought in others of his own ethnic background to work with him in the exploitation of the silver deposits. Once again, as at Aguaje, many people of various backgrounds rushed to the scene, either for work or in hopes of getting rich quickly. But again, the owners of the mines were Basque, Juan Bautista de Anza being chief among them.

Anza was at Tetuachi for close to two years—from 1719 to 1721. Even though it was only a short stay, it was the beginning of the Anza family's roots at Arizpe and in the Sonora River valley. Arizpe, a well-established, early Spanish mission community, was not more than ten miles north of Tetuachi. It was while mining at

Nuestra Señora de Aránzazu de Tetuachi that Anza made many of his first important acquaintances in Sonora. It was also there that he became embroiled in a heated controversy that literally bespoke life or death for the Spanish population of the area.

Between 1710,[81] when Gregorio Álvarez Tuñón y Quirós first became capitán vitalicio at the Presidio of Fronteras, and 1722, when the conflict between him and his fellow Spanish citizens of Sonora reached a frenzied climax, his professional associates and landed neighbors were predominantly Basque.[82] Álvarez Tuñón was the third person appointed permanent lifetime captain at Fronteras,[83] but there had also been an interim commander, none other than Anza's Basque associate at Aguaje, Martín de Ibarburu.[84] Although much of the conflict with Don Gregorio involved Juan Bautista de Anza, it had started well before Juan's arrival on the frontier. In fact, it started even before Álvarez Tuñón became captain of the presidio, when a number of enraged citizens petitioned to have his uncle, Jacinto Fuensaldaña, removed from the same captaincy.[85] It is certain that such Sonora veterans as Ibarburu and Juan Mateo Manje[86] had adequately informed Anza of this captain's shortcomings. In fact, many local residents felt that Don Gregorio was in the process of bringing about the "ultimate ruin of the province."[87]

He did not live at the presidio, but instead at Jamaica, the site of a silver mine he was exploiting far to the south on the Moctezuma River. Most of the presidial soldiers were forced to be off someplace else most of the time, working for him on his ranches or in his mines, leaving no one to protect the frontier from the ever-increasing raids of the dreaded Apaches. The captain was collecting wages for soldiers who had been dead for years, and pocketing the money. Honest men throughout Sonora, and especially in the north, were becoming more and more disgruntled with Captain Álvarez Tuñón. Others, however, were willing to be party to his schemes and conspiracies. Don Gregorio did not like the Jesuit missionaries. They were too vocal—far too willing to tell his superiors about his fraudulence and un-Christian-like behavior. Worse yet, they refused to let him have any more tapisques to work in his mines than the very minimum for which the law provided.[88]

The first recorded complaint against Álvarez Tuñón came in the form of a letter written to Antonio Bezerra Nieto by a group of irate citizens from the real de minas at Nacozari in 1718. They complained of Don Gregorio's total neglect of his presidial responsibilities and requested Captain Bezerra Nieto to inspect the situation.[89] He did, and ordered Captain Álvarez Tuñón to send his lieutenant, Juan Bautista de Escalante, with a squadron of men to guard the passes leading into Sonora from the Apache country.[90] Nothing came of it, however, and the captain's excesses continued to increase.

Besides the Jesuits, there was another group that Don Gregorio despised—the vizcaínos, or Basques. Father Joseph María Genovese, a Swiss Jesuit and father visitor to the northern missions, provided a graphic picture of Don Gregorio's prejudices: "These good citizens are so molested and vexed with the tyranny of the alcalde mayor, as they struggle forward, so injured by Don Gregorio's continuous neglect, especially those of the Basque nation (of which there are many and very honorable ones in this province). Regarding these, Don Gregorio has said he will not stop until all the Basques are reduced to tanateros in his mine."[91]

The alcalde mayor at this time, of whom Father Genovese spoke, was Álvarez Tuñón's brother-in-law, a man by the name of Rafael Pacheco Zeballos.[92] Although these two men had had their own differences in the past,[93] they seem to have been united in their conspiracy to make themselves wealthy at the expense of Sonora. Both were in debt to, and not on the best terms with, two former Sonorans who were now living in Chihuahua, José de Zubiate and his son-in-law, José de Aguirre.[94] Zubiate was one of the earliest settlers of Sonora, introducing some of the first cattle into that province,[95] and Aguirre had been its alcalde mayor between 1715 and 1717.[96] Both were powerful and influential Basques. Both of the governors of Nueva Vizcaya during the period in question, Manuel San Juan de Santa Cruz[97] and Martín de Alday, were Basque. Alday and Zubiate were *paisanos* and close friends, having been born and raised in the same town in Gipuzkoa, Spain.[98] All of this seemed to matter little, however, to Don Gregorio. He had his organization of supporters, including another possible in-law by the name of Juachín José de Rivera.[99] The captain went about his business as though his superiors would never ask for a day of reckoning.

As tension continued to escalate, both the Basques and the Jesuits needed a spokesman that could pull them together and lead the fight against this unscrupulous captain, whom they felt was going to bring about the downfall of Sonora. That turned out to be Juan Bautista de Anza. Living at Nuestra Señora de Aránzazu de Tetuachi, he was right in the middle of the situation. With the background in litigation that he had gained in the old country, he knew how to proceed.

In 1719 Gregorio Álvarez Tuñón y Quirós was alcalde mayor of Sonora.[100] Rafael Pacheco Zeballos was justicia mayor.[101] Pacheco Zeballos served notice in early March that he was going to appoint Juachín José de Rivera, a well-educated young man originally from Guadalajara, as his lieutenant. Almost immediately, three Basques, Juan Bautista de Anza, Francisco Javier de Barcelón, and Pedro de Alday, along with Manuel Domínguez,[102] filed a formal statement that Rivera should not be allowed to hold public office. According to them, he lacked the necessary *nobleza y limpieza de sangre,* or "nobility and clean blood." They leveled the grave charge that he was the son of a *mulata,* a lady of African blood.

It is doubtful that Juan Bautista de Anza had his own *prueba de nobleza,* or "proof of nobility," as of yet, but it was on the way. The forty-one-folio document had been posted on September 19, 1718, in Hernani by his father. It bore the signatures of Alcalde Miguel de Ogillurreta and one of the town regidores, none other than Juan's lehengusutipi, Francisco de Beroiz. It contained the sworn testimony of an impressive list of five important people in Hernani: Ignacio Antonio de Leizaur, Juan de Galardi, Nicolás de Zuaznabar, Sebastian de Lubelza, and José de Arratia. The document guaranteed that "hera notorio el orijen y deszendenzia nobleza limpieza y pureza de Sangre de Juan Bautista de Anza"—"the origin, noble descent, and cleanliness and purity of blood of Juan Bautista de Anza is widely known." [103] The problem was, it was most likely still sitting on the dock at Cádiz, waiting for transport to Vera Cruz and Mexico City.

That may well be why there seems to have been no further pursuit of the litigation when Pacheco Zeballos went through with Rivera's appointment in spite of the protest: "[The appointee must] have the endowments, nobility, intelligence, approval, and trust that is required, and because these and others are met in the person of Don Juachín José de Rivera, by this writing, in the name of His Majesty, and mine in his Royal Name, by the authority that I have and that is granted to me, I nominate and appoint the said Don Juachín José de Rivera to be my lieutenant chief justice and captain of war." [104]

Juachín José officially became interim deputy to the justicia mayor by title handed down from Governor San Juan de Santa Cruz in Arizpe on March 11, 1719.[105] He, too, set out to prove his own limpieza de sangre, probably in part to satisfy his critics, but mainly because he planned to be married in a few months. His soon-to-be in-laws would be as interested in his clean bloodlines as were his critics. He obtained a declaration, given under oath, from Manuel Ballesteros, Joseph San Ibañes, and Gregorio Fernandez, three natives of Guadalajara living in Sonora. They all three swore that they knew Rivera and his mother, Teresa de Rivera. She was a native of Guadalajara and an española of good lineage. The fact of the matter was that Juachín José was not the son of a mulata, but an *expósito,* or "abandoned infant." As far as he was concerned, he was of *buen calidad,* or noble character, and there was no basis for the charge and slander that he was the son of a mulata. In a letter to the Basque governor of Nueva Vizcaya, Juan Manuel San Juan de Santa Cruz, he explained:

> Your Lordship may be assured that my place of birth was the city of Guadalajara, where I was trained as an escribano. The false charge they have leveled against me is that I am the son of a mulata, which has absolutely no basis in fact. Speaking with complete truth, sir, I am an expósito, abandoned at the

home of Francisco de Río Frio, who died shortly after my birth. I was then passed to the care of Don Diego de Arcarazo, who raised me. At the age of eighteen I came to know that my mother was Doña Teresa de Rivera, a resident of the said city. She confessed that I was her son and told me that I was born out of wedlock to her and Señor Don Antonio Vidal y Alvaro. This is not any speculation of mine. I am certainly only an expósito and nothing else.[106]

Events apparently reached an impasse during the next year. Juachín José heard cases in his jurisdiction, while those opposed to Don Gregorio, in whose web Rivera seems to have been caught, held their peace. That situation, however, would come to an abrupt halt with the changing of the guard.

A fairly large group of people gathered at Aconchi on Wednesday, January 31, 1720. General Gregorio Álvarez Tuñón y Quirós, outgoing alcalde mayor, was there making sure everything ran the way he wanted. Also present, to take Álvarez Tuñón's place, was the incoming alcalde mayor, Miguel Álvarez de la Bandera. Outgoing justicia mayor Rafael Pacheco Zeballos was there, and Juachín José de Rivera, Pacheco Zeballos's deputy, was also in attendance. The church was well represented by Father Visitor José Ruiz Calderón and Vicar Francisco Páez y Guzmán. A number of other local residents were also present. Don Gregorio officially handed over the office of alcalde mayor to Álvarez de la Bandera. Pacheco Zeballos presented Rivera with a paper conferring upon him, by order of Governor San Juan de Santa Cruz, the title of justicia mayor. It appeared that Don Gregorio had orchestrated the changing of the local government to suit his liking and to keep it within the family. Don Juachín José had been placed in office "without any contradiction or opposition."

On Friday, February 2, a procession rode north through Banámichi and up the canyon to the real de minas of Motepore, where Rivera lived. There the residents received him "with great happiness and cheering, manifested in various demonstrations." Nowhere, in the various surviving letters and other documents does Juachín José de Rivera appear to be presumptuous or arrogant. Perhaps all the fanfare among his friends gave him courage, however, because the very next day he wrote a letter to the vizcaínos at Tetuachi informing them of his appointment.[107] If he did not already know it, he would quickly learn that they were not as impressed as his friends.

The following day, February 3, he received a stinging reply from them:

Lord Don Juachín de Rivera

My dear sir, we, the undersigned, being gathered in the place called Nuestra Señora de Aranzazu de Tetuachi, having received the dispatch from Your Honor with the notice that you have given that the lord governor of this New Kingdom of Vizcaya has honored you with the title of chief justice of this province, and that you are in possession of the office, to which we say, united with the voice and warning of many other residents, that we protest and do not consent to Your Honor being the chief justice until you give proof to the lord governor of what we ask by public voice, heard throughout all of this said province, in not concurring with Your Honor's appointment. As per the order of the lord governor, the preeminent requisites and laws that are obligatory to obtain such a superior office are not being placed before those of us [108] who are obedient in payment of our land taxes and quick to report for the causes that assist in the service of His Majesty and the good of this province.

God keep you many years. Aranzazu, February 2, 1720. Kissing the hand [109] of Your Honor, Your Servants

Francisco Xavier de Barcelón (rubric)
Joseph de Goicoechea (rubric)
Antonio de Miranda (rubric)
Juan Bauptista de Anssa (rubric)
Juan Domingo de Berroeta (rubric) [110]

From this point, things deteriorated rapidly. A meeting was called among the Basques and other interested citizens to drum up opposition to Rivera. Rivera, on the other hand, did everything he could to block it. After all, it was illegal for anyone but the alcalde mayor to call such a meeting. He tried to get influential "Spaniards" behind him. Joseph Sagade, Andrés de Padilla, and Juan Antonio Maldonado all signed a document in his behalf. The vicar even came out in open support. Don Juachín José complained bitterly: "Every charge brought against me has been governed by a blind passion that has attended Don Juan Bautista de Anza, because of a judgment I issued against Don Pedro de Alday. He has also been obsessed because he did not want a case to be heard before me, concerning the sale of a half-share in a mine, between an Indian (who made the sale) and Don Manuel de Hugues." [111]

Rivera pointedly summed up the situation as he and the followers of Don Gregorio saw it. He accused Juan Bautista de Anza of being the "principal cause" of an open rebellion brewing in Sonora, and stated: "It is public knowledge that the said Don Juan Bautista de Anza has always been a violator of public peace and welfare and a troublemaker in whatever part of the province he has lived. Today, as I am writing this, it is known by honorable men that the said Anza is going about dispatching letters to the people asking them to rise up against me. I, also, have seen the exchange of letters conceived by the said Anza and the people who have united together at his call." [112]

A lot of people had banded together under the leadership of Anza. In Tetuachi, alone, according to Rivera, thirty-four citizens had signed a statement against him. Other communities throughout Sonora were banding together, maybe not so much in opposition to Rivera, but in opposition to his resolute allegiance to Álvarez

Tuñón. In order to break the alliance, since Rivera had shown that he was not the son of a mulata and since the disputants could not seem to prove that he was unqualified for the position, Anza now switched the opposition's argument from "limpieza de sangre" to one of "illegitimacy." Juachín José protested that despite his illegitimate birth both of his parents were noble Spaniards.

On February 6, thirty armed men, under the leadership of Juan Bautista de Anza, rode into Motepore shouting their opposition to Rivera and demanding that he be immediately removed from office. The vicar arrived soon after in an attempt to save the peace.[113] Word was sent to General Álvarez Tuñón, who on February 10 dispatched a letter to the governor at Parral, also blaming Anza for all of Sonora's troubles.[114] It was too late, however.

Word from furious citizens at Fronteras had come in, blaming everything that was happening on Álvarez Tuñón and a conspiracy between him and Rivera. They spoke of the "uselessness" of the presidio at Fronteras in protecting them against the incessant murders and stealing of horses by the "the enemies from the north," the Apaches. "And, who is the cause of all this evil?" they asked and then answered, "The Captain, Don Gregorio!"[115]

Juan Mateo Manje was dispatched to Mexico City,[116] and Pedro de Alday was riding posthaste to Parral to carry the protest to Governor San Juan de Santa Cruz.[117] Vicar Páez y Guzmán quietly convinced Rivera to step down and save the peace in Sonora. Once he agreed to that, Anza and his belligerent Basque contingent disbanded and rode back to their homes. Juachín José sat down that same afternoon, and with quill pen and ink wrote a long and involved letter to Don Gregorio in Jamaica,[118] informing him of the day's events. Although he had agreed to step down to prevent bloodshed, he made a vow to Don Gregorio "to defend your honor and mine, even to the loss of my life."[119]

Although the first battle in the struggle appeared to be over, on paper at least, the underhanded tactics of Don Gregorio's licensed hooligans continued. Much of the documentation of the period that speaks out against Álvarez Tuñón or Rivera was written anonymously, evidently in fear of reprisal. Sometimes authorship can be determined either by handwriting or by a rubric at the end of the document, but otherwise the authors will forever remain anonymous. One such document tells an interesting story of an attempted reprisal by Juachín José after the confrontation on February 6. On the following Sunday, while Anza and other devout people were attending Mass, Rivera and a group of armed men covertly approached one of his mines at Tetuachi. Finding no one present but a youth guarding the mine, Rivera determined to arrest him. The story is best told in the words of the original author:

> We will only add that in five days he attempted to arrest, in the name of the king, one of Juan Bautista de Anza's mine guards, because Anza was one of

those who would not consent to him being admitted as justicia mayor. Thinking that he could perhaps provoke the guard by calling him some improper names, Rivera said that, as judge, he knew all about him. In response to this the young man refused to be taken, to which Rivera began to demand that he come "in the name of the King, Our Lord!" The young man broke and ran, hiding himself among a string of pack mules. In pursuit of him, this Moorish magistrate began to shoot at him, yelling at those who had accompanied him to fire their *arcabuces*.[120] This and other outrages have been committed by the said Juachín in the short time of just a few days.[121]

Anyone could see that the Spanish citizenry of Sonora was on the verge of open civil war. Don Gregorio and his henchmen, evidently cautious about their ability to squelch the rebellion, backed off. Things quieted down for a while. It would be another two years before the pot would again boil over, and another four years after that before Mexico City would finally take notice. Only then would Don Gregorio be stripped of his commission and ordered to stand trial in Mexico City. He would die before that ever happened, but he would go to his grave much chagrined that the "miserable boy"—that "vizcaíno troublemaker"—the one called Juan Bautista de Anza, would be awarded his lifetime captaincy.

In an interesting turn of events, Juachín José de Rivera later became secretary of governance and war under the second governor of Sonora, Agustín de Vildósola,[122] one of the Basques firmly entrenched on the side of Anza and the others in the Álvarez Tuñón controversy.[123] Although Juan Bautista de Anza continued his efforts to oust Álvarez Tuñón, after the February 6, 1720, confrontation his actions would come more from the sidelines. As in many similar circumstances, he was probably able to accomplish more from the outside than he could from the middle of the conflict. Regardless, by leaving Tetuachi, he would be able to prepare himself to step in and take command when Álvarez Tuñón got his just due. Until then, it would be up to Anza's own group of schemers and conspirators, the members of Sonora's Basque community, to take the lead. Beginning in the latter part of 1721, Anza would have other priorities that would capture his attention and other duties that would take him elsewhere.

## The First Apache Campaign

*Testigo es de esto el Cap$^n$ D$^n$ Juan Bap$^{ta}$ de Anssa, Alferes oy del Precidio de Xanos, y entonses Teniente de Sonora y Cabo delos Vezinos q yvan âla tornada — autor desconocido, transcribido por Manuel José de Sosa . . .* Witness to this was Don Juan Bautista de Anza, second lieutenant today of the Presidio of Janos, but then lieutenant of Sonora and commander of the citizens who went on the campaign—unknown author, transcribed by Manuel José de Sosa.[124]

Little is known of the first recorded Apache campaign in which Juan Bautista de Anza took part.[125] Nothing is known about his militia appointment beyond the above quotation, but as lieutenant of Sonora he was in command of the militia troops that went on the campaign. At best, there were only three or four veteran soldiers who went with the expedition, but one of them was probably the overall commander of the campaign. The numbers of Spanish citizens and Indians who went was not recorded. Captain Álvarez Tuñón, of course, was not present. Outgoing alcalde mayor of Sonora, Miguel Álvarez de la Bandera, and his deputy, Cristóbal de Leon,[126] had undoubtedly planned the expedition, in conjunction with Anza. January, however, was the time for changing political offices, and the new alcalde mayor, Francisco Pacheco Zeballos,[127] had just taken the reins of government and was, thus, Sonora's new commander in chief of the militia. Brother of Rafael Pacheco Zeballos, he would hold the position that year, while his brother would have it the following year. It appears, however, that since he was just coming into office and Álvarez de la Bandera was leaving, Anza, as lieutenant of Sonora, was left to command the troops in the field with whatever help he could get from the presidials at Fronteras.

Sometime in January of 1721, citizen militiamen came together at the mission visita of San Miguel de Bacoachi. It may have been a bit early in the history of the north frontier for the Spanish citizenry to have learned the Apache tactic of attacking during the full moon, a technique that Anza's son and namesake would perfect a generation later. However, if the militia had come to understand the efficacy of sneaking up on an enemy at night and attacking by the light of a full or semifull moon, they would have been watching the phases closely. Knowing that the full moon in January of that year would come on Monday, the thirteenth, they would have planned the campaign around that date. Judging from the wording used by the scribe in writing this *informe*—"[the expedition] left here in silence"[128]—it is possible that this offensive was planned in just such a manner.

Regardless, an undisclosed number of the citizenry, an equal or larger number of Opata Indians, and the three or four soldiers already mentioned, rode out of Bacoachi to the north, pack mules and provisions in tow. Under the direction of Father Cristóbal de Cañas at Arizpe,[129] a large number of pack and saddle animals had been gathered for the campaign at Arizpe, Chinapa, and Bacoachi. Missions farther to the south including Huepac, Banámichi, and Sinoquipe, under the direction of their missionary, Antonio Leal,[130] and possibly Aconchi and Baviácora, had also sent livestock and provisions. The only thing provided by the Presidio of Fronteras in the way of supplies was one box of *bizcocho,* or "hard tack," and it came back unused because of the good supply of victuals sent by the missions.

Beyond this, nothing is known of the campaign other than the fact that it went north. It very likely went into what is today the state of Arizona and possibly into the mountains known as the Chiricahuas. Certainly many operations after this one were staged against the Apache stronghold in the Chiricahuas. Those later campaigns, generally led by trained military officers, often have detailed diaries recording what took place on a daily basis. Had Juan Bautista de Escalante, lieutenant at Fronteras and known to have previously kept such military journals, been on this expedition, we might know more about it today.[131] Even if Alférez Juan Antonio Durán had been present, a campaign journal might have been kept, since he was able to read and write.[132] In his absence, however, it is possible that Anza was the only literate person in the group, and he may not have been instructed in the importance of keeping military diaries.

In any case, either he did not keep a journal or else it has never surfaced. It is therefore not known whether the campaign was in any way successful or not. It is not even known if it was the first campaign in which Juan Bautista de Anza was involved. Certainly, with the early date of January 1721, it was one of his first. It was the beginning of Anza's career as a soldier. It was the beginning of his education in, and eventual vast knowledge of, the topography of today's northern Sonora and southern Arizona. And it was the beginning of continual campaigns against marauding Apaches led by men named Juan Bautista de Anza, father and then son. It would be another sixty-eight years before the Anza-led operations ceased.[133]

# Chapter Four

## The Cavalry of the Frontier

### San Felipe y Santiago de Janos

*El teniente general Ju.º Bautista de Anssa hijo legitimo de D.ⁿ Ant.º de Anssa, natural de la villa de Hernani, en la provincia de Guipuzcoa, de buen cuerpo, blanco, de rostro poblado de barba, pelicastaño lacio, de veinte y nueve años, poco mas o menos y costa su asiento en dos dias del mes de agosto de mil setecientos y veinteun años* . . . The first lieutenant, Juan Bautista de Anza, legitimate son of Don Antonio de Anza, native of the village of Hernani in the Province of Gipuzkoa, [is] of sound body, white, bearded, [and has] faded auburn hair. [He is] twenty-nine years of age, more or less, and entered the service on August 2, 1721.[1]

The Presidio of Janos[2] in the present-day state of Chihuahua, unlike most of the presidios of its day, was truly built like a fort. Housing for the soldiers surrounded a courtyard that was some ninety yards square. Each room of the barracks opened onto the square, where a double wall near its front enclosed a smaller compound. Thus, those entering the main gate on the southeast end of the structure passed through the gate in the heavy adobe wall into a plaza that was about twenty yards deep by ninety yards wide. Passing through the next gate, one entered the main courtyard. To the left, on the southwest side of the compound, was a door leading into the presidial chapel. The church had its own walled patio attached to, but outside of, the main structure. Across the main square to the northwest was a door leading into the captain's house. Like the church, it was attached to the fortified complex but was built outside of it. It had its own small plaza, and its front door opened off of the main road coming in from El Paso del Norte and Sonora. This was the home of Captain Antonio Bezerra Nieto and his wife, Catalina Gómez de Silva.

The Janos River ran past the main entrance toward the northeast. It split into two forks just above the presidio and joined again in one channel a little farther along its course. This left an open floodplain, about three hundred yards deep, that all had to cross if approaching the presidio toward its main gate. On both sides of the fortified compound along the northern side of the river were other adobe houses in which the citizenry, including some of the soldiers, lived. Thirty yards from the northeast corner of the fort was a dam of stone and timbers built into the river, where water was diverted out of the main channel into an acequia to irrigate the numerous fields and farms below the presidio.

This was farming country. Unlike much of Sonora, with its small patches of fertile land sandwiched in between rugged mountains and fast-flowing rivers, this was an area of rolling hills in wide, sweeping valleys. Above Janos to the southeast were the even larger agricultural valleys of Casas Grandes and San Buenaventura. So, although it lacked in mining and mineral resources, this country was rich agriculturally. It was also a hub for traffic coming from Chihuahua, Durango, Mexico City, and any other points to the south. Once traffic left Janos, it split off for either El Paso and Santa Fe to the north, or Sonora to the west.

Antonio Bezerra Nieto had lived in the captain's quarters at Janos since late 1713 or early 1714, and he had been living at the presidio itself since at least 1688.[3] Where he came from prior to that is unknown. There is some evidence that he was involved in the reconquest of Nuevo México after the pueblo revolt.[4] His wife, Catalina Gómez de Silva, came from one of the prominent Spanish families of the San Buenaventura Valley.[5] Antonio and Catalina appear to have had, at the very least, five children. There were four sons, Tomás Antonio, Felipe, Pedro, and Gaspar, and a daughter, María Rosa.[6] At times, other relatives lived with Antonio and Catalina at Janos. In fact, at least three of Catalina's siblings, Nicolasa, Pedro, and José Gómez de Silva, are known to have lived at the presidio.[7] However, it was the daughter, María Rosa, in whom Juan Bautista de Anza took an interest.

It may never be known whether he was attracted to Janos by the prospect of a military career or the possibility of obtaining a bride. Possibly he was attracted by both, for he certainly obtained them both there. Anza joined the cavalry on August 2, 1721, and was living at Janos that fall, where he served as alférez and married Captain Bezerra Nieto's daughter, María Rosa. This was the Apache frontier and the home of their allies, the Suma, Janos, and Jocome Indians.[8] Because of burning and plundering and constant upheaval over a period of many years, records of the era are scarce. Neither a marriage document nor a record appointing Juan as alférez has ever been found, but through letters written at that time both events can be pinpointed to within a few weeks of the new year.[9]

There was an earlier marriage before this one,[10] but Anza's first wife, María Valenzuela, evidently died. Although little original documentation about the marriage, or liaison, has surfaced, the available evidence is conclusive.[11] It is also supported by the fact that two daughters of Juan Bautista de Anza, María Manuela[12] and María Gertrudis,[13] about whom very little documentation has ever been found, possibly resulted from this previous marriage. Further research may someday tell if these two daughters and the lady who was probably their mother, María Valenzuela, lived with Anza at Aguaje or Tetuachi. It would also be interesting to learn who cared for the two little girls between the death of the first wife and Anza's marriage to María Rosa Bezerra Nieto, or if there was not a death but a nonmarital connection.

There has also been some confusion about Juan Bautista de Anza being stationed at Santa Fe, New Mexico during the same period.[14] Although he may have been detailed there for a short time, he served continuously at Janos, first as the alférez and later as its lieutenant, from 1722 until 1726, and can be documented as having been there during each one of those five years.[15] Thus, if he went to Santa Fe, it was on some detail as a soldier from the Presidio of Janos.

Although he lived at Janos, he continued to operate mines at Aguaje and Tetuachi, and bought pre-existing mines at Basochuca. He also evidently continued to operate supply stores at the mines, but there is no evidence that he had yet started to become involved in owning and operating vast cattle ranches there. He did, however, get involved to some extent in agriculture and stock raising at Janos.

His business operations never approached those of his father-in-law in size, mostly because he was only there for five years. He did have one recorded hired couple, a mulato by the name of Julian de Ortega and his wife, Catharina, a Suma Indian—a small number of employees compared to the recorded twelve families and two single workers who were employed by his father-in-law during the same time on two haciendas, one at Janos and one at Casas Grandes. It would appear that most of Bezerra Nieto's hired help were Indians, simply because they did not have last names. However, there was one family and one single man who were listed as Suma Indians, two Apache families, and one family of Janos Indians. Both of the mayordomos for his two haciendas were either Spanish or mestizo, Antonio Rodriguez and José Sambrano. One woman, Antonia de los Santos, was recorded as a slave, but her ethnic background was not provided.[16] Although these numbers probably do not reflect everyone who worked for Antonio Bezerra Nieto and Juan Bautista de Anza, they give an indication of the sizes of their operations and cultural makeup of those working for them.

Of course, now that he was an officer in His Majesty's frontier cavalry, Juan was expected to devote all his time to the service, even though it was well known that a presidial soldier's pay was so small that he had to work part-time as a vaquero, or at some other job, to be able to feed and clothe his family. One of the first things that he probably did upon arrival at Janos was to send to the old country for someone to manage his mines for him. Unfortunately, no correspondence between Juan and his cousin, Pedro Felipe de Anza, has ever surfaced. Although it is likely that Pedro Felipe wanted to come to America anyway, it is even more likely that Alférez Anza sent for him. At any rate, Pedro Felipe was at Janos living with Juan Bautista and María Rosa by the spring of 1724.[17] He quickly took over administration of the Anza mines and was manager for Juan, and later his widow, for many years.

*Pedro Phelipe de Anza* [signature]

This, of course, freed up Anza for more pressing duties. Trying to hold the frontier was a full-time job for any junior officer. The hundreds of mountain passes through which the enemy could flow during a raid or attack always needed to be watched and guarded. It was usually the junior officers who were sent forth with a handful of soldiers to carry out such reconnaissance duty. It was a dangerous way of learning the lay of land and the habits of the enemy, but it was guaranteed effective if one lived through it. Juan Bautista de Anza would quickly rise to the occasion, learning under the watchful eye of some of the master cavalrymen of the frontier.

The Janos presidio was a crack unit of battle-hardened veteran soldiers, many of whom had lived on the frontier all of their lives. Unlike the unorganized and untrained compañía volante that Juan had become accustomed to in Sonora, these men knew what they were doing and could teach him well. Furthermore, this unit was well manned and fully staffed.[18] Each soldier was in possession of the required arms necessary to carry out his duty, and each owned the required ten horses and one pack mule. In compliance with his commission as alférez, Juan brought to the garrison the fifteen horses and one pack mule required of an officer at Janos.

Antonio Bezerra Nieto, Anza's father-in-law and commanding officer, was a presidial veteran of over thirty-four years and had been commanding this presidio for nine of those years. Although Bezerra Nieto seems to have stayed behind at Janos during the great Pima campaign of 1695, his lieutenant, Francisco Ignacio Gómez Robledo, had been appointed secretary of war for the expedition and kept faithful records of everything that occurred.[19] Five other veterans of that campaign, Cristóbal Fontes, Francisco Grijalva, Juan Marqués Rodriguez, Francisco Xavier Rodriguez, and Antonio Contreras,[20] still served at the Presidio of Janos and were now associated with Juan Bautista de Anza. They and many of the other soldiers had thousands of hours of reconnaissance and combat experience in other areas and theaters. Juan could not have asked for a better body of men to instruct him in the techniques of frontier warfare.

Of course, there were other soldiers in the garrison that were as new to the king's frontier cavalry as was Juan. The sergeant at Janos, next in command under Anza, was Diego Laines, formerly from San Juan Bautista, Sonora. Like Anza, he had first met Captain Bezerra Nieto on that inspection tour of Sonora back in 1718, and he had just recently signed on with the company. There were other Bezerra *parientes*, besides Juan, serving in the garrison. Antonio's brother-in-law, José Gómez de Silva, a younger brother of Catalina, was an *alférez reformado*, or "semiretired second lieutenant" in the garrison, and Pedro Bezerra Nieto, the captain's son, was one of the newest recruits in the unit.

In total, the presidio was manned with a full complement of fifty soldiers and officers. These men had a monumental task in continually riding escort, guarding the mountain passes, conducting reconnaissance expeditions, and fighting for their lives when necessary. It was now up to Juan Bautista de Anza to take an active role of leadership in these activities. He would do just that over the next several years, advancing in rank to lieutenant when Francisco Ignacio Gómez Robledo retired. For the present, however, there was a more urgent duty to be taken care of—one that was left pending when he left Sonora.

## The Incessant Conflict with Don Gregorio

*Este escaravaxo ynmundo quiere lavarse las manos con la sangre de 22 gloriosos martires de la Compania de Jhs. que a manos de los Barvaros la derramaron desde la entrada por Guadiana hasta reducir a la Yglesia esta Prov$^a$ y yntroducir en ella el estandarte de la paz de Jesuchristo de donde lo quiere arrancar y derribar este malvado, y colocar en su lugar la Vandera del Demonio— Martín de Ibarburu . . .* This filthy dung beetle wants to clean his hands with the blood of twenty-two glorious martyrs of the Company of Jesus, spilled at the hands of the barbarians, from the time of first entrance at Guadiana until the Church tamed this province and introduced the Standard of Peace of Jesus Christ, from where this vile person wants to tear it down and demolish it and raise in its place the banner of the devil—Martín de Ibarburu.[21]

In a way, Martín de Ibarburu, Juan Bautista de Anza's old neighbor at Aguaje and past interim captain at the Presidio of Fronteras, started the next round of battle in the incessant conflict with the deceitful, conniving, and arrogant Gregorio Álvarez Tuñón y Quirós. Anza had moved to Janos and could hardly be blamed by the perfidious captain for what was taking place now. In fact, Don Gregorio had no one to blame but himself, for in reality he was the one who started the latest controversy. Don Martín was only reacting to an affront that the captain had made against the entire community of Sonora, especially the Jesuit padres and their supporters.

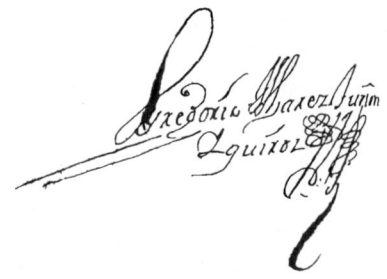

A weeklong citizens' conference had been held in the community of San Juan Bautista beginning on Wednesday, January 14, 1722. Don Gregorio's henchman, Alcalde Raphael Pacheco Zeballos, had called the meeting to discuss ways of nurturing and defending the Province of Sonora and advancing the work of the Church. Although Don Raphael had arranged for the gathering, it was obviously under the direction of Álvarez Tuñón. Over several days, monies were collected to send Don Gregorio to Mexico City to present Sonora's case before the authorities there.[22]

It was after this general citizens' meeting that Don Gregorio made three serious mistakes. First, he called a secret meeting of a select few of the citizenry—illegal even by that day's standards—to convene the night after the general meeting was adjourned. Secondly, he made the mistake of gravely maligning the Jesuits in order to promote his scheme for obtaining more tapisques for his mines. And thirdly, he seriously erred in inviting some Basques, Juan Domingo de Berroeta, José de Goicoechea, and Francisco Antonio de Lassa, to attend the meeting. As far as is known, these three were the only vizcaínos in attendance.

Everyone at the secret meeting was asked to sign a pact demanding that more tapisques be released from the missions to work in the mines. The Jesuit missionaries had refused to give up one Indian more than the 4 percent they were required by law to send. In order to make his proposal and system attractive to the powers above him, it was necessary for Don Gregorio to make the Jesuits and their system look bad. Contained in the instrument, which almost everyone in attendance was coerced into signing, were many accusations against the missionaries.[23]

Juan Domingo de Berroeta was the first to break the silence. Writing from Bavicanora on January 27, 1722, to Cristóbal de Cañas, the father visitor of Sonora, he detailed everything that had taken place at the meeting, describing pointedly his disdain for those who attacked the padres' reputations: "With infernal hypocritical cunning and with the appearance that it was for the common good, these few citizens, sly and crafty men, have introduced and planted into the hearts of many of the simple to avenge their passions on the Reverend Fathers."[24] He described the miserable conditions in Sonora and blamed it all on Don Gregorio. He described how he had spoken out in opposition to the perpetrators of this great slander against the padres and how, even though they had tried to force him to sign the statement, he had refused. After his refusal came threats that they would see him "in court, in prison, or on the scaffold." Therefore, he did sign a statement of "two or three lines" written below everyone else's signatures, stating that he did not sign the main document because he would only be in Sonora long enough to clear up his business debts, then he was leaving. "Surely God will understand," he reasoned.[25] He also spoke of another vizcaíno in attendance: "My countryman, Don Joseph de Goicoechea, fared better than I did. Indeed, they agreed to his excuse that he should not have to sign because he was not a resident. In finalizing the document, however, they returned to him two or three times, urging him to sign as a witness, but he left without signing, saying that his hand hurt."[26]

Goicoechea had a few words to say on the subject himself. He too wrote Father Cañas from Bavicanora the day after Berroeta, stating his feelings about the meeting and gave a classic statement of his and many other Basques' feelings toward the reverend fathers of the Society of Jesus: "Respecting what we owe to all the priests belonging to the Sacred Company of Jesus, I would sacrifice in your defense to the last drop of blood in my veins."[27]

The only other known Basque in attendance at the meeting was Francisco Antonio de Lassa. He signed the document under duress and then remained silent about it for over two years. Finally, on March 20, 1724, he swore out a deathbed statement that he had not known if there was any truth in the accusations made against the Jesuits and claimed that he had signed the statement against his will and in fear of his life.[28]

It was after the first two letters from Berroeta and Goicoechea brought the proceedings of the secret meeting to light that Martín de Ibarburu, under the pseudonym of "El Anciano de la Soledad," wrote an inflammatory, thirty-one-page letter to his "compatriots and countrymen of the Province of Sonora," urging them to rise up against this blight on their society. Even though El Anciano did not sign the missive with his true name, to those among the Basque community of Sonora, the heavy, flowing hand and elaborate rubric of Don Martín was unmistakable.[29]

In this remarkable document, El Anciano detailed all the problems of Sonora for the past several years. The writing is flamboyant, and although Don Martín dedicated a half-page out of the thirty-one to calling on his fellow Basques to meet and iron out a united front, most of the rest of the document consists of a vehement maligning of Álvarez Tuñón. Don Martín was not bashful in his choice of words or sarcasm, directing his remarks to "mis hixos"— "my sons." He lashed out brutally at both Don Gregorio and Don Rafael, accusing them of a variety of misdeeds, including an attempt to "atapar sus cacas"—"cover their shit." His contempt for them and all others that opposed the fathers of the Company of Jesus is obvious:

> Another consideration, in only the eight days that these two firstborn of Satan were friends,[30] they have brought the province into rebellion, removing the

tranquility, the liberty, the reputation, the wealth; having tried, judged, sentenced, and censured that which had been, as if they had always been united. Oh, tender hearts with gall of dragons! Oh, viperous tongues! You need not tell me, my fellow countrymen, why they hid and concealed everything so much in this, their meeting, closing doors and windows and stationing guards. If you do not know, I will tell you. Are not these the mysterious secrets and ceremonies of the Pharisees? If you do not understand, I will demonstrate. Look at those who work wickedness, mocking the light. Such are the meetings of the Lutherans in Germany, such are those of the Huguenots in France, and such are those of the Protestants in Jamaica,[31] and always against the fathers of the Company of Jesus.

This letter, Don Martín's own "viperous" call for action and unity, accomplished its purpose.[32] A meeting was convened and a united statement was hammered out in opposition to Don Gregorio's schemes. It was signed and sent to Father Visitor José María Genovese on February 20, 1722. This meeting was even more secret than the one at San Juan Bautista. The place where it was convened was given simply as "The Province of Sonora." Of the seventeen men known to be in attendance, at least thirteen were Basques: Manuel de Aldamiz, Juan Domingo de Berroeta, Juan Bauptista García de Echave y Barrutia, José de Goicoechea, Martín de Goicoechea, Martín de Ibarburu, Juan Miguel Madraz y Velasco, Antonio de Miranda, Cristóbal Olacho, Juachín Ignacio de Ozaeta Gallaistegui, Baltazar de la Peña, Agustín de Vildósola, and Juan Manuel de Zelaya. One other person who signed the document, Cristóbal de Leon, was of unknown heritage. Peña also signed for Diego Bañuelos, and Berroeta signed on behalf of Juan de Leon, both also of unknown ethnicity. The only other person in attendance, and the one who dutifully wrote and compiled the statement for everyone to sign, including himself, was the *escribano eclesiástico*, Manuel José de Sosa.[33] His ethnic heritage has never been determined, but he was a brother-in-law of Antonio Bezerra Nieto, married to Nicolasa Gómez de Silva.[34]

Not only was the meeting secret, but it appears that a number of letters, dictated to and written by Señor Sosa, were secretly produced as a result of this meeting. Although the originals, with their signatures, have never been found, it is fortunate that Sosa, and possibly one other scribe, made copies that still exist. By studying to whom they were written, even though the events that followed this meeting seem to have been kept secret to prevent Don Gregorio and his henchmen from knowing what was taking place, one can begin to understand the opposition's strategy.

It is difficult to document the whereabouts of Juan Bautista de Anza during this period. There seems to be a blank space in the documentary record from the latter part of 1721 until the beginning of 1723. It was at this time that he moved to Janos and took up residence there, but his name does not appear in any of the Janos documentation of that period. But by studying closely the letters relating to the

Álvarez Tuñón case, it becomes apparent not only where he was, but that he was still very heavily involved in the struggle to oust Don Gregorio from Fronteras. A copy of one letter, transcribed by Sosa and obviously written to the attention of Viceroy Baltazar de Zuñiga, is revealing. Although somewhat lengthy, it bears quoting in full because of the clear picture it gives of the customs of the time and the sentiments of the people of Sonora, at least of the Basque community. It describes the forces that were at work in Sonora, each trying to gain a foothold in political and economic power. It also starts to paint a picture of Juan Bautista de Anza's role in this controversy:

Most Illustrious Lord[35]

In speaking with the exalted person of Your Lordship our smallness will be magnified by the unskillfulness of our language,[36] although some of us were born in ancient Spain and others in the cities of this Nueva España. Out of a sacred respect for Your Lordship, we do not wish to disturb. Our fear is that in the greatness of your authority, you will not communicate a word with us. Your well-known charity will ascend to new heights if you deign favor a few poor, simple, and loyal vassals of the Catholic Majesty of the King, Our Lord (may God protect him), by hearing our humble petitions and declarations. Therefore, Sir, the undersigned citizens of this Province of Sonora, trusting in Your Lordship's innate condescension, kneel reverently at your feet by means of this written entreaty, and say without blind passion overpowering our hearts or extinguishing the light of truth, we submit ourselves to your judgment.

We lament without relief from ever-increasing fatalities. Every day on these roads we see the dead bodies of its inhabitants, perpetual hostilities, continuous and excessive robberies of horses, depopulated sites and habitations, mining operations shut down by fears and dangers, caused by the enemy invasions. Every footstep is a danger, every departure from our homes a hazard, even though there was security in times past.

All of this is because of the negligence of Captain Don Gregorio Álvarez Tuñón y Quirós, commander and leader of those called the compañía volante. He is callous to the common anguish of his fifty enlisted men, forgetful of his precise obligations, holding only in remembrance his own particular feelings. Indeed, Sir, the foundation of his neglect in these matters is that for many years he has lived thirty leagues[37] distant from the presidio,[38] his legitimate residence, while it has been under command of a lieutenant.[39] His extortion is in his soldiers' assistance in his mines and silver refineries, and the pack trains that carry their metals. He claims his delinquency is gallantry, saying that anyone who has silver to ingratiate himself will have the benevolence of princes. His captaincy has secured his well-established credit, a system that is for prosperous but ineffective businessmen, although totally contrary to serious Catholic honesty and the loyal spirit of Your Lordship.

In collecting the wages for his fifty assigned cavalrymen, he remits reports every year on which can be seen the signatures of those who are not, and never were, soldiers. When those original papers are compared with the report of people here who know which designations were valid over the past ten or eleven years, some of them (and not a small number) do not even exist. Many live in their homes away from the presidio and scarcely know the meaning of the words "sword" and "lance." Some are occupied on his cattle ranches and others in hauling firewood in carretas and smelting his metals. Still others are employed in the care of his person as messengers and delivery boys. Some, without shelter, horses, or arms, make stockings from the linings of their *cueras*,[40] and for every one good arcabuz among them, there are ten that will not shoot. Deserters from their garrison because of the exorbitant cheating and price setting of their captain, they are reduced to the necessity of working for a pittance in the mining camps.

The Apache enemies visit us boldly and repeatedly, to our confusion and damage, all for lack of a commanding officer with determination, interest, and valor. Every retaliation against them, made by his lieutenant, is brief and without speed, range, or organization. In all of this, Sir, we petition Your Lordship, who is endowed with royal civility and compassion for our miseries, to deign provide, with appropriate foresight, that which such calamities require—for the augmentation of the Royal wealth and conservation of this province and its missions. The reverend Jesuit fathers, whose richly adorned churches are protected from damage only by their own watchfulness, currently administer these missions. Owing to the fear felt by all, in view of the success of the enemy in their totally profane destruction, the missions have been deserted by the Christian Indians, their ancient parishioners vexed by the enemy's arrogance and victories, and unhappy with the profound indolence of the captain. When the enemy destroys one mission, they all perish.

Sir, over and above these clauses, which express our suffering, when compassion is born within Your Lordship; beyond the persuasiveness of a swift and efficient remedy, when zeal and charity super abound *(super abundan)* in Your Lordship; beyond extensive narratives that would be imprudent and injurious to the sublime comprehension of Your Lordship—we desire for you to examine these events closely.

For your happiness, we ask our Divine Majesty to grant prosperity to the person of Your Lordship. We are in need of your grand magnificence in the Province of Sonora.

(If this writing is suitable, the date—month, day, and year—with the normal courtesy of "Kissing the Feet,"[41] etc., will be added, after which it will be signed by Anza, Alday, Manje, Miranda, Berroeta, and others[42] that make up the leaders of this community, not leaving space for everyone to endorse it, but only those that have always been known to sign.)[43]

The final copy of this letter was undoubtedly signed and sent to Mexico City. It was probably the cover letter for the informe entitled "Respuesta a Varias Calumnias y Postulados de la Cecular asamblea de San Juan"—"Response to Various False Charges and Postulates of the Secular Meeting of San Juan"—a nine-folio answer to the charges that had been made at Don Gregorio's secret meeting.[44] And it is likely that the "Respuesta" was copied, at least in triplicate, and sent to Governor Martín de Alday in Parral and Viceroy Baltazar de Zuñiga and Jesuit Provincial Alejandro Romano in Mexico City. The copy of the "Respuesta" that exists today is also undated and unsigned. Another unsigned, five-folio letter, which carries the date of February 22, 1722, and is addressed to the governor of Nueva Vizcaya, probably also went in the same pouch as far as Parral in present-day Chihuahua, where Governor Alday had his residence.[45] One other letter from the vecinos of Nacozari that describes the same basic negligence, fraudulence, and enemy depredations may have been included.[46] These letters were all written in the singular hand of Manuel José de Sosa, and some carry the sender's address as "Province of Sonora," just like the one signed by the junta on February 20 and sent to Father Genovese.

All of this correspondence is obviously a product of that particular secret meeting. It all tells the same basic story and attempts to both discredit Álvarez Tuñón and to present another side to the story that he intended to present in Mexico City. Even other correspondence may have gone out in response to Don Gregorio's intrigues, traveling in a single *pliego*, or "packet of letters." Who carried that pliego to Parral and Mexico City is somewhat more illusive. We have to turn to the Jesuit priest at Bacadéguachi and a letter that he sent to the Jesuit provincial in Mexico City for the answer:

My Father Provincial Alejandro Romano

The bearer [of these letters] is a son-in-law of General Bezerra, a fine admirer of our company and an honorable Basque, called Don Juan Baptista de Anza. Because of the storm Don Gregorio has raised against the missions, the presence of the said Anza can serve us greatly, which he has promised me. I inform Your Reverence that this struggle has gone on for two years, because of which the said Anza, with other Basques and other residents, zealous of the good of the land, made a complaint against Don Gregorio that contains many accusations.[47] The said Anza, who is one of the principals and knows Don Gregorio very well, has observed his soldiers many times. At various times, he has given them charity, the miserable wretches having been degraded to such a condition. Indeed, the fruit of the land has been destroyed more each day. Because of the insufficient escort, the roads, mines, and gold can be robbed by the many enemies at any time. Now there is no one else here other than the poor Indians of the missions.[48] These villages under my care are so terrorized that by night they are on fire, and I believe the enemy will destroy them by this means. May the Lord assist us. In our Holy Sacraments, I am in your service and stand ready to fulfill Your Reverence's every desire.

San Luis de Bacadéguachi, April 20, 1722. A minor servant and subject of Your Reverence.

Nicolas de Oro[49]

*Nicolas de Oro*

The letter was written both as an introduction of Juan Bautista de Anza to the father provincial and also as an introduction to the other letters that Father Romano would be receiving in the same pliego. By now, the correspondence going to him included at least one other letter from Father Oro written on March 8, 1722,[50] one from Antonio Bezerra Nieto,[51] probably the "Respuesta," and a lengthy summation of everything by Sonora's father visitor, José María Genovese.[52] This last was a point-by-point answer to the thirteen charges that were leveled at the Jesuits and the missions by Álvarez Tuñón, and copies were probably destined to the governor and the viceroy, as well as to the father provincial. Father Genovese had pulled together numerous letters from the other Jesuits in Sonora and their various supporters and consolidated and summarized them all in one lengthy report.[53]

Father Oro, missionary at San Luis de Bacadéguachi, one of the closest missions to Don Gregorio's mines at Jamaica, was the victim of some of the captain's most pointed criticism. Don Gregorio saw the potential for a tremendous amount of Indian labor at Father Oro's mission, but the good padre refused to allow him to take to his mines one Indian more than the specified number allowed by Spanish law. So, besides the letter that Father Oro wrote introducing Anza to the father provincial, he wrote one in support of his own reputation. Bezerra Nieto's letter was also written in support of Father Oro's good character. Antonio had known and dealt with Father Oro for thirteen years and wrote a flowery description of his many virtues. The following year he would write a similar informe in support of the Jesuits and the missions.[54]

Now, in the latter part of April 1722, Juan Bautista de Anza was on his way to Mexico City carrying all of the petitions, letters, and reports generated in Sonora in February, March, and April against the wily Don Gregorio Álvarez Tuñón y Quirós. Not only was he carrying testimony of numerous people condemning the captain, but he was also taking his own personal witness, accrued over some seven years of living in Sonora.[55] He was traveling as an official representative of the people of Sonora as well as an official army courier, the alférez of His Majesty's Royal Presidio of San Felipe y Santiago de Janos. Furthermore, he was under orders from, and traveling with the total approval of, his commanding officer, Captain Antonio Bezerra Nieto.

As Anza traveled southeast across the Sierra Madre to Parral and on south to Mexico City, his detested counterpart, Don Gregorio, was also traveling south. The captain was traveling to Mexico City as planned, but his travel arrangements had taken on a completely new aspect. Although it probably appeared perfectly normal to an outsider, Don Gregorio's entourage was strange indeed. An entirely new companion was traveling with him. In addition to the seven soldiers of his asistencia, and whoever else happened to be riding south with the group, the party was joined on the first day of its departure from Jamaica by General Don Andrés de Rezabal. Don Andrés had been involved with military operations in Sonora since 1678,[56] and was presently governor and military commander of the Presidio of Sinaloa. He traveled now under orders from the Viceroy Baltazar Zuñiga, marqués de Valero, with Don Gregorio as his prisoner.[57] Adding insult to injury, General Rezabal was an old-country Basque.[58]

General Rezabal had quietly arrested Don Gregorio near his home at Jamaica.[59] He had allowed the captain time to complete the necessary arrangements for the journey to Mexico City, and had arranged the arrest so that all during their three months of travel it never appeared that Don Gregorio was his prisoner. Immediately upon their arrival in Mexico City on either the third or fourth of July, 1722, the viceroy had Captain Álvarez Tuñón committed to prison. However, his imprisonment did not last long. By July 24, the viceroy had acquitted and released him. Stating that the only accusation against him came from a "privileged person," the marqués absolved him of all charges.

Exactly where Juan Bautista de Anza was while this was taking place is unknown, but he must have arrived in the city after Don Gregorio's release. It is unlikely that he was the "privileged person" referred to. With all the letters that he was carrying from both privileged and underprivileged persons, the viceroy would not have considered his presentation of the case of the vecinos of Sonora to be that of a single person. Furthermore, since Don Gregorio was arrested on March 11, 1722, whoever filed the case against him did it well before this particular phase of the struggle began. In fact, the charge may well have dated back two years to when Juan Mateo Manje made his whirlwind trip to Mexico City in protest of the appointment of Juachín José de Rivera as justicia mayor of Sonora.

Regardless, at this time both Don Juan and Don Gregorio knew the other was there to present an opposing story to his own. Don Gregorio hired a lawyer and presented a convincing case of the needs and potentials of the province, convincing at least to someone who had never been to Sonora and did not know the situation. He had the advantage of being an inside man, part of the political system. Juan had the advantage of the backing of many prominent and powerful individuals in Sonora and his commanding officer in Nueva Vizcaya. Gregorio had the experience of many years of working in the system, albeit surreptitiously. Juan had the confidence of youth. Gregorio probably underestimated his adversary, even though that "boy of little more than twenty-five years" that he had complained about so bitterly in 1720 turned twenty-nine this summer. Maybe he was starting to realize that the "boy" was there to stay. Juan, on the other hand, knew that he and his cohorts would have difficulty dislodging Gregorio from his securely wedged position as captain of the compañía volante of Fronteras.

Don Gregorio and his entourage of seven soldiers were gone from Sonora for just over a year.[60] Anza's time away from Janos was probably close to that. Whether anyone went with him is unknown, but it would be nice to think his new bride, María Rosa Bezerra Nieto, was traveling with him.

Sonora was to be well represented in Mexico City in 1722. Not only did Anza and Álvarez Tuñón make their appearance there, but so did Agustín de Campos, the stalwart Jesuit missionary of twenty-nine years at Mission San Ignacio de Cabórica.[61] Although he went to Mexico City for an entirely different reason—one that has nothing to do with the present story—his trip was the very beginning of another saga in which Juan Bautista de Anza would become entangled some fourteen years later. At most, Don Juan and Don Gregorio might have heard through the grapevine that Father Campos was on his way to Mexico City. If they had heard anything, it was probably that the good padre had been called south by his superior, Father Provincial Alejandro Romano, for some minor discipline. Both Anza and Father Campos set out to present their case before Father Romano, but it may be that neither of them met with him (certainly Campos did not), because there was a change that summer, and Father José de Arjó was appointed father provincial in Romano's stead.[62]

Anza carried a letter of introduction for his meeting with the father provincial, whoever that might have been when he got there. Father Campos certainly needed no such introduction. He knew both Fathers Romano and Arjó very well. The three of them, in company with thirty other Jesuits, had traveled to the New World together. That trip had started on September 12, 1691, when they boarded the same ship, piloted by the master seaman Vicente Álvarez, back in Cádiz, Spain.[63] Father Romano, the provincial who called Campos south, was four years Campos's senior, a native of Patti, Italy.[64] Father Arjó, who heard Campos's case and apparently acquitted him of any wrongdoing, was a year younger than Campos. He was a native of Tarazona, Aragón,[65] possibly the same province in which Campos was born.[66] While Father Campos was away in Mexico City, it was two Italian Jesuits who watched after his mission—Fathers Luis María Marciano and Luis María Gallardi.[67]

Father Campos left San Ignacio on April 9, 1722,[68] probably just about the same time that Anza left Janos. The difference was, Campos seems not to have been in a hurry. He may have gotten wind that his countryman was going to be replacing Father Romano, because he certainly took his time getting across Sonora on his way to Mexico City. On the other hand, Anza and Álvarez Tuñón were in a hurry. Don Gregorio was in Mexico City by the first days of July, and Don Juan arrived there probably no later than the first part of August. Father Campos, on the other hand, traveled as far as Mátape and spent the summer there. He did not get started on his journey again until the morning of September 22,[69] probably about the time the other two men were making preparations to return to the north.

Their routes were also different. Both Anza and Álvarez Tuñón traveled to Mexico City via Parral and Durango. Father Campos, on the other hand, followed the coastal route from Sonora through Sinaloa. Their modes of travel also may have been different. The two military officers probably went on horseback, at least as far as Parral. From there they may have continued on horseback, or gone by coach. Father Campos, on the other hand, traveled in his own private coach. He was assisted by his trusted driver, a Pima Indian called Lázaro Chihuahua, another person who would become ensnared in the Campos affair fourteen years later.[70] Anza went as a representative of the vecinos of Sonora. Father Campos went at the behest of his superior, Father Provincial Alejandro Romano. Don Gregorio went as a prisoner of Don Andrés de Rezabal.

Both Campos and Álvarez Tuñón came back to Sonora and continued serving in their current positions. It would be another four years before the bureaucratic wheels in Mexico City finally rolled over and crushed Don Gregorio's little empire, showing the successful effects of Anza's trip. It would be fourteen years before Father Campos would be asked to leave San Ignacio. Although that particular event was the result of an entirely different matter, his present call to Mexico City would be continually brought up and held against him. Mexico City was even a pivotal point for Anza. Although the Álvarez Tuñón controversy did not directly effect his demise, what took place in Mexico City set Anza on a course of military action that probably would have been different had Don Gregorio won out in the end. It would be another eighteen years before the Apaches stopped Anza's career ascent.

Father Campos arrived back at San Ignacio and picked up where he had left off on Monday, May 24, 1723.[71] We know that Juan Bautista de Anza was back home at Janos by at least Thursday, April 8, 1723, because on that day Gregorio Álvarez Tuñón arrived in Janos, presented papers showing that he had been ordered by Governor Martín de Alday to inspect the presidio, and ordered that the troops were to be mustered for inspection on Saturday. Captain Antonio Bezerra Nieto dutifully sat down and wrote up a muster roll that listed Anza as being present at the presidio with all his arms.[72] (For the muster roll of the Janos Presidio on April 10, 1723, see table 1 in the appendix.) So, of the three Sonorans who went to Mexico City in 1722, Don Juan was the first one back, with Don Gregorio hot on his heels.

Regardless of the ignominious circumstances of his trip to Mexico City, Don Gregorio came back to Sonora under full cover of military authority and importance. In December, with Indian invasions in the Province of Coahuila resulting in numerous deaths at Santa María de Parras and in other locations, Governor Alday was forced to go on the campaign against the belligerents. At the same time, he was obligated, in his position as governor of Nueva Vizcaya, to personally inspect all the presidios of his jurisdiction or assign some other officer to accomplish the same. Alday had already met with Álvarez Tuñón when he was on his way to Mexico City. Knowing that the captain had been acquitted of the charges brought against him, and that he would be returning to Sonora after the first of the year, the governor sat at his desk in Parral on December 15, 1722, and signed orders naming Don Gregorio "inspector general" of the presidios of Nueva Vizcaya and her provinces. These orders were sent south to the Presidio of Nuestra Señora de la Límpia Concepción del Pasaje where Governor Alday was the capitán vitalicio. There, his son, José Romualdo de Alday, who was interim captain during his father's absence as governor, would present the orders to Don Gregorio on his way north.[73]

Álvarez Tuñón arrived at Pasaje on a Thursday, February 25, 1723, with the seven members of his asistencia who had gone to Mexico City with him at the expense of the king—his brother-in-law, Francisco Xavier de Miranda, José Ponce, Francisco Felix Corella, Baltazar Hugues San Martín, Francisco Espinal, and two other unnamed soldiers.[74] Don Gregorio accepted his appointment and immediately set about carrying out his assignment. As with other military assignments he had been given, he carried it out quickly and probably with a total lack of thoroughness. Three things point to this: the speed with which the inspection was performed, the fact that the accounting of each soldier and his equipment was supplied by the presidial captains rather than being gathered firsthand by Captain Gregorio, and the fact that he had never been conscientious about anything else. In all, Don Gregorio traveled over six hundred miles and inspected seven presidios in just forty-three days.

Being prejudiced against the Basques, Álvarez Tuñón would have felt somewhat intimidated by the situation. Five of the seven presidial captains with whom he had to deal were certainly Basque, the exceptions being José de Sarmiento, captain of the Compañía Volante de Campaña—"the Flying Campaign Company"—stationed at San Bartolomé, and Captain Bezerra Nieto at Janos. And those two may well also have been Basque. However, his reports of the inspection reveal his self-importance and his typical arrogance.

The inspection started at Pasaje with Captain Alday.[75] Five days later, on Tuesday, March 2, Álvarez Tuñón's party was at San Pedro de Gallo, where he examined Captain Juan Bautista de Leizaola's troops. Since Captain José de Berrotaran was also there at the time, Don Gregorio took his report and did not even bother going on to his Presidio of Santiago de Mapimí. Instead, he continued on to Cerrogordo and began the inspection of Captain Bentura de Álvarez y Zubialdea's soldiers the following Monday, March 8. On March 11, he investigated the compañía volante at San Bartolomé, and on March 17 he was examining the troops under the command of Ignacio de Zubiate, son of Don Gregorio's old financier and adversary José de Zubiate, at San Francisco de Conchos. Then, after a fast 275-mile journey north, he was at Janos on April 8, 1722.[76]

Captain Bezerra Nieto presented him with the list of all his troops that afternoon, and the following day Don Gregorio summoned four of the soldiers to interview them about conditions at the presidio. He asked questions such as how many soldiers the presidio had and what their wages were. He asked if Janos had its full number of soldiers and if they were properly armed. He wanted to know if the soldiers were well disciplined—an odd question coming from a commander such as himself. The soldiers were asked about civil or criminal charges that they might want to bring against their captain or other officers or soldiers. They were asked if a pension or other taxes were being deducted from their wages. Finally, Don Gregorio asked what are always termed *generales*, "general questions" about their age, length of service, and other personal information.

As might have been expected with the animosity between Don Gregorio and Juan Bautista de Anza, the latter was not one of the soldiers chosen for the interrogatories. Furthermore, if a true cross section of the garrison was the goal, it was certainly not achieved with the four soldiers that Álvarez Tuñón chose for questioning. Anza had been a member of Janos's cavalry for only a little over a year now, and there were others who were about as new to the service as he. None of them were interviewed, however. In fact, the only ones chosen for the inquiry were probably the oldest soldiers in the garrison, with the most years of service. Those questioned ranged from sixteen to twenty-three years older than Anza, who would be turning thirty in a couple of months. Between them they had the remarkable cumulative record of 111 years of military service at His Majesty's Royal Presidio of San Felipe y Santiago de Janos. Two of them, Francisco Griego and Francisco Pacheco, were squad corporals. Cristóbal Fontes was just a soldier, but with twenty-seven years of service, and Juan López de Ocanto was the corporal of the guard. None of the four was able to read or write.

The men were called one at a time into a room facing the presidio's secondary plaza. After giving the sign of the cross and swearing to tell the truth, they were interrogated with seven predetermined questions. They all testified that the garrison was fully manned and each man was well equipped with arms, horses, clothing, and supplies. The soldiers, they said, were well trained and disciplined, and each man was fully fit for the service. No one knew of any civil or criminal actions that needed to be filed against anybody. Each enlistee was paid 450 pesos annually, from which the only deduction was an eighteen-peso tax levied by the royal officials of Zacatecas. That fee was partially for the soldier's pension fund and partially to help offset the costs of maintaining the compañía volante of Coahuila. Each of the four soldiers also reported that the presidio was able to supply sufficient escorts for all the mule packers, freighters, and travelers moving on the roads "between Nueva España and Sonora." All gave glowing reports about their captain, telling proudly how he, at his own expense, was helping maintain a colony of the Janos Indians at the presidio and through this munificent program had greatly advanced the peace between the Spaniards and the native populations.

When each interview was complete, Don Gregorio and two members of his asistencia waited while the scribe finished recording the witness's answers to each of the questions. Then, each of the three affixed their signature and rubric to the document and the next witness was called in. At the completion of the interviews, the Presidio of Janos was reported as being fully in compliance with all rules and regulations. Captain Álvarez Tuñón sent word by courier across the presidio compound to Captain Bezerra Nieto that he would review the troops early the next morning, Saturday, April 10, 1723, before leaving for Fronteras.

The next morning at daylight, Juan Moreno, the company trumpeter, standing in the middle of the main presidio plaza, sounded the call to muster. As the men appeared from the barracks, carrying all their arms and equipment, they lined up by rank and length of service. Alférez Juan Bautista de Anza, standing beside *clarinero* Moreno, ordered the men to proceed to the holding pen where the *caballada* was being held, catch their mounts, and saddle up. Inspection would be in two hours. The company lieutenant, Juan Ignacio Gómez Robledo, was on an Apache detail with some soldiers in the north. Sergeant Diego Laines was somewhere south of Janos with another detachment of troops, riding escort for a heavily-laden mule train plying its way north. Although the company's three corporals and the other alférez, José Gómez de Silva, were all present, Anza was the senior officer and it was his responsibility to prepare the troops to pass in review.

The area where the horses were being held was partially a natural pen formed by rock outcroppings at the upper rims of an arroyo. Sections between the rocks had been filled with willows from the river bottom and ocotillo cactus to prevent escape. The narrow, upper end of the arroyo had been fenced off with a stockade of mesquite posts. At the wide, lower end of the wash, the five soldiers who were presently on guard duty over the caballada were spread out, holding a long grass rope to keep the horses above that point. They had driven the herd in that morning before daylight and were waiting for the rest of the troops to arrive.

When all was ready, five or six men at a time, again by order of rank and service, would enter the corral and stand in the middle of the caballada. As the band circled the handful of soldiers, each man would toss a rope around the neck of the horse he intended to ride as it trotted by him. He would then lead his mount for the day out of the corral and another soldier would take his place, until each was outfitted. Outside the corral, each man proceeded to the pile of equipment he had left lying on the ground. The horses were quickly bridled and saddled. Then the soldiers proceeded to put on their equipment. Swords were strapped on and cueras laced up. Each man put on his *espuelas*, or "spurs," if he did not already have them on, and tied on his leather *botas* that protected his feet and legs from cactus and brush. Alférez Anza then gave the command, "monten sus caballos," and everyone mounted up.

At a few hundred yards distance, on a flat parade ground, Captains Bezerra Nieto and Álvarez Tuñón were waiting, also on horseback. As the cavalrymen fell in behind Alférez Anza, he led them in a line past the two officers. Each man saluted stiffly with a partially clenched right fist over the left breast. As the procession rode past the two captains, it circled back around and lined up in front of them. When everyone was in place, horses and men standing at attention, Moreno, at the end of the line, sounded his trumpet. Anza nudged his horse forward and formally presented the troop. Of the Janos full complement of fifty soldiers, thirty were present. Nine were with Lieutenant Gómez Robledo guarding the mountain passes against Apache invasion. Five were with Sergeant Laines escorting the supply train northward. And four were with the *correo* providing mail service. Twenty-five, including Anza, were standing at attention, facing the two officers. The other five, assigned to the caballada, were still holding the extra horses.[77]

Alférez Anza called each man out, one at a time. As his name was called, the soldier would ride forward until his horse was standing directly in front of Bezerra Nieto and Álvarez Tuñón. There he would give the same salute with the fist over the heart. He would then state his name and rank and announce how many horses and pack mules he owned and the condition of his arms. When all of the soldiers in line had passed in review, several of them rode back to the corral and exchanged places with those of the caballada detail so they could present themselves before the "inspector general." Trained, fully equipped, and ready for action, these men looked sharp. Anza could not have helped but gloat a little as each man rode up to pass in review. These soldiers were in a class above those whom Don Gregorio commanded. Alférez Anza must have felt deep satisfaction in presenting these experienced, well-disciplined, battle-hardened soldiers to a man who looked upon him as a mere boy and an upstart troublemaker.

The struggle between the two men would continue. Because of corruption in the system, Gregorio would not be easy to topple from his prominent position of power. The poor vecinos of Sonora would continue to suffer for a time yet. The bureaucratic wheels would turn ever so slowly, but they were beginning to do so in Mexico City and elsewhere. Information was coming into high government offices from many different sources about the outrages being committed in Sonora. Even now, as the review of the Janos soldiers continued, Álvarez Tuñón had received the message that his own presidio at Fronteras was under a military inspection and that he had finally come under suspicion of insubordination and disobedience.

Twenty-two of his own soldiers under command of Alférez Juan Antonio Durán had just arrived to escort him back to Fronteras.[78] They brought word that the *sargento mayor de armas* of Sonora, Domingo Picado Pacheco, was waiting at Cuquiárachi for him to return so that his soldiers could be mustered and pass in review. Don Gregorio might have been more concerned if the sargento mayor had not been his own godson[79] and in total and unequivocal collusion with him. There had been some friction between the two of late, however, and Gregorio may have felt some erosion of his self-confidence.

He and his troops headed back to Fronteras the following Monday. They arrived at the presidio on Friday evening, April 16, where Don Gregorio found a letter waiting for him that had been addressed the day before at the Mission of Cuquiárachi, eight miles southwest of Fronteras. It was signed by Picado Pacheco. The sargento mayor was ordering Álvarez Tuñón to muster his troops for a review as soon as he arrived back at the presidio. Don Gregorio sent a return letter by one of his soldiers the next day, Saturday, informing Don Domingo that he would have his troops mounted and ready for review Sunday morning at eight o'clock sharp. Normally, it seems, Álvarez Tuñón held such reviews and troop musters at Cuquiárachi[80] where he could better hide the untended condition of the presidio. Evidently, however, he was not concerned about what Don Domingo would say in his report, and so he ordered this inspection to be held on the parade ground in the valley below the presidio complex.

The troop review took place, but little information was recorded and everything about it was the antithesis of the review at Janos the week before. Sargento mayor Picado Pacheco, who was a resident of San Juan Bautista, rode over to Fronteras from Cuquiárachi early Sunday morning for the inspection. He left his wife and family behind at the house that was maintained for him at the mission[81] and returned there in the evening. Afterward, he remained a few more days at Cuquiárachi to complete his report and then went south to Santa María Baseraca with an escort of ten of Don Gregorio's soldiers and a corporal. Finally, that summer he traveled south to Durango where he completed his final report.

Don Gregorio need not have had the slightest concern about what Don Domingo would say about the troop review of April 18. The sargento mayor hardly mentioned it in his report. What he told about his trials leading up to and after the official review, however, was more than sufficient to have convicted both men and sent them to prison. He lamented the fact that although twenty-two soldiers had ridden south to meet Don Gregorio on his way home from Mexico City, he and his wife and family had been forced to travel to Cuquiárachi without any escort because there were no soldiers at the presidio.

He had arrived at Fronteras on April 2 and tried to conduct a review of the troops, but only twelve soldiers could be located. The alférez and twenty-one others were on their way to meet Álvarez Tuñón. Seven had been gone with the captain to Mexico City for over a year. Three had been living at home for that length of time and were unavailable for the muster. One soldier was stationed in the Pimería Alta as a token guard for that vast expanse of territory, and one position was vacant because of a death. With so many soldiers absent, the sargento mayor suspended the review until Don Gregorio's return. "Still," he maintained, "that accounted for the fifty soldiers"—though in fact it does not. If Lieutenant Escalante, who presented the soldiers for review that day, was not among the twelve to be found at the presidio before the muster, the total was forty-seven enlistees. If he was one of the twelve, there were only forty-six soldiers accounted for.

The sargento mayor also included other incriminating evidence in his report. He told how the captain's brother-in-law, Francisco Xavier de Miranda, had never been a soldier but was listed as one. Miranda lived at Jamaica with Don Gregorio and had been paid as a soldier over the last year as he traveled to Mexico City and back with the captain. The sargento mayor told how the presidio had been too short-handed to supply a guard for his trip back to Baseraca, and how the lieutenant had had to send some Indians to guard the caballada so the soldiers assigned to its care could be freed up to ride escort for him. He even included in the report Don Gregorio's letter, written the day after his arrival back at Fronteras, in which he said that the reason for the shortage of soldiers at the presidio was because the lieutenant and several of the enlisted men had been assigned to guard Domingo Picado Pacheco's own mines at Jamaica!

Surely such a report would work its way slowly up to some official who would be incensed by its contents. That person was the newly appointed viceroy of Nueva España, Juan de Acuña, better known as the marqués de Casafuerte. He took office on October 15, 1722,[82] and very likely received the reports and letters that Juan Bautista de Anza had carried south from Sonora. Although Fronteras may well have been the worst presidio in the entire system, there were problems at the other northern garrisons as well. The entire system was costly, inefficient, undermanned, and often exploited by the presidial commanders. It did not take the marqués long to act. On May 25, 1723, he petitioned King Felipe V for a complete and thorough inspection of all the northern presidios. That permission was granted on February 19, 1724.[83]

Because of the tremendous distances across Nueva España, Texas, and New Mexico, because of the large number of presidios to be inspected, and because Fronteras was one of the most remote of the presidios, on the far northern reaches of Spanish dominion, it would yet be more than two years before Don Gregorio's day of reckoning. But this time a brigadier general was on his way. The cunning captain of Fronteras would not be able to deceive him as he had done so many others in the past. And when that day finally came, Don Juan Bautista de Anza—that young boy, that troublemaker, that miserable Basque whom Don Gregorio so thoroughly despised—would be there to pick up the pieces.

## Deaths, Births, and Letters from Home

*En seis de Sept$^e$ de mil setecientos y veinte y tres a$^s$, yo, el liz$^{do}$ fran$^{co}$ Xav$^r$ Ponze de Leon como cura enterré del cruz alta a D$^a$ Greg$^a$ Gomes de Silba mujer del Cap$^n$ D$^n$ Antto B$^a$ N$^{to}$ se le administraron todos los st$^{os}$ sacram$^{tos}$. doy fee — Fran$^{co}$ Xav$^r$ Ponze de Leon* . . . On September 6, 1723, I, Licentiate Francisco Xavier Ponce de León, as priest, interred with high cross, Doña Gregoria Gómez de Silva, wife of Captain Don Antonio Bezerra Nieto. All the Holy Sacraments were administered to which I faithfully attest—Francisco Xavier Ponce de León

As events progressed at Janos and Juan Bautista de Anza became accustomed to his life as a soldier, rising in rank to the office of lieutenant, all was not a seemingly endless battle to save Sonora. All was not fast-moving Apache campaigns and riding escort for dusty mule trains and freight wagons. Trips to Mexico City were rare events. There was also normal life—a life with family and friends in which the tension and struggles of the turbulent world outside could be forgotten, momentarily at least. For all intents and purposes, Juan's life as a husband and father began at Janos. Although, as already mentioned, there was a previous wife, or liaison, from which the two little girls, María Manuela and María Gertrudis, resulted, it was a short-lived arrangement. If María Valenzuela was a legitimate wife, the marriage might have ended with her death in one of the plagues that hit Sonora on a regular basis in those years. Death from childbirth is certainly another possibility. Even death by Apaches is not remote. Maybe that was the final factor that drew Juan into the military. Regardless, he had ended up at Janos, totally involved in the life of a soldier.

By then, Spain must have seemed little more than a dusty image in his memory. Even if he were to leave Janos, it would take months—maybe even a year or more—to return to his old home in Hernani. A visit to his family was not an option. He could entertain no hopes of ever seeing them again. It was necessary that he fully integrate himself into the new family into which he had married. And that is what he did, accepting all the pleasures, trials, responsibilities, and heartaches that came with being a husband and father in that day and age.

The death of his mother-in-law just a few months after his return from Mexico City came as a devastating blow. Her funeral Mass was held on Monday, September 6, 1723. In the short time he had known her, Juan had come to love Doña Gregoria as his own mother. She had been so like his mother in many ways. A friend, writing many years later, captured the essence of the family's affection for her:

And, more especially, [the memory] of the lady, . . . Doña Gregoria Gómez de Silva [will live forever]. Well, I cannot pass over this lady in silence. I will say that she was a matron of praiseworthy manners, of which the principal one was her devout Christianity, endowments, which she inherited from her noble birth, being of the most illustrious families of the Buenaventura Valley.[84]

As the body was lowered into the grave, her family took hope in her exemplary life and the fact that she had died peacefully at home in receipt of all the final holy sacraments. Still, it would be difficult moving forward without their beloved matriarch of so many years, especially for Don Antonio who was destined to be a widower for another ten years. But life went on in this remote military base on the fringes of Spanish society.

Remote as Janos was, Juan did stay in contact, after a fashion, with his homeland. Letters from Spain were always welcome, but they also brought a certain amount of anxiety when they arrived. One or two a year, at best, could be expected, and one never knew whose grave illness or death they might announce. Yet, even though family members back home did pass away, there was always news of new family members being born as well. Written correspondence also evoked a certain amount of melancholy as one learned about old friends and acquaintances and what they were doing with their lives.

Letters from home sometimes also brought requests for money, for nearly everyone who came to the New World improved their situation. Unfortunately, such correspondence between private family members was rare, and it seldom survived the centuries. Formal government, military, or church-sponsored communication often survived by being filed in a secure archive somewhere. Although no private missives between Juan Bautista de Anza and his family back in Hernani have ever been found, one formal government document that he received is still in existence. It can almost be considered personal since it came from people he knew well and loved.

The dispatch was written from Hernani in the latter part of 1721 when Anza was in the process of removing from Tetuachi to Janos. However, with Anza's frequent moving about in some of the most remote areas of all Nueva España, making it difficult for the correo, or "mail service," to even find him, it is relatively certain that he was already the alférez at Janos when he received it. Correspondence between parties on the two continents, especially if one of them was on the far northern frontier of Nueva España, took a long time. It might be a full year before one received a reply.[85] The dispatch came from the town government of Hernani, and probably had a note penned in the margin, at least from his father, if not also from his lehengusutipi, Teodoro de Zuaznabar, both of whom were serving on the town council at the time:

My Lord

Due to difficulties caused by the misfortunes of war and finding ourselves restored to the desired dominion of the majesty of Lord Don Felipe V, our most beloved King, may God protect him, and finding the structure of this, our parochial church of San Juan Bautista with several cracks in need of repair, especially in the entryway, where a few years ago at my own expense[86] a portal was built with four large columns and placed by the altar of the image of that same saint. There remains to be constructed, because of lack of means, an arch to cover and protect the work, which also lacks two images of St. Peter and St. Paul between the columns. The sacristy suffers from leaks, it being difficult to repair since its roof is lower than that of the church. It should be raised so they have the same slope. The interior of the church is a disgrace and needs to be renovated and whitewashed the way it used to be. The main door really needs a wooden screen to direct the breeze toward the altars. This, among other urgent needs, suffers from the delay in transferring funds, since what little is left over each year is being applied to the completion of the bell tower, which in order to be completed will require more resources, and for that reason a part has been set aside for the work on the cemetery and for the organ. This makes it necessary for me to appeal to Your Honor and to others of my children, having called a general meeting of my residents. With complete confidence and due consideration I beg Your Honor to please bear in mind this pressing need of our parish for the means of dispensing alms and for other pious works and the urgency of obtaining assistance in this necessity. And if it is seen fit to attend to this matter, a little more or less than one thousand one hundred escudos would be needed according to the estimates of those learned in such things, leaving the bell tower for another time when some benefactor shall feel so moved. I hope Your Honor will give serious attention to my supplication while I assure Your Honor at the same time of my desire to serve you in any way you wish, and I pray that our Lord God will keep Your Honor for many years in happiness. From my town hall, November 22, 1721.[87]

Copies of this same letter had gone out to at least twelve native sons of Hernani—the Zuaznabars in Argentina, Nicolás de Lecuna, Juan de Torres, Sebastian de Miner, and Miguel de Amasorrain, all in Mexico City, and the Borrote brothers in Mexico City, Querétaro, and Valladolid, Mexico. Although others received copies of the letter, Juan Bautista de Anza was the only native son to receive a copy at Janos, Chihuahua. Indeed, as far as is known, he was the only native son of Hernani in all of Nueva Vizcaya.[88]

Unfortunately, as is generally the case with occurrences that took place so long ago, we have only one side of the story. The record of how much money, if any,

Anza donated to the cause has been lost. A number of those who received the request responded with sizable sums, and a few of their replies still exist.[89] Knowing of Anza's great love for the church and his family back in Hernani, we can only assume that he, too, sent as much as he could afford.

In a land so remote as the northern reaches of Nueva Vizcaya in the first quarter of the eighteenth century, the receipt of a tiny piece of paper, with the familiar signature of a loved one back home, could bring immense joy, regardless of the actual text of the letter. When that text told of some achievement or moment of happiness in the life of the loved one who wrote it, the receiver's happiness was magnified tenfold. The same was true when those in the old country received notice from an adventurous son or daughter who had moved half a world away. So it must have been with great satisfaction and delight that Antonio Anza and Lucia Sasoeta, in distant Hernani, received word from their eldest son about his marriage or the birth of a grandchild, even though the news probably reached them several months to a year after the event.

Juan and María Rosa's first child was a son, whom they named Francisco Antonio. As was customary for the time, he was probably baptized on the same day he was born. What is unique about his baptism is that it is recorded twice on the same day with all the same participants. The only difference in the two baptismal entries is that the baby's uncle, Tomás Antonio Bezerra Nieto, deputy priest at the Janos presidio, wrote the first, and the priest, Francisco Xavier Ponce de Leon, wrote the second. Each man claimed in his particular excerpt that he was the one who baptized the new baby. It is inconceivable that Ponce de León wrote his entry thinking that Bezerra Nieto had forgotten to record the baptism, because his is written immediately below that of Bezerra Nieto's. The only logical explanation is that both men wanted to have the honor of baptizing the child, and so he was baptized twice that day. Bezerra Nieto's entry was recorded as follows:

> On the seventeenth day of the month of January, 1725, I, the bachiller Thomas Anttonio Bezerra Nietto, deputy priest of this Royal Presidio of Janos, baptized Francisco Anttonio, a Spanish child,[90] the legitimate son of the legitimate marriage of Don Juan Baptista de Anza and of Doña Maria Rosa Bezerra Nietto, Spaniards. His godparents being Don Anttonio Bezerra Nietto and Doña María Muñoz. And I signed as evident on the said day, month and year mentioned above.
> Bachiller Thomas Anttonio Bezerra Nieto[91]

Their next child was born just over two years later. By then Juan Bautista de Anza had become captain at the Presidio of Santa Rosa de Corodéguachi. It is possible that María Rosa had not even moved to Fronteras yet, or she may have returned to Janos to engage the services of a familiar midwife for the birth. Regardless, María Margarita, or Margarita, as she seems to have been known, was born on June 29, her father's birthday, in the year of 1727, at Janos. Had she been a boy, being born this close to the feast day of San Juan, in a desert land so dry and in need of the saint's intervention in sending rains, she most likely would have been named Juan Bautista, like her father. That opportunity would not come to her parents for another nine years, however. Father Ponce de León faithfully recorded little Margarita's baptism in the Janos baptismal registry as follows: "On the twenty-ninth of June of the year 1727, I, the licentiate Francisco Xavier Ponze de Leon, priest, baptized and anointed with holy oil Maria Margarita, a Spanish child, the legitimate daughter of Don Juan Baptista de Anza and of Doña Maria Rosa Bezerra. Her godparents were Bachiller Thomas Bezerra and Doña Anttonia Granillo, which I certify. Francisco Xavier Ponze de Leon"[92]

Margarita was born at a time of transition. Her father was probably not present at her birth because the family was in the process of moving and he had nearly overwhelming responsibilities in a new appointment. Margarita's arrival marked the end of the family's residence at San Felipe y Santiago de Janos. A new chapter in their life as a frontier cavalry family was about to begin at Santa Rosa de Corodéguachi, alias Fronteras.

## Santa Rosa de Corodéguachi

*Tanbien Participa a V.S. Como de la Visita que se hizo en el Presidio de Sonora, Resulto deponer desu empleo al Cap<sup>n</sup> D.<sup>n</sup> Gregorio y dejar el Comando de aquellas Armas ami Th.<sup>e</sup> D.<sup>n</sup> Juan Baup<sup>ta</sup> de Anssa quien Con deseo de desempeñar Su obligazion y encargadolo nrô Visitador Passo aestte Presidio por provisiones dettodo—pues nada allo en el de Sonora y oi se restituyo a su Plaza—Antt.º Bezerra (rúbrica)* . . . I also inform Your Lordship about the inspection made at the Presidio of Sonora. It resulted that Captain Don Gregorio was relieved of his commission and my lieutenant, Don Juan Bautista de Anza, was left in command of those troops. With a desire to perform his obligation, and charged with such by our Visitor, he left for that presidio with provisions for everyone. Indeed, none were to be found in Sonora—but today he has re-equipped his garrison—Antonio Bezerra (rubric).[93]

The official decree that established the Presidio de las Fronteras de la Provincia de Sonora was handed down in 1692. During most of the next ten years the garrison was a *compañía volante*, a true "flying company" without a permanent base of operations or headquarters. When a permanent location was finally decided upon, it was the site of a large, flowing spring known as Corodéguachi, in the valley of Cabullona.⁹⁴ The saint's name of Santa Rosa was chosen for the site. The buildings of the presidio proper were constructed on a high promontory overlooking the spring and the valley. In time, both the saint's name and the name of the beautiful spring, bubbling up in the desert, would be dropped in favor of brevity. Sometimes the presidio would be referred to as Santa Rosa de Corodéguachi, alias Fronteras, but eventually it would be known as simply "Fronteras."

Across the valley to the east stood the imposing, rugged Sierra Espuelas, the "Spur Mountains," the northern end of the great Sierra Madre, or Continental Divide. Some one hundred fifty miles to the east was the Royal Presidio of San Felipe y Santiago de Janos. Forty miles south lay the Real de Minas of Nuestra Señora del Rosario de Nacozari. The northernmost mission to the Opata Indians, San Ignacio de Cuquiárachi, was a mere eight miles west, and a little bit south. Farther to the west, scattered over hundreds of square miles, were the missions of the Pimería Alta. To the north was an unimaginably vast and mostly unexplored wilderness, from the shadows of which came the dreaded Apache. By the turn of the century, the españoles had ventured far enough into this foreboding mountain and desert country to become aware of the great Apache stronghold in the Sierra Chiricahua in present-day Arizona.⁹⁵

Distant, remote, and lonely, on the most northern reaches of Spanish civilization in Sonora, life would have been almost unbearably harsh at Fronteras, even without Apache raids, especially for someone raised in Hernani, Gipuzkoa. As Juan Bautista de Anza stood at his new home at the point of the hill where the Fronteras presidio stood, he could turn around 360 degrees and see more open territory than he had ever imagined existed in the entire world when he was a boy growing up in Spain. Not only was it more vast than anything he had ever dreamed, but he was responsible for it—every last square league of it. And everything that could be seen from the presidio hill was only about a tenth of all the country for which he was accountable. The responsibility of protecting the settlements to the south from the enemies to the north was staggering. The vastness of the great Sonoran desert was unfathomable. The remoteness of this frontier territory was intimidating. The view was absolutely breathtaking.⁹⁶

In fact, that was possibly the only redeeming quality this godforsaken outpost had when Anza took over as its captain. From the guardhouse, which adjoined the captain's house, the sentries posted there on a twenty-four-hour basis⁹⁷ could see for vast distances in any direction. No Apache attack could be staged on the presidio itself without the entire community knowing well beforehand, giving everyone plenty of time to prepare. Like a medieval castle on a hill, the presidio was nearly invulnerable. Unlike its ancient counterpart, the buildings were not made of stone, but their sun-dried adobe construction was more than sufficient to stop Apache arrows.

The presidio was situated on the eastern point of a long, fingerlike ridge that pointed out into the valley on an east-west plane. The captain's house and the guardhouse sat at the easternmost point on the southern side of the narrow ridge. Anza built a presidio chapel that nearly adjoined them on the north.[98] It constituted the building farthest to the east on the north rim of the ridge. The soldiers' barracks ran in a line down both the north and the south rims of the ridge. There was a large plaza adjoining the captain's house and a smaller one farther to the west between the rows of barracks. Both plazas were partially enclosed by the barracks. Sometime after Anza's appointment as captain of Fronteras, a tower was constructed on the guardhouse, allowing for even greater visibility,[99] and the walls and buildings that constituted the presidio were repaired, improved, and expanded. Although it was built somewhat after the manner of a fort, the real fortress was the steep ridge on top of which it sat. As far as is known, no attempt was ever made by the enemy to breach its security.

As at all such Spanish colonial military installations, homes of the vecinos who farmed and ran livestock in the area sprang up just outside the walls of the presidio proper. This served a twofold purpose: first, it provided better protection for the families of the settlers, and secondly, the presidio was a ready market where supplies and farm produce could be sold. This community of vecinos and their small adobe houses was situated in the valley between the base of the presidio ridge and Corodéguachi spring, about a quarter of a mile to the southeast. On the far side of the community from the ridge was a flour mill located at the spring. The water in the area and deep fertile soils made the valley a prime agricultural area. There might have been a bustling community, even before Anza arrived, had people felt safe in living there. Sadly, due to the many years of neglect by its captain, Don Gregorio Álvarez Tuñón y Quirós, and even to some extent his predecessors, that was not the case.

Juan Bautista de Anza first arrived on the scene late one Tuesday afternoon, October 29, 1726.[100] This was not the first time he had been there, of course. In fact, on several occasions he had come to the presidio with pack trains of supplies for the soldiers' families, the product of his own charity and that of his commanding officer and father-in-law, Antonio Bezerra Nieto.[101] This time was different, however. As lieutenant of the Presidio of Janos, and with a squadron of soldiers from that garrison, he was escorting an important dignitary from Mexico who had been on the road for two years inspecting the presidios of northern Nueva España, Brigadier General Pedro de Rivera. This little detachment with their important visitor had been on the road for six days, but rather than stopping at Fronteras, they continued right on past the presidio for eight more miles and camped that night at Cuquiárachi.

Inspector General Rivera had arrived first at Janos, on his return trip from Santa Fe through El Paso, over two weeks before, on October 13.[102] There he had found the soldiers "were so equal that there was no one among them who was not ideal." He determined that Captain Bezerra Nieto "was well-suited to his position and ably discharged his duties." Furthermore, "the soldiers lacked none of the equipment that their jobs demanded."[103] That would certainly not be the case at Fronteras.

General Rivera was not unaware of the chaos that reigned in this frontier outpost. He had certainly heard many stories about its shortcomings from disgruntled citizens, especially Anza and Bezerra Nieto. The marqués de Casafuerte, viceroy of Nueva España and the man who had appointed Rivera inspector general, had undoubtedly made him aware of all of the written information that Juan Bautista de Anza had carried to Mexico City over four years previously, and other correspondence that had continued to flood his office. Probably nothing could have prepared him, however, for the miserable conditions that he was about to witness.

Likewise, Captain Álvarez Tuñón was not unaware that the brigadier general was coming. After all, the inspector had been on the road examining presidios for just a few days under two years, having left Mexico City on November 21, 1724.[104] Word had undoubtedly reached Don Gregorio months in advance of the arrival of the expedition of inspection. Typically, however, the derelict captain did nothing to prepare the presidio for the general inspection until a few weeks prior to the general's arrival. Then, he arrived hurriedly from his home in Jamaica and, in a flurry of activity, tried to snap everything into shape by borrowing guns, cueras, and horses from the vecinos, and barking out meaningless orders to soldiers who barely knew who he was.[105]

The hearing started promptly the day after Rivera's entourage arrived at Cuquiárachi. On Wednesday, October 30, word was sent to Fronteras by escribano Francisco Sanchez de Santa Ana announcing the beginning of the inspection and its purpose. The inquiry would take place at Cuquiárachi and all witnesses would come there to provide their testimonies. All soldiers were ordered to remain at the presidio until the inspection was completed. As had occurred at all the other presidios inspected by Don Pedro, the captain, Don Gregorio, and his officers were sent a distance away to wait out the inspection. In this instance, they were ordered to the nearby village of Teuricachi. They were not to leave there and they were not to come to Cuquiárachi until summoned. This precautionary measure was taken so that the soldiers might testify without fear of intimidation by their captain.

At the mission, General Rivera conducted the interrogations while escribano Sanchez de Santa Ana rapidly wrote down everything that was said. Numerous witnesses were called and questioned. Various citizens were on hand throughout much of the investigation. Well-known and beloved old-timer Juan Mateo Manje was there much of the time representing the vecinos. Lieutenant Juan Bautista de Anza, from Janos, and two local vecinos, Manuel de Berryessa and Juan José Ramirez, sat as witnesses for the entire proceeding.[106] How it must have rankled Don Gregorio that the man he had labeled an "upstart boy" was there, seated beside the brigadier general for the duration!

General Rivera was at Cuquiárachi for thirty-five days. As a professional soldier and administrator who had been on the road inspecting presidios for two years, it did not take him long to see through the flimsy facade that Don Gregorio had tried to construct at the last minute. Possibly even more telling than the many hours of condemning testimony that he heard was the fact that early on the second day of the hearings, before that day's interrogations started, Sergeant Nicolás Sanchez and Corporal Diego de Barrios showed up at the general's door at Cuquiárachi with a written petition. The soldiers at the presidio were hungry. Since they were being required to remain there, they had no way of providing food for themselves. The general responded immediately by requisitioning wheat, corn, and beef from Father Ignacio Arceo, the missionary at Cuquiárachi.[107] With this incident and just a few days of questioning the soldiers, he was able to say:

> Since no one cared for the presidio, the soldiers continuously lacked food and clothing. With what supplies they have been furnished at high prices, the soldiers bartered with the Indians for more urgently needed items. Because they had to use their supplies for bartering and because of the high prices of goods, the soldiers were continually in debt. These soldiers were so demoralized because of the lack of inspiration from their commander that they never ventured from the vicinity of the presidio. While the soldiers were inside, they experienced the hostilities of the Indians, who knew how ineffective their weapons were, so they attacked the province at will without fear of reprisal. Thus, this garrison suffered problems that eventually led to its ruin.[108]

Just two weeks after his arrival at Cuquiárachi, after having heard testimony of soldiers, vecinos, and Captain Álvarez Tuñón himself, Inspector General Rivera charged Don Gregorio with fifteen counts of misconduct, embezzlement, and fraud. The charges were presented to Don Gregorio on Tuesday, November 12, and he was given until the following Monday, November 18, 1726, to respond. His response was long and rambling, supported with mostly irrelevant documents, and in the end it was nearly all meaningless. When his presentation was over, General Rivera immediately found him guilty of two of the charges, removed him from his captaincy, placed him under house arrest, and ordered him to stand trial on the other thirteen charges in Mexico City where the viceroy, the marqués de Casafuerte, would sit in judgment.[109] Of this the general later wrote:

> The captain was given a copy of the charges against him so that within a set time he might prepare his defense. Although the amounts [i.e., the money Don

Gregorio was collecting for soldiers that did not exist] had already been reviewed and found to be in good order, I reviewed them again after the inspection because of the caliber of the company. The soldiers were not only ill equipped, but many were unfit for the service. I charged the captain accordingly, but he could not defend himself against the charge, or any other, even though he presented a lengthy argument. I therefore decreed a final judgment ordering that the wages of one of the garrison's positions be deducted from the captain's pay. This position was fictitious, as was sworn to by the person who theoretically occupied it. Furthermore, the captain was ordered to produce documentation accounting for 14,654 pesos, the yield of thirty-four positions over a period of seventeen years.[110] It was known that he had embezzled the salaries of two positions each year. I thus found him guilty on two counts, and the remaining thirteen charges I have sent to Your Excellency[111] for review. Finally, I suspended the captain and ordered him to appear to hear the sentence pronounced.[112]

There is nothing to indicate that Don Gregorio's responses to the charges lasted longer than one day. Juan Bautista de Anza had sat as a witness for the entire proceeding—both that day and the many days of testimony prior to it. Thus, it may have been on that Monday afternoon, November 18, 1726, after General Rivera had pronounced sentence on Don Gregorio, that he turned to Anza and informed him that he was being raised in rank from lieutenant to captain, and that henceforth he would be interim captain of the Presidio of Santa Rosa de Corodéguachi, alias Fronteras, with the possibility of becoming capitán vitalicio through good faith and conduct. Regardless of how the moment came, it must have given Don Juan, and others who were there to hear his appointment, great satisfaction in knowing they had finally won the difficult and extended battle to bring integrity back to Sonora and obtain the appointment of a presidial commander who would have the interest of the province at heart. It seemed that finally everyone, with the possible exception of Don Gregorio, could heave a sigh of relief. The struggle was over.

Among the many things that General Rivera did between his appointment of Juan Bautista de Anza as captain of the Fronteras presidio and his leaving Cuquiárachi to inspect the Presidio of Sinaloa, was to instruct the new captain in his duties and provide him with a detailed document of regulations for the management of the presidio.[113] After so many years of neglect and mismanagement, gaining the confidence of the soldiers and the vecinos of Sonora and bringing the presidio onto an equal plane as a fighting force with the other garrisons in the north would be a long and difficult task. However, the general had confidence in the new captain and passed that sentiment along to the viceroy.

Brigadier General Pedro de Rivera left Cuquiárachi and Fronteras on Saturday morning, December 2, 1726, on his way to his next site of inquiry, the Royal Presidio of San Felipe y Santiago de Sinaloa.[114] Juan Bautista de Anza had been living at Fronteras as its captain for almost two weeks by then. He had been making arrangements to put the physical structure of the presidio into shape. He had also spent the time getting acquainted with his men—interviewing, counseling, and instructing. His own work ethic and enthusiasm were already starting to rub off on them.

However, shortly after Rivera left, Juan did also. The entire garrison was drastically in need of supplies and provisions, which he and a small detachment of his new soldiers would obtain in a fast trip to Janos. There he would tell his father-in-law of his new appointment and take leave of the Janos soldiers who had ridden to Fronteras with him as part of General Rivera's escort. He and his new soldiers would load several pack trains of mules with the much-needed provisions, supplied through the stores of the Janos presidio and the generosity of Anza and Bezerra Nieto.[115] Then, they would hurry back to Fronteras to continue placing things in order and to commence fulfilling the mandate given to Captain Anza by General Rivera, to start patrolling and protecting his territory of responsibility.

If on the 150-mile ride from Fronteras, Juan mulled over the details of moving his young family to their new home, those plans were somewhat frustrated when he arrived back at Janos. It was a happy frustration, however, because María Rosa also had important news for him. She was pregnant with their second child.[116] If Juan had been planning a quick removal of his family to their new home, he probably had second thoughts now. His two daughters by his previous union were very small, and little Francisco would be turning two years old in just a few weeks. That could probably be coped with, but Fronteras was no place for a pregnant wife and certainly not the environment in which to give birth.

It is therefore likely that Juan went back to Fronteras alone with his soldiers and Rosa waited out her time with the children at Janos. Fronteras was still an extremely dangerous place. Much had to be done to get the buildings into shape and make them livable as well as secure. There was much to be done to start giving the enemy a new image of what this garrison was going to be like in the future. Reconnaissance and retaliatory expeditions would have to be mounted. The ragtag soldiers desperately needed training. Supplies had to be obtained so that when the cavalry left on a campaign they would be well dressed, equipped, and armed, and the enemy would understand the danger of defying this new regime.

One of the charges that had been brought against Don Gregorio by General Rivera was that he had totally failed to respond to and help put down a Seri uprising in southwestern Sonora.[117] It had taken place the year before, and a number of vecinos had been killed.[118] Rivera had also charged that Captain Álvarez Tuñón had often failed to respond when the "enemy," meaning Apaches, had attacked.[119] In the new list of regulations that the inspector general left for the management of the Fronteras presidio, Captain Anza was specifically ordered to rectify the situation:

"Because of the carelessness of the army of this presidio and because of the cleverness of the enemy of these frontiers, they have committed continuous thefts of horses, cattle, and other things, penetrating right to the presidio itself. It is ordered that the armies be continually on the move, with one squadron inspecting and visiting the passes and areas where the enemy comes, for this presidio was built for that reason."[120]

Captain Anza rode back to Fronteras from Janos and set about complying with this mandate with a vengeance. There can be no question that the Apaches who had been plaguing the settlers of northern Sonora knew within just a few months that something was very different. Suddenly, the cavalry was everywhere, watching every pass and loping out hot on the heels of every raiding party. Even though no force or measure seemed capable of fully curtailing the guerrilla tactics of the Apache, no longer was there free access to anything and everything. No longer was it just the Opatas, Pimas, and Spaniards whose lives were in danger. Now there was retaliation for every single strike that was made.

There had been some retaliatory expeditions mounted before, but almost without exception Lieutenant Juan Bautista de Escalante or one of the junior officers had led them, and they had never gone far before the soldiers ran out of food. Now the commander was generally at the head of any retaliatory campaign. It would be unfair to say that Don Gregorio never led an Apache campaign, because there is evidence of one as remembered by Father Agustín de Campos of Mission San Ignacio: "In those years gone by, Father Gallardi was on a campaign against the Apaches with Captain Don Gregorio Álvarez, at the latter's request. All three Fathers[121] concurred by sending Spaniards, horses, and supplies to help impede the many and extremely grave injuries and terror that we received each day from the said enemy."[122]

This recollection concerning one paltry crusade conducted by Don Gregorio in the seventeen years that he was captain of the Fronteras presidio stands in stark contrast to a statement made by Don Juan Bautista de Anza a mere year and a half after Rivera's inspection and Juan's appointment to the captaincy. His campaign journals have been lost, but he did report that "I have also made three campaigns against the Pimería and the Seris to calm certain disturbances among them, and I have always done so with the approval of the province's subjects."[123]

Opata, Apache, Pima, Seri, or Spaniard—it made no difference—Sonorans everywhere now knew that they were marching to a different drummer. Some were happy about it and some were not, but Spanish law was now going to be enforced. Gone were the days of cheating on the king, in whatever manner, and not having to answer for it. The Royal Presidio of Santa Rosa de Corodéguachi, alias Fronteras, was taking its place on the map, and its new commander, Don Juan Bautista de Anza, would soon be known by regional peoples everywhere, be they friend or foe.

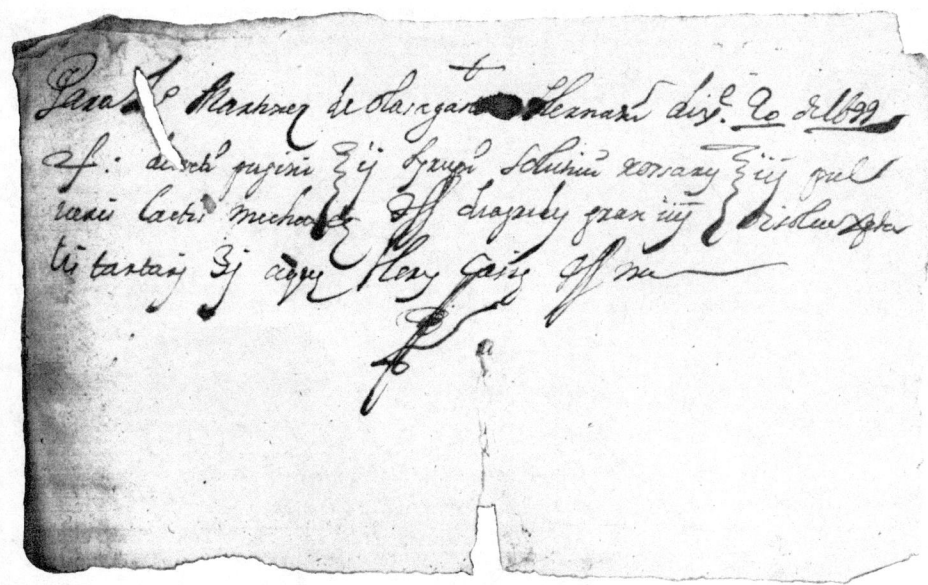

Prescription for five different herbs, written by Dr. Agustín Zabala "for Juan Martinez de Olasagasti, Hernani, December 20, 1699," and filled at Antonio de Anza's pharmacy. Note Dr. Zabala's unique rubric after the text. (HUA, E-7-I-9-5, Demanda interpuesta por Antonio de Ansa contra Teresa de Portugal, viuda de Juan Martínez de Olasagasti, 1701, folio 24.

*Letter from Juan Bautista de Anza to Father Visitor Nicolás de Oro, Motepore, July 11, 1729; see chapter 5 for translation.* (AHH, Temp. Leg. 17, Exp. 21, Anssa to Oro, ff. 37-37v.)

allo fazilidad Respecto a la Pobreza de los PP.
pues aunque en tuburama se dize taxo es mucha la Cortedad que tiene: sobre lo demas
se me hizen algunas Razones (en Caso de que
a los Seris Saquen a tierra firme) en que me
pareze no Combenia Concurriesen a la facción
pero Como Ignoro las Ideas de Vs. Cavallero
no quiero ablar ni preuenir nada y esto ba
de Comuersazion = El R.do P.e R.or Somosa me
dizen hira a la faccion por orden del d.ho P.e Prov.l
q.e Dios n.ro S.r Consiga para su Santo Servi.o
Sobre la Preuencion de algunos S.res y de los PP.
Dhos que no Salgan Soldados de mi Compañia,
las Razones que dan me parezen muy fuertes,
y podran Seruir las d.has para que no que-
dan Imbernarlos, mas no para dettener al
presentte Respecto al Orden de n.ra m.s Ex.ca
Si os bien saue la flag.d en son buenos quiera n.ro
fortuna Conzedermelo = toda via me allo Sin
poder Conseguir la Conclusion de n.as d.ras
puede Ser que para S.n tiago logre, despacho Correo luego a Mex.co siseofrece alguna Cosa
havisseme V.S.ma y mandeme Con el seguro
de que Sera obedezido pues Soy Su Vm.de
Criado: N.ro S.r g.de a V.S.ma m.s a.s Motepe
y Julio 11 de 1722 = B L P de V S.

Juan Bauta de Anssa

*Last page of a four-page letter from Juan Bautista de Anza to Father Provincial Andres Nieto, Motepore, July 28, 1729; see chapter 5 for translation. (AHH, Temporalidades Leg. 17, Exp. 21, Anssa to Nieto, F. 65).*

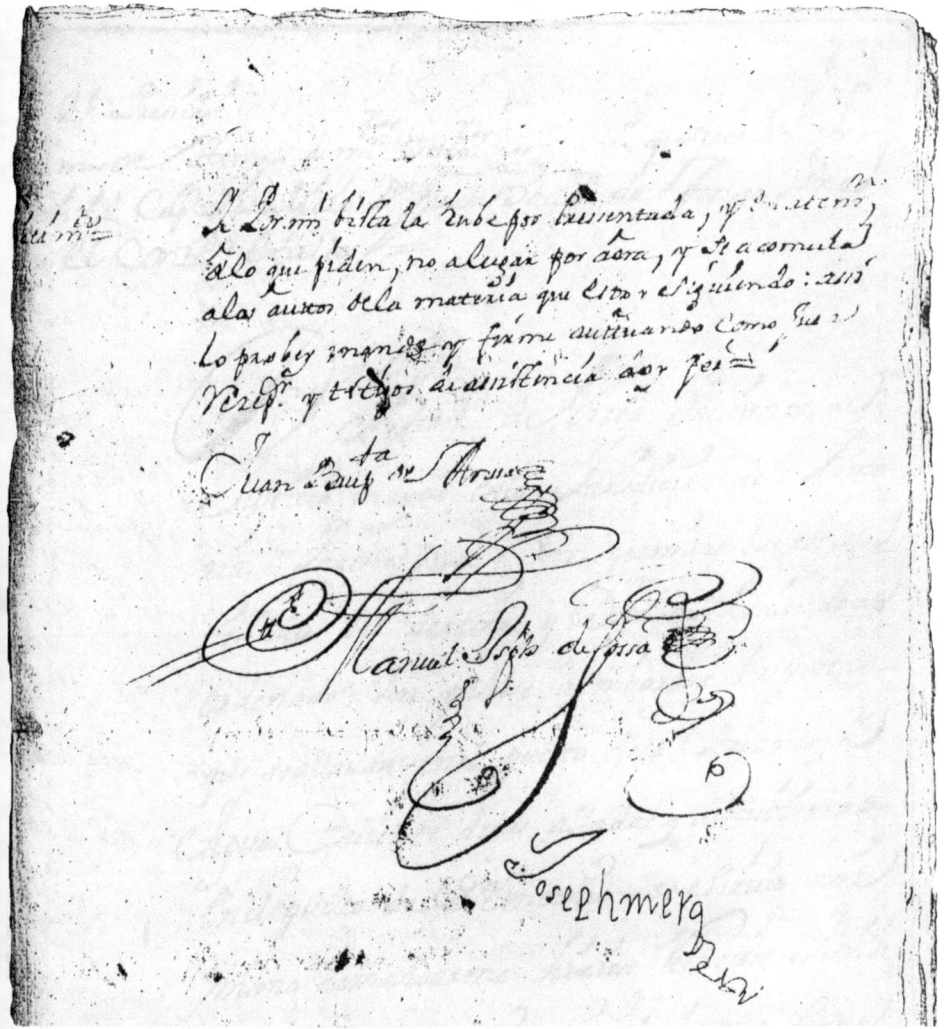

Captain Juan Bautista de Anza's statement of December 3, 1736, in which he certifies receipt of a request from fifteen Agua Caliente residents for the return of the impounded Arizona silver. Note the signatures of Anza and witnesses Manuel José de Sosa and José Romero. (AGN Minería 160, Leg. 1, Testamento de Juan Bauptista de Anssa, Arizona, diciembre de 1736, folio 87).

Presidio of Fronteras, subject to the government of Sonora, situated at 31° 17' north latitude and 255° 24' longitude from the Tenerife meridian. Explanation: A. Captain's house B. Guardhouse, C. Church, D. First plaza, E. Second plaza, F. Mill. NOTE: All of the construction is of adobe. Scale: 200 toesas (1335 feet). Joseph de Urrutia. Note that although the diagram does not indicate it, the mill site (F) is the location of the spring where the original Opata ranchería (Santa Rosa de Corodéguachi) was situated and where the Caballería de las Fronteras first took residence in the early 1690s. (Courtesy British Library, Picture Library, London)

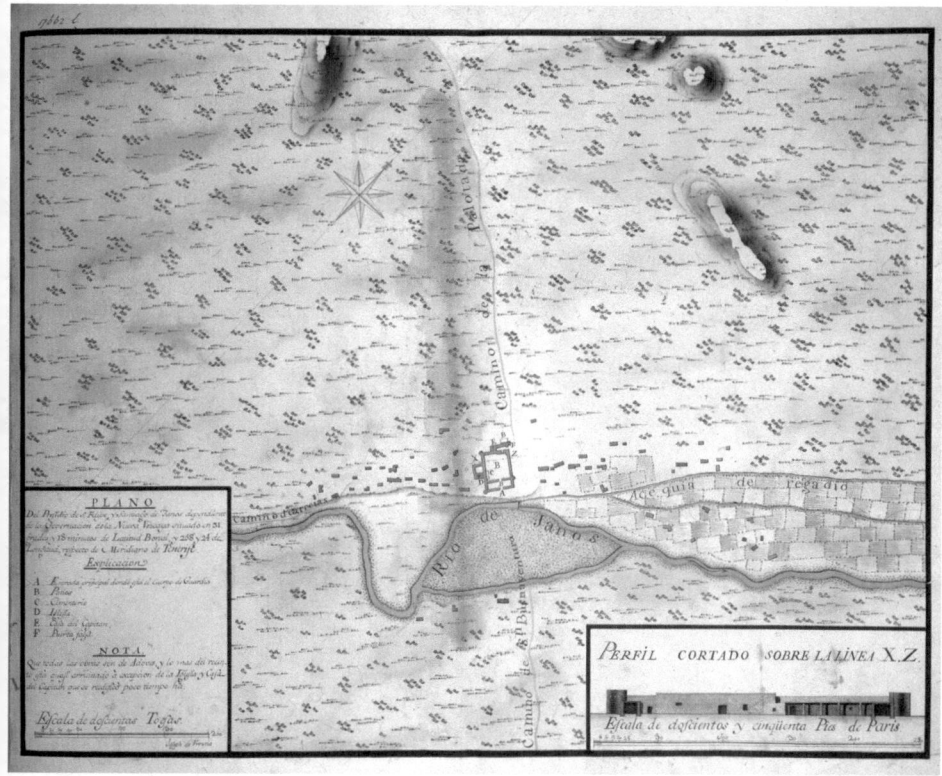

Presidio of San Phelipe y Santiage de Janos, subject to the government of Nueva Vizcaya, situated 31° 18′ north latitude and 258° 24′ longitude from the Tenerife meridian. Explanation: A. Main entrance where the guardhouse is, B. Courtyards, C. Cemetery, D. Church, E. Captain's house, F. False door. NOTE: All the construction is of adobe, the entire compound being nearly in ruins, with the exception of the church and captain's house, which were repaired a short time ago. Scale: 200 toesas (1355 feet). Legend in the lower-right-hand corner: Profile drawn along a line from X to Y. Scale: 250 pies de París [approximately 266 feet]. Joseph de Urrutia. (Courtesy British Library, Picture Library, London)

# Chapter Five

## Apaches, Livestock, Politics, and Jesuits

## *Midnight Marauding*

*De dhas sierras espian los cavallos mulas y rezes q andan en los campos y de noche recogen y los lleban y si ven pasar algunas personas por algunos puertos estrechos salen a matarlos* — Juº Baup<sup>ta</sup> *de Anssa (rúbrica)* . . . From the said mountains they spy out the horses, mules, and cattle grazing in the fields, and by night they gather and drive them off, and if they should see anyone passing through the narrow canyons, they ride out to kill them—Juan Bautista de Anza (rubric)[1]

The territory for which Juan Bautista de Anza found himself responsible as captain of the presidio at Fronteras was so vast as to stagger the imagination of any European of his day. It was ten times the size of his native Basque country. It was twice the size of Portugal and one-third the size of the entire country of Spain. It covered over 100,000 square miles. And he was expected to protect it with fifty men!

His area of responsibility ran north from Fronteras past the Chiricahua Mountains to the Gila River in present-day Arizona.[2] It ran west to the Colorado River and the Gulf of California. It went south at least as far as present-day Guaymas, Sonora, and east to the present-day border of the state of Chihuahua. It contained numerous river valleys that drained down immense canyons to the Gulf of California. Some of the rivers ran directly south and west to get there. Others like the Santa Cruz and the San Pedro ran north for 150 miles before connecting with the Gila, which then ran west and south to empty into the gulf. It crossed at least a half-dozen mountain ranges, and its lower elevations were composed of extensive inhospitable desert. Most of the land in the north and west was unexplored and had been seen only by a few soldiers on reconnaissance expeditions or punitive forays.

Don Juan, in his wildest dreams, also could have never imagined the many tribes of indigenous peoples who lived there. In the northwestern corner of the territory lived the tribes the Spaniards called the Yuma,[3] O'opa, Cocomaric O'opa,[4] and Papabi O'otam, or Papagos.[5] People known to the Spaniards as the Seri Indians lived in the southwest section, along the coast of the Gulf of California.[6] South and east of Fronteras were the Opatas and Eudeves,[7] and in the center of it all were the Pimas.[8] This last group comprised several subgroups, recognized by the Spaniards as Pimas Altos (Piatos), Sobaipuri,[9] and Pimas Bajos (Sibubapas). Another group with whom Anza dealt was the Yaqui.[10] They seemed to be everywhere in Sonora but were not indigenous to this northern country. And, of course, from the northeast came the dreaded Apaches.[11]

The Apaches were the scourge of the Spanish frontier. Mounted on horseback, they seemingly appeared out of nowhere and were gone just as fast, leaving death and destruction in their wake. They were guerrilla fighters, and no effective means of combating such tactics had ever been developed. As presidial captain at Fronteras, Captain Anza dealt with them, or the consequences of their activities, on an almost daily basis. The pressure never let up. Both preventive and punitive expeditions and campaigns had to be mounted constantly. It was a job that would keep him busy for the rest of his life. And when he was gone, it would occupy his son for most of his life. It was the captain's greatest challenge—one that would prove fatal in the end.

In a report to Governor Manuel Bernal de Huidobro in 1735, Juan Bautista de Anza related many of the difficulties that he had experienced as captain of Sonora's only presidio. "Only those who have attempted it know how difficult it is to apprehend [the Apaches]," he lamented. "Our troops usually march in search of them at night so they cannot discover us by the dust of our horses."[12] It is even likely that Captain Anza and his soldiers learned the technique of traveling by night from the Apaches. In fact, Rowland translated the above statement of Anza's as, "[the Apaches'] entrance when they invade our territory is customarily made at night so they will not be revealed by the dust raised by their horses."[13]

Either translation is correct, depending on where the translator chooses to place the period that Anza did not provide. And either statement was correct. The Apaches regularly attacked in the dark. Often guided by the full moon, they could move at nearly top speed through open country, but their dust cloud would be relatively invisible. The vecinos would not know they were coming until the Apaches were on top of them. It was a technique that the Spaniards would eventually adopt and use increasingly as years went by, until maneuvers during the full moon were almost a monthly occurrence somewhere in Sonora.[14]

Even when the soldiers of Fronteras went out stealthily at night under cover of darkness, however, the Apaches often discovered them before they could make a raid on the Indian camp.

"Despite these precautions," Anza pointed out, "they often discover us by scouting the countryside on fast horses or on foot, whereby they cover the ground almost as quickly as on horseback."

"This discovery habitually occurs the day after the troops depart [from the presidio]," he said, "because they know the troops do not take to the trails for any other purpose. Within two hours Apaches great distances away are aware of our presence because the first to find our tracks raises the alarm and others take up the cry wherever tracks are found."[15]

The Apaches generally lived in small, scattered communities, often long distances from the missions and communities that they raided. Small scouting parties of two or three seem to have been ubiquitous in the high vantage places where they could spy on the Spaniards and easily warn their own people when the cavalry was out in search of them. For many Apaches, raiding was a way of life, but it did not become fully developed until after the arrival of the Spanish. There is no evidence to show that Apaches made extensive raids anywhere in what is today Sonora or Arizona prior to the coming of the Spaniards.[16] However, with the arrival of these Europeans and their new way of life that centralized everything around a mission or other settlement, tightly knit, immovable communities with their accessible commodities became the targets of Apache raiding. Domestic horses and cattle were easy prey for these marauders, whether the attack was carried out after dark or in broad daylight. By the time Anza arrived in Sonora in the early 1700s, Spanish missions and settlements were quickly becoming Apache supermarkets—and heaven help the poor, unsuspecting vecino who got in the way of the shoppers![17]

Describing the Apache way of life and the insurmountable odds faced by the Spanish settlers, Anza said: "They live in small, dispersed rancherías, both in their own lands and when they seek the protection of the impregnable mountain ranges along the frontier. Hence, if they are found, only a small number are seized.... And even though they always inhabit regions of great strategic advantage, they attain even greater advantage by taking positions where they cannot be attacked, in a land as vast as the ocean, with their backs secure."[18]

Juan Bautista de Anza must evidently have had a vague notion of how extremely vast the Apache territory was. If he had visited El Paso del Norte and Santa Fe, which he probably had, he knew that people that far away also spoke of the Apache—Apaches that came and raided from lands even farther north and east of those two Spanish settlements. Just how far north or east of the Spanish settlements of the day the Apachería extended was unknown to Anza and everyone of his generation. Agustín de Vildósola, Anza's close friend and associate, also writing in 1735, provides us with an idea of the Sonorans' general understanding of the Apache homeland.

"The Apache nation," he said, "is so widely spread out from the Chiricahua, distant about twenty or thirty leagues from the presidio of Fronteras, it extends as far away as New Mexico, which amounts to about 300 leagues, and over which frontier they live broken up into rancherías divided one from another."[19]

Not only did the Apaches have the advantage of the vast, inhospitable Sonoran Desert and the land beyond, with all its many varied mountains, canyons, arroyos, and valleys, but they had the benefit of the Apache way of thinking—something that the average early Spanish settler of Sonora could scarcely comprehend. To the Apache, a small, hard-riding, fast-moving guerrilla band that did not stop for the purpose of engaging someone else in battle was far superior to any Spanish army or cavalry force that could be thrown against it. The soldiers of Fronteras and other presidios in the early years of the eighteenth century soon began to understand why.

Furthermore, the Apache warrior traveled much lighter than did the Spanish presidial soldier. The evidence all seems to indicate that he carried no supplies with him during his raids, but rather lived off the land. Thus, there were no bulky packs or cumbersome pack strings of horses or mules to slow him down. The few arrows that he carried and the scanty breechcloth that he wore were meager protection from Spanish weapons, but since he relied on speed to protect him, it really did not matter. The Apache raider would appear out of nowhere, grab what he wanted, and disappear into the shadows before the presidial cavalry soldier could get mounted up, let alone pursue or fire upon him.

Under attack, Captain Anza's soldiers were better protected and possibly more organized. Surely, the captain had provided his men with the military training that they never got under his predecessor. Furthermore, he had supplied them with the armor and weapons they needed. Each wore a heavy leather cuera that was capable of preventing most Apache arrows from entering the torso. A heavy rawhide *adarga*, or "shield," was carried on the left arm and was also effective in deflecting Apache arrows. For the most part, however, the armor was only useful or necessary when under direct attack, and the Apache never attacked unless they had superior numbers. If the numbers were significantly superior, no amount of armor would do any good.

Certainly there were times when Anza and his frontier soldiers managed to corner and attack small bands of Apaches, at which time their cueras and other gear proved very effective against the onslaught of enemy arrows. When the engagement was at a relatively close range and less mobile, the cavalry's muskets and pistols were also highly effective. However, in a normal galloping chase after a band of raiding Apaches, there was little hope of unseating an Apache warrior from his horse by means of powder and ball. If Anza or one of his soldiers could actually catch up to their quarry, a long, lightweight, metal-tipped lance proved to be far more deadly—a technique learned from the Apache and improved upon by the presidials with their use of metal lance points.

Captain Anza and his frontier soldiers eventually came to know that the Apache way was capable of causing damage that their own forces were nearly incapable of preventing, as evidenced by Anza's melancholy narration: "When they come to plunder it is in small groups. These groups penetrate deep into our province by following different routes along the more than one hundred leagues that border upon it. We have tried to pursue them, but we have not succeeded because they take refuge in the uninterrupted mountain ranges that surround this province. The country is so rugged that not even a track can be immediately recognized."[20]

Small raiding bands were the norm. However, the Apaches were fully capable of putting together a large army when it suited their purposes. According to Vildósola, "at times they gather and enter in bands of one, two, or even three hundred warriors, whom it is not easy to oppose with few men." He continued: "They do not lack courage, nor at the same time are they wanting in knowledge of the art of war in the encounters that occur, nor do they use arrows alone but also lances and barbed pikes with very long shafts."[21] Captain Anza agreed with this assessment, as he explained in his account that "sometimes . . . they gather in large numbers to mount a major attack against travelers, soldiers, or settlements. This happens especially when they come together with others of the same tribe from farther north."[22]

The modern-day person cannot comprehend the continual fear and anxiety under which Anza and his contemporaries lived, brought about by this continuous raiding and plundering. While it may have been somewhat easier for the next generation to accept as a way of life, having grown up knowing nothing different, it must have been extremely trying for those in the captain's generation, who came from such a totally different way of life. On the other hand, to put everything in perspective, there were no more violent deaths (i.e., murder) in Anza's day than there are in our own time. Violent deaths on our highways today kill twice as many people per capita as did the Apaches in Anza's day.[23] In the back of our minds we know that we can be killed in a car wreck, and we take precautionary measures to avoid it. Juan Bautista de Anza and his contemporaries knew that they could be killed by Apaches, and took precautionary measures to avoid that. As with the dangers of our day, people of those years must have pushed their fears to the back of their minds. As Don Juan pointed out, the concern was always there: "With good reason the inhabitants of the province are fearful of seeing themselves destroyed by such a cruel and pernicious enemy. Yet, since it is difficult to know where the Apaches are going to vent their fury next, it is difficult to guard against them."[24]

Guard against them he did, however, or at least he tried mightily. Many settlers moved away from Sonora because they truly were unable to withstand the constant fear and pressure. But none ever faulted Captain Anza, as they understood all too well the near hopelessness of his, as well as their own, situation. Agustín Vildósola summed it up nicely when he said, "[it is not] possible . . . that the one sole presidio of Corodéguachi, which is the only protection of this province, can keep in check so obstinate an enemy through greater vigilance and activity which its commander might possess."[25]

Anza had only fifty soldiers, total. There was a militia organized in every village and community, the soldiers of which were more than willing to help, but they were generally both poor and poorly equipped, making their service of little consequence. As the Apaches raided, stealing and destroying private property that belonged to Indians of other tribes, or to the Spaniards, and killing those who stood in their way, Sonorans began to look for alternatives. For the Pima and the Opata, who had never been anywhere else or known any other way of life, the only option was to hold on and hope for the best. Mestizos and other groups were in a similar predicament and soon found themselves living more like Apaches than the cultures from which they came. Landowners, on the other hand, had the option of trying to stick it out, or getting out while they still had their fortunes and their lives. The exodus started in Anza's day and would only grow as things got worse. As he put it: "Several cattle and horse ranches have been abandoned because of attacks by the Apaches and their allies. The ruins of these ranches are still visible. The Apaches have stolen and slaughtered great numbers of cattle and horses. They have murdered Spaniards and friendly Indians, and have besieged villages." [26]

Although some people left Sonora in fear, others came to take their places in even larger numbers. So, the population of the province grew rather than declined. The demographics, however, changed. As the Apache raids got worse, people living on outlying ranches and in remote mining camps abandoned them for the relative safety of larger population centers. Juan Bautista de Anza saw only the very beginning of the difficulties. Yet, as he observed the mounting hostilities, he was able to say: "I have done my duty in opposing these raids, but with the forces under my command it is not possible to put an end to the damages they cause and can cause in so vast a province as this." [27]

Even in the worst of such trying times, the Spanish settlers agreed on one thing, again summed by Agustín de Vildósola: "It is well known by all of us that in nothing is there omission on the part of Don Juan Bautista de Anza." [28]

Not only was there nothing amiss in Captain Anza's performance of his duties, but he and his father-in-law pioneered a program fifty years before it became official Spanish policy and was fully implemented on the northern frontier under the name of *establecimientos de paz*, or "establishments of peace." [29] These two captains from Janos and Fronteras, at least as early as 1732, began attempting to attract the Apaches to a peaceful way of life by providing them with food, clothing, and shelter. Although it was probably Captain Bezerra Nieto's idea, Captain Anza fully agreed with the plan and attempted to implement it. Although it did not work, the attempt was made, as here described by Captain Anza:

> While on campaign or in pursuit of stolen horses, I have punished our enemies in various ways for the murders they have committed. I did this in order to curb their attacks. A good number of the enemy have therefore come and offered peace to Captain Don Antonio Bezerra, who was captain of the Presidio of Janos in 1732. (They did the same on other occasions as well.) Captain Bezerra sought to attract them to a more civilized way of life by granting them sufficient supplies of food and other gifts. At the same time, however, they and other bands of their nation continued to enter the province to commit their usual attacks. In October 1733, they offered to make peace with me. I accepted

their offer and released the women and children who had been captured a few days earlier. Two days later, they attacked again just as we expected.

In compliance with the repeated mandates of our lord and king (may God protect him), the instructions of Viceroy Marqués de Casafuerte, and the requirements of Christian charity, I have sought to gain the Apaches' goodwill. I have done so by employing the methods that usually achieve that end—sending them horses, loads of food, coarse cloth, blankets, and knives. A few families began to arrive. Lately as many as eighty men and women have camped within four gunshots of the presidio under my command. Other families are nearby. We have been bribing them with food, clothing, and whatever else they covet (as is public knowledge) and have planted a field of corn so they can enjoy the harvest. Yet in spite of all this, they departed under the pretext of going hunting, running off a few horse herds along the way. About the same time, the Apaches at the Presidio of Janos did the same. They offered peace in order to massacre its inhabitants. I suspect that the Apaches intended to do the same thing at the presidio under my command.[30]

So the struggle continued, year after year, in an attempt to find some way to bring peace to the northern frontier. For fourteen years, from 1726 until his death in 1740, Captain Anza never let up in pursuit of that goal. How could he possibly have imagined such a life when growing up in the peaceful mountains of Gipuzkoa? If he wanted adventure by coming to the New World, he certainly got it. And there was so much more to Sonora than just the Apaches.

## Guevavi to Sópori

*Parezio presente Ju° Nuñez yndio de Nacion opata Natural del real de minas de San Ju° Baup*<sup>ta</sup> *y residente por tiempo a mas de dos años en los ranchos de Guebavi y S<sup>n</sup> Matheo de la dha Pimería Pertenesientes al señor Cap<sup>n</sup> D<sup>n</sup> Ju° Baup*<sup>ta</sup> *de Anza y en el servicio de Manuel Joseph de Sosa — Pedro Verdugo del Castillo (rúbrica)* . . . Appearing in person was Juan Núñez, an Indian of the Opata nation, native of the Real de Minas de San Juan Bautista, who has lived for more than two years in the said Pimería, working for Manuel José de Sosa on the Guevavi and San Mateo ranches that belong to Señor Capitán Don Juan Bautista de Anza—Pedro Verdugo del Castillo (rubric)[31]

Juan Núñez was an Opata Indian. The son of José Núñez and María Nicolasa Ruiz, he was born in the Real de Minas de San Juan Bautista in central Sonora. He first came to the San Luis Valley of northern Sonora in the late 1720s or early 1730s. He went to work as a vaquero on the extensive ranch properties of Juan Bautista de

Anza in 1730 or 1731.³² The job would last over thirty years and would involve working for two generations of the Anza family. Surely Juan Núñez must have been a good employee or the Anzas would not have kept him around so long. On the other hand, his employers must have been good to work for; otherwise he would have quit them long before. As it was, from the above statement we know that he was living at the Guevavi and San Mateo ranches at the time of his marriage in 1734. We also know that after the death of the senior Juan Bautista de Anza, he followed the family a few miles south up the river to their new headquarters on the Divisadero Ranch. And when the Apache problem got so bad during the early years of the younger Anza's captaincy that he asked the residents in the San Luis Valley to move closer to the presidio, Juan Núñez packed up his family and moved to Tubac.³³

When Juan Núñez married María Rosa Samaniego, the mulata widow of Pablo Samaniego,³⁴ at Mission Los Santos Angeles de Guevavi,³⁵ he had been working for the Anza family longer than there had been a missionary at Guevavi to perform marriages. Even though Father Kino established it as a mission in 1691 and a small church had been built a few years later, Guevavi had proven to be a difficult place to keep a resident missionary. It was not until the spring of 1732 that a permanent missionary arrived, escorted by Captain Juan Bautista de Anza and a squadron of soldiers.³⁶

Actually, Captain Anza and his soldiers escorted three new Jesuit missionaries to their assigned missions that spring. They placed Father Ignacio Keller, a Moravian-born priest, at Santa María Suamca near the headwaters of the Santa Cruz River. An Austrian, Juan Bautista Grazhoffer, was installed at Guevavi, and Father Felipe Segesser von Brunneg, recently from Lucerne, Switzerland, was taken to San Xavier del Bac, the northernmost established mission on the river. Although Father Grazhoffer was the missionary assigned to Guevavi, he died after only a year, and it was probably Father Segesser who performed the marriage of Juan Núñez and Rosa Samaniego.

*Phelippe Segesser*

Prior to the arrival of the entourage of soldiers, various Pima officials, and priests at Guevavi that spring of 1732, Captain Anza had made an earlier trip and, with the help of some of his soldiers, had constructed a house for Father Grazhoffer to live in. Now, probably at the end of April 1732, Anza was ready to install the newly arrived missionaries at their assigned missions. Leaving Fronteras they evidently traveled north to the San Pedro River. Although the records are scanty, it would appear that Captain Anza had set out to show the three missionaries the entire area over which they would be in charge. They were at a ranchería called Quino on the morning of May 3, 1732. That was on a Saturday. It appears the company visited several of the Sobaipuri villages in the area before turning west to the rancherías of Sonoitac and Obtuavo.

San Ignacio de Sonoitac, on the north side of the mountains, had already been designated a visita of Mission Guevavi. San Jago de Obtuavo, on the other hand, lay on the south slope of the mountains and had been designated a visita of Santa María Suamca. In the early morning hours of Friday, May 9, 1732, Mass was said at this latter ranchería in preparation for a full day's work that lay ahead. Father Keller could see down the valley to the south where his designated cabecera, Suamca, lay. Although he would claim in later years that when he arrived there was nothing there except the native village, from Obtuavo he could see where it was across the river. If what took place at Obtuavo that day was any indication of what future baptisms would be like, Father Keller's joy must have been nearly uncontainable. There must have been several hundred people at the open-air Mass that morning because, for the rest of the day, Father Keller and his associates were kept busy baptizing ninety-two children of the gentile Pimas who occupied the village.[37]

From this baptismal record comes an indication of who some of the people were in the party besides Captain Anza and the three fathers. There were at least a dozen already Christianized Pimas in the group, including Domingo Tuvante, Joseph Ytasi, and a man called San Jago. Eusebio Aquibisani, appointed by the Spaniards as captain general of the entire Pima nation, was also present. They and their fellow Pima officials acted as godfathers for many of the baptisms. Also standing as godfathers for a number of the children were Captain Anza's soldiers. Militia lieutenant José Romero, who was on permanent assignment in the San Luis Valley where he lived, was one of them. Cristóbal Barrios, whom Anza had elevated to the rank of sergeant,[38] and Xavier Moraga, who seems to have been on permanent guard duty at Terrenate, were also part of the military escort. Even Captain Anza was godfather that day for a bright-eyed little Pima girl with raven black hair whom Father Keller gave the Christian name of Juana María when he baptized her.

When the exhilarating day was finished, the expedition traveled on down the valley to Suamca to spend the night. Camped in the open-air with few conveniences of any kind, the fathers must have had mixed emotions about their new assignments so far removed from the homes they had recently left in Europe. On the other hand, by this time Don Juan must have been fully used to the inconveniences of the New World.

Over the next couple of days the little party traveled on down the river, around the bend, and through the San Luis Valley to Guevavi. Here were two large Pima rancherías, almost adjoining each other and spread down the valley for a considerable distance. The mission had been assigned to the one called Guevavi. The other, of similar size, was called Gusutaqui, or Gutzutag.[39] Once again, here at Guevavi, the natives turned out in large numbers estimated to be approximately a thousand. A new cross was planted and muskets were fired in celebration. It was probably Father Campos of San Ignacio, a number of years before, who had baptized Francisco Cobesia, one of the local Pima who had been the native governor of Guevavi since at least 1728.[40] Now, in an elaborate ceremony, Francisco was reaffirmed as the local governor and presented his *bastón* of authority. High Mass was sung and speeches were given. Captain General Aquibisani spoke at length to his gentile brethren. Even Captain Anza, as described by Father Visitor Cristóbal de Cañas in a letter to the bishop of Durango, addressed the crowd:

> Through a skillful interpreter the captain delivered to more than a thousand Pimas who gathered that day from its cabecera and visitas a pious and effective oration explaining to them the cause, purpose, and motive of his coming, which was to present to them, in the name of the King our Lord, Felipe V, whom God guard, a father minister to teach and impress upon them Christian obligations, to baptize their children, and instruct adults so that they might gain the same benefit and partake of the rest of the services offered, as do the natives in the other missions.[41]

Juan Bautista de Anza was well known to these people. He had owned and operated the Guevavi Ranch for several years. For exactly how long is uncertain. None of the original *títulos de merced*, or Spanish "land grants," for any of the Anza holdings are still in existence. However, it is known that the Figueroas, Grijalvas, and other families began to move into the San Luis Valley, just south of Guevavi, about the time or shortly after Juan Bautista de Anza became presidial captain at Fronteras. Diego Romero and his four sons, Nicolás, Ignacio, Cristóbal, and José probably came even earlier. It is likely that the Romeros had established the Santa Barbara Ranch shortly before Anza became captain. In fact, they probably requested military protection because they were so totally isolated from the rest of the Spanish world of the early 1720s. Captain Anza responded by commissioning José a militia lieutenant and then assigning him to stand guard over the San Luis Valley. It is also possible that the Romeros and others started to move into the San Luis Valley precisely because Juan Bautista de Anza had been made captain of the presidio and arrangements were made to protect their holdings.

It is doubtful that Anza's predecessor at Fronteras ever saw the San Luis Valley. But immediately upon his takeover, Don Juan set about fulfilling his commission to protect the Spanish citizens everywhere in his jurisdiction, including the Pimería Alta. There is no evidence that he owned any stock ranches prior to his appointment as captain at Fronteras. Hence, he saw the potential for a whole new business when he first set eyes on the San Luis and upper Santa Cruz River valleys. It was probably in the late 1720s that he began his livestock ranching career, and as far as we know, the Guevavi Ranch in present-day Arizona was the first that he started.

Evidently the earliest settlers in the San Luis Valley had taken the best lands there, so Anza went further north to Guevavi, at the south end of the upper Santa

Cruz River valley, to establish his stock ranch. Exactly where the ranch was located in relation to the villages is uncertain, but it had to be close by. Judging from where the present mission ruins and the current Guevavi Ranch are located, it was probably a half mile or so to the north of the mission, where a house had been constructed for Captain Anza's foreman. Manuel José de Sosa was a longtime friend and relative by marriage. He had been the escribano de número at the Presidio of Fronteras since Anza's captaincy began. It is not known how many children he and his wife, Nicolasa Gómez de Silva, had, but their last two were born while they were still working for the Anza family on their ranches, after the death of the captain.[42] We know that the Sosa family was living at Fronteras in May of 1726.[43] Sometime after that they moved to Guevavi to become probably the first permanent European settlers in what is today the state of Arizona.

Juan Bautista de Anza continued to expand his ranching operations, moving further north down the Santa Cruz River. Next in line from the Guevavi Ranch was his San Mateo Ranch, located at the confluence of Sonoita Creek and the Santa Cruz River[44] near the Pima Indian village called Toacuquita, which would one day become the Jesuit Mission of Calabazas.[45] Due west from there, in the mountains between Guevavi and Arivaca, he established the Sicurisuta Ranch,[46] not to be confused with the ranch called Sicurisutac[47] (which, as far as is known, Anza never owned) in the mountains between the San Luis Valley and Ímuris. Finally, going still further north, Anza established the Sópori Ranch near Arivaca.[48]

Captain Anza hired Juan Manuel Bais, a longtime San Luis Valley resident, as his foreman on the Sópori Ranch. Juan Manuel and his wife, Josefa de Luque, continued to work for the Anza family at Sópori well after the captain's death. After Juan Manuel died in 1747, María Josefa married Manuel Vicente Salazar in 1749 and they continued to operate the ranch for the Anzas. In fact, even after María Josefa was left a widow a second time, she continued to live on the Sópori Ranch, probably until she died.[49]

Little is known about any of these operations, but it would be safe to assume that both cattle and sheep were grazed on them. Contrary to the Hollywood image, Anza probably ran a lot more sheep then he did beef cattle. Certainly, mission records of the time show greater numbers of sheep on the mission ranches than cattle.[50] Therefore, besides having vaqueros, or "cowboys," he also must have hired a number of *sabaneros*,[51] or "herdsmen," to care for his sheep. It would be pure speculation to try to quantify the number of workers hired on the Anza ranches, but clearly they were numerous. Probably the majority were Native American, and even though we know Don Juan hired Opatas, like Juan Núñez, and Yaquis, the majority were undoubtedly Pima, because this was Piman country.

There is an excellent chance that a number of the Pimas in attendance on the day that Father Grazhoffer was installed as the priest at Guevavi were either Anza's employees or workers for other ranchers in the San Luis Valley. These included vaqueros, sabaneros, arrieros, cargadores, *herreros,* and *boyeros*—"cowboys, herders, mule packers, freighters, blacksmiths, and ox drivers"—as well as cooks, gardeners, carpenters, and a long list of other workers necessary to keep livestock ranches in operation. Here was the beginning of a grand *mestizaje,* or "mixing of races." Opatas, Yaquis, and Pimas intermarried with one another and with the Apaches and *Nijoras*[52] who were brought in from the outside. All of these tribes intermarried with the Spanish population of the San Luis Valley and surrounding areas, a large percentage of which was already mestizo.

The proximity of this Indian population to Spanish settlements in the San Luis Valley may be one of the reasons why Father Grazhoffer was stationed at Guevavi and why it continued to remain the cabecera. With his headquarters at Guevavi, the father had at least four visitas to look after, including Sonoitac, Tumacácori, Tubac, and Arivaca. The numerous Pima rancherías that fell under his jurisdiction included Ati, Bacarica, Bacuacucan, Comacavitcam, Mamturss, Piticai, Raum, Seug Bag, Seug Tuburss, Sópori, Spibah, Stonssutag, Taupari, Tutup, Toacuquita, Toamuqui, Tonacbi, Tuhto, Tupssi, Tutumac, Unbas, and Vaicat. Almost all of these villages were located to the north of Guevavi along the Santa Cruz River, east up Sonoita Creek, or northwest between Tubac and Arivaca. Thus, Guevavi lay at the far southern end of its own jurisdiction. Tumacácori or Tubac would have been the logical choice for the cabecera if ease of visitation was paramount. On the other hand, if population had been the deciding factor, Sonoitac always had more people than did Guevavi.[53]

Guevavi did have some semblance of a physical plant already constructed. While its utility was doubtful after all the years without a resident priest, there may have been enough physical structures there that the deciding authorities felt there would be less work in remodeling than in starting from scratch at a new site. However, it appears that the main reason Guevavi was chosen as the cabecera was because the Spanish population also needed a church. There had been a time when the bishop of Durango had ordered the Jesuits not to minister to the Spaniards but rather to spend their time working strictly with the native peoples. That had changed with a new bishop, and now the missionaries were expected to care for the needs of the Spanish population as well. It is likely that the ranchers in the San Luis Valley, and especially Juan Bautista de Anza, had an influence in obtaining the appointment of a missionary to Guevavi.

There were probably as many baptisms performed at Guevavi that day as there were recorded at Obtuavo just a few days previously, though unfortunately those records have not survived. Things must have looked bright for everyone, particularly the ranchers, on that warm May morning in 1732 as Guevavi's new missionary was introduced to his neophytes. Little could Father Grazhoffer have known that within the space of a year he would be dead, possibly the victim of poisoning. Father Segesser, who was waiting that morning for his chance to continue on to San

Xavier del Bac, could not have known that he would take Father Grazhoffer's place. For a little over a year he would minister at Guevavi until he himself became so sick with fever that Captain Anza had to come with some soldiers and carry him back to Fronteras. There the captain's wife, skilled in the use of local medicinal herbs, would nurse him back to health.

Between the time that Father Grazhoffer began his ministry at Guevavi and Father Segesser left the same mission, sick and debilitated, there would be a small uprising of sorts. In July of 1734 the Pimas at Suamca, Guevavi, and San Xavier all fled their missions, taking with them cattle and horses and ornaments from the churches. Captain Anza and some of his soldiers would rush to the scene to bring peace back to the Pimería Alta. As he got Father Segesser and his neophytes resettled back at Guevavi, little could he have known that a few short years later his family would be living at the southern end of that mission's jurisdiction. Nor would he have guessed that his youngest son, the junior Juan Bautista de Anza, who was not even born at the time, would attend Mass at the Guevavi church regularly while helping with the work on the Anza ranches from Guevavi to Sópori.

## Even in Death

*No por esso epensado jamas sacar las Alajas de las Yglesias; sino solo avaluarluas; teniendo ânimo fino de poner de mi bolsa qualquiera exzessa q resultase de precio enôbsequio de la div.$^a$ Mag$^d$ y sus Cultos — Juan Baup$^{ta}$ de Anssa (rúbrica)* . . . For this reason I have never thought to remove the furnishings from the churches, other than for appraising them, being of a mind, instead, to pay whatever difference in price there was from my own purse in compliance with the Divine Majesty and His church rituals—Juan Bautista de Anza (rubric)[54]

Juan Bautista de Anza probably thought that his troubles were over when Gregorio Álvarez Tuñón y Quirós was removed from the captaincy of Fronteras and he was given that commission himself. Certainly, when Don Gregorio died, he must have heaved a sigh of relief, thinking that now, after all those years, he and Sonora were finally rid of the problem. Sadly for Anza, it was not to be. That Captain Anza was a devout Catholic and had the deepest of devotions for the Company of Jesus and the Jesuit fathers is a well-established fact. That he always got along with them and they with him is pure fantasy. They were human, and so was he. It seems that Don Gregorio—even in death—brought out the best, or the worst, of human characteristics in everybody.

It had all started on September 22, 1727. The viceroy advised the captain of Fronteras, Don Juan Bautista de Anza, the highest-ranking military official in Sonora, to preempt the Álvarez Tuñón properties for the payment of fines that had been levied against him in the viceroy's final decision, handed down after the court had heard all the arguments in the case. Although Don Gregorio had not traveled to Mexico City, he had hired lawyers to represent him there. They fought a hard, uphill battle and, in the end, lost everything, including their own right to practice law for a specified period of time. Don Gregorio was permanently removed from his lifetime captaincy and fined 24,431 pesos plus court costs.[55] This was the amount that would be taken from the properties that Anza attached.

We cannot know what kind of a fight Don Gregorio might have put up to prevent Captain Anza from attaching and selling his goods. The disgraced captain died on March 30, 1728.[56] However, his death might have simplified matters in one way, it seems to have vastly complicated things when the greed of other people began to kick in. Anza, who in his typical loyalty to the king's authorities attempted to accomplish what he had been assigned to do, found himself being condemned from all quarters for his handling of the estate. Evidently a number of people felt that Don Gregorio had owed them something and were willing to circumvent the due process of law to get it—certain Jesuit missionaries not excluded.

Juan Bautista de Anza's interim captaincy of the Fronteras presidio ended on April 26, 1729, when the king appointed him capitán vitalicio.[57] He had gone south from Fronteras to the Real de Minas de San Antonio de Motepore in July as part of his preparations to help in a general expedition against the Seri Indians and an invasion of Tiburón Island in the Gulf of California. While there, plagued by rumors and accusations about his handling of the Álvarez Tuñón estate, he wrote a letter to the father provincial, Andrés Nieto, in Mexico City. It appears to be a quiet plea for reimbursement of monies spent and payment for appropriated items, as well as a general plea to the father to disregard certain individuals who were spreading false rumors about the captain. At the same time, it provides a great deal of insight into the human nature of both Anza and his associates.

Juan Bautista de Anza seems to have worried a lot about money, a character trait of his youngest son and namesake as well. Both also worried about their reputation, as evidenced by the senior Anza's letter to the father provincial:

My Dear Sir:

The suspicion is well founded that obliges me to trouble Your Reverence with the coarseness of my writings.[58] Reverend Father, I have always esteemed, through the devout love of a son, the most sacred religion of the Company of Jesus. Because of this love I have always pledged to stand against her enemies, without revering at any time the respect of any person of my own standing. I know, and neither are they yet ignorant in Mexico, of the efficacy of compensating, through the litigation of Don Gregorio's estate, for the false accusations made by a certain person of distinction.[59] Although I have not been educated in this sentiment, I feel in every case to praise my mother for how I justly respect all the religious of the Company of Jesus and [for my desire] to protect the virtue, religion, and unity of the reverend fathers in these territories.

I do not know what deficiency of mine has presently placed me out of favor with some of the very reverend father missionaries, whom I imagine have already passed judgment upon me. Indeed, it has been said, without revealing the names of the persons who said it, that I have transgressed the commission that the Most Excellent Señor Marqués de Casafuerte[60] gave me months ago in regard to the property of the deceased Don Gregorio.

It should be known, then, Most Reverend Father, that the alcalde mayor of this province[61] took charge of the possessions of the said deceased and sold them at public auction, from which some of the reverend father missionaries removed various furnishings for public worship. This caballero[62] reported to His Excellency[63] what was executed at that time. The belongings of Don Gregorio, amounting to 12,500 pesos, were inventoried, appraised, and sold. The amount was held in trust by a credible person, according to the orders that His Excellency sent to me in his dispatch. Because of the many disputes that I predicted would be forthcoming in the execution of his mandate, it was received with great concern on my part. Upon my forming of the said trust, the heirs were informed of their recourse. Over 25,000 and some odd pesos were needed for the amount owed His Majesty.[64] I did not remove all the goods, furnishings, slaves, etc. that existed when Don Gregorio died from the possession of whatever persons held them until the said amount was reported to me. There are now no more than 300 and some pesos left in trust and nothing for the satisfaction of the heirs.

I am compelled to obey the orders I received, which has resulted in all the complaints against me. Because they ignored the contents of the letter sent to me by His Excellency, some of the reverend fathers think a decision of malice on my part came about through instructions from my friends. Even the influence of other reverend fathers, the highest ranking in the province[65] (and this has hurt the most), says the same concerning the decree of His Excellency. Clearly, His Excellency does not need guidance from anyone, and neither do I, even though I am lacking in understanding.

I have not been guided, Most Reverend Father, by the influence of someone in the Sacred Company of Jesus, although I have consulted a priest upon some points of procedure. He advised me that such counsel should come from the learned who can simply and prudently guide me in practice, because moral theology, although it goes hand in hand with jurisprudence, follows another route, very distinct from the judicial, and I am unable to ascend such a theological mountain. I acted accordingly, sending mail to Parral.[66]

This is the truth in everything, Reverend Father Provincial, and it is not born of human malice, so tortuously mistrustful. I have also not had advice from any of the other fathers concerning my actions; neither in my actions have I neglected the Holy Religion of the Company; nor could I even have imagined the infinite number of disputes that would take place, of which I have no doubt Your Reverence has been advised. I anticipate that Your Reverence's wise ears have been filled with the noise of false charges made by some people to discredit me.[67]

It is true, Reverend Father, that I wrote to the very reverend father visitor,[68] by request of a priest who removed some of the furnishings, always imagining that the father visitor would respond to me by returning the price of the furnishings if they were delivered to him. Although the said reverend father visitor has not responded as I had hoped, it was my intent to return to the señor alcalde, with urgency, the amount that had been received. Without doing so, this tyrannical curse will only continue to oppress us. Indeed, this urgency has arisen from a justified petition filed by certain parties. For this reason I have never thought to remove the furnishings from the churches, other than for appraising them, being of a mind, instead, to pay whatever difference there was from my own purse in my desire to please and worship the Divine Majesty.[69] Reverend Father, acting on the appraisals of the value of these furnishings that are in the possession of Their Reverences, it never appeared to me to be conducive to the credit of the father missionaries, or myself, to neglect this business cost. This amount will remain without liquidation at the mercy of whatever false charges may be leveled against me. Indeed, the account has remained in balance, to the condemnation of my critics, who have acted as my very devoted judges, using uncompromising justice at times and audacious tolerance at others.

The truth is, Reverend Father, I am worthy of forgiveness if I have erred in something. Certainly my error was born of misunderstanding (incapable as I am, not versed in commerce, and totally unschooled in the professions), and not of my will, which has always been firm in the desire to please all the father missionaries. This is especially true of Your Reverence, and by it I am very obedient to all your wishes. I remain prayerful that the Divine Majesty will extend the most useful life of Your Reverence for many long years and I make no excuse for my expression of great confidence, as the least of all your servants, that His grace will put my pleas into prompt execution. In the royal mining camp of San Antonio de Mótepore on July 28, 1729.

Very Reverend Father, your most humble servant kisses the feet of Your Reverence.
Juan Bautista de Anza (rubric)
To the Most Reverend Father Provincial Andres Nieto[70]

The conflicts evidently worked themselves out in time and the matter was forgotten. It is interesting, however, to view how two people, Anza and Cañas, both considered to be honest, upright Spanish citizens, reacted to the same set of circumstances. Anza had been involved in the squabble with Don Gregorio for nearly ten years. He had seen people die because of Don Gregorio's negligence. His mining businesses had deteriorated. He had spent countless hours of his own time and probably thousands of his own pesos in attempting to rectify the situation. Yet, he wanted to implement the viceroy's orders to the letter and see that the king got the money owed him before Don Gregorio's creditors or heirs. Even so, one can detect a feeling of sympathy for the heirs in the letter.

Cristóbal de Cañas, the father visitor stationed at Arizpe, whom Anza mentions twice in the letter, had also been involved in the conflict with Don Gregorio for some ten years. He had seen the missions deteriorate because of Apache depredations that Don Gregorio did not even try to prevent. He had taken the brunt of Don Gregorio's contempt for the Jesuit missionaries. He, too, had spent countless hours writing letters in the attempt to have Don Gregorio ousted. Yet, he appears to have condoned the "stealing" of items belonging to the estate. When Captain Anza approached him about payment for the various furnishings that some of the priests had taken, he refused, forcing the captain to pay for them out of his own pocket in order to make the accounts balance.

Greed and corruption were obviously not limited to the lawless element of Sonora. Even Jesuit priests could succumb to such temptation. It is to Anza's credit, however, that he did not do what is common to too many people. He did not become disgruntled with the organization because of the actions of a few of its members. Rather, he continued to hold the Company of Jesus in highest regard, and within a few short months was himself admitted as a brother into the order. Furthermore, even though the incident cost him in both money and anxiety, he evidently never held it against Father Cañas and continued to associate with and respect the priest for the abilities and good qualities that he had. Any animosity that may have developed between the two over this incident seems to have been forgotten just seven years down the road when Captain Anza turned to Father Cañas for legal advice on how to handle the "Arizona" silver discovery.

So, within seven years the whole incident was probably forgotten and the living had gone back to speaking to each other on friendly terms. The dead, on the other hand, would not soon be forgotten. Whenever anyone spoke of hard times in Sonora, Don Gregorio's name would come up, and even though Captain Anza and most of the others of the day were far too pious to ever vocalize it, they were ecstatic that he was gone.

## Tiburón Island

*Esta fue la causa del alzam.*<sup>to</sup> *que tanto nos dio que hazer hastaq*<sup>e</sup> *pasando el Capp*<sup>n</sup> *D.*<sup>n</sup> *Ju*<sup>o</sup> *Bap.*<sup>ta</sup> *de Anssa a la isla del Tiburon fue el s.*<sup>r</sup> *servido se mejoraron las cosas, y que dentro de poco tiempo se sosegara la Nacion* — Nicolas de Perera . . . This was the cause of the uprising that inflicted us with so much work until, crossing over to Tiburón Island, Juan Bautista de Anza was the man who made everything better, and in a short time pacified the nation—Nicolás de Perera [71]

The Apaches, as mentioned previously, were not the only native group to cause concern in Captain Anza's jurisdiction. Even before Anza had taken command of the Presidio of Fronteras, the Seris had started to rebel against Spanish encroachment on their territory. Anza's predecessor at the presidio, of course, had refused to send his troops on a 300-400-mile round-trip campaign to help put down that insurrection, one of the many reasons for which he was relieved of his captaincy. This fact likely delivered a message to Anza that, regardless of distance or lack of manpower, he was responsible for his entire jurisdiction and all of the peoples inhabiting it.

In their zeal, the Jesuits attempted to Christianize the Seris, who lived in the most inhospitable, harsh, and, to the Spanish way of thinking, uninhabitable territory in all of Sonora, if not the world. But the Spaniards probably would not have been interested in the Seri's hot, wind-swept, desert sea coasts and rocky islands if it had not been for the discovery of pearls just offshore near Tiburón Island. With the discovery, two vastly different cultures came into close contact with each other.[72] As the number and frequency of those contacts increased, Juan Bautista de Anza found himself involved more and more in actions against the Seris. His thoughts about them are typical of the time: "Our troops are [often] far away fighting the Seri, who are even more cruel than the Apache. It is well known that the Seri have burned homes and hunted down boats, killing young and old like. If every effort had not been made to repel them, they undoubtedly would have wiped out a large part of the province. Because of their familiarity with the region, the Seri knew and continue to know how dispersed the inhabitants are, and how easily their homes can be set ablaze."[73]

In the first days of July 1729, the governor of Sinaloa, Manuel Bernal de Huidobro, sent word to Anza requesting troops from his presidio to be part of an expedition to Tiburón Island. The governor also sent similar requests for native auxiliaries to the missionaries of Sonora. There had been some disturbances the previous year around the pearl beds in the Gulf.[74] The expedition was intended to intimidate the rebels along the coast, remove any belligerents from Tiburón Island, and convince the Seri everywhere to come settle at the Mission of Pópulo, where Father Nicolás de Perera was the resident missionary. The governor requested troops and supplies for one month beginning at the end of August. Father Perera would go as chaplain on the expedition. While Bernal de Huidobro was invading Tiburón Island, Captain Anza and a detachment of his troops, along with 200 Pima auxiliaries to be sent by Father Campos of San Ignacio, would patrol the coast.[75]

Father Campos balked. It was planting season for the Pima. Captain Anza was shorthanded and was receiving orders from two different commanders—the viceroy in Mexico City and Governor Bernal de Huidobro—even though they seemed to be in agreement. Increasingly, he found himself caught between the conflicting views of the Jesuit hierarchy and the civil government. In a letter to then Father Visitor Nicolás de Oro, a hint of his frustration can be sensed:

My Dear Sir and Master:

> The Reverend Father Agustín[76] has given me charge of this pliego that was placed in his hands. I am persuaded (according to what he has advised me) that it speaks of the soldiers that will leave our presidio as auxiliaries for the troops of Sinaloa in the reduction, or conquest, of Tiburón Island. As Your Reverence knows, the governor of Sinaloa[77] is in Pópulo. He wrote to me, telling me to leave the presidio in care of the garrison and send the rest of the soldiers, and I should go also. The order that the viceroy[78] sent me on the subject says that if the governor needed some soldiers, I should free them up, taking care not to cause a shortage; and that, in the meantime, the company that is on the expedition to Tiburón should secure the coast with my soldiers. In obedience to this, I have dispatched a squadron, and shall soon join them to comply with the last part of the order.
>
> The said governor has entreated me to intercede, by my limited authority with the fathers of the Pimería, to send 200 Pimas, armed and supplied for one month for the said expedition. I have written to Their Reverences on this particular. I don't know what the results will be, however, since supplying the auxiliaries will not be easy, considering the poverty of the fathers. Although they harvested the wheat in Tubutama, it was a very small amount that was gathered, and the Pima have given me some excuses about this. I think they do not want to take part in the expedition, in case the Seri attack inland. But ignore the ideas of this caballero.[79] I do not want to say or predict anything. This is just by way of conversation.
>
> The Reverend Father Rector Somoza[80] tells me the expedition will only go by order of the reverend father provincial, whom God, Our Lord, has appointed for His Holy Service. The reasons that the said fathers have given me concerning the solicitation of some soldiers and why they do not want the soldiers of my company to come[81] seem very sound to me. They can inform you why they do not want to put the soldiers up for the winter. I will bring thirty men, and no more, to maintain the present numbers with respect to His Excel-

lency's order. The Lord well knows that my desires are good and I hope he will grant them to me for my success. I am still without power to follow through in completing these orders. It can be that they will be left for Saint James to manage.[82] I will dispatch mail to Mexico, then, to see if they can offer some advice.

Advise me Your Reverence and send me orders, with the sure knowledge that they will be obeyed. Certainly I am your humble servant. Our Lord keep Your Reverence many years. Motepore, July 11, 1729. Your humble servant and friend kisses the feet of Your Reverence.

Juan Bautista de Anza (rubric)[83]

Anza stayed on at Motepore until the end of July. Sometime in August he left for the coast to participate in the expedition. Bernal de Huidobro was there with a detachment of his soldiers. Anza's fellow Basque, Sargento Mayor Agustín de Vildósola, was there with a contingent of militia soldiers. In spite of grumbling on the part of some, the Jesuit missionaries did supply auxiliaries and a lot of food and supplies.[84] Alcalde Mayor Gabriel Prudhom Butrón y Mujica, another of Sonora's Basque alliance,[85] who claimed there were 800 men at the final tally, was also there with militia troops.[86] The numbers looked good and the troops seemed well enough supplied, but the campaign was little more than an exercise in futility from the beginning.

The governor never did cross over to Tiburón Island. Failing in that goal because of bad weather, his troops captured a Seri ranchería of twenty-seven inhabitants. They also managed to convince 151 Seri to accompany them back to Pópulo. As soon as the troops headed back to Sinaloa, however, the Seri left the Mission of Pópulo and attacked and killed the pearl fishermen who had originally requested the expedition. Had it not been for Captain Anza, the entire expedition would have probably been a dismal failure. He and his troops did make the amphibious landing on Tiburón Island after the governor was gone. They did punish the rebels there. And they did convince 700 Seri to settle in the Mission of Pópulo.[87] Unfortunately, no military journal of that invasion has ever been located. Anza personally summed up the entire matter by saying: "We were able to punish and terrify the enemy. This was particularly fortunate because the Seri have so many refuges on Tiburón Island as well as in the estuaries, mountains, and thickets [of the mainland]. As is well known, there is a total lack of water and pasture in those places. Soldiers and horses therefore cannot remain on campaign as long as is necessary. Because of such difficulties, the Indians have dared to mount their uprisings."[88]

What little is known about the actual invasion of Tiburón Island comes from the pen of Anza's Bizkaian friend, Agustín de Vildósola:

The burden of war was laid on Captain Juan Bautista de Ansa, who with a military force attacked said island in some *canoas* by means of which he ferried across the men (although not many could be conveyed) and some supplies and bridled horses. The amount of labor which he and his men, and some Yaqui Indians whom he had taken along on this expedition because they knew the sea, expended on this occasion is incredible, and after they had returned to land they endured no less in opposing the hostilities of this so rebellious a nation, which by the burning of houses, the death of men and the destruction of ranches, and because of arrogance over some successes in attacks made, threatened the province to the great fright of everyone until by Divine Clemency in some encounters their state of mind was changed and they desisted in their intent.[89]

## A Jesuit Brother

*Quando soy herm°, y enauda que algunos P P. emfermos conlicencia delos Superiores, aian hido â cura, y combalencia âella—Juan Baup^{ta} de Anssa (rúbrica)* . . . When I am a brother, with permission from the Superiors, I will aid in the healing and convalescence of any sick fathers—Juan Bautista de Anza (rubric)[90]

Juan Bautista de Anza was made a brother in the Jesuit order sometime prior to November 4, 1729.[91] Very little is known about why or how this took place, or what it even meant for that matter. In fact, from what little information we have, it is impossible to tell exactly how the situation came about. We are told by secondary sources that Anza "petitioned to be admitted as a Jesuit Brother" and that "his request [was] granted."[92] Although this may be true, there is no other evidence that Anza made any kind of a petition. All we know is that he was admitted as a brother into the Society of Jesus. From all appearances he did not go through any of the normal procedures to become a Jesuit, and therefore the honor might have been bestowed upon him in recognition of some service that he had performed—like his help with the recently completed Tiburón Island campaign. His run-ins with the Jesuits over the Álvarez Tuñón affair couldn't have helped his appointment. Since so little is known about the matter it is probably best to take his words and let it go at that: "Through the kindness of Reverend Father Minister Juan Antonio de Oviedo, I have been honored to be admitted as a brother into the Holy Company of Jesus, with no other merit than he has considered the great affection that I have professed, for the general reason that I am a Basque, and especially because, since childhood, an intimate friendship with the reverend father missionaries of these provinces, for the space of the twenty-four years that I have assisted in them, has reigned in me to the present."[93]

There has been speculation about the capacity in which Don Juan served. Since he was already married, had four children, and continued to live at home, he could not have made the customary vows of poverty, chastity, and obedience to enter the priesthood.[94] (It has even been said that Anza could not have been made a brother, since the Jesuits do not have a third order and never did.)[95] Whatever formality was executed to bring Anza into alignment with the Company of Jesus was probably one of the proudest moments of his life, considering his great love for the Society of Jesus. Unfortunately, the only record we have of the matter comes from a letter that Anza himself wrote to the Jesuit provincial of the time, José Barba. Even that letter does not take as its main subject matter Anza's acceptance into the Society of Jesus. It was written about an incident with Father Campos several years later, but information about Anza's brotherhood can be gleaned from it.

For example, we are told that he did not take all the vows, nor was he able or expected to perform all the sacraments: "I have obtained . . . relief from my obligations in the case of religious offerings. For the sake of respecting my smallness, I have been thus empowered."[96]

Evidently as part of his duties, the captain's house at Fronteras was to be converted to a type of convalescent home for aging missionaries. They could go there to spend their last days in relative comfort, with health care provided. María Rosa Bezerra Nieto was known for her abilities with soothing and medicinal herbs, so Anza's wife was to be a partner in the endeavor. He requested that "[Father Campos] be permitted to come to my house (and this applies to all my beloved fathers) so that my wife will be able to assist and apply some remedies and other graces that she has obtained, which she, in truth, finds for some of the sickly."[97]

One of the choicest tidbits possible to glean from this letter of Anza's is the great devotion that he had developed for the peoples of the New World with whom he now associated. He again provides us with a glimpse of his enduring devotion to his religion and his country. Even though he was a soldier and continually involved in battles with the Apache and other belligerents, there is the sense that peace for everyone in Sonora was always on his mind. That, coupled with the great service that he and his soldiers were providing in protecting the missions, may be the foremost reason why he was chosen to become a Jesuit brother. "With much sincerity I prayed to the Holy Patriarch[98] that he might obtain from Our Lord tranquility for everyone. And, although I am a great sinner, he heard me. And this Pimería being so large, wherever I have been, what I have wanted to say has been precisely dispatched to the various rancherías, officials and families, to persuade the Indians to remain calm. . . . It is certain that this nation[99] respects me. It must be so as I love them so very much."[100]

## The Father Campos Dilemma

*Hallarme ya en este Pres$^o$ de fronteras casa del Cap$^n$ D$^n$ J$^u$ Baut$^a$ de anssa n$^o$ h$^o$ de missas conducido con silla de manos por mis hijos Pimas — Joseph Ag$^n$*

*de Campos Ihs* . . . I am already settled in at this Presidio of Fronteras at the house of Captain Don Juan Bautista de Anza, our brother for the Mass, brought here in a sedan chair by my Pima children—José Agustín de Campos, IHS[101]

The fires had burned low in the little camp that night, and most of the people were already asleep. As soon as evening prayers were said, Father Nieto[102] had gone into the tent that the soldiers had set up for him and Father Campos. There he had curled up under his blanket and was sleeping soundly. At a short distance from the tent were a half-dozen Pima Indians, also sleeping soundly in a state of near exhaustion. Several soldiers, wrapped in their blankets, were trying to catch a couple of hours of sleep before their turn at sentry duty. There were also several sentries posted on the high points around the little valley, gazing down toward the camp and keeping an ever-vigilant eye open for marauding Apaches. It was too dark to see much of anything. It was barely ten o'clock, but the sun had been down for an hour and a half and the moon would not be up until midnight. The soldiers who were standing as sentries were not terribly concerned. If there was to be an Apache raid tonight, in all probability it would not come until there was moonlight, by which time they would have been relieved of their duty by some other poor souls who would have to be twice as vigilant. It was Monday night, April 30, 1736.

Juan Bautista de Anza and José Agustín de Campos[103] sat on the ground by the only fire that had not been reduced to embers. The captain would probably rather have been sleeping, but the old padre had developed a talkative streak and was pouring out all of his frustrations of the past few months. Anza lent a sympathetic ear, but did not say much himself. There was no need. Father Campos just needed to talk. He felt better just knowing that Don Juan was there listening, whether he agreed with him or not. The captain was most likely aware of nearly everything the old man was saying, anyway, making it easy for him to just nod his head in agreement or interject a quiet word or two of understanding. This was not really a conversation that Captain Anza would have wanted anyone else to hear. Most of it was probably factual. If anyone was aware that the Jesuit fathers had human weaknesses, certainly Anza was. There was nothing he could do about it, however. His duty was to keep the peace in his jurisdiction, which was what he was trying to do by taking this frail old padre home with him. Although he could not do anything about Father Campos's complaints, he could compassionately listen to them and make sure that what was said did not go beyond their smoldering campfire.

Not that anyone was likely to hear them. The piousness of both men dictated subdued tones when speaking of such scandalous subjects. All of the soldiers were too tired to care, having spent nearly two months in the saddle alongside their dauntless commanding officer. The Pima, who had been carrying Father Campos in a sedan chair for the past week, were also far too exhausted to care about what the two men were saying. The sentries and the people in the ranch houses were too far removed from the camp to hear anybody's conversation, even if they did care. The people in the houses were typical ranchers and farmers. They had put in a hard day's work and were trying to get rested up for the one tomorrow.

The houses, the shadows of which could barely be seen in the distance from the flickering campfire, were typical of all the farmhouses in the region. They were mere adobe huts with mesquite and grass roofs. This was Terrenate, the oldest and northernmost ranch on the frontier in this part of the world.[104] Martín de Elizondo and his wife, Antonia de Luque, and their six children lived here along with numerous hired hands.[105] Antonia was a sister of María Josefa de Luque, wife of Anza's foreman on his Sópori Ranch. Elizondo was Basque, as were several others of the hired help. It was something like a family reunion anytime that Anza came by.

Terrenate was established as a ranch, probably by José Romo de Vivar or Juan Munguía Villela, prior to 1680. Romo de Vivar had livestock operations at San Andres de la Cananea and San Lázaro below Suamca by that date. Munguía Villela, son-in-law of Sonora's first alcalde mayor, Pedro Perea, and alcalde mayor himself from 1652 to 1654, ran cattle where the future Mission Suamca would be.[106] Since Terrenate lies between Suamca and Cananea, it is only logical that it was also a stock-raising headquarters at that early date, established by one of these gentlemen. Perea, Munguía Villela, Romo de Vivar, and a number of their associates were Basque,[107] as evidenced by the names they gave these ranches. San Lázaro, of course, is generic, but Cananea is a common name from the vicinity of Karrantza in Bizkaia. *Terrenate* is a typical descriptive compound word. A *terren* is an earthen tub, or basin. *Ate* means door, or passageway. Thus, *terrenate* possibly means gateway to a basin. Nothing could be more descriptive of its location.

It was too dark now for Captain Anza and Father Campos to even see as far as the creek that ran below the ranch houses. As their party had crested the ridge coming in from Santa María Suamca, however, they would have looked down on Terrenate to see, stretching out below and far into the distance, a most stunning and beautiful view of an enormous basin. Far below, on the west corner of the valley, was Cananea. On the horizon to the south, the Crestones above Arizpe could be seen. Across the colossal valley to the west were the Sierra Espuelas and the Sierra Madre, with Fronteras tucked out of sight in a pocket. Bordering this magnificent valley on the north was the Sierra Huachuca.

Here at the ranch was the spring that constituted the headwaters of the Terrenate River, known today as the San Pedro. According to Juan Mateo Manje, writing in

1697, that nearly endless valley below was known as the Llanos de Terrenate—the Plains of Terrenate.[108] In a letter written at Tetuachi and directed to the new governor of Sonora[109] nearly a year before this spring night in 1736, Manje had pointed out that this site where Anza and his party were camped was an "estancia yherma que vulgarmente llaman Terrenate"—a "grassland ranch commonly called Terrenate."[110] That was on July 8, 1735. Manje had written the letter requesting Governor Bernal de Huidobro to establish a new presidio at Terrenate. Within four months, in response to the governor's request for other opinions, Captain Anza, sargento mayor of the Sonoran militia, Agustín de Vildósola, and outgoing Sonora alcalde mayor Gabriel Prudhom Butrón y Mujica had all written letters in support of Manje's petition.[111] One day a presidio would stand here, but for tonight the only people in the world were the captain and the distraught, talkative old padre, sitting on the ground beside their small, flickering fire.

The old man was fretting about the possibility of being excommunicated for alleged misdeeds. He was well aware that the governor had been excommunicated,[112] and since he had taken sides with the governor over what he considered a trivial matter, he was afraid that he too might be cut off from the Church.

"I am well aware of the conspiracy of several of the fathers against me,"[113] he told Anza. "They have secretly dispatched mail to Mexico many times condemning me—months before I knew about it. If they haven't gotten a response, it is not my fault.[114]

"I hope His Reverence will favor me in everything for my greatest honor," Father Campos continued, "which would be to return to San Ignacio from where I have been banished with such shame and reproach in front of the lay Spaniards and Indians."[115]

Anza felt certain that would never happen, but he kept his peace and let the old man ramble on.

"Is the authority of a father visitor of Sonora greater," he was asking, "or is that of the father provincial above all?"[116]

Of course, the father provincial could override Father Visitor Marciano's orders, but it was doubtful that would happen in this case. Besides, no one expected Father Campos to live long enough for a letter from him to actually reach Mexico City. Regardless, Captain Anza had promised him that as soon as they arrived at Mission Cuquiárachi he would see that the old padre had the opportunity to write all the letters he wanted to.

In the meantime, they were camped at Terrenate and, at their current rate, another two or three days' travel lay ahead of them. As Father Campos babbled on, the captain's mind must have wandered back to when all this had started, nearly two months before. On Sunday afternoon, March 11, Don Juan had been sick and lying on his bed at his home in Fronteras[117] when José Romero, the militia lieutenant from the San Luis Valley, had been ushered in to talk to him.[118]

José told him that the vecinos in the San Luis Valley had been informed that Father Campos was to be replaced at San Ignacio. The vecinos had misgivings that the entire Pima nation would be aroused over the affair and come to the aid of their beloved old missionary.[119] They had heard that Pimas from the mining camps at Aguaje and Soledad were on their way north to block the removal of Father Campos.[120] Diego Romero, José's father, had mounted up at the same time that José had. He left the San Luis Valley for the real at Agua Caliente to notify the miners there and the vecinos at the Arizona Ranch, and to convene a meeting among them to try to determine what should be done to prevent a general uprising.[121]

José was carrying a pliego of letters from Father Campos. One was addressed to Captain Anza; others were destined for Campos's superiors in Mexico City.[122] As well as Anza was acquainted with Father Campos, and as much as he loved the old man, something looked suspicious to the captain. He was well aware of protocol. Letters addressed to the father provincial in Mexico City by a missionary were to be routed through the father visitor, his superior. Anza was most likely also aware of the long-standing animosity between Father Campos and his superior, Father Visitor Marciano. Campos's letter to Anza asked him to intercede, as a Jesuit brother and as a man of great authority in the province, with Father Marciano and to write letters on his behalf to Father Provincial José Barba in Mexico City. The entire matter did not sit well with the captain, and he resolved to pick himself up out of his sickbed and organize an expedition to the Pimería Alta the very next morning.

José Romero had no more than left Anza's bedside when another messenger arrived, this one sent by Father Visitor Marciano. He brought a request "asking [Anza] for the aid of [his] arms to contain the Pima Indians who were hindering the departure of Father Campos." The father visitor had sent Father Nicolás de Perera, missionary at Pópulo, accompanied by Father Ignacio Keller of Suamca, to install Father Nieto at San Ignacio and escort Father Campos back to Cucurpe. Once again, Anza was most likely aware of Father Campos's displeasure with Father Perera. The father visitor, however, "believed that [Anza] might be able to restrain some vecinos who had cooperated with Father Campos" in his effort to remain at San Ignacio.[123]

*[signature]*

Even though Captain Anza did not have orders from his own superiors, this looked like the makings of a serious civil disturbance and possible uprising of the Pima. The captain sent out orders that very evening for a large detachment of soldiers to ready their arms, horses, and pack mules. They would leave the next day as soon as they could get organized.

Early the following morning the company traveled south to Arizpe, and then over the mountains to Cucurpe. There Captain Anza met with a still-shaken Father Perera and heard his version of what had happened. The missionary said he had left Cucurpe for San Ignacio by order of his superior, Father Visitor Marciano, over a week before on Monday, March 5, 1736. He was accompanied by Father Nieto. Father Perera was to gently and charitably bring Father Campos back to Cucurpe, and Father Nieto was to stay at San Ignacio and take over the administration of the mission. They found the old missionary sick and in bed upon their arrival at San Ignacio late that afternoon. On Tuesday morning after celebrating Mass in the church, they went in search of Father Campos, whom they found seated outside in a ramada even though it was a cold, windy day. Father Keller arrived from Suamca shortly afterward to assist in the transfer.

The native governor of Tepoca, who was also there at the time, informed Keller that Father Campos had held a tlatole with the Indians. Supposedly the old padre had told them that he did not want any other missionary to come to San Ignacio. He had always loved them and supplied them with necessities, and he wanted to die with them. Not content with that, he had sent a dispatch to various Spaniards asking for their help.[124]

By now a large number of Pimas had gathered around and were talking with Father Campos in their native language. Although Perera and Nieto could not understand a word they were saying, Father Keller was somewhat familiar with the Pima language and picked up on some of the conversation.[125] He gathered that Father Campos had sent out spies on Monday night to see if Father Perera's Opatas were following him to help in forcibly removing the old padre. He had sent messengers to Ímuris telling the Indians there to come with bows, arrows, and *macanas*, or "war clubs."[126] Of course, when this was brought to Father Perera's attention he emphatically denied that his Opatas were coming.[127]

Throughout that day and the next, while Father Campos lay sick in bed, armed Pimas arrived from various quarters. It soon became apparent that they were under the leadership of Lázaro Chihuahua, Father Campos's former coach driver and now native governor of Tubutama. Lázaro was also in conspiracy with the native governors of Ímuris and San Ignacio. Father Perera's disdain for Chihuahua was obvious. "He is an Indian worthy of nothing but chastisement," he had told Anza.

At Cucurpe, Anza heard how scared Father Perera and the others were on that Wednesday. They asked the Pimas on Tuesday night to come to the church the next morning for Mass where they could discuss the entire matter and resolve it to everyone's satisfaction. Instead, at the first ringing of the bell the next morning, the Pimas fled to the mountains.[128] They continued to gather in the hills around San Ignacio in a very menacing fashion throughout the day until Perera begged Father Campos to send them away. At eleven o'clock that night, however, they were still there. They were saying that Father Perera was planning to remove Campos violently and that they themselves would take him from the town.[129] A large group of them had gathered at the house of Francisco de Neyra,[130] where the padres had been staying. As the Indians continued to become more menacing and belligerent, Father Perera finished up a letter he was writing to Father Marciano at one o'clock in the morning with the plea, "please don't forget me in your prayers!"[131]

The three padres retreated south down the river to the neighboring village of Sasabac, where they spent the remainder of a sleepless night. Early the next morning, Father Campos sent the Pimas away, but Father Perera suspected that they had his and the other fathers' horses. He went back to San Ignacio and asked that they be returned. Father Campos called Juan de Villa and Juan José Martín, his house servants, and sent them to get the horses for Father Perera. When Villa and Martín returned with the horses to Sasabac, the three priests made a hasty retreat back to Cucurpe.[132]

Now, a month and a half later, as Captain Anza and Father Campos sat by their waning fire at Terrenate, the old missionary painted a somewhat different picture about the interaction between the three priests and the Pima Indians.[133]

"[That] night," he said, "they ordered the native governor of San Ignacio to bring all of the Indians into the church for Mass the next day, where they would talk with them, and so on. At the same time, they hid chains inside the church.

"The Pimas knew everything they were doing," Father Campos continued, "and when the bell rang in the morning for Mass, they had scattered, saying that no one would come into the church.

"The fathers commanded that the bell be rung over and over again. Even though they kept calling them to come to Mass, the Pimas responded that they did not want to. All they wanted was to burn houses and churches, and they were ready to fight. That night the Pimas had taken their families into the hills in back of the church where they remained in sight of everyone.

"What would have happened if those fathers had done something inside the church?" the old padre wondered. "How many deaths would have resulted?

"How sacrilegious!" he continued. "Why, even a squadron of soldiers could not have helped those padres inside the church!"

Shaking his head now in disbelief, Father Campos thought back to the odds that presented themselves that Wednesday morning. "While each one of them seized an Indian, the rest would have opened the doors and run outside to get their arms. There were more than a hundred armed Indians at that time. [The next] day there were more than three hundred.

"To whom can these unpleasantries be attributed?" he queried. "Would not the three fathers have died?"[134]

Anza knew it was so. It did not really matter, though, because no one had been hurt and the incident was now quickly drawing to a close. The question of who was at fault was a more difficult one, but that did not really matter either, because the old missionary had gone on to another subject. As he sat on the ground lamenting, Father Campos was thinking about how impolitely he had been treated from the beginning.

"A couple of married girls of the gente de razón," he was saying, "who were born and raised in these villages of the legitimate marriage of Xavier German and Rosa Manuela [sic] Garcia [135]—she has been dead for a number of years [136]—without any cause, they had come to my house to help medicate me with back rubs, hot towels, and so on.

"Father Perera said loudly in front of me, and to me, 'We will help Your Reverence—Father Keller, Father Nieto, and I.'

"Never in my wildest imagination had I ever thought that our most benevolent brothers would elevate themselves to this extreme kindness!" Father Campos interjected sarcastically. "Then they told me they had come to take me to Cucurpe by order of Father Visitor Marciano, and that my mission would be turned over to Father Nieto.

"I was down in bed. How could I deliver my mission to him?"

Anza was probably thinking that bed would be a good place for the old missionary right now. Who would have dreamed that this Jesuit priest could almost single-handedly bring about a revolution in the Pimería Alta? There had been plenty of guilt on the other side, too, but everybody had tried to act the best they could with the information they had. Besides, the poor old bald padre was thin and debilitated, and in his advanced age he was getting a little senile.[137]

Captain Anza had not gotten the full picture from Father Perera at Cucurpe. He had first left that mission with his soldiers to go on to San Ignacio to see what more he could learn. When he got there he found that Father Campos was in Ímuris, surrounded by a large number of his Pimas. He did find in San Ignacio, however, "a goodly number of Indians of different villages and rancherías who, having given [him] the customary greeting, begged [him] to leave their Father Campos with them."

Anza "reprimanded the action they had taken, manifesting to them that they ought to have accepted the superior of their father." To this, "they gave some excuses, confessing to have acted in ignorance."[138]

At that point, the captain and a few of his soldiers turned back to Cucurpe, and from there, with the blessing of Father Perera, headed south to Ures to meet with Father Visitor Marciano to discuss how best to handle the situation. Of this part of the drama, Anza said:

> Having recognized the restlessness exhibited by the Indians here and in the rest of the Pimería, I thought it would be useful in securing tranquility to go

in person to entreat the said father visitor to plan the departure of Father Campos. To accomplish this I went to the village of Ures. I arrived there on Holy Monday [April 2] and met with His Reverence. Finding myself in the presence of the Superior, I made known the inconveniences and the final outcome that could be avoided. He responded that he had no authority to commission me to arrange the departure of the father, subject to both Majesties, the faith of our Religion, and his superiors. With his resolution, then, I returned [to Cucurpe]. There I found Father Perera with whom I had communicated as previously mentioned. At this time I received notice from my officers that each day the boldness of the Indians was strengthened to resist the removal of the father.[139]

Captain Anza arrived back at Cucurpe somewhat discouraged by the politics of the whole mess. Father Marciano could not commission him to take charge of the matter because Anza was a military officer. Only the governor of Sonora, Manuel Bernal de Huidobro, Anza's commanding officer, could give that order. No one wanted that—it was best that the governor not even know about this dilemma if it could at all be kept quiet. The governor's role in this drama is another story. Anza had learned from the father visitor that the entire problem had come about because of correspondence between Father Campos and Governor Bernal de Huidobro. The governor was an avowed anti-Jesuit who had tried to bring reform to the mission system. Father Campos had sided with him, and had refused to sign a letter condemning the governor's actions, which his fellow missionaries in Sonora had willingly signed.

Everything went rapidly downhill from that point. The exchange was alarming. Father Campos sarcastically accused his fellow Jesuits of being a "council of geniuses."[140] Father José Toral aimed a barbed comment at Campos for siding with the governor. "The father would not even know him, except he is his rigorous paisano," Father José complained.[141] Toral was the missionary at Banámichi. He and Cristóbal de Cañas of Arizpe and Juan de Echagoyen at Baviácora were schooled in the law and everyone turned to them for legal advice. Now the father visitor had turned to them hoping that they could give him some counsel.

Father Echagoyen wrote five different letters from Baviácora stating his opinion as to what should be done with Campos, signing two of them with only his given name.[142] Father Cañas, like Echagoyen, never set foot anywhere near San Ignacio[143] while this letter-writing episode was taking place, but he offered the opinion that "the said father has gone from abyss to abyss in this entire incident until I don't know if he is enraged, crazy, or just absentminded. The only thing certain is that I have marveled at all of his writings, letters, and responses—his intentions and excesses."[144]

"It is unimaginable that such boldness, such language, and such little respect should be found in a Jesuit, even the most wayward," Father Toral had written from

Banámichi. "Father Campos values ignorance," he protested.¹⁴⁵ Certainly Father Campos was not the only one who was sarcastic.

Tiring of the accusations that were being leveled against him, Father Campos complained bitterly to the father visitor. "Father Campos says this, Father Campos says that," he grumbled. "You cannot find any such thing among my original letters."¹⁴⁶

The situation finally deteriorated to the point that Father Visitor Marciano had decided to replace the old workhorse, and sent Father Perera to San Ignacio. In the middle of the conflict, Father Campos had requested that he be allowed to remain at San Ignacio until the following month. Perera had agreed to the request before retreating to Cucurpe. Father Marciano had already sent for Anza, who came but lacked authority to do anything. While he was in Ures, Father Marciano told Anza that he had named Father Toral superior over the matter, and had given him the authority to administer Campos's removal from San Ignacio when the month was up.¹⁴⁷ So, there sat Anza, back in Cucurpe, with a possible uprising brewing among the Indians, and all he could do was wait until Father Toral arrived before he could ask him how he might help.

Father Toral arrived at Cucurpe from his mission at Banámichi on Thursday morning, April 19, 1736. He and Captain Anza sat down to discuss what could be done about Father Campos.¹⁴⁸

"I was mindful," Anza said, "of having been informed that Father Campos had asked that he be able to stay until this month, a time more favorable for him to be able to leave, with regard to his illness, and that he be allowed to put the order into execution himself, thereby maintaining, in this way, the honor of the old padre."¹⁴⁹

The captain felt that the delay had bought time with which to better plan the removal of the old missionary. He sent for his foreman at the Guevavi Ranch, requesting that he come talk with Father Campos. Manuel José de Sosa was an ecclesiastical scribe, well known to and loved by all the missionaries. Anza had hoped that he might be able to reason with the old priest.

Father Toral, on the other hand, was concerned about the delay. "He has built bulwarks and guard towers around the house where he is staying," Toral said, "and has placed sentinels along the roads to inform him when the fathers will be returning to remove him."¹⁵⁰

Even though Anza had previously received reports from "his *cabos*" (corporals) saying an uprising was certain, he doubted there had been either sufficient time or organization on the part of Campos and his followers for things to have gotten quite as serious as Father Toral thought they were. Regardless, Toral requested an escort, reminding himself and Anza of the sticky political situation they were in. Anza could not march in and remove Father Campos without a request from the Jesuit superiors or orders from his own.[151]

"A requisition is necessary if I am to provide a guard. I cannot provide the auxiliaries you ask for without it," the captain informed him.

"In view of your response, then," Toral retorted, "I will have to leave unprepared and without a means of executing the orders from my superiors. If, by chance, the Pimas, instigated by the devil, cause the death of one of the fathers, it will all be blamed on Your Honor because of your decision."

Both captain and priest knew that Anza was stepping beyond the law (answering "extrajudicially," as Toral put it), when, after a moment's pause, he gave his thoughtful reply.

"I will go personally with my company to help you, Father," he responded. "I will protect you in whatever might happen."

Early the next morning, Friday, April 20, 1736, Fathers Toral and Keller left Cucurpe with an escort of several soldiers. They traveled to Mission Dolores where Father Keller was informed by one of the natives that Lázaro Chihuahua would kill all the fathers and any Opatas that came to Ímuris to "sack" Father Campos. The fathers continued on northward to Mission Remedios where they set up camp for the night. There they would wait for word from Captain Anza as to when they should enter Ímuris.

Captain Anza and the rest of his soldiers also left Cucurpe early on the morning of April 20. They traveled northwest across the mountain pass to Magdalena, and by evening they had moved up river where they camped at some waterholes south of Ímuris. That night, the captain sent two spies into the village to try to determine the situation. They soon came back with "the Alférez"[152] and word of impending war. Anza immediately dispatched a messenger galloping over the mountain to Remedios to warn the fathers that, due to conditions in Ímuris, they were not to come until further notice.

The next morning, Saturday, April 21, 1736, the soldiers' camp was stirring well before daylight. With Captain Anza in the lead, they rode into Ímuris just as the sun was about to rise from behind the rugged mountains to the east. As they rode past the many sullen Pima faces watching them, the little squadron must have been relieved by what took place next. Chances are, Anza could hardly believe his good fortune when Manuel José de Sosa walked out of Campos's house. Standing by Don Juan's horse, he looked up at Anza and said the old padre was desirous to talk to him. He is "repentant and in tears, and kissing his robe," Anza was informed.

The captain stepped down from his horse and, handing the reins to one of his soldiers, strode with Sosa into the adobe hut to meet with Father Campos. There, in the close quarters of the little house, Anza quickly determined that the old father missionary was truly repentant. While the details of what took place are unknown, three concessions were made by Anza, subject to the approval of Father Toral, in exchange for Father Agustín agreeing to leave his beloved San Ignacio.

No one knows how long the negotiations lasted, but when Anza came out of Father Campos's house, he ordered the soldiers to mount up, and they made a hasty retreat back over the mountain to Remedios. There, in another small adobe structure, the captain met with Father Campos's fellow Jesuit and superior, José Toral. "I knelt at his feet," Anza said, "asking that he would grant me all grace to be able to do what I had come to beseech of him." [153]

The captain then presented the three concessions that he had made to Father Campos and asked Father Toral to approve of them. First, he asked that Campos not be sent to Cucurpe. The old man had a morbid fear of being imprisoned there, and with good reason. Confinement had been the original plan when Father Perera had been sent to San Ignacio to get him the first time.[154]

Secondly, Captain Anza requested that none of the fathers except Toral accompany him to make the final arrangements with Campos. This evidently implied Fathers Marciano, Perera, and Velarde, because in the end Fathers Keller and Nieto were among those who saw the Campos's departure.

The captain's final request was that he personally be allowed to take Father Campos home to Fronteras with him. There the old father would be able to live out his life under the care of Anza and his wife, "which, considering his condition," the captain concluded, "will not be many years." [155]

Father Toral, seeing an easy out to an extremely complicated situation, readily agreed to all of Anza's proposals, with one reservation. He did not have the authority to say that Campos could stay at Fronteras until he died. Only the father visitor could make that decision. He would, however, grant that the old missionary could go home with Don Juan temporarily, until Marciano could make the final decision.

The next day was Sunday. After Mass, and undoubtedly numerous prayers for tranquility, Anza, the soldiers, and the fathers all left Remedios to travel back over the mountain to Ímuris. Everything was peaceful and quiet as they pitched their camp in the little village that night. The next morning dawned clear and sunny. Even though Father Campos appeared to be gravely ill, he moved about with the aid and support of a couple of his beloved Pima neophytes, helping direct the final preparations for his departure. A sedan chair had been brought to the mission, probably from Ures, to be used in carrying the disabled old fellow to Fronteras. Even though the chair was normally used only for dignitaries like the bishop, on his visits to the various jurisdictions, it is doubtful that Father Campos had illusions of royal treatment. The thought of being carried over a hundred miles in a jarring, tightly enclosed sedan chair, through desert heat and across treacherous mountain terrain, was enough to make the heart of a younger man falter.

In spite of everything that had gone on over the last several months, preparations for the final transfer of Mission San Ignacio went smoothly. It had been decided that Father Gaspar Stiger would take the place of Father Campos. Father Nieto would accompany Anza and the soldiers as far as Cuquiárachi to assist the aging missionary. Several young Pima men were chosen by Father Campos to carry him on his long journey. By evening everything was in order. Captain Anza and Fathers Nieto and Keller sat down by candlelight to write a letter to Father Provincial José Barba in Mexico City, informing him of what had taken place. Father Toral also wrote a letter that night, but his report went to Father Visitor Marciano. Anza was evidently so tired, and the lighting was so poor, that he mistakenly misdated his letter, writing April 21 instead of April 23, 1736.[156]

Early the next morning as the expedition was preparing to leave Ímuris, Father Toral made a sarcastic remark about Father Campos having been unable to walk by himself during the preceding days, yet this morning he walked "without the aid of his *gomesillos*" (young boys who guide the blind). "His whole sickness was pure fiction," he sneered.[157]

Regardless, it was the last time that Father Campos ever saw his beloved Pimería Alta. Anza and his soldiers were mounted horseback, while the Pimas walked, two at a time, carrying their beloved father in the sedan chair. This was how, after a full week of difficult traveling, Captain Anza came to be sitting in front of the campfire at Terrenate listening to the aged priest ramble on. Don Juan had been promising the old gentleman ever since they left San Ignacio that as soon as they reached a mission where there was writing paper, he would be allowed time to record his complaints and send them to the father provincial. By a sheer quirk of fate—or maybe it was by design—Father Campos missed his first opportunity to record his frustrations.

Leaving Ímuris, the group had traveled slowly up and over the mountain pass to Remedios, where they spent the first night. The next day they began working their way up the valley toward Mission Cocóspera and eventually went out across the Divisadero, an oak-covered, sandy, alluvial fan, to Santa María Suamca. They probably arrived at that mission sometime in the late afternoon of April 28, a Saturday.

Not being burdened with the responsibility of carrying Father Campos, Father Keller, missionary at Suamca, had evidently traveled ahead of Captain Anza's group, because he was there to greet them when they arrived at his mission. That evening Father Campos went to his house to pay him a visit. Father Keller, a congenial host and much younger than the aging Campos, offered the old man a cup of mescal, an intoxicating native liquor made from the agave plant.[158] There were some Pima Indians there that evening. Father Campos probably knew them. If not, he certainly had the ability to converse with them in their own language, and they quickly became happily acquainted. Here is what happened in Father Campos's own words:

"Father Keller is very amiable. When I arrived at his house he committed a treachery with me that is unimaginable. When I entered his house at Santa María de los Pimas he gave me some mescal. I had wanted to write some declarations by favor of Captain Don Juan Bautista de Anza, but some Indians called on us that night and gave us two or three earthen jugs of mescal brandy. There went my declarations. My critics were too big of a challenge under those conditions. What kind of answers could I have given to the arguments in their letters and writings?"[159]

Sad, comical, and pathetic as it was, Father Campos had missed his first opportunity to strike back at those he felt were persecuting him. Now, as the old missionary sat at Terrenate pouring out frustrations that he had kept inside for so many years, Juan Bautista de Anza was getting an education in history, sociology, and religion in one short course. The old man's mind was wandering back fourteen years, to when he had been called south to answer charges that he felt were spurious at that time also.[160]

"In that other exile in the year 1722," he was saying, "Father Marciano was the principal cause. Twenty of my thirty cattle that were left at San Ignacio were not to be found on my return. Of the five hundred horses, sixty of the herd were separated out and gone, the work of Father Marciano. That my church was stripped of its furnishings does not speak well. Everyone has forgotten what was registered in the sacristy of San Ignacio at the time of the general visit. When they were looking for two chalices and couldn't find them, it was this same Father Marciano who said to Father Visitor Echevarria,[161] 'Why are you worried about a chalice—is it gold?'"[162]

"The other time they exiled me," he continued, "I never said a word that would have dishonored Father Marciano. The only thing I ever said was that in the ten months that he was in the Pimería, I provided him with 740 head of cattle from my mission farm and ranches."[163]

Anza, of course, knew little about that incident as he had been in Mexico City himself, concerned with a completely different agenda.

Campos went on. "These fathers and my superiors—and this is not to contradict them—but they know, as does Father Toral, that in my expulsion from these lands to Mexico . . . I was fully obedient and totally humble. Neither in my writings, nor by word of mouth, can they show even the least neglect of my duty."[164]

Although Father Campos assured Anza that he had not neglected his duties, he could certainly show where his accusers had. One of the things that really galled him was their inability to speak the Pima language. Of course, he was one of the best ever at communicating in native language, so his judgment of his fellow Jesuits may have been a bit unfair.[165]

For example, "Father Velarde has lived more than twenty years in the Pimería Alta, at the Mission of Dolores," Campos grumbled. "Take note of the language of the nation that he knows—you will find that in those twenty years he has not made half of a small speech or sermonette to his Indians [in their own tongue]."[166]

Furthermore, "Marciano has lived for fourteen years or more, first among the Pimas Altos, and now with the Pimas Bajos. And has anyone investigated how many talks, how many sermons or sermonettes he has given in the church to his parishioners?"[167]

Once he started on Father Marciano, Father Agustín could have gone on all night. Captain Anza probably did not want to hear it. Nobody wanted to hear it. Campos had not even wanted to say it and had kept quiet about it for many years. Nobody would pay heed to him now; he was just a crazy old man. Perhaps if some of the problems he knew about had been worked out, however, the mission system would have been in better condition. Possibly it would have been on better terms with the political arm of the government.

"The scandals of Father Marciano"—he was now shaking his weary old head—"all those years of living with a sorceress—first in Tecoripa and now in Ures where he has brought her. His affair with her was scandalously publicized everywhere in the country, and now he has two sons by her who are growing bigger every day. Besides that, he has two publicly known mistresses these days in the village of Ures. They are natives of that town. Father Marciano has the first concubine and their two sons living with him, as well as the rest of the sorceress's family. What extremely excessive costs must he have in maintaining his home?"[168]

And "Father Perera," he continued, "always has two single Seri Indian women with him. He takes them from valley to valley, from river to river, from village to village, and even among the Opata. And if somebody comes to the place or village where he has them with him to try to return them to their village, they won't be with him because he hides them somewhere else—if he can, at the house of Juan de Acosta in the *bosque* along the river. When the governor of Pópulo came to ask when they would be returned to his village, he couldn't find any trace of them. Why Father Perera has them or for what purpose he keeps them, only he knows. Whether these two, Father Visitor Marciano and Vice Visitor Perera, deserve to be publicly censured as mistress-keepers is not for me to judge. Everyone—the young and the old, Indians and Spaniards, from all villages and reales de minas—they all know about it."[169]

"Father Velarde also has a family in his same village of Dolores,"[170] he said, nearly in a whisper now. "From what I understand, he now wants to move from Dolores to Cocóspera where it will be more convenient for him, and especially the Spanish señora who is constraining him [to stay there]. He has already sent her there. Her name is Ramos García, and he had a son by her last March. They call him Xavier Moraga to hide the name Velarde."[171]

"I don't know," he continued to shake his head, "if this desire of those fathers, so offensive and with such rudeness and full of scandal before Indians and Spaniards alike, will be true zealousness for the glory of God? Or will it end in contention and shameful dishonor?"[172]

Captain Anza did not know either. As he helped the rickety old padre to his tent that night, neither of them could have guessed that some thirty years down the road, for offenses real or imagined, their beloved Company of Jesus would be expelled by the king from the entire Spanish world. They would both be dead and so would many of their brothers in the order. Father Campos might have felt a trace of satisfaction had he known that Father Perera would still be alive to be arrested at that time. Not only that, but he would be old and sick, just like Campos was now, and would have to be carried away on a stretcher. Anza, on the other hand, would probably have felt a twinge of sadness had he known that his son and namesake, with whom his wife was now seven months pregnant, would be the one to arrest Father Perera and carry him away.

For now, the important thing was to get to bed. They had a couple more hard days ahead of them before arriving at San Ignacio de Cuquiárachi. There, Father Nieto would leave for a new assignment in the south. Father Carlos de Rojas would be Father Campos's host for a few days, providing him with paper and pen.[173] He would finally get to have his say. Being so old and sick, however, he would have to finish his letter to the father provincial when he was finally settled in at Fronteras on Monday afternoon, May 8, 1736.

## Passing of the First Generation and Arrival of the Third

*En Primero de Maio de mil setecientos y treinta y tres años el R.$^{do}$ P. Preci.$^{de}$ fr. Fran.$^{co}$ Llavero licencia Parrochi, enterro + de cruz Alta Vigil.$^a$ y Missa a D.$^n$ Ant.$^o$ Bezerra Nieto Capitan Vitalicio de este R.1 Precidio, q$^n$ dejo Poder especial p$^a$ Testar a su hijo B.$^r$ D$^n$ Thomas Bezerra N$^{to}$ subcura dio porcion fallesio, aviendosela administrado los s$^{tos}$ sacram$^{tos}$ de la penet.$^a$ eucharistia y extrem.$^a$ uncion; fue el dho casado con D$^a$ Gregoria Catharina Gomez de Silva; y paraque conste lo firmó conmigo: Fr Fran$^{co}$ Llavero = Fran$^{co}$ Pedro Romano* . . . On the first of May 1733, the Reverend Father President, Fray Francisco Llavero, with parochial license, interred by High Cross, wake, and Mass, Don Antonio Bezerra Nieto, captain for life of this royal presidio, who granted special power to his son, Bachiller Tomás Bezerra Nieto, deputy priest, to receive his last will and testament and divide his estate. He died after the Holy Sacraments of Penance, Eucharist, and Extreme Unction were administered. The said captain was married to Doña Gregoria Catalina Gómez de Silva, and for these truths we signed: Fray Francisco Llavero = Francisco Pedro Romano[174]

His wife, Gregoria Catalina Gómez de Silva, had been dead just short of ten years when the old veteran Antonio Bezerra Nieto passed away on May 1, 1733. Word spread quickly on the frontier by couriers on fast horses, but it is doubtful that the Anza household in Fronteras knew about the death in time for María Rosa to attend her father's funeral Mass some one hundred fifty miles away. Undoubtedly various eulogies were given at the time of the funeral, but none have survived the ages. Therefore, the testimony of Manuel Vásques, given twenty years later at Nacosari, will have to suffice:

> Captain Antonio Bezerra Nieto and Doña Gregoria Gomez de Silva (who enjoy the presence of God), who were well known in this province and outside of it, were very noble persons of famous services. Captain Don Antonio Bezerra was always associated with the Royal Presidio of Janos, having, at the same time as his official visit here, obtained the assignment of visitor general for this Province of Sonora from His Majesty. He died in this office of visitor general as well as in his employment as captain. He conducted himself with great veneration and honor in the service of His Majesty, and it is commonly acknowledged that his memory will live forever.[175]

The distance was so great between Fronteras and Janos—at least for women with new babies, or old men who did not feel like being jarred around by a saddle horse or bumping over nearly impassable roads in a dead-axle wagon or thorough-brace carriage—that Captain Bezerra Nieto possibly never saw his newest granddaughter before he died, even though she was more than a year old. Gregoria de Anza, as everyone knew her when she got older, was born on March 30, 1732, at Fronteras. Either Father Verdugo del Castillo, parish priest for the jurisdiction of Nacosari, which included Fronteras, was unavailable, or else Carlos de Rojas, Jesuit missionary at San Ignacio de Cuquiárachi just happened to be at the presidio when the birth occurred, for it was he who baptized the new baby and recorded the event as follows:

> On March 30 in the year of our Lord 1732, I, Carlos Rojas of the Company of Jesus, missionary of this district of San Ignacio de Cuquiárachi, with license from the honorable priest Don Pedro Verdugo del Castillo, in the new church[176] of the Royal Presidio of Santa Rosa de Corodéguachi, solemnly baptized and anointed with holy oil Josefa Gregoria Juaquina, legitimate daughter of Señor Don Juan Bautista de Anza, captain for life of the said presidio, and his wife, the Señora Doña María Rosa Bezerra Nieto. Her godfather was Señor Don Agustín de Vildósola, militia captain for His Majesty in this Province of Sonora, for which truth I sign—the Jesuit Carlos de Rojas, Minister of Doctrine for His Majesty[177]

There may have been other children born to Juan Bautista de Anza and María Rosa Bezerra Nieto between the years 1726 and 1732 at Fronteras, but records for that period have never surfaced. We are fortunate that copies of Gregoria's baptismal record and that of her younger brother, Juan Bautista, exist in archives in Spain. Spanish citizens had to be very careful that they properly documented themselves for a variety of reasons—owning land, obtaining the best employment, becoming a military officer, and so on—so duplicate copies of vital records often exist somewhere besides just their point of origin. Someday, records of other Anza children may be found in archives outside of Sonora, but for the present we know of only two children born while the family was living at Fronteras.

Even though Gregoria de Anza was not born in time to remember her grandfather, Antonio Bezerra Nieto, she certainly entered the world in time for him, and even her grandparents in Spain, to receive word of her arrival. That was not the case with the next Anza baby. His maternal grandfather had been dead for three years when he arrived. His maternal grandmother, Lucia de Sasoeta, died the fall before his birth. In fact, word of Lucia's passing on November 28, 1735,[178] probably reached Fronteras about the time the baby arrived, mixing the sad with the joyous. On the other hand, word of new little Juan Bautista de Anza's arrival on July 7 of 1736 probably reached Spain sometime before his paternal grandfather, Antonio de Anza, passed away on June 17, 1737.[179]

Antonio Anza's death marked the end of an era. Nearly a month after his passing, on July 10, María Estevan de Anza wrote to her two younger brothers, Juan Bautista in Fronteras, Sonora, and Juan Felipe in Sevilla, Spain, to inform them of what had taken place. Their youngest brother, Nicolás, one of the parish priests of Hernani, had been in attendance at the funeral Mass and was involved in everything that took place regarding the estate of the deceased. There being no heir interested in operating the Anza botica, María Estevan and her husband, Juan Domingo de Larreta, had hired José de Miranda, a maestro boticario, to inventory everything in her father's drugstore. Then they had sold all the drugs, bottles, and tools of the trade. They removed the little sign that read "Antonio de Anssa, Boticario," which had hung on that door for forty-eight years. The time of being able to purchase Anza-formulated remedies in Hernani and vicinity had passed.[180] The last of the first generation had passed from this life—the last of the third generation had just arrived one year previously.

This youngest member of the third generation, Juan Bautista de Anza, always claimed that he was a native of Fronteras, Sonora. That is where his family was living when he was born and where he spent the first four years of his life. However, all evidence indicates that he was born at Cuquiárachi, Sonora, eight miles away.[181] The new baby's baptismal entry is crucial here: "On the seventh of July of the year 1736 in the Church of San Ignacio of Cuquiárachi with license from its own parish priest,[182] I solemnly baptized and anointed with holy oil Juan Bautista, legitimate son of Captain Don Juan Bautista de Anza, and of Doña María Rosa Bezerra Nieto. His godfather was Don Pedro Felipe de Anza, in testimony of which I signed—the Jesuit Carlos de Rojas, Minister of Doctrine for His Majesty."[183]

Baptism was so crucial to Catholic doctrine that every effort was made to baptize a newly arrived baby immediately after its birth. In fact, it was so crucial that if a mother was about to, or did, die before the baby was born, it was to be taken by caesarian operation and the waters of baptism were to be applied.[184] This could be done by anyone of the Catholic faith and the ceremony ratified by a priest afterward. In a very small percentage of cases, when a baby was born very late at night, the baptismal entry will reflect a baptism performed one day after the birth, probably in the early morning hours after the priest arose for the day. Sometimes on the frontier, a baptism might take place two or three days after the birth, but this is seen more often in the baptism of Indian babies from outlying villages. Sometimes, the Indians got around to it when they got around to it, but Catholicism was so ingrained into the Spanish community, and especially in devout families like the Anzas, that arrangements for baptism were made well before the birth of the child.

None of the exceptions apply to the birth and baptism of the junior Juan Bautista de Anza. Neither he nor his mother was in danger of dying, so no emergency baptismal procedures were performed. Even if that had been the case, the child would not have been taken eight miles to Cuquiárachi in such an emergency. Anyone at the presidio could have performed the baptism, but if such a thing had happened, it would have been reflected in the baptismal entry.

Father Pedro Verdugo del Castillo was the logical one to have performed the baptism had young Anza been born at Fronteras. Father Pedro was assigned to the jurisdiction of Nacosari but appears to have lived at Fronteras and acted as chaplain for the soldiers. Even had he been on the campaign with the cavalry, there was no shortage of priests at Fronteras as there might have been at other places on the frontier. Agustín de Campos was there and certainly capable of performing a baptism. In fact, it would have been a great honor for the old priest, and just as much of an honor for the family to have had their old friend baptize the new baby. The fact that neither Father Castillo nor Father Campos baptized him is a strong indication that Juan was not born at Fronteras. Furthermore, had he been born at the presidio, and if there had been no priests available, it is much more likely that Father Rojas would have ridden to Fronteras to perform the baptism rather than subjecting the new baby to eight miles of travel in the heat of the summer. That is what the father had done for Juan's sister, Gregoria, four years previously when he baptized her at the presidio rather than at his mission.

Women often traveled somewhere besides their homes to have their babies, perhaps for safety or so that the mother could be with family and give birth in familiar surroundings. More often, however, it was for the purpose of obtaining the services of a trusted midwife. Juan's older sister, Margarita, was born at Janos even though the family had moved to Fronteras. Taking everything into consideration, it is almost certain that Juan Bautista de Anza was born at Cuquiárachi, even though the family was living at Fronteras.

The new baby was probably born that Saturday morning of July 7, 1736, or the night before. There being only eight miles between Cuquiárachi and Fronteras, a messenger on a fast-trotting horse could easily have arrived at the presidio within an hour, carrying news of the birth. In another two or three hours, the family could have easily gathered at Cuquiárachi for the baptism. There in the small mission church located on a slight knoll above the creek that ran down to Fronteras, Juan and María Rosa and their five other children watched as Father Rojas performed the baptism at the small stone *pila,* or "font," at the rear of the church. Pedro Felipe de Anza, the new baby's first cousin, one generation removed, was godfather for the ceremony. Father Rojas had informed him of the spiritual duties and obligations inherent in his position, and he agreed to care for and watch after the new child, as well as provide instruction in Christian doctrine and other learning, should anything happen to the child's natural parents.

The Día de San Juan, or feast day of John the Baptist, had fallen on Sunday that year. The weeklong ceremonies commemorating this beloved saint had ended on the Saturday previous to the new baby's baptism. It was appropriate, then, that he should be given the name of Saint John the Baptist, the same name as his father. In this desert country, where rain was so scarce, it was also appropriate that he be given a name associated with water and the beginning of the rainy season. It was a joyous day.

There is one other person of that earlier generation that the young Juan Bautista de Anza would not remember but would grow up hearing stories about. In fact, as he grew up he probably felt a closer tie to Father Agustín de Campos than he did to his own grandparents who had lived in Spain. Even though the old man was not a blood relative, he was like a member of the family for the first year of the young boy's life. Although he was not truly a grandparent, the old workhorse of the Pimería Alta was in the same generation as the grandparents, and Juan's older brother and sisters probably looked up to him as though he were their grandfather during that year he spent in their home. Unlike the baby's true grandparents, Father Campos actually saw and held the latest addition to the Anza family.

A young child will often bring happiness to an old person who has begun to feel that he has outlived his usefulness and, as senility begins to set in, reverts back to thinking of things in his early childhood. One can hope this was the case, at least, because Father Campos's life was anything but happy during his final year. He continued to worry about being excommunicated for his misdeeds. He continued to dream of returning to his beloved San Ignacio. His last known letter, written in a shaky hand, reveals a physically worn-out old man. His mental faculties, however, were still sharp and his thought patterns clearly understandable, though heart-wrenching. He was again at Cuquiárachi for a brief visit.

> The presidio, which is governed by Don Juan Bautista de Anza, is two leagues from here. Well, I have only a white rag for underwear, nor do I have sheets for my bed. And this is the way my condition has been at the presidio, Your Reverence, from the time I first arrived there. In view of this, then, and other things, I gave my best, Your Reverence, in being a strong servant. I ask that I be allowed to go briefly to my mission that I might look for a way for them to make me a couple of shirts. But with this order of Father Toral, I cannot leave here. Only in the presidio, where I celebrate a few Masses, are they moved to provide me this old rag through charity, seeing the abject poverty of a very sad priest.[185]

It was almost a year later on July 24, 1737, while on a brief visit from Fronteras to the Opata mission of Santa María de Baseraca,[186] some fifty miles away, that Father Campos died. Father Nicolás de Oro provided the funeral Mass and served notice of the old missionary's death.[187] The passing of Father Campos came one month after Antonio de Anza died at his home in Spain, but word of the missionary's death was received at Fronteras several months before the notice of the passing of old Aitona Antonio. By the beginning of 1738 the Anzas of Sonora were aware that the previous generation of the Anza and Bezerra Nieto families was gone, and the passing of Father Campos marked the end of a generation of pioneer Jesuits. A new age was beginning.

# Chapter Six

## The Final Years

## *Arizona*

*En el Puesto del Arisona en Veinte y ocho dias del mes de Noviembre de mil setecᵒˢ treinta y seis Yo dicho justicia maior En Virtud del mandato en auto antesedente pase a las Casas y morada de D. Bernardo de Urrea Teniente de esta jurisdicion y depositorio de las platas — Juan Baupᵗᵃ de Anssa (rúbrica)* . . . On the twenty-eighth day of November 1736, I, the said justicia mayor, by virtue of the mandate in the preceding decree, went to the houses and residence of Don Bernardo de Urrea, deputy of this jurisdiction and trustee of the silver, in the place called Arizona—Juan Bautista de Anza (rubric)[1]

From Don Juan Bautista de Anza, Captain for Life of the Presidio of Fronteras, to the Most Illustrious Señor Doctor Don Benito Crespo of the Order of Saint James[2]

Most Illustrious Lord:

I am ever mindful, Most Illustrious Lord, of the favors you have seen fit to bestow upon me. I should like to reciprocate, to the extent that my small talents will permit, with news I shall relate that I believe you will find especially pleasing since the circumstances could result in the augmentation and spread of the Holy Gospel where it was planted at the insistence of the burning zeal of your illustrious self.

Soon after the missions of the Pimería were founded, there were discovered some small mines of limited production in three areas,[3] news of which I gave to the late viceroy,[4] and showing, Most Illustrious Lord, how pleased he was, he began to recompense by this means our most pious Monarch for what he had advanced from the Royal Treasury for the maintenance of the reverend missionary fathers.

Toward the end of last October, between the Guevavi Mission and the Arizona Ranchería, there were discovered some balls and slabs of silver, one of which weighed more than one hundred arrobas,[5] a sample of which I am sending to you, Most Illustrious Lord. There were others found as well, but mixed with tailings and other metal, with a total of more than 200 arrobas. By the time I was made aware of the matter it had disappeared. Some pieces that I saw appeared to have been smelted. Acting in my capacity of justicia mayor, I impounded them, disputing whether His Majesty was entitled to more than would be assigned to him from regular mines, since these pieces had been found lying loose, less than one-quarter to one-half vara deep.[6] Whether my decision was proper according to the ordinances will have to be decided by His Excellency, the viceroy.[7] When I arrived it had already been excavated and there were found afterward no more than ten or twelve arrobas, but discoveries of mines continue in other hills.

So sudden and unexpected was this discovery that all prudent and capable men take the position that the Lord our God has permitted it so that with this as an enticement, further penetration of the frontier can be made and the banner of our redemption planted, bringing the good fortune of that day to so many people, as some express. I also wish to consult Your Excellency in this. I am directing a relative[8] with this dispatch to Mexico City and to remit a little of the silver to Your Most Illustrious Lordship. Needless to say, I covet the cooperation of Your Most Illustriousness with your Holy Prayers and other diligences that, as this enterprise has begun, it will have a happy outcome. Since what you desire and what you do for the redemption of souls is well known, I ask and direct my pleas for its materialization to Divine Providence, that there be conceded to Your Most Illustrious Lordship many long years in sound health. In greatest acquiescence from the Presidio of Santa Rosa de Corodéguachi, January 7, 1737.

Most Illustrious and Reverend Lord, your most attentive servant who venerates you kisses the feet of Your Most Illustrious Lordship

Juan Bauptista de Anssa (rubric)[9]

The foregoing letter marks the first announcement to the world that a place called Arizona existed on the northern outskirts of Sonora and the Pimería Alta. Prior to the delivery of this letter to Durango, and another that Anza wrote to the viceroy six days later and sent to Mexico City with his foreman and clerk Manuel José de Sosa, no one other than a few locals and some other Sonorans had even heard of it. It was nothing more than the ranch headquarters of one Bernardo de Urrea, a rancher, storekeeper, miner, and Anza's deputy justicia mayor for the Pimería Alta. Although Urrea undoubtedly had employees, some of whom will be mentioned later, the record only shows two people to have lived at Arizona prior to 1736—Bernardo de Urrea and Manuel Cortés Monroy. However, thanks to Anza using Urrea's house as a headquarters, and his table as a judge's bench and place for writing decrees and mandates in a highly unusual court hearing and investigation, Arizona[10] would soon be a household word throughout the length and breadth of Nueva España.

Moreover, in just a few years, the name would become a legend, passed down from generation to generation, even until today. It became a symbol of vast mineral wealth, even though it was far removed from the great silver discovery that brought it fame. One hundred and twenty years after Anza's letter to Bishop Crespo, promoters of a new and distinct United States territory, to be formed by the lands of the Gadsden Purchase, would choose the name "Arizona" for what would eventually become a state of the Union. Although the choice of the name fell to a man named William Claude Jones,[11] he would have never heard of the word had it not been for Juan Bautista de Anza. In that sense, Anza is responsible for the name that the forty-eighth state bears. Had he not chosen to hold his court of inquiry at Bernardo Urrea's house located at the place called Arizona, and to send out numerous proclamations, decrees, and court orders with that address, hardly anyone would have heard of it. It would just be the sleepy little ranch that it still is today, located at the bottom of a deep canyon in northern Sonora, about ten air miles south of the present international border—south of a state that would undoubtedly have been named something else.

The story began in late October of 1736 in the rugged canyon country of northern Sonora, about equidistant between the Spanish settlements in the San Luis Valley and a newly established real de minas called Nuestra Señora de la Límpia Concepción del Agua Caliente. The San Luis Valley and the Guevavi Mission lay about fifteen miles to the northeast. Agua Caliente was roughly fifteen miles to the southwest down a tortuous canyon that would eventually be known as the Planchas de Plata, or "Slabs of Silver" Canyon. Gabriel Prudhom Butrón y Mujica, alcalde mayor of Sonora from July 1727 until July 1735, may have had something to do with the founding of Nuestra Señora de la Límpia Concepción del Agua Caliente, but there is no evidence to prove such a claim. There is no documentary evidence to show that he ever even owned a mine, anywhere. It is known, however, that he was physically at Agua Caliente just prior to his leaving office in March of 1735, as evidenced by an informe he wrote from there. The *realito*, or "little mining camp," as it was known, may have been started as early as 1733 or 1734. However, disregarding the so-called Prudhom map, which was obviously put together after the fact to try to prove something in court, there is no evidence of mining in the area until March 4, 1735, the date of Prudhom's report.[12]

In the spring of 1736, during the time of the previously discussed Father Campos dilemma, there seems to have been fairly extensive prospecting, at least, and possibly some mining, in the area. Again, however, there is no record of any silver, gold, or any other mineral actually being found and produced there. That Spaniards of the San Luis Valley were involved in the venture is evident from the fact that Diego Romero was sent down from his Santa Barbara ranch to alert the prospectors and miners about the impending removal of Father Campos from San Ignacio. Miners known to be living at Agua Caliente in the fall of 1736, who were originally from

Guevavi, Suamca, and the San Luis Valley, included Juan Antonio de Rivera and José Ximenez.[13]

*[signature: Juan Antonio de Rivera]*

A larger number of the miners who were living at the realito at that time, however, were originally from San Ignacio and Sasabac. These included Juan Felipe Martín, Claudio Antonio Segura, Francisco de Longoria, Nicolás Alfonso de Ochoa, Juan Contreras, and Juan Lorenzo García.[14]

The names of eighteen men who were living in the area in the fall of 1736 appear in the original documentation. As was typical of those early frontier mining camps, a disproportionate number (exactly half in this instance) of those residents were Basque, one was Yaqui, and the other eight were of Spanish or other European origin. The nine Basque residents were José Fermín de Almazán, Francisco de Longoria, Alfonso de Ochoa, José de Osorio, Nicolás Quiros y Nerea, Claudio Antonio Segura, Pedro Regala de Urias, Bernardo de Urrea, and José Joaquín de Usarraga.[15]

There were also a sizable number of mestizo, Indian, and other workers living at Agua Caliente that fall.[16] Some were hired by the resident miners, others by absentee employers. These men probably did the majority of the physical digging and scouring of the surrounding mountains in search of mineral deposits. One such person was a Yaqui Indian of about fifty years of age named Antonio Siraumea, who lived at Agua Caliente with his wife and children.[17] He was employed by one of the miners, evidently as a barretero or tanatero, for the sum of 100 pesos per year.[18] He apparently did some prospecting on his own time, however, because that is what he was doing one day in late October of 1736.

Struggling through some of the most inhospitable, rugged, and harsh mountain terrain in northern Sonora, he stumbled upon a ball of yellowish metal, laced with silver.[19] The chunk of metal was lying in the soil, partially exposed, beside a large boulder. Antonio dug it up and carried it fifteen miles down the mountain to his home at Agua Caliente. He gathered up his children and took them back to where he had found it, to help him search for more. They did not do any digging, but rather searched the surface looking for other pieces of silver. One of the children found a slab of virgin silver intermixed with other metals that weighed nearly fifty pounds. Shortly after that, Antonio found another ball that weighed about seventy-five pounds. It, too, was laced with other metals, but the silver was in greater quantity than in the first chunk he had found.

How long he and his children searched before others arrived on the scene is not known. Since only he and they went back up the mountain without notifying anyone else of his discovery, however, it seems obvious that secrecy was his intent. Unfortunately for him, however, Agua Caliente was like any other such frontier mining camp—everyone's eyes were on everyone else. Antonio would later bitterly complain that almost immediately several other people arrived at the site and began discovering chunks of silver, at or just below the surface of the ground.

Almost immediately, disputes began to break out over who had the right to dig where. Antonio or one of his children hurried back down the canyon to get a couple of friends named Dionisio Cuchusuamea and Bartolillo, also Yaqui Indians, to come help them. Three of José Caballero's laborers, evidently at the request of Antonio, also began digging in the same vicinity as Antonio and his children and friends, and helped to hold back any claim jumpers. Caballero was one of the absentee employers of Agua Caliente, who lived with his wife, Luisa Chamorro, and their children at San Ignacio.[20] Luisa and her brother, Juan Chamorro, were "free Negroes,"[21] and had lived at San Ignacio for more than ten years.[22] Juan was presently residing at Agua Caliente where he was foreman for Caballero's mining interests there. With his ear evidently to the ground, he and several of the workers had arrived at the discovery site hot on the heels of Antonio Siraumea and his children.

Word spread quickly, but in the first couple of days after the initial discovery, it got no farther than down the canyon to Agua Caliente. Of course, the miners, prospectors, and workers at that realito were the first on the scene following Siraumea. One of the fortune seekers in the earliest wave of prospectors and miners that flooded the area was José Fermín de Almazán, evidently the foreman for, or at least an employee of, Lorenzo de Velasco. Both men were Basque. José Fermín was residing at Agua Caliente, but Velasco and his wife, Sabina Moraga, and their children lived at Santa Ana, south of San Ignacio.[23] Almazán had the extreme good fortune to discover the largest slab of silver that the site produced. Unlike Antonio Siraumea, however, he did not have the good fortune to be working for himself on the day that he found it. Judging from the favors Velasco and his wife bestowed upon others, it can be assumed that they compensated Almazán well for his discovery. However, the written record does not show him having received any of the silver or any compensation other than his salary.

At a distance of probably several hundred yards from where Antonio Siraumea found the first ball of silver, Almazán was searching in a rather large arroyo between two small hills. Turning over two stones, one of which he termed "large" and the other "medium-sized," he saw what appeared to be a slab of silver beneath. He must have become more and more amazed with each scoop of earth that he removed. There, lying less than a foot beneath the surface of the soil was a gigantic sheet, or plank, that appeared to be virgin silver without slag. It was so huge that neither human nor beast could move it. Later, after it had been cut into several manageable pieces that could be weighed as separate units, its total weight was calculated at one and one-quarter tons. With the exception of some gravel that was embedded in its surface and a couple of small streaks of other metal that ran through its center, it was nearly pure silver that gave the appearance of having been smelted.

Antonio Siraumea immediately claimed his rights under Spanish law as first discoverer of the site and requested a percentage of the massive slab. By this time, Bernardo de Urrea, in the capacity of deputy justicia mayor, was on the scene and demanded a percentage for the king. Under normal circumstances that tax would have constituted 20 percent, but as they were unable to weigh the huge block, an estimate was the best they could accomplish, to which José Fermín agreed. With hammer and chisel, roughly a fifth of the silver was cut away from the slab. The smaller piece was then broken into several smaller chunks—some for Siraumea, some for the king, and a small amount in payment to Urrea for undisclosed services rendered. Siraumea took his piece to his house at Agua Caliente and Urrea took his to his home at Arizona. With his share, which amounted to 130 *marcos*,[24] together with some other silver he had from previous transactions, Urrea rode over the mountain to the San Luis Valley. There, at Diego Romero's Santa Barbara Ranch, he paid part of an outstanding bill to his *aviador*, or "supplier" of trade merchandise, for his supply store at Arizona. His aviador appears to have been Diego Romero.

News of the astonishing silver discovery spread like wildfire from the San Luis Valley. Within just a few days miners, prospectors, day workers, fortune seekers, and the normal complement of riffraff were soon arriving at what had been, only the week before, a remote, uninhabited wilderness known only to the Apache, if anyone. Word traveled as far as Tetuachi in the east and at least two miners arrived from there, Francisco Pérez Serrano and Francisco López. From further south down the Sonora River, at the real de minas of Motepore, Santiago Ruiz de Ael, a merchant and Inquisition official, quickly dispatched his clerk, Nicolás López de Sequeiros, and an Indian helper, Dionisio, to the site of the new discovery. Silver seekers also arrived quickly from the mines and villages of southern Sonora. José de Mesa and José de Usarraga arrived from the vicinity of the mission communities of Pópulo and Los Ángeles.[25]

Usarraga's son, José Juachín, was on the scene before his father. He was evidently living at Arizona at the time of the discovery and working for Bernardo de Urrea, as he acted as Urrea's assistant in all the duties that he performed as deputy justicia mayor during the days following the silver strike. Another of Urrea's assistants, who wrote most of the decrees and dispatches signed by Urrea at the time, was José de Osorio. Urrea, Osorio, and the Usarragas were all Basques who maintained a close-knit association with one another. Many other people of diverse and various ethnicities—including mestizos, Yaqui Indians, Spaniards of numerous regional backgrounds, and at least one person of African descent, Juan Chamorro—were soon camped at the discovery site and digging up the area.

The entire area was in chaos, with people turning over rocks and picking and digging practically on top of each other. López de Sequeiros's Indian employee, Dionisio, borrowed a crowbar from Antonio Siraumea and proceeded to dig just a couple of paces away from where Siraumea and his helpers were digging. He and one of

José Caballero's employees evidently uncovered a chunk of silver practically together and at the same time. Dionisio claimed it. Caballero's hired man claimed it. Siraumea asserted that they were digging on his claim and took it away from them. Although the slab weighed nearly three hundred pounds, he managed to transport it to Agua Caliente and lock it in his house.

In the meantime, Santiago Ruiz de Ael and several arrieros were on their way to the discovery site with a heavily laden string of pack mules. Realizing the tremendous amount of money to be made by selling merchandise to the miners that would be gathering there, Don Santiago rode over the mountains from Motepore to Cucurpe and on to San Ignacio. There he spent the night at the home of José Caballero. José de Mesa, on his way to the silver strike from the south, was also spending the night there. The next day, Caballero, Mesa, and Ruiz de Ael all headed north. They arrived at the site of the discovery after dark. Ruiz de Ael found the camp of his clerk, López de Sequeiros, and pitched his tent alongside. Dionisio, the Indian servant, came in just as Ruiz de Ael was going to bed. Not wanting to disturb Don Santiago, Dionisio told him he would talk to him in the morning.

Early next morning, Dionisio explained the circumstances to Don Santiago, as he understood them, concerning the piece of silver that Siraumea had confiscated. Thirty-four-year-old Don Santiago, being a notary for the Holy Office of the Inquisition, and his clerk, López de Sequeiros, also being an escribano, recorded Dionisio's statement in writing in the presence of a half-dozen witnesses. Because of pressing business matters that he had in various parts of Sonora, Santiago planned to send López de Sequeiros back to Motepore to look after his affairs. First, however, with Dionisio's statement in hand, they rode down the canyon to Arizona and presented the case before Deputy Justicia Mayor Urrea.

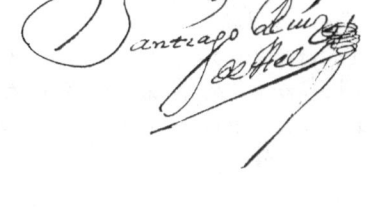

Don Bernardo prepared a legal document and then he and Ruiz de Ael went to Siraumea's house at Agua Caliente. Siraumea and his friend and helper, Dionisio Cuchusuamea, were there. Don Bernardo questioned them and got the story that the silver had been discovered by one of José Caballero's hired men, and that Siraumea's claim to the slab of silver came from his being the first discoverer, and the fact that Caballero's servants were helping him. Under the pretext that no one had paid the "king's fifth" on the piece of silver, and that no one had a legal mining claim in the area, Urrea confiscated the silver and gave it to Don Santiago. He then obtained a sworn statement from Don Santiago that he would settle the matter with José Caballero. López de Sequeiros loaded the silver on a pack mule and headed back to Motepore with it. Antonio Siraumea, feeling his rights as the first discoverer were being trampled, was enraged.

Don Bernardo went back to his home at Arizona and sat down at his table to write a letter. He had probably lived in the jurisdiction of Nuestra Señora de la Límpia Concepción del Agua Caliente longer than anybody. He may well have been living at Arizona prior to the establishment of the realito. In fact, it is likely he who gave it the Basque name, *Arizona*, meaning "the good oak tree."[26] He had the biggest, nicest, and most secure house of anyone in the little valley. However, he was just thirty years old at the time and inexperienced in matters of mining. As deputy justicia mayor, he did not know how he should proceed legally. He could not have known at the time that no one else was sure either. Even the highest tribunals in Mexico City would not know what to make of the fantastic discovery when they were informed of it. Don Bernardo did realize that the discovery, and the pandemonium taking place in the hills in back of his house, was bigger than his ability to manage them. Although lacking in experience, he was conscientious. Justicia Mayor Juan Bautista de Anza would say of him, "The deputy of that jurisdiction, Don Bernardo de Urrea, is a good man and that is why I chose him. He also has the respect of the Pima and, even though he is without experience, there was no one else adequate for the job."[27]

So, Don Bernardo sat down to compose a letter to his chief, setting out the facts of the discovery as he understood them.[28] He requested advice on how he should proceed in collecting the king's fifth. He needed information on how to lay out mining claims. He was concerned about Antonio Siraumea's claim as the first discoverer of the *planchas y bolas de plata*, and how he should proceed to protect the Yaqui's rights. When the letter was complete, he sealed it and dispatched it by fast courier to be delivered personally to Captain Anza, and no one else.

Fast courier or not, it took the letter several days to reach the captain. To begin with, there were a hundred miles of hard travel to get to Fronteras from Arizona. The first day saw the mail carried up out of the canyon and over the mountain to the Romero Ranch at Santa Barbara. The next day it arrived at Terrenate. If all went well, the day after that the courier probably camped within fifteen or twenty miles of Fronteras. Then, on the fourth day he arrived early in the day at the presidio, only to find that Anza was not there. The captain was performing legal duties as justicia mayor somewhere in the Sonora River valley.

The next day, with a fresh change of horses, the courier made a long, hard ride over the mountain past Basochuca and Guepavérachi and on into Arizpe. There he learned in the evening that Anza was not there, either. He had gone up river to the mines at Bacanuchi. The following morning, after another change of horses, the courier wended his way up the Bacanuchi River to the real de minas. He arrived late in the afternoon to find Captain Anza encamped there with several soldiers, holding court in his campaign tent. The courier delivered his letter and waited while Don Juan read it. Then it was time for some intensive interrogation. Don Bernardo's letter certainly did not tell everything about the unique discovery, and the courier tried diligently to answer all of the captain's pointed questions.

When Anza was fully satisfied that he understood what had taken place, even though he and the other miners at Bacanuchi had never heard of chunks of silver lying practically on the surface of the ground, so huge they could not be moved, he determined it was necessary to go investigate the matter. He closed down the court, postponed all pending business, and ordered his soldiers to make ready to leave in the morning. It was a beautiful fall evening, Tuesday, November 13, 1736.

On Wednesday morning, Captain Anza and his soldiers folded up their tents, rounded up their horses and pack mules, saddled and loaded up, and headed down the Bacanuchi River. About halfway down the river to its junction with the Sonora River, they turned east through the rugged cactus and brush-covered hills to Mission San José de Chinapa. Arriving there in the late afternoon, they set up camp and settled in for a few days. As Anza had ridden along that day, the events of the fantastic silver discovery in the Pimería Alta must have been foremost on his mind. There was no precedent for it of which he was aware. The question of how to settle Antonio Siraumea's claim as first discoverer had been Deputy Urrea's prime concern, but to Captain Anza, who was familiar with mining law, there were intriguing questions of greater concern.

If this were a vein of silver that could be mined, then the Yaqui probably had a valid claim. However, large slabs of apparently pure, or nearly pure, virgin silver, lying loosely scattered about near the surface of the soil, did not sound like any vein that Anza had heard of. Could this be a hidden treasure, buried in the ground by some prehistoric people? The captain was aware that the rules concerning such treasures were different than mining laws. On the other hand, it almost sounded like someone had been conducting a clandestine mining and smelting operation. If this discovery had uncovered such illegal activity, then it would be necessary to search out and arrest the guilty parties involved in the scheme, close down their operation, and confiscate all of the silver for the king. If there were really as many people already at the discovery site as the courier had reported, searching and digging without legally notarized mining claims, then the task that lay ahead would be a difficult one. As he rode toward Chinapa that day, Don Juan formulated a plan of action.

That evening after his campaign tent had been pitched, he and the two officers of his asistencia, Corporals Francisco Xavier Escalante and Juan Antonio Ramírez, sat up by candlelight late into the night composing three letters. Escalante acted as scribe and wrote down the thoughts that Anza jointly formulated with him and Ramírez. When the writing was complete, Captain Anza signed each one and Escalante and Ramírez signed as witnesses. The next morning a soldier would be dispatched down the Sonora River on the fastest horse in their caballada. The letters would be delivered to the three Jesuit priests who were Sonora's leading authorities in matters of the law. The first would be delivered to Cristóbal de Cañas at Arizpe. The second would go to José Toral at Banámichi. The final letter would be taken farthest down the river to Juan de Echagoyen at Baviácora. The letters spoke of the unusual characteristics and unique circumstances of the silver discovery. Anza described what he planned to do in detail and requested any legal advice that the three fathers might be able to offer.

At the crack of dawn on Thursday the fifteenth, the designated courier sped down the Sonora River at a fast trot. Anza also dispatched a couple of soldiers to Fronteras with orders for more presidials to come immediately to Chinapa, prepared to travel with him to the Pimería Alta. Then, probably sensing the gravity and implications of the coming endeavor, he retired again to his tent with the two officers of his asistencia. There, as he waited for responses to his letters from the three Jesuit authorities, he began to compose the documents that would tell the story of one of the most unique silver discoveries in the history of North America.

By midday the messenger was at Arizpe and had delivered the letter to Father Cañas. As the courier hurried on down the river, the father began researching the authorities that he had on such matters. Although the missionaries often complained that their libraries were lacking in both number and quality of books,[29] the number of volumes that each mission library possessed is surprising. Father Cañas found in volume two of *Obras del Doctor Torresilla* that all of any treasure that might be found belonged to the king. He determined from law I, title 13 contained in book 6 of *La Recopilación de Indias* that for almost all nations of world, a treasure belonged to the king of whatever country it was found in. Before he went to bed that night, Father Cañas had formulated his thoughts and written and signed his response to Anza's letter. That same evening, the captain's courier caught up with Father Toral at Banámichi, and early the next morning he actually found Father Juan de Echagoyen north of Baviácora at Aconchi. Father Juan assured the messenger that he would have his reply ready to take back to Captain Anza the following morning.

Both Fathers Toral and Echagoyen worked on their responses throughout the day and into the evening of Friday the sixteenth. Father Toral consulted the *Escritos de Santo Tomás* and extracted pertinent information about treasures from the *Curso Moral*, volume III, treatise 12, chapter 2, and *Villalobos*, volume II, treatise 10. He also consulted *Cardinal Lugo* and *Diana*. Father Echagoyen, on the other hand, consulted Torresilla as Father Cañas had done. He went further, however, in quoting from *Padre Mendo* and showing how the *Curso Salmantino* allowed that a quarter of a treasure belonged to its finder in treatise 12, *Justicia y Ley*, section 3, number 98.

Once again, soon after dawn on Saturday the seventeenth, the official courier jogged his horse north out of Aconchi with Father Echagoyen's letter in his saddle pouch. At Banámichi he had just a few minutes' wait while Father Toral, grumbling that he was being rushed, hurriedly finished his written response and signed it. With that letter added to the pliego, the messenger hurried on north to Arizpe where he added the final letter from Father Cañas to his collection. By late afternoon he was at San José de Chinapa where Captain Anza had time to read and study the letters and give the order that all of his soldiers should be ready to move out in the morning after daylight Mass.

As Anza repeatedly read over the three letters that evening, he learned that Father Cañas thought he was right in thinking the discovery might be a treasure. The padre encouraged him to go see for himself. Father Echagoyen, on the other hand, felt that the pieces of silver that had been discovered were too big to be a treasure. He, like everyone who lived in Sonora in those years, was familiar with a legend that Montezuma had fled south toward Mexico City from this, the north country. Father Cañas had pointed out that the legend said the ancient Mexicans had buried much wealth as they escaped through Sonora and, that after a hundred years, ownership by those who originally possessed it was forfeited. Since it had been much more than a hundred years since Montezuma had taken his flight from the north, the silver now belonged to the king. Father Toral also thought that Montezuma had passed through the Pimería Alta on his way to Mexico. Although Father Echagoyen did not dispute the point and also pointed out that both Montezuma and Atabaliba had great quantities of silver, he felt that the pieces discovered in the Pimería Alta were much too big for any refining or transporting equipment that they might have had. Father Toral added weight to Echagoyen's argument when he pointed out that he had actually seen a piece of the silver that was brought to Tetuachi and traded to Agustín de Vildósola through his supply store there. That particular piece had some white pebbles in its interior, which seemed to give it the appearance of natural virgin silver.

Anza had said in his letter to the padres that he was of the opinion that Antonio Siraumea should receive a portion of each of the chunks of silver that had been discovered. Father Cañas argued, however, that in his opinion, giving the Yaqui some of each piece would be unjust since, if the silver was determined to be a treasure, a quarter of what Siraumea had found, at best, would belong to him as the finder. Father Toral, on the other hand, argued that the Indian had no rights whatsoever because he did not register his discovery as a mine. He did, however, urge extreme care on Anza's part in determining the rights issue, reminding him of the "stupid little dolt of Tubutama,"[30] who had discovered the piece of silver where the newly established realito of Oquitoa now was. He had shown it to a deceitful Indian and asked what it was. The Indian had told him it was nothing worthwhile and asked where he had found it. Then the scoundrel had gone to the site of the discovery and claimed it for himself as the first discoverer. In all, Captain Anza received arguments that went in all directions and provided a lot of legal jargon but no real answers to his dilemma. The concluding statement made by Father Echagoyen in his letter gives an idea of the superstitions and religious fervor of the era:

> Finally, an incident comes to my pen. Although it may cause you laughter, I have to mention it. Out of the balls and sheets of silver there may be some deceit of the devil and all the vapor [speculation] will stop like the coins of gold put in the path of the angel San Francisco in order to deceive him.... The devil can form apparent mountains of silver, and he can show very great treasures. For our well-being, we can fear from him and the witches of the Pimería some entanglement. In all, we must [rid] ourselves and much more of the devils who are great miners, as they also say (without reason) that the miners are some devils.[31]

Probably before he had ever received the letters from the Jesuit authorities, Juan Bautista de Anza had made up his mind that whether the discovery was a treasure, a clandestine mining operation, or simply a vein of silver, the king would receive tax monies from it. It was not the devil that Anza thought had placed the silver there:

> I believe (and there are plenty of discrete persons who agree with me) that the Most High Lord has permitted the discovery of the said balls and slabs to reimburse His Majesty for the endowment he made to the missions of the said Pimería,[32] for by this means the natives are saved and his power is extended to the gentility of the said unknown lands, and human means are necessary for this to happen.[33]

As soon as Mass was over in the little mission church at San José de Chinapa that Sunday morning, November 18, 1736, Anza and his soldiers mounted up for the long ride north and east to wherever it was they were going, for surely none of them had ever been there. Escalante and Ramírez, the two officers of Anza's asistencia, and probably as many as twenty other soldiers made up the expedition. They were leading a sizable pack string of mules and driving a substantial caballada of extra horses. After a grueling ride, they camped the night at Rancho Terrenate. The next morning they rode over the hill to Santa María Suamca and then on to Mission Guevavi. Whether they crossed over San Antonio Pass or followed the Santa Cruz River in its sweeping curve around through the San Luis Valley on their way to Guevavi, Anza stopped long enough at Santa Barbara to pick up his alférez in that region, José Romero. Forging on past the mission, the party camped Monday night at Anza's Guevavi Ranch. There, the captain asked his friend and foreman, Manuel José de Sosa, to accompany them to the discovery site to act as his scribe and witness.

On Tuesday morning the company, now having grown by at least two men and probably more, struck out through the rugged, unfamiliar country toward the site where Antonio de Siraumea had made his astounding discovery just a couple of weeks earlier. Although the going was difficult, the distance was relatively short and the party found itself in the midst of the frenzied silver rushers by midafternoon. Here was bedlam at its best. Camps and makeshift brush shelters were scattered everywhere. The hills on both sides of the ravine were scratched, plowed, and dug up as though ten thousand javalinas had come through rooting up agaves. There seemed to be no organization as to where anyone was digging or searching for more silver. Everything was in complete chaos. Captain Anza estimated that there were over two hundred people scratching and digging in the dirt. Santiago Ruiz de Ael, who had arrived several days before and by now had moved his headquarters down the canyon to Agua Caliente where he set up a store to sell supplies to the miners, estimated that there were more than four hundred people on the site.[34]

Anza called a halt and ordered his soldiers to set up camp. Those prospectors who stopped long enough to notice that the cavalry had arrived probably sensed that the free ride was over—and it truly was. Authority had arrived in the form of Captain Juan Bautista de Anza, and regulation was on its way. As soon as the captain's campaign tent was set up, he, Sosa, and others of his asistencia gathered inside. As Anza gave orders, soldiers scurried in and out of the tent. As he dictated, Sosa wrote down his every word. One of the first things Don Juan did was to give the site a name so they would not have to keep calling it "este puesto del descubrimiento de las bolas y planchas de plata virgen en el distrito de la Pimería Alta"—"this place of the discovery of the balls and slabs of virgin silver in the district of the Pimería Alta." The name the captain chose, not surprisingly, was that of his own patron saint, San Antonio de Padua.

The next thing that he did was to dictate an order to his deputy justicia mayor for the mining district of Agua Caliente. As soon as Sosa had written it down and it was properly signed, a soldier was dispatched with it to Urrea's house in Arizona. Don Bernardo received and read it that very evening:

Don Juan Bautista de Anza, Captain for Life of the Royal Presidio of Santa Rosa de Corodégauchi and Justicia Mayor of this Province of Sonora for His Majesty (may God guard him):

By the present [dispatch] I command and order that Don Bernardo de Urrea, my deputy of this jurisdiction, go to the house and residence of Antonio, the Indian of the Yaqui nation, and that he make a statement about the silver that he may have found in this place where various balls and sheets of virgin silver have been found. [Urrea is to take statements] as well from all other persons, whatever their class or condition. He shall notify them that they must make similar statements and that all the quantities [of silver] that are still here will be weighed in the presence of witnesses and will be given to [the deputy] himself, because it is known that the house of his residence is the safest in the realito he serves. He will give a receipt for what he receives to the persons who may make a statement and hand over [the silver]. They must hand it over precisely and punctually under penalty of the loss of their properties and corporal punishment, which the most Excellent Viceroy of this kingdom will impose, to whose judgment I leave it and to the Real Audiencia of the kingdom. Those who resist will be caught and held in security with guards at their own expense. It is necessary for me to make this provision in fulfillment of my obligation to His Majesty (may God guard him) in case the treasure belongs to him, as it is not of the nature of mines, which have not been found up to the present. The [portions] belonging to the finders [will be given] to them, being certain of the fairness of the ministers who will attend to it in the most judicial way. If some persons have dispatched some portions of the silver found in this jurisdiction, they will make a sworn report, as I have made clear.

If by the end of today or yesterday they have made a remittance, the said deputy will order that those portions be returned to the senders so they can be presented before me, bringing everything they may be carrying of this kind. He shall also declare that no one is to leave this camp and its jurisdiction under the same penalties. If the deputy had some portion of silver, he will report it with a sworn statement relative to this treasure, or discovery, so that all [the reports] will stay together. An account must be given with the fidelity to which he is obligated as a minister and vassal of His Majesty like all the rest of the persons who have an interest. This is written [at the place] of the discovery of balls and sheets of virgin silver, District of Pimería Alta, on November 20, 1736. I authorized it and signed with my assisting witnesses by the power that is conferred upon me, to which I attest.

Juan Bauptista de Anssa (rubric)
Pedro López de Zequeiros (rubric)
Manuel Joséph de Sossa (rubric)[35]

On Wednesday morning, November 21, Don Bernardo sent written acknowledgement of the order back up the canyon to Anza by the same courier that had brought him the dispatch. He then began taking depositions at Arizona and weighing silver at Agua Caliente. Captain Anza began taking depositions and examining discovery sites and chunks of silver at San Antonio de Padua. The first person that he called to his headquarters for interrogation was Francisco López, a resident of Nuestra Señora de Aranzazu de Tetuachi. After giving his oath to tell the truth, sealed by his giving the sign of the Holy Cross, Francisco told the captain that he had found a slab of silver the day before that weighed an arroba and five or six libras. He had uncovered it at the bottom of an arroyo, about eight or nine inches below the surface of the ground. He swore that he had seen only two other persons, Juan Carlos López and Antonio de Ocampo, find pieces of silver in the same vicinity. When his statement was complete, it was read to him and he was asked to sign it, but he did not know how to write.

While Francisco's deposition was in progress, a soldier had interrupted the proceedings to inform Captain Anza that Antonio Siraumea had arrived at San Antonio from his home at Agua Caliente. Anza immediately sent for him, and the Yaqui was waiting outside his tent door when the first interrogation was completed. Unfortunately, the illiterate Siraumea spoke no Spanish. An interpreter was sent for, and one of the soldiers quickly came back escorting one Ignacio Dominguez, a mestizo fluent in the Yaqui language. Although Dominguez was illiterate, Anza received his oath of good faith as an interpreter, and then proceeded to take Antonio's deposition. The captain found the Yaqui still angry about the slab of silver that Don Santiago had taken from him, and began to get the picture of how the silver discovery had taken place, including how the great rush of treasure seekers had overrun the area.

By the time Siraumea's deposition was complete, one of the cavalrymen had located José Fermín de Almazán and escorted him to Anza's campaign tent. Francisco López and Juan Chamorro were also waiting outside with pieces of silver they had found. Anza took sworn statements from Almazán and Chamorro and viewed the silver that López and Chamorro had brought to the tent. Almazán, however, did not have anything to show the captain because, as he testified, the slab he had discovered was much too large to move. Don Juan adjourned his court and he, Sosa, several soldiers, and a number of curious bystanders went with Almazán a short distance and over a hill from where the main prospecting activity was taking place.

There in an arroyo between two hills, Almazán showed Anza the incredible ton and a quarter slab of silver he had found, now chiseled into several huge chunks. Although no one knew at the time what its weight was, they estimated it fairly closely.

"I determined by its composition that it is virgin [silver] without any slag, and only where it was in contact with the soil is it seen to have any gravel," Anza dictated.[36]

In the afternoon, when the examination of the silver that Almazán had discovered was complete and all depositions were properly signed and notarized, Captain Anza and his party went up the same arroyo to the north. At a distance of about three musket shots, they visited the camp of José de Mesa and his party. There, Mesa showed him a "ball" of ore that Don Juan estimated to weigh about three arrobas. "It is composed of metal," Anza said, "interlaced with dirt and impurities in a class of rock that miners call slate."[37] The captain was evidently not impressed by it, especially after having seen the other samples of nearly pure silver. He gave no indication that he thought Mesa's piece of slate contained any silver. He did not impound it, and it never showed up on any of the lists of silver pieces compiled over the next several days.

By the time Anza was through with Mesa it was getting late in the afternoon. He retired to his tent to help Sosa in the compilation and completion of documents generated that day, and in the preparation of decrees and letters that would go out the next day. Early the next morning they finished up a letter to the three Jesuit priests, informing them of what had taken place thus far and requesting further advice.[38]

The captain was thoroughly confused at this point. If he determined the discovery to be a hidden treasure, he was undecided as to how to interpret the law concerning the king's portion thereof. Law number 2, title 12, in book 8, volume 3 of the *Recopilación de Indias* said that half of any treasure belonged to the king after one and a half percent had been taken out for the smelter. "I find myself perplexed," Anza wrote to the three padres, "as to whether I must regulate the present circumstances to enforce what is provided in the expressed law, or not, and if I should give half to those who found the slabs and balls of silver, as the ordinance mandates."[39]

When the letter to the padres was completed and duly signed in triplicate by Captain Anza and his asistencia, it was dispatched by soldier courier to the Sonora River valley. Then, Don Juan and Don Manuel went back inside the tent and finished formulating an official decree. While they were doing that, soldiers scurried about the prospectors' camps, informing everyone that Captain and Justicia Mayor Anza had ordered all—Spaniards, mestizos, and Indians—to appear at his tent that afternoon. When the appointed hour arrived, Captain Anza and escribano Sosa stepped outside with the completed decree, to face what seemed like several hundred grimy, callous miners. Anza read the decree in a loud voice as the prospectors listened intently:

> To proceed with accounting and so that His Majesty will not be deprived, I must order, and I do order, that all persons who discovered and found the said balls and slabs will appear before me and make a declaration concerning them, and put them on deposit. Also, all those who are found in possession of the silver will make the same declaration, whether it was through sale or gift that they came into possession of it, so that all may be accounted for. All those camped in and inhabiting this place will be made aware of that which I cite in this decree, which is that he who hides a treasure will lose what he found as well as half of his goods, because at no time can anyone claim ignorance. Those who might have left this jurisdiction with any part of the silver will be made to appear before me, or before my deputies, in order to make a declaration and hand it over, or declare to what person they gave it. All this will proceed under solemn oath.[40]

When Anza had finished reading the decree, he asked if all understood the implications of what they had just heard. After everyone's questions seemed to have been satisfactorily answered, he asked if they would comply with the order. All acknowledged that they would. Captain Anza spent the rest of the day taking depositions, viewing places where any metal ore had been found, and examining chunks and pieces of silver. He noted that any of the silver that had been melted appeared to have some carbons and charcoal in it.[41]

The next day, Friday, November 23, Bernardo de Urrea rode into camp with a packet of documents he and his escribano, José de Osorio, had compiled the day before in taking depositions and weighing and impounding the silver that had made its way to Agua Caliente. Captain Anza went over all the paperwork with Deputy Urrea, including Don Bernardo's own written statement concerning the silver that he had in his possession. That completed, the captain took his deputy's declaration, given under oath and sign of the Holy Cross.

On Saturday, Lorenzo Velasco showed up at San Antonio with a string of pack mules and a 200-pound piece of silver that he had evidently taken to Santa Ana. He told the captain that José Fermín de Almazán had told him that he was required to deposit it with the authorities. Anza would later comment that it was either out of simpleness or because Velasco thought that since the silver had metal impurities he did not have to show it, that he had not previously declared it. Velasco's signature shows him to have been very poorly educated, but simple he probably was not. When all was said and done, and the silver was returned to its finders, Lorenzo owned the entire piece that Almazán had found. With it, he converted his holdings at Santa Ana into what was probably the biggest and most dynamic ranching operation in all of Sonora. He and his wife, Sabina Moraga, would employ what was likely the largest workforce in the province.

Returning to the present situation, however, Friday afternoon, all of Saturday, and the next several days were all spent in spreading the word that since no one had filed a legal mining claim, they were all there illegally and they had one month to pack up their equipment and vacate the premises. Since no one knew the legalities of the discovery or what percentage of the silver belonged to the king, no one would be allowed back onto the site until after an official decision had been made in Mexico City. Then, all would get their just due. Legal mining claims would be allotted if the discovery were determined to be a mine. In the meantime, soldiers were placed around the perimeter of the camp to make certain that no one carried anything away that was not theirs, or silver that had not been declared.

Finally, the following Tuesday, November 27, Anza moved his camp fifteen miles down the canyon to Bernardo de Urrea's Arizona Ranch, leaving the majority of his soldiers to stand guard over San Antonio de Padua.[42] On Wednesday he went to Don Bernardo's house and spent the day examining, weighing, and documenting every piece of silver that had been impounded. The chunks were in many sizes and shapes and their containers were just as varied. Some were in buckskin pouches. The pieces owned by Alfonso de Ochoa were in a heavy leather tanate. Some of the pieces had been too heavy to weigh on Don Bernardo's scale. Captain Anza had evidently brought a larger scale and by means of a pole tripod, ropes, and Ochoa's tanate, they managed to hoist each piece high enough to get it accurately weighed.

Over the next two days the inventory continued. Through the graciousness of his deputy, Anza was able to move his command post out of his tent and into an actual house. Not only were living conditions less primitive, but the cooking was probably better, provided by Don Bernardo's wife, María Ana Gallardo. Besides, their six-week-old son, little Bernardo Gaspar, probably reminded the captain of his own small son, Juan Bautista, whom he had left at home several weeks before. It was a tense situation. The miners and merchants were not happy at having to forfeit their silver, and some of their grumblings had reached the ears of Don Juan. The decrees that he was about to send out would bring even more criticism. Visiting with his good friends in the evening, however, probably helped ease the tension. Certainly, in his spare moments when the captain had the opportunity to hold little Bernardo Gaspar, who had just been taken to San Ignacio the month before to be baptized,[43] he was able to forget the stressful business at hand.

To better determine what the chunks of silver were—if they had been smelted or if they were natural—Anza appointed two inspectors. First was his old friend, Francisco Xavier de Miranda. Then he appointed a local who lived at Arizona, Manuel Monroy. Miranda was a thirty-six-year-old militia captain. Monroy was a thirty-eight-year-old *platero*, or "silversmith," by profession.[44] After Captain Anza had administered an oath of honesty, the two men went diligently about taking samples and smelting them to determine their purity.

The work of smelting and documenting the results kept everyone busy through Friday. Anza still had to hear the dispute between Santiago Ruiz de Ael and Antonio Siraumea over the piece of silver that the Yaqui had carried home with him and that Don Santiago had confiscated in the name of his employee. On Saturday, December 1, Anza had both men escorted to Don Bernardo's house. He took Don Santiago's deposition first. Then he swore in the illiterate Alfonso de Ochoa as an interpreter and heard Siraumea's declaration. It may have looked suspicious to the captain, but the Yaqui told him, through the interpreter, that he had ceded all rights to that particular slab of silver to Don Santiago. Whatever the arrangement was, it would come back to haunt Anza in a soon-to-be-filed court case.

Don Santiago presented the captain with a written petition for the return of his silver, claiming that he had accepted it in good faith as payment for merchandise sold. Now the merchandise was gone and he had to pay some large bills incurred in order to transport food and supplies to San Antonio de Padua. Anza told him that he would take it under consideration.

December 2 was a Sunday and everyone must have rested—at least, there were no documents signed that day. Early the next morning, however, Anza received the final reports from Miranda and Monroy about their silver-smelting project. He issued an order to Urrea to return Don Santiago's silver, which Don Bernardo did later that afternoon. However, Anza included a strong stipulation that Don Santiago could not have it smelted or trade it in any way until a decision was handed down from Mexico City. The captain also issued orders to Don Bernardo placing him in charge of the silver and everything concerning it while it was at Arizona. Then he gave orders to the members of his entourage to mount up.

Just as Captain Anza was about to step up onto his horse, Francisco de Longoria came rushing up and handed him a petition signed by fifteen residents of Agua Caliente.[45] They, too, were requesting Anza to return the silver and lift the embargo. Anza told him that he did not have time to read it right then, as he was on his way back to San Antonio de Padua. He would take it under consideration, however, as "receiving judge" and would add it to the other documents being collected for his and the viceroy's and the higher court's consideration. Then he mounted his horse and he and his party rode back up the canyon to finish some final details at the site of the discovery.

Francisco Xavier de Miranda had ridden back up the canyon with the captain's entourage to test and smelt some of the silver that had been left there. Once on site, Anza appointed another old friend from the early days at Tetuachi and a fellow combatant in the struggle against Álvarez Tuñón to assist Miranda with the project. Andrés de Padilla received the oath of his commission from Anza "before God Our Lord and with the sign of the Holy Cross." While the two inspectors set about their business, the captain located José Fermín de Almazán. He and Almazán and a group of soldiers and prospectors went to the arroyo where the ton and a quarter slab of silver lay, now in several still unmanageable chunks. After much sweat, and hammering, chiseling, and sawing, the men turned it into numerous workable pieces. It was discovered while cutting the pieces that there was a narrow band of metal refuse in the very center of the huge slab. Anza sent orders for Miranda and Padilla to come sample a portion of it, and then placed the entire collection under guard.

While the two inspectors completed their assaying, Anza issued orders to a number of his soldiers to prepare to break camp in the morning. A majority of the detachment was told to stay where they were. They were to both guard the diggings and facilitate the removal of the last of the fortune seekers and prospectors. This latter group of soldiers would be under the command of Corporal Francisco Xavier Escalante, and he, in turn, would be under the command of Don Bernardo de Urrea. They would guard the place called San Antonio de Padua until such time as a large enough pack string would arrive to remove all the silver from both there and Arizona, and further orders could be issued.

Early on Tuesday morning, December 4, Capitán Vitalicio Juan Bautista de Anza, escribano Manuel José de Sosa, Alférez José Romero, Cabo Juan Antonio Ramírez, and a few others, including Anza's deputy justicia mayor for the district of Motepore, Andrés de Padilla, mounted up early and rode up and over the summit to the San Luis Valley.[46] Before they left, Captain Anza had given last-minute instructions to Corporal Escalante and the soldiers remaining behind with him. Upon arrival in the San Luis Valley, the party went directly to Diego Romero's Santa Barbara Ranch, where they set up camp.

The following morning, Anza and Sosa began drafting decrees, reports, and dispatches. They sent for more mules from Fronteras to help carry the enormous quantity of impounded silver back to the presidio where it could be kept in a safe place and guarded. Reports were dutifully written of everything that had taken place over the past couple of weeks. Nicolás Alfonso de Ochoa, who had homes at both Agua Caliente and San Ignacio, showed up with another piece of silver and a petition that he be allowed to keep it. More dispatches were sent to and received from the three Jesuit padres on the Sonora River.

Anza still did not know what to call the discovery: a natural silver deposit or a treasure that had been buried by some prehistoric people. Father Echagoyen had advised him that even though he personally thought it was a natural deposit, because it was so unique and did not fit any of the criteria for a mine, it would have to be called a treasure and belong to the king. At this point, it appears that the captain had ruled out the idea of a clandestine smelting operation. Regardless of how the silver got there, a myriad of laws governed its disposal and who had rights to any portion of it. While the silver was stored safely at the presidio, the captain would send samples of it along with all the documents he had been compiling, and would continue generating and collecting, to Mexico City for his superiors there to make a decision in the matter. Then, he would happily carry out their orders, whatever they might be.

On the thirteenth, another decree was written ordering merchants everywhere throughout Sonora to turn over any silver they had taken in trade that had originated at San Antonio de Padua. Anza duly signed numerous copies of it, with José Romero and Manuel José de Sosa as witnesses, and it was dispatched the next day to his deputy justicia mayores throughout Sonora. Deputy Andres de Padilla had already left Santa Barbara for his district of Motepore. His orders, and those for him to send on to Opodepe and San Juan Bautista, were included in the pliego to Agua Caliente. The following morning, Saturday, December 15, Deputy Bernardo de Urrea received the pliego at Arizona. He made the decree known to the miners at Agua Caliente and dispatched the other copies on to the various districts. Francisco Pérez Serrano, who was still at Arizona, was asked to deliver the decree to Tetuachi, but instead he wrote a strong protest requesting that the embargo be lifted and asked that this document be included with the pliego that Don Bernardo would send back to Anza.

Back in the San Luis Valley, Pérez Serrano's petition was not the only one that Anza received. The miners were getting more and more disgruntled, as they realized it might be months or even years before they would see any silver again. Although Nicolás Alfonso de Ochoa was illiterate, he found someone to write another petition for him, again requesting that the silver he had found be returned to him. Urrea included both his and Pérez Serrano's petitions in the next pliego of letters that he forwarded to Anza. Also in that pouch of letters, dated December 17 and 18, were assay reports from Manuel Cortés Monroy describing each of the samples that he had removed from the various chunks and slabs of silver. The captain had been waiting for these before he left to return home to Fronteras. If the officials in Mexico City were to make anything resembling an informed decision, they would need the minutest details of the silver content of the various pieces. Deputy Urrea personally delivered all this information, plus a report that he picked up from Corporal Escalante at San Antonio de Padua. He arrived at the Santa Barbara Ranch on the afternoon of December 19. Also included in the packet of letters that Don Bernardo delivered to Anza on that day was a petition and mining claim registration from Francisco de Longoria. He claimed to be concerned that the rush of undisciplined people at San Antonio de Padua had so defaced the slope where the silver had been found that it was becoming impossible for real miners to accomplish their work. Longoria was afraid that if the area were not mined properly it would be impossible to determine if there was a true vein of silver buried beneath the surface slabs. He claimed that sixty days had passed since the discovery of the first silver and, since no one had filed a legal mining claim, it was his right to do so. After all, he and a few others had continued to search, using proper mining techniques and with the permission of Captain Anza. He, therefore, filed the following claim: "By royal ordinance for the greater augmentation of the royal fifths of His Majesty, in his royal name and in the matter permitted, I register that depression and slope from the crest of the hill down to the arroyo, with no other intent than to be able to work it in the proper form and disposition for its best maintenance, and to survey its center to see if it might have a vein or veins that would produce gold or silver for the common good."[47]

At this late date, Anza simply added Longoria's petition to the already bulging bundle of documents that he was preparing to send to the viceroy, with the comment that he felt Longoria might have the right to such a claim, provided it did not interfere with the rights of the first discoverer, Antonio Siraumea. The pack mules had arrived from Fronteras and the arrieros had gone to Agua Caliente and San Antonio de Padua and removed all the silver to Anza's camp at Santa Barbara, under guard of a heavy contingent of soldiers. The letter that Don Bernardo delivered to Anza from Corporal Escalante informed the captain that, "no one is left on the hill that is called San Antonio de las Bolas y Planchas de Plata and no more silver is being found by anyone."[48] The "Holy Festival Days" were approaching, and Captain Anza wanted to be home with his family. He was also anxious to get reports compiled and sent off to the viceroy, the bishop, and others. So, he issued orders that evening to all those who were going with him to Fronteras to be ready to move out in the morning. He and escribano Sosa sat up late that night going over the final reports from Monroy and organizing all the documents into a package that would eventually travel to Mexico City.

Captain Anza reiterated his orders to Bernardo de Urrea to keep a tight seal on the hill called San Antonio. Manuel Monroy had also arrived at Santa Barbara that afternoon, and Don Bernardo received a final sworn declaration from him telling of the high percentage of pure silver contained in the slabs and chunks. Anza again spelled out his orders that no silver would be returned to anyone until the viceroy had made his decision, in spite of the fact that numerous people were clamoring for an end to the embargo. The preliminary plan was for Sosa to come to Fronteras after the first of the year where he would help Anza finish the final report and then travel to Mexico City with it and some samples of the silver. In the meantime, Christmas was approaching and everyone was eager to be home with their families.

Early the next morning, Saturday, December 20, 1736, the arrieros struggled to load the heavy and various-shaped slabs of silver, as well as all the tents, bedrolls, cooking pots, tools, and other paraphernalia that had accumulated over the last month and a half. Captain Anza and his trusted escribano, Manuel José de Sosa, said goodbye until after the holidays. Sosa mounted his horse and, with José Romero and a couple of other soldiers as escorts, rode down river to Guevavi. When the camp was fully broken down and packed, Anza and his soldiers formed an escort in front, behind, and on the sides of the long pack train and the caballada of extra horses and headed up river toward San Lázaro. Numerous members of the Romero family and their hired help—men, women, and children, with dogs barking—came out to wave goodbye to the departing cavalcade.

The Christmas holidays passed without incident and without being recorded, by Juan Bautista de Anza, at least. Although the silver discovery of the Pimería Alta was undoubtedly at the back of his mind the entire time, Captain Anza did not continue with the formal proceedings until after the first of the year. On the other hand, his deputy at Motepore, Andrés de Padilla was busy throughout the holidays taking depositions from merchants who had accepted silver from San Antonio de Padua in trade.[49] In fact, he completed and signed a lengthy report and declaration of intent on Christmas Eve, reporting that he had received Anza's decree from Don Bernardo and explaining how he intended to proceed in carrying out the order.

A couple of days after Christmas, he rode north to Nuestra Señora de Aránzazu de Tetuachi to obtain a statement from Sargento Mayor Vildósola. Don Agustín operated a large mercantile business at that real de minas. When Padilla arrived on the scene and read him the decree impounding all the silver generated at San Antonio de Padua, Vildósola quickly agreed to cooperate. His Basque clerk, Blas de Gortazar, who had recently arrived from Gipuzkoa, was assigned to make a complete inventory of all the silver that he had taken in trade. Juan Chamorro had traveled all the way to Tetuachi from Agua Caliente with some of the silver he had found, probably to pay Vildósola for part of an outstanding supply bill that he or his brother-in-law, José Caballero, had amassed. Likewise, José de Leiva, a poor lobo from the San Luis Valley, had come to Tetuachi to trade some silver he had acquired in Don Agustín's supply store. He actually liquidated his bill and Vildósola had given him some change. An Indian named Salvador, from the village of Sinoquipe, had also traded San Antonio silver to Vildósola at Tetuachi for some merchandise and cattle.

Even though Vildósola was allowed by Padilla to keep the silver he had taken in trade, he was barred from spending or smelting any of it until a final decision could be rendered in Mexico City. Unlike some of the other merchants who had the same embargo placed upon them, Don Agustín was not critical of Anza's methods in administering the unusual situation. He dictated a lengthy declaration, which Gortazar carefully recorded, commending Captain Anza for his handling of the situation: "Justicia Mayor and Captain for Life Don Juan Bautista de Anza is a person in whom abounds knowledge and experience, by which he knows what is conducive to the well-being of these provinces." [50]

Don Agustín's was certainly not the majority opinion among the merchants and miners of Sonora. In fact, he appears to have stood by himself in such thinking. Although ethnic unity can be seen among the Basques of Sonora in certain aspects of the San Antonio silver story, any solidarity there may have been vaporized over the prospect of losing the wealth that they had visualized. It only appears that those who were financially sound complained the least and those who were living hand to mouth cried the loudest. Don Agustín and Don Juan had been friends for years, and Don Agustín stood firmly behind the captain in all of his policies concerning the matter. On the other hand, Francisco Pérez Serrano, another Basque who had been with Don Juan from the earliest days at Tetuachi, disagreed with the captain and had voiced his opinion strongly from Agua Caliente: "What may seem reasonable to the justicia mayor is a great injustice to commerce and the common good." [51]

Pérez Serrano expressed his opinion freely in hopes that the higher authorities in Mexico City would quickly override the embargo put in place by Captain Anza. Nicolás Alfonso de Ochoa, another Basque vecino, presented his petitions in a similar fashion. Although neither man berated Anza, they begged the officials to veto his actions and return the silver to those who had found it. The fifteen miners of Agua Caliente, of whom half were Basque (Alfonso de Ochoa being one), respectfully disagreed with Anza's actions. They said they understood why the captain had done what he did, but pled for a swift return of the silver. The merchants of Motepore were not so understanding. Evidently taking a day off in celebration of the new year, which fell on Tuesday, Andrés de Padilla took depositions and impounded silver from the Motepore businessmen on December 31 and January 2. Then, on January 3, he recorded their irate petitions. Francisco Salmón gave an accounting of the silver that he had received on the last day of the year. Juan Chamorro and Salvador, the Indian from Sinoquipe, had also traded some of the silver from San Antonio with Salmón. He had also received some of the silver from an Indian of Cucurpe, whose name he did not know, and from Antonio Ocampo. On January 2, Padilla took statements and accountings from Pedro Camargo, Luis de Mendivil, and Santiago Ruiz de Ael, who, by this date was back at his home in Motepore. All three, of course, had traded in the silver from San Antonio de Padua. Mendivil was the only one of the group who was Basque, but he stood firmly with his fellow merchants in opposition to Anza's embargo. On Thursday, January 3, all four tradesmen of Motepore filed a lengthy, joint petition requesting that the embargo be swiftly lifted. Evidently unaware of what Captain Anza had been through in attempting to obtain interpretations of the law from the three Jesuit missionaries on the Sonora River, the four men were less than complimentary of his abilities: "Don Juan Bautista de Anza, captain for life for His Majesty in the royal presidio of this province and justicia mayor of the same, came to the said discovery site with zeal for His Majesty and formed the opinion that [the silver] belonged to His Majesty as a special thing, unheard of in this new world. Being unfamiliar with the royal laws of His Majesty (God keep him), and not being supported by any author, either ancient or modern, he seized through embargo the balls and pieces, both large and small, of the metal silver that had been found." [52]

Although Don Santiago was the most vocal, filing his own lengthy statement, he was careful how he worded his own petition. Having served for a number of years as an official of the Inquisition, he was well educated and wrote his complaints in such a way as to show himself in good light, while not necessarily ridiculing Captain Anza. He concluded: "If my petition is not granted, grave inconveniences to my business will result, which seems unjust to me. Indeed, I would be unable to supply, as I presently am, seven mine owners and their operations, four of whom also operate silver smelters." [53]

Don Santiago intended to go beyond a mere statement that might not be seen by officials in Mexico City for several months. He was in the process of filing a lawsuit to force the end of the embargo. In the meantime, however, he fully kept his bases covered with the statement he made to Padilla. He claimed to have, and probably did have, a greater interest in the San Antonio silver than any other merchant. It was he who had outfitted the enormous pack train with provisions that he sold to the miners at San Antonio, Agua Caliente, and Arizona. He had purchased goods from Francisco Salmón and had also traded with Miguel Martínez and Fathers Nicolás de Perera and Gaspar Stiger. Not only did he owe them money, but he had purchased 800 fanegas of wheat and corn from Lázaro de Verdugo in Culiacán in order to supply the miners at San Antonio de Padua. There were outstanding bills on both the grain and the freight charges for delivering it.

Beyond these expenses, Don Santiago had taken pity on Antonio Siraumea. He had brought the Yaqui and his family with him to Motepore, and was caring for them at his home until such time as Anza should lift the embargo. Antonio's wife was sick and in bed, and the poor Indian would go hungry if not for Don Santiago's charity. In fact, Don Santiago even arranged for Siraumea to dictate another statement, declaring his poverty and lack of understanding of Spanish law and his dire need to have his silver returned to prevent starvation. This time nobody bothered to point out who his translator was. Andrés de Padilla obediently accepted everyone's petitions and collected them into a pliego of documents, which he sent north to Anza at Fronteras on January 3.

Manuel José de Sosa arrived at Fronteras on Saturday afternoon, January 5, 1737, in company with Bernardo de Urrea and some others. The next day, Sunday, was set aside for attending Mass at the presidio chapel and visiting with old friends. Anza may have gone over some of the documents in the ever-growing pliego, but chances are that was reserved for the next day.

On Monday, January 7, Juan Bautista de Anza, his own mining foreman and cousin, Pedro Felipe de Anza, Manuel José de Sosa, and Don Bernardo busily set about organizing all the new documents and getting them in order to take to Mexico City. The first order of business for Captain Anza, however, was to dictate a letter to Bishop Crespo of Durango, to inform him of the happenings of the last couple of months. With his spiritual obligations out of the way, the next day was free for putting together the report for the viceroy and his advisers and court in Mexico City.

Bernardo de Urrea dictated and signed one last statement on January 8, giving an inventory of all the silver that he had personally impounded at Agua Caliente. Anza had respectfully read all the petitions and complaints that Padilla and Urrea had collected, and signed an affidavit certifying that he had received each one. Since he had read each of the requests asking for an end to the embargo, and undoubtedly was privy to much of the gossip as to who thought what about him and his decisions as justicia mayor, he sat down with Sosa and Cousin Pedro Felipe to construct a letter that would answer all the criticisms.

"I have been accused of conducting the said embargo incorrectly," he said, "which some have vocalized in obnoxious voices."[54] He then went on to answer each of the charges and objections that had been leveled against him, pointing out that he understood the miners' and merchants' plight. He had never said that the merchants had not traded in good faith, and he was fully aware that the articles traded would have been consumed or used, but since this was such an unusual occurrence, they would have to be patient. He praised Antonio Siraumea's piety and sympathized with his poverty. However, he was also well aware that Antonio earned a wage of 100 pesos per year, and had serious doubts that the Yaqui would starve. Whatever the outcome in Mexico City, Anza felt that Siraumea should be rewarded for being the person who made the discovery. At the very end of the document, Don Juan provided the reader with a fleeting glimpse of his own sensitive feelings concerning the controversy caused by his decision to impound the silver: "Permit me to offer these arguments for the counsel of the Most Excellent Viceroy and the Royal Lord Ministers so they might know what I have suffered from some people over the embargo that I have decreed, although some of it has come from interested persons, through their good courage and disposition, as can be inferred from their responses and allegations."[55]

When the six-folio document was complete, Captain Anza signed it with Manuel José de Sosa and Pedro de Anza as witnesses. Over the next five days, with the aid of his associates, the captain compiled a detailed list of all the silver, to whom it belonged, how much each piece weighed, the relative purity of each chunk, and whether it appeared smelted or natural. Anza also compiled his own two-folio opinion of how the silver should be distributed and to whom it should belong: "A greater profit for His Majesty and the common good is to be realized in this silver find. . . . What common good could there be if a particular person (who might even be from a foreign land) was to find one, two, four balls, or more, worth 100,000 or 200,000 pesos? By the same token, even three or four more, and they could be carried to their houses without anything belonging to anybody!"[56]

Anza then pointed out how much more good would come from the majority of the silver being placed in the king's coffers. "The king," he said, "pays a great deal from his treasury for missionaries and soldiers in this Province of Sonora, in that of Ostimuri, in the kingdoms of Nueva Vizcaya and Nuevo México, California, and Province of Sinaloa and Tarahumara."[57] Clearly, Anza felt that the people were reaping a great benefit from the services provided by the king, and that whatever this unusual find was called, the king should get the lion's share.

During this time, Anza also dictated and signed orders placing the care and safety of any future silver finds in the area of San Antonio de Padua "in the hands of Don Bernardo de Urrea, deputy of the jurisdiction of the Pimería,"[58] who left Fronteras on Friday morning to return to Arizona. Finally, on Sunday, January 13, the full and complete fourteen-folio report to Viceroy Juan Antonio de Vizarrón y Eguiarreta was completed and Anza signed it. The next day, Don Manuel José, in his meticulous and beautiful penmanship, completed another document that was just as long and detailed, requesting permission from the viceroy to lead an expedition of discovery to the north and west in search of other lands and a road to California. When it was complete, Anza also endorsed it with the signature of his full title of nobility and rubric.

Now all that was left to do was to bundle the entire pliego of documents, which by now was two inches thick, into a saddlebag, along with a couple of small samples of the silver to be taken to the bishop of Durango and the viceroy of Nueva España. Another bag would carry a change of shirt and socks, a small supply of dried meat, and probably a knife and cup. The idea was to travel light and fast. It was crucial to get this information to the viceroy and the high court quickly. Anza and Sosa spent the next several days making the preparations. Don Manuel José was the one chosen to make the delivery and present the case before the viceroy. He would go *corriendo la posta*, as he called it, or "riding relay" to get there as fast as possible.[59]

It was not until the middle of the week of January 20 that a small party of riders left Fronteras. The escribano, accompanied by Captain Anza, his cousin Pedro, and a few soldiers, rode out over the pass toward Arizpe and the Sonora River. Sosa's escort accompanied him only as far as Tetuachi, however. Anza still operated mines there and had business to tend to. The little company arrived there on January 26 in the afternoon. Captain Anza wrote one last note of explanation concerning the myriad of documents and included it with the full pliego.[60] The following day was Sunday and everyone spent it relaxing and visiting, but Monday morning they were all out at daylight, bidding farewell to Don Manuel José as he trotted away down the Sonora River on the best horse that the Caballería de las Fronteras could provide.

For Sosa it would be a long, grueling ride. For Anza, it would be a long, suspenseful wait, with a number of vecinos grumbling and grousing about him. Although he probably did not see it as an advantage, events in Sonora would soon preoccupy him with more pressing problems than the fantastic silver discovery at San Antonio de Padua.

### Agustín Aschuhuli

*Luego q$^e$ el referido Capitán Ansa llego a entender tan grill perturbaz" y sus motivos; sin otra escolta que la de 29 soldados y doze Paysanos armados gue le acompañaron se determino a emprehender el Sosiego de esta altelaz$^{on}$, y venciendo la larga distancia de 140 leguas gue havia de su estancia al expresado parage en 26 de Mayo logro apreender en el Pueblo de S.$^n$ Jph de los Guaymas a dho Aresibi ô May$^{mo}$ fingido — Juan Antonio Arzpo de Mexico (rúbrica)* ... As soon as the aforementioned Captain Anza became aware of the general disturbance and what motivated it, without any other escort than the twenty-two soldiers and twelve armed countrymen who accompanied him, he determined to undertake the pacification of this disturbance, and overcoming the long distance of 140 leagues from his ranch to the said place on May 26, he was able to apprehend the said false prophet, or mayordomo, in the village of San José de los Guaymas—Juan Antonio [de Vizarrón y Eguiarreta], Archbishop of Mexico (rubric)[61]

Early in March of 1737, soon after Manuel José de Sosa had arrived in Mexico City, Juan Bautista de Anza was at one of his ranches in the Santa Cruz River valley. He was probably there because Don Manuel José was in Mexico City and not taking care of business at home, operating the Anza ranches. While there, the captain received word of some kind of disturbance to the south in the Pimería Baja. He dispatched an officer to determine the seriousness of the problem and, after finishing up his business in the Pimería Alta, headed back to Fronteras. A letter that he wrote to Viceroy Juan Antonio de Vizarrón y Eguiarreta the following June is one of only two known first-person accounts of what took place next:

Most excellent Sir:

It has seemed fitting to me that I should bring to Your Excellency's attention one of the most extraordinary cases ever heard of in the kingdom, which has occurred in this vast Province of Sonora.

It began to be rumored last March in the country that is inhabited by the contiguous nations of the Guaymas and the Pimas Bajos that there had appeared a prophet of the God Montezuma, offering them many gifts. The natives were told by this Guayman Indian, who said he was Montezuma's mayordomo, or prophet, called *arebisi*[62] in their language, that they should assemble in his presence to receive the gifts. He went on to say that if they failed to do so they would experience great punishments, which he described. At this news they abandoned the villages in which they lived and the mining camps where some of them found employment and went to the place he indicated. It should be added, however, that tlatoles, or voices of caution, had come from here in the Pimería Alta.

In view of this I decided to send someone to both districts to observe their movements, and so I sent my alférez[63] to Pimería Baja, since Alta was quiet. A few days after his arrival, he advised me that the restlessness had settled down and that the Indians were back in their villages. He said that the Reverend Father Felipe Segesser, minister missionary from Tecoripa,[64] and my deputy justicia mayor, Don Francisco de Aldamiz,[65] had gone to visit them to impress upon them the bad thing they had done in deserting their villages and churches, and that, in all compassion, they were forgiven. And the padre preached and spoke on the matter and how it should be considered, and they assured both him and my alférez that they were disabused of the illusions that had deceived them.

It was all deception, however, because on the night of May 8 they once again deserted—with the exception here and there of an Indian or a village—men, women and children, with the elderly and the infirm carried on *tapestles*,[66] convinced that they would be healed. Others were persuaded that it was the will of the aresibi, and that if they disobeyed they would be turned to stone. This is according to an Indian who was taken prisoner.

It is admirable that in the hundred leagues between the villages and rancherías in which these two nations are situated, they should all leave at the same time, taking their horses, mules, cows, goats, and sheep as well as some that were scattered from the missions or belonged to some Spaniard.

This news was a source of consternation to this entire province and that of Ostimuri. Moreover, other tribes were responding positively to the appearance of the said Montezuma and I feared that they would follow the same course, resulting in a general uprising that might spread to other provinces and cause the loss of those tribes. I left this presidio without delay, as the situation required, to prevent such malicious consequences. I had twenty soldiers of my company and seven from Sinaloa, who were at the Seri frontier, and twelve well-armed vecinos financed by Sargento Mayor Don Agustín de Vildósola and other merchants who had some resources.

With such limited forces, not deeming it wise to excite the suspicions of the other tribes, I left by the route leading to where I had been told the gathering was to be, near the South Sea,[67] about 140 leagues[68] from the presidio in my charge. Passing by various Opata villages, having arrived at their watering place, I encountered some of the Indians of the conspiracy who presented themselves to me asking pardon for their desertion, protesting that they had been deceived by the illusions engendered in them by the aresibi. At the same time, however, others declared that the day of San Juan had been cited for additional acts of trepidation (by the Indians). Since others had made the same declarations earlier, I doubted the veracity of their repentance and believed they were moved by their own desires, for since they knew of his deception, why had they not arrested him? They replied that it was because of fear of the Indians he still had in his assemblage. I also came to understand that he had plans to come here to Pimería Alta to spread his doctrine.

I continued the march, and along the way I received news that the aresibi himself was to pass by a certain camp on that same day, May 28. At that notice I dispatched twenty-five soldiers, leaving the rest of the people and the supplies in the charge of my alférez. I quickly set out in his pursuit and came across his trail about four in the afternoon. From the tracks I determined that he was riding a mule and driving some cows, accompanied by three riders on horseback. We were able to follow the tracks until ten o'clock in the evening, at which time we lost them when they took to rough terrain.

The next day I returned to find the tracks again. I followed them, and at half a league from the village of San José de Guaymas, the native governor there came out to meet me. We greeted each other, and I asked where I might find the aresibi, or mayordomo, who claimed to be from Montezuma. He answered that he was there in the village. Having been notified the day before by two Indians that I was asking for him, the governor persuaded him to wait for me. I went to look for him, and in fact found him in a room, conversing with Andrés of the Pima nation, captain of Belen. Upon determining that he was the same person who had caused so much commotion, I had him made prisoner, since the said governor, who should have been in charge, had not done so. The governor excused himself by saying that he was afraid. I suspected that he and the other Guayman Indians, confronted by such arms, had counseled him and persuaded him to wait for me, all in accord with the will of the Lord our God.

Statements of various persons regarding the affair were taken while we were on the march. All witnesses declared that he sent out collectors, and that he spoke in person to the Pima and Guayman Indians, intimating that he was emissary of the god Montezuma who had created the sky, earth, and water and all the things therein. He told them that they should come into his presence on the day he indicated in the place he had prepared ahead of time, and that all who failed to believe would be turned to stone, as I have said. He said that the world was thin as paper and would end soon. In the new world that Montezuma would make, the Indian dead would be resurrected as Spaniards and the latter as Indians to serve them. The food and raiment that he would give them would be sweet and fragrant. The two nations gave such credence to these and other illusions that, if one had not witnessed it, it would be hard to believe.

He placed his throne near the water flowing into the sea. There was a house made of straw mats, and inside was a figure, or idol, which he said was the God Montezuma. He issued a ban against entry by either humans or animals on pain of death and ordered that any who entered should be killed with arrows. The only persons he permitted to dwell therein were six unmarried girls of from fourteen to sixteen years of age, the prettiest ones in the assembly that I knew of. Four to five thousand persons of both nations were congregated there. He opened the curtain in front of the door and displayed the figure, which they viewed by moonlight, since he never showed it by day. It was dressed in black with a surplice of white cloth, and on its head was a miter or bonnet. He repeated to them that this was their god who would give them the promised gifts, etc. He also assured them that they had no need to fear the soldiers, because even they would be turned to stone, the same as all those who failed to believe in him. All were required to kneel before him, at the sound of a little bell, and recite some of the prayers of our Holy Mother and Church. The Indian women especially offered him their rosaries and medallions and anything of value. The Indian men willingly sacrificed their cows and smaller livestock for those in attendance, as well as for the prophet, who made them believe that the idol also ate, using the ruse of putting the dishes in a hole and burying what was brought in them.

There was abundant music, composed of harps, guitars, and violins, along with a lot of fireworks and dancing, which made it festive. This went on for several days. On one of those days, two mestizos arrived, sent by my deputy from the mining camp of Aguaje with some collections, and to observe the disturbance. They were respected by the Indians, as was another coyote of the same nation, who had good references and was sent as well by Deputy Aldamiz and his father minister, the aforementioned Father Felipe [Segesser]. At the same time, these three pretended to go along with the act and knelt down before the idol, excusing themselves for doing so for fear of being killed. Other Indians have confirmed this and added that the mayordomo gave the idol tobacco cigars. From the smoke that was emitted, it appeared to be smoking them. He gave some of these same cigars to the Indians who took turns taking a draw and then returning to the feet of the idol, which was on a chair decorated with ornaments taken from the sacristy of Belen. These acts continued until eleven or twelve o'clock at night. During the day the mayordomo gave out gifts, pretending that they came from Montezuma, and at the conclusion they seemed to disappear without being touched by human hand. They told an infinite number of similar tales, but those related here are the substance of the matter.

I went to hear his confession, asking him the necessary questions to determine the sentence. He openly acknowledged having stirred up the two nations and confessed to almost all that I have recounted here. He used as his excuse that the Devil ordered him to do it, and he obeyed. He admitted that he now knew the God whom he had assured the people was the creator of all things, which is what he took him for, was really a demon, since he had not made good on his promises. I ordered him to tell me where he kept the idol he showed to the Indians, and the applicable gifts. He answered that they had disappeared, a position that he maintained for some time. Knowing of his maliciousness I gave him a few blows with my cane to get him to confess. He indicated where they would be found and I actually obtained them there. The house of the Devil was there. He had [the idol] in a little basket, wrapped in cotton. The rosaries and crucifixes and other jewels with which they had endowed him were in a large basket.

I determined to bring him to justice in consequence of the grave offense he had committed; the adoration he had caused in the people for the figure, or idol; the damnable sect he had tried to introduce, mixed with some of the things of our Holy Religion; the damage he had caused and could cause in the future if he continued to live, in effecting the perdition, not only of the two nations, but of others of this province. I put [the punishment] into effect, having first administered the sacrament of penance, on the first day of this month[69] in the aforementioned village of Guaymas, where I had him hanged from a tall palm tree.[70] It was remarkable that until he breathed his last the Indians were half-expecting him to turn us to stone or bring the world to an end by means of his false God. They even asked me to take him to a Spanish community to have him executed, but I did not consent to the request. I wanted to make a present example of him, whereby they might be undeceived by the illusions that he instilled in them, and so that no supporter of his should rise up and claim that he was still alive in the presence of the God Montezuma, like the false Prophet Mohammed. I did other material acts in the presence of the Indians so that they would remain undeceived, and apparently they were successful. The said aresibi, named Agustín Aschuhuli,[71] was apparently about forty-five years of age.

Finished with this task, I went to several Indian villages that had been deserted but were now the most crowded. People were lying in the open where some, unfortunately, were dying, having contracted smallpox and other infirmities. They confessed that a great part of this severe calamity was the result of their own foolishness for having believed such an evil Indian. [I am convinced] that if he had lived, he perhaps would have made them believe that they would shortly be resuscitated. I also would conjecture that, having persuaded the Indians to desert their villages to rob them, he became fearful of punishment and instigated the uprising.

I called together all the other native officers of the deserted villages, and many other Indians who were in Tecoripa for the feast of Pentecost.[72] There the said father missionary, after they made the act of contrition, absolved them and performed the function of burning the idol and all the gifts they had offered to it. At the conclusion of this fervent ceremony, I entered and administered the penance of lashes, to which they willingly volunteered their backs—men, women, and children—confessing that they deserved even greater punishment for their folly, and rendered me thanks.

I recall having pointed out to Your Excellency in a consultation that the Indians of these districts await the coming of their Montezuma. This has been verified. Perhaps the disenchantment of this episode, seen firsthand by some and heard about by others, will serve as a powerful antidote for their belief in these demonic illusions and their ministers, the *hechiceros*,[73] and cause them to give credence to the Catholic doctrine that the missionaries preach to them.

For my part, I am going to enlighten the other nations that inhabit this province regarding these happenings. Presently, here in the Pimería Alta, I am attending to the business of both Majesties. May Divine guidance guard the important life of Your Excellency for the many years that the kingdom will need you for its greater glory.

Pimería Alta, June 25, 1737. Most Illustrious and Excellent Lord, your most humble servant is at the feet of Your Excellency.

Juan Bauptista de Anssa (rubric)[74]

So, the disturbance was over. Anza most likely headed back home to Fronteras from Tecoripa. After only a brief stay at the presidio, however, he made another trip to the Pimería Alta, from where he wrote the foregoing account. He probably went there to make a general inspection of the region, as well as to check up on his ranches. It was now nearing the end of June. The viceroy had made his decision in Mexico City concerning what should be done about San Antonio de Padua and its silver. Manuel José de Sosa had been paid for his services a couple of weeks before[75] and was now riding north, on his way home after nearly three and a half months in the bustling city. It would still be three weeks, however, before he would arrive at Fronteras, when Captain Anza would hear the results of what had taken place in Mexico City.

## The Petition

*El Alcalde Ma.*[or] *Probisto por su Magestad D. fran.*[co] *de Garrastegui me âvisa delos Comfines dela Prov.*[a] *q ba êntrando en ella y q Viene cometido âmi por la Real Audiencia de Guadalajara y êl Govierno* — *Juan Bauptista de Anssa (rúbrica)* . . . Don Francisco de Garrastegui, the alcalde mayor appointed by His Majesty, informs me from the border area of the province that he is exploring it and comes to me by order of the Royal Court of Guadalajara and the government — Juan Bautista de Anza (rubric)[76]

One of the letters that had been carried south by Manuel José de Sosa for review by Viceroy Vizarrón was a nine-folio petition from Juan Bautista de Anza to be granted the commission to explore the country between Sonora and California.[77] The discovery of the silver at San Antonio de Padua had proven a theory held by many Sonorans that there was vast mineral wealth in the province and the unexplored lands to the north — in their minds, at least — wealth that was just waiting to be discovered. The latest and last alcalde mayor of Sonora, a Basque by the name of Don Francisco de Garrastegui,[78] who lived at Motepore, had informed Anza that it was his right under the law, as justicia mayor, to go in search of that vast wealth and had commissioned him to do so, pending the viceroy's approval.

Sonorans were confident not only that there was great mineral wealth in the land beyond the borders, but that many and diverse tribes of native peoples lived in its vast expense. Jesuit Father Kino, on several *entradas*, had visited the seemingly endless, unmapped terrain to the north and west some thirty years previously. Each time, he had returned with glowing stories of docile indigenous farmers living on the banks of the Gila and Colorado Rivers. He had also crossed the Colorado River and proven once and for all that California was not an island, but a peninsula. However, not everyone had felt Kino's report was sound — perhaps weeks in the hot desert sun had disoriented him. Loyal and supportive to his superior in every other way, Father Campos for one had not believed that Kino had truly crossed the Colorado and stepped into California. Having never known Kino personally, Juan Bautista de Anza likely followed the lead of his good friend Campos. "It is thought that California is probably an island," he had dictated to his escribano, Manuel José de Sosa, as they were compiling the petition to the viceroy for Anza to sign.

It really did not matter, however, because the point was that an extremely unusual and wealthy silver strike had been made on the farthest outer limit of Sonora. Truly, there must be even greater wealth further to the interior and, certainly, there would be new indigenous peoples to bring to a knowledge of the Spaniards' "true" God.

In his attempt to convince the viceroy to authorize and fund the commission granted by Alcalde Mayor Garrastegui to explore into the unknown, Anza spoke of gold, silver, pearls, and even quick silver that had been found in Sonora and at the "South Sea." He reminded the viceroy that he had personally met with Father Visitor José de Echevarria, a fellow vizcaíno, at the padre's request, to compile accounts of others that had explored or seen parts of the vast terrain. The captain spoke of Juan de Oñate, Francisco Vásquez de Coronado, Andrés de Medina Davila, the marqués de Manziera, Miguel Delgado, Father Kino, and Juan Mateo Manje. Had not their explorations and reports shown the need for a much more thorough and comprehensive penetration into the wilderness beyond Sonora? Although he was extremely busy in his duties of protecting, monitoring, and judging the frontier, Anza offered his services for the cause:

> It is certain, Sir, that no presidio of those in the kingdom has to attend to more than does this one in my charge, since it is located in the harshest country, because it is on the frontier, and of all those in this province, it [is] at more risk than the others from the enemy Apaches. Some soldiers of the Presidio of Sinaloa and of my company are on guard watching the Seri on their frontier, as well as attending to the Indians of the Pima nation. Although [the Pima are] of good disposition, because of the Holy Gospel having been introduced, the enemy of the human race has caused some disturbances, but they can be quieted with some ease. I have no misgivings about them, as in general [the Pimas] are obedient and, finally, are tillers of the soil, which does much for tranquility.
>
> These inconveniences, which are evident, could be obstacles for me not to present any project for the discovery of new lands and nations. But, Excellent Sir, a compulsion that I cannot reject moves me to the contrary and to a battle to which God Our Lord orders me. I protest before [the Lord] that I have no interest in human conveniences or ambition to do it for myself. There are others with more efficiency and endurance who can achieve what I am certain will yield to the service of both Majesties. I am aware that many projects proposed in preceding years (and with much ardor) have not been effective because of the difficulties experienced in practice, in various judgments and cases, and that much money has been spent in order to begin. And here begins mine—to dis-

cover [the land] as far as the Colorado River and to go some leagues into the interior. [This project] cannot cost much.

These [expenses] could be achieved by some pious persons here. I shall help with some cattle, horses, mules, and little gifts for the Indians. The greatest difficulty is to make two canoes in order to cross [the Colorado River] (as well as the Gila), which has abundant water. This plan would be aided by taking two or three carpenters, as there cannot be a lack of thick trees. The nations on its banks and other places will understand if they are fertile and the conveniences that they offer. And, with the truthful report that will be taken [to Mexico City], notice will be given to His Majesty. [If it is agreed] that some town is to be built on the Colorado River, it will be a step toward facilitating the discovery of the Seven Cities, the Gran Teguayo, and Quivira[79] and [exploiting] the wealth it can have in it and [what is] on the land (if what the reports say is true) and if there is an exit to the Sea of the North. And, most necessary of all, is the chance to secure the salvation of souls, which ought to be the principal object. The first activity can be pursued with fifty or sixty men at arms, which has been offered, and a hundred friendly Pimas, detaching a small squadron of soldiers of the company in my charge. And some other people [could be] collected from other places. The Jesuit fathers would be pleased to be ready, something all those who are in the missions of this province want very much, as [they are] zealous of the good of souls and of the service of our King and Lord.[80]

It was always a great honor, and possibly a path to prestige, political importance, and wealth, to be designated *adelantado*, the leader of an exploratory expedition into new and uncharted lands. Now that a concrete reason for further exploration to the north and west could be advanced, it was not only Juan Bautista de Anza who was interested in being commissioned to lead such an expedition. José de Mesa, a resident of Los Ángeles on the San Miguel River in the Pimería Baja, filed suit against Francisco de Garrastegui before the Real Audiencia de Guadalajara.[81] The suit sought first to block the commission of Juan Bautista de Anza to lead an expedition of exploration and instead grant that right to Mesa. Secondly: "The writing and resolutions presented by Don José de Mesa, in his name and in that of Don Francisco de Longoria, as empowered by the Province of Sonora, say that the powers that are provided are given by the citizens of that province only for the purpose of having recourse to the Real Audiencia de Guadalajara against Don Francisco de Garrastegui, the designated alcalde mayor of the Province of Sonora, in order to suspend him from the possession of his employment."[82]

If Mesa could force the removal of Garrastegui from office, it would nullify the alcalde mayor's approval of Anza to lead the expedition. Although Longoria, and the other unseen and unheard "citizens," seem to have been involved in the case in name only, it is interesting that the conflict, on paper at least, was between four

Basques: Anza, Garrastegui, Mesa, and Longoria. The Real Audiencia examined the evidence of the case that summer of 1737. Mesa presented written evidence of his long service to the king as a citizen of Sonora, and of numerous battles he had fought against the Seri and Apache in defending the Spanish settlements in the south. It was he who discovered the silver at San Antonio, he maintained. All this, he felt, qualified him to advance the frontier into unknown lands.

The Real Audiencia, under mandate by the fiscal, or state attorney, also ordered depositions be taken from three of the Sonora residents. When the court received all of the paperwork, they apparently were not overly impressed. They found that all the documents, so meticulously collected by Anza and Sosa, were in order and told a very different story than Mesa was attempting to present. His witnesses had "made deposition of inference, credulity, and vague hearsay,"[83] according to Fiscal Ambrosio Melgarejo in Mexico City. Melgarejo further found that

> Concerning the claim of Don José de Mesa that there should be conferred on him the position of captain, notwithstanding the instruments he presents, one perceives that he, on occasion, had aided in the defense of that land. There is no record that he has any military rank that would justify conferring on him the position of captain at this time. The principal merit he alleges is being the discoverer of the silver that was found in the Pimería. This is contrary to what is recorded in the principal decrees, in which it is patent that the first discoverer was an Indian of the Yaqui nation named Antonio Siraumea. The most that the witnesses provided by Mesa proved was that he was one of many who went to seek silver after it was discovered by the Indian.[84]

Most likely, Captain Anza was oblivious to all of this as he scurried about Sonora that summer, taking care of his myriad of duties as commander of the troops in Sonora and justicia mayor of the same. He was probably aware that Mesa had opened the litigation but likely was not concerned. He had been acquainted with Mesa for many years and knew that he had never done anything to warrant being commissioned to execute such an undertaking. Besides, if Anza truly had no "ambition to do it for myself," as he is quoted as saying above, then it really did not matter who led the expedition. The important thing was that the job get done.

José de Mesa, of course, lost his bid to be commissioned a captain and lead an expedition into the vast wilderness beyond Sonora. Fiscal Melgarejo ordered further study into Captain Anza's proposal. Several things would come up over the next several years, however, that would preclude the expedition actually being mounted. To begin with, Anza, in carrying out the orders he was about to receive from the viceroy concerning the disposition of the impounded silver, would invoke the ire of fiscal Melgarejo, causing an almost certain delay in an already slow process. Even without that impediment, however, the viceroy would be gone and Anza would be dead before the slowly grinding government wheels would crank out a decision.

The verdict would come nearly forty years later. It would be a favorable resolution for Captain Juan Bautista de Anza, but not the present one. A different viceroy would make the decision, in a different generation and in a different political climate. The commission would be granted to explore beyond Sonora into California, but it would be conferred on the Juan Bautista de Anza who was presently one year old.

## Return to San Antonio de Padua

*Ordeno al referido cap.ⁿ D.ⁿ Juan Bap.ᵗᵃ de Ansa pace luego con los mineros mas expertos de aguellas sercanias gue sean de su m.ᵒʳ satisfas.ⁿ â reconocer el panino y qualidad de tierra de la cañada donde se hallaron las platas y de sus contiguos — Juan Antonio Arzpô de Mexico (rúbrica)* . . . I order the said captain, Don Juan Bautista de Anza, to immediately go survey the makeup and quality of the land in the canyon where the silver was found, and the surrounding countryside, with miners whom he is fully satisfied are the most expert of those regions—Juan Antonio [de Vizarrón y Eguiarreta], Archbishop of Mexico (rubric)[85]

Juan Bautista de Anza, returning from the Pimería Alta, and Manuel José de Sosa, returning from Mexico City, arrived at the Presidio of Fronteras about the same time, the second week of July 1737. Sosa was carrying orders from the viceroy, signed on June 8, telling Anza to return to the site of the fabulous silver discovery with the most knowledgeable miners of Sonora, and to determine with them, once and for all, whether the silver had come from a natural vein, or if it was a hidden treasure.[86] While Anza had been busily engaged in preventing a general uprising in the Pimería Baja, Sosa had spent a long, tiring, and tedious spring in Mexico City, waiting for the viceroy and his councillors to come to a final decision in the matter of the "bolas y planchas de plata."

It was an age-old case of hurry up and wait. Don Manuel José had left Tetuachi early on the morning of January 28. He had ridden hard for twenty-six days straight, changing horses at mail stations all along the way, and had arrived in Mexico City on Friday afternoon, February 22.[87] With a distance between Tetuachi and Mexico City of just over 1,300 miles, that was an average of fifty miles per day— an accomplishment that took place 123 years before the establishment of the Pony Express![88] Upon arrival in Mexico City, however, he had to wait for over three months for Viceroy Vizarrón's final decision so he could turn around and "run the post" all the way back to Fronteras.

Sosa had presented the documents and samples of the silver at the viceroy's office shortly after his arrival in Mexico City. There, the entire packet was turned over to

Fiscal Licenciado Ambrosio Melgarejo on March 2. Melgarejo had his assessment of the situation to the viceroy in eighteen days.[89]

The licenciado was of the opinion that a sample taken from the Almazán slab was not from a vein. In his opinion, the silver had been smelted or had been beaten by hammers "as the ancient Mexicans were known to have done." He was "persuaded by the ancient tradition" of the passage of the Mexicans through that area and of their "marvelous wealth and art for working large pieces of silver." He deduced that God, as the natural creator, could not have formed the slabs of silver in the place where they were found. Since there were no known "producing mines in the Pimería Alta," he was of the opinion that the silver was an ancient treasure and, therefore, the king should get it all.

In considering whether Antonio Siraumea should get some of the silver as a reward for discovering it, Melgarejo quoted law stating that the finder was obligated to report his discovery to a justicia. Failing to do that, the discoverer lost his rights. The fiscal was not impressed by the Yaqui's plea for recompense due to his abject poverty. After all, he had spent six arrobas (150 pounds) of the silver without having filed the required report with the justicia. The licenciado suggested that Siraumea should "consider himself sufficiently thanked" by being allowed to have used that much of the silver, not to mention the pardon he was granted for not having filed the said report. Licenciado Melgarejo did find extenuating circumstances for Siraumea and the other miners and prospectors of Sonora through a classic, and seemingly timeless, statement about adherence to the law: "Although ignorance is not an excuse according to one canonic rule and other civil laws, this manifestly has an exception for the stupid, those under age, and others who, through the weakness of their abilities or by the impediment of their profession, are worthy of being excused for ignorance of the laws, mainly because the number [of laws] has so increased that it appears impossible to know them all, and no one is obligated to do the impossible!"[90]

In the end, the fiscal seemed rather unsympathetic to the needs and pleas of the poor people of Sonora. Although he granted that the merchants had acted in good faith, it was his opinion that "because of all that, Your Excellency would do well to declare that the said silver belongs and pertains entirely to His Majesty, ordering that it be sent by the said captain, with the greatest haste and by whatever means is most convenient, to the Royal Silver Bank of this court so that the large slabs can be sent as they are to Spain, because of the peculiarity of their size and quality."[91]

As soon as the viceroy had read Melgarejo's opinion, he forwarded it on to the Real Acuerdo, a cabinet of six legal advisers. When they had had sufficient time to form an opinion, one concluded that the silver came from a "very rich mine" and should be treated as such. The other five were of the opinion that it was from a mine, or vein, but that further study was needed to be certain.

During this time, Diego Gonzales de la Cueva, chief assayer of Nueva España and weigh master of the Royal Silver Bank, was assaying the samples of silver that Sosa had carried with him. His findings were anything but conclusive. He determined that silver from the Almazán slab had been smelted by human hands and that it was a hidden treasure. On the other hand, samples from the smaller chunks, he determined, were created naturally in a vein in the earth.

Once he had everyone's opinions in hand, Viceroy Vizarrón quickly made his decision. In keeping with the majority opinion of his Real Acuerdo, he dictated orders to Captain Anza to take the most knowledgeable silver mining experts of Sonora back to the discovery site at San Antonio. There, they were to determine for certain if the silver was from a natural vein or if it was truly a hidden treasure. The orders were signed by the viceroy on June 8, 1737. How soon after that Sosa left with the dispatch is unknown. Nor did he record how quickly he made the trip back north to Fronteras. The only thing known for certain is that he wrote a letter on July 19, which he and Francisco Xavier Moraga signed as witnesses with Captain Anza, acknowledging Anza's receipt of the viceroy's orders. However, Anza informed Vizarrón that since all the expert miners of Sonora lived at least fifty or sixty leagues from San Antonio de Padua, it would be the sixth or eighth of August before he could accomplish the task.

Letters had already been sent to five of Sonora's top silver miners, ordering them, by virtue of the viceroy's mandate, to meet Anza, probably at Santa Barbara or Guevavi, to go with him to San Antonio to make the determination. Don Francisco Xavier Miranda was a thirty-six-year-old militia captain and alguacil mayor of the Santo Tribunal. Don Andrés Sanchez Padilla was a sixty-four-year-old miner who had been associated with Captain Anza for more than fifteen years. Don José Nuñez was a forty-four-year-old miner. Don José de Usarraga was fifty years old, a miner, and a militia alférez. Ignacio Sambrano was very knowledgeable in mining and was also about fifty years old. Anza at this time was forty-four years old.

True to his word, Captain Anza had them all congregated on the hill at San Antonio de Padua early on the morning of Thursday, August 8, 1737. Anza's escribano, Manuel José de Sosa, one of the officers of his asistencia, Francisco Xavier Moraga, and his deputy justicia mayor for the San Luis Valley, fellow Basque José de Olave, were also there. There were likely another half-dozen to a dozen soldiers with them. The party had most likely gathered at the San Luis Valley on August 6 and then ridden over the mountain to San Antonio and camped there on the evening of August 7, because early on the morning of the eighth, the mining experts were surveying and analyzing the discovery site. Captain Anza and his soldiers began a systematic reconnaissance of the surrounding hills, valleys, and arroyos.

The process took four days. Anza and his men scoured the countryside from Arizona to the San Luis Valley. They found no tracks or evidence anywhere that indicated the existence of a clandestine mining and smelting operation. Anza interviewed the native Pimas of Saric and other rancherías downstream from Agua Caliente and Arizona. They denied any knowledge of activity in the area, claiming that they never went there due to its being too rugged and infested with Apaches.

Back at San Antonio on Monday, August 12, Captain Anza and his trusted escribano, Sosa, took separate statements from the five experts who had also completed their investigation. Miranda felt that the silver was not a treasure, but was ore, produced in ten or twelve veins. Padilla, who had stated the winter before that he thought the silver was a treasure, now did an about-face and certified that it was natural ore. Nuñez agreed that it was ore from several simple veins. Usarraga seemed to think there was no question that it was ore and not a treasure. Finally, Sambrano also agreed that it was ore, created naturally from several veins.

Being a typical military man, Anza never once mentioned his personal feelings about the findings of the five mining experts. Considering the fact that he had so wanted to see the majority of the silver go to the king's coffers, their decision must have come as a great blow to him, since the silver would now have to be given back to the original finders. However, there is much room for speculation about the decision. Anza and Padilla, at least, had previously been very vocal in their opinion that the silver was a treasure. Now, for some reason, they had changed their minds. Were the mining experts truly in opposition to Anza's thinking in the matter? Had Anza acquiesced to pressure and criticism from such men as Santiago Ruiz de Ael and Nicolás Alfonso de Ochoa? Were Anza and the experts in conspiracy to return the silver to the original finders that it might be exploited in some way? Had the experts really discovered anything new to indicate there was truly a vein of silver anywhere in the area? Was everything truly aboveboard? All such questions will probably remain forever unanswered. They baffled the minds of interested parties in Anza's time and have continued to do so ever since.

Regardless, the following day, August 13, Anza and Sosa completed a statement showing there was no evidence that any illegal mining or smelting had taken place in the vicinity. Then, with that document and the statements from the mining experts in hand, they and most of the others in the party rode down the canyon to Agua Caliente. They set up camp at the real de minas where, on Wednesday, Captain Anza and escribano Sosa again began producing decrees. Since the five inspectors had found the silver not to be a treasure, Anza put everyone on notice that he would comply with his orders and return the impounded silver to its finders. There had been many expenses incurred, however, for which everyone would be taxed accordingly and, of course, the king's fifth would be subtracted from the total weight of each ball or chunk. Anza termed the expenses "personal and procedural costs, guards and transportation, and mail that was sent to Mexico City."[92]

Anza also sent notice to Antonio Siraumea to meet him at San Antonio de Padua on Friday, at which time he would assign the Yaqui his legal mining claim to the discovery site. That morning, Anza, Miranda, Padilla, Nuñez, Sosa, and Bernardo de Urrea, accompanied by Siraumea and possibly others, rode back up the canyon to San Antonio de Padua, where a 160-vara claim[93] was surveyed, marked, and turned over to the Yaqui "to his satisfaction." That project completed, everyone rode back down the canyon to Agua Caliente where Anza and Sosa remained at least until the following Thursday.

Captain Anza sent out notices that, having granted Siraumea's mining registration, he was now ready to grant others as previously registered, a process that took place over the next several days. Letters were signed and sent out dictating procedures for the return of everyone's silver and for collecting the king's fifth. When Anza went home, he stopped at all the various towns and rancherías on his way back to Corodégauchi to announce the resolution at each place.

Anza was back at Fronteras by September 30, 1737, and all of the silver had been returned to its original finders, with the exception of a nearly 300-pound piece that had been chiseled off of the slab found by Almazán and purchased to be sent to the viceroy for further investigation. Anza contracted with an old friend and fellow Basque, Tomás de Garnica, a longtime cargador on the camino real into Santa Fe, to transport this piece of silver on the first leg of its journey to Mexico City. Garnica carried it by mule train as far as Chihuahua City. There, he turned it over to Mexican freighter Juan Manchón Moreno, who transported it the rest of the way to Mexico City and delivered it to Domingo Gomendio, Anza's Basque supplier and financier.

Captain Anza sent his final report to Viceroy Vizarrón on October 6, 1737. He reported everything that he had done and informed the viceroy that there were now several miners working the site. Some new silver had been found, but it seems to have been minimal. Although Juan Bautista de Anza had no further association with the silver from San Antonio de Padua, the controversy did not end. When Licenciado Melgarejo received Anza's report he was livid. He was the man who had commended Anza for his promptness and good management of the affair previously. He had even recommended that the viceroy personally thank the captain, which the viceroy did, in the name of the king. Now he furiously called Anza incompetent. He fumed that the five mining experts were incompetent. Applying the same assessment to nearly everyone that was or had been involved in the case, he stopped just short of accusing the viceroy of incompetence!

New investigations were started. Maps were called for. Other experts were called for, but viceroys changed and government wheels turned slowly. Over the next ten years other expeditions were suggested, and some even mounted, to go to San Antonio de Padua to determine what had really happened. Anza and many of the others who were there at the time died before any investigation ever took place. No one ever found any more silver, to speak of, in the area. Although no great amount of wealth seems to have passed from the owners of the silver to the next generation, not entirely pleasant memories did. Almost thirty-five years after Juan Bautista de Anza's death, his son of the same name, who may not have had even a fleeting memory of his father, had the following to say:

> Seven to eight leagues distant from this village[94] to the northeast is the place of Arizona, known for the balls of virgin silver that were found in the year of 1736. Some weighed 150 arrobas. This peculiarity has been doubted, but certainly many people are still alive who possessed them. I can also provide documents that verify it, in which my father, with advice from individuals skilled in the law, impounded them because it appeared to him that they belonged to His Majesty. His conduct was not entirely approved by the Acuerdo in Mexico City, but it was by the Royal Council of Castilla.[95]

Another author, a Jesuit writing in the year 1760, was even more graphic in his description of the matter: "La Cuesta de las Bolas[96] is the name of the place where they found those astounding pieces of virgin silver in 1737, some of them weighing more than fifty quintales.[97] But from the greedy disputes and suits that were brought over them, they have disappeared, and neither in the bowels of that hill nor in the possession of those who found them, nor in the hands of their heirs, has any trace[98] of them been found."[99]

Although the silver seems to have been gone after just one or two generations, the story, and mystery, of the fantastic "bolas y planchas de plata" would linger for generations. (For a list of the Basques involved in the famous "Arizona" silver discovery, see the appendix at the end of the book.)

## The Bishop's Visit

*Pueblo mision de nrâ S$^{ra}$ de los Remedios de Banámichi, y Diz.$^e$ de 13 de 1737 a$^s$. Visitado reconocido, y probado, por el Ill.$^{mo}$ S.$^r$ D.$^r$ D.$^n$ Marttín de Elizacoechea Obispo de Durango Reyno de la Nueba Vizcaya del consejo de su Mag.$^d$ etc. quien lo Rubrico en la visita general de este su Obispado en que estta entendiendo Doy Fe = R.[rúbrica del Obispo Martín de Elizacoechea] — Antemi Don Pedro de Echenigue [rúbrica] S.$^{rio}$ de Gov.$^{no}$ y Vis.$^{ta}$ — Joseph Toral M. de D.P.S.M. . . . .* Village mission of Nuestra Señora de los Remedios of Banámichi, December 13, 1737. Visited, examined, and proven by the Most Illustrious Lord Doctor Don Martín de Elizacoechea, Bishop of Durango, Kingdom of Nueva Vizcaya, of the Council of His Majesty, etc., who signed with his rubric during the general visit of this, his diocese, in which he is presently engaged. I certify it. = Rubric [of Bishop Martín Elizacoechea]—before me, Don Pedro de Echenique (rubric), secretary of governance and visitation—Joséph Toral, minister of doctrine for His Majesty[100]

The missions of the Pimería and Opatería, which Captain Anza was now charged with protecting and defending, fell under the jurisdiction of the Bishopric of Durango, established in 1620.[101] As bishops changed over the years, the rules often changed and some of the bishops were more supportive of the far northern missions than others. This was also true of the Spanish communities that sprang up in the vicinity of the missions. For example, just after the turn of the eighteenth century and several years before Anza arrived in Sonora, Bishop Ignacio Diaz de Barrera, concerned with the sparseness of Jesuit missionaries in the north, and feeling their workload was already overwhelming in just trying to care for the missions, forbade them from ministering to non-Indians.[102] The next bishop, Pedro Tápiz,[103] evidently left his predecessor's decree in place. This edict left a great void in the lives of the Spanish populations of Sonora and surrounding areas. Parish priests were even in shorter supply than Jesuit missionaries, leaving the people with no one to baptize their children or perform marriages or funeral services, no one to hear confessions or administer other important ordinances.

That had all changed when Bishop Benito Crespo y Monroy was officially instated as bishop of Durango on December 20, 1723, in Mexico City.[104] It had been many years since a prelate representing the Holy See had visited the far north, but Bishop Crespo made it one of his top priorities to learn firsthand what was needed on the frontier. His official visit to Sonora occurred in 1725.[105] One of the new bishop's first actions was to repeal the rule not allowing Jesuits to minister to the Spanish communities.[106] He soon became the most ardent supporter of the missions in the north and vigorously promoted mission expansion. It was he who later, in 1732, assigned the three missionaries to begin work at Santa María Suamca, Los Santos Ángeles de Guevavi, and San Xavier del Bac in the northern Pimería Alta. It was he who Juan Bautista de Anza praised for providing those three missionaries, and for establishing the cabeceras at Suamca and Guevavi, so close to the Spanish communities of the San Luis and upper Santa Cruz River valleys. Bishop Crespo, however, was now gone. He had been promoted to the office of bishop of Puebla de los Ángeles. Although he had set about providing hospitals and doing other great works there, the dreaded *matlazahuatl*, or "typhus," broke out in the summer of 1737. It spread quickly east to Puebla, and by August 3, 1737, Bishop Crespo was among the estimated 50,000 victims in that city.[107]

Juan Bautista de Anza had been in Mexico City just one year previous to the appointment of Bishop Crespo. However, by the time of the bishop's appointment in 1723, he was living at Janos and actively engaged as alférez of the presidio. When Bishop Crespo made his official visit to the north in 1725, it is unlikely the two men saw each other, unless Anza had the extreme good fortune to be assigned as one of the escorts on Crespo's tour of inspection. If Anza did not have that opportunity, he probably never saw Bishop Crespo in person. Their acquaintance was strictly through the mail. However, when the change was made in the bishopric on September 5, 1736, after a vacancy of two years,[108] Captain Anza would get to meet the new bishop personally.

Like Benito Crespo, the new bishop, Martín de Elizacoechea, made it a top priority to visit the missions on the north frontier. He arrived in Chihuahua about a year later, with Sonora as the next stopping place on his itinerary. Captain Anza, as military commander of Sonora, was honored to provide his escort through that province. The captain probably met Bishop Elizacoechea at Janos and escorted him back to his own presidio at Fronteras. The bishop undoubtedly had a carriage for much of his journey, for transporting his entourage and luggage, but it was likely left behind when he was escorted across the mountains from the Opatería to the Pimería. If that was the case, the carriage probably went from Janos to Fronteras and then down the Sonora River to Ures, where it waited until after the inspection of the Pimería Alta. Then, the bishop would have ridden in it from Ures to Álamos, where Anza turned the duties of his escort over to another officer.

For the inspection of the missions of the Pimería Alta, it is likely that Bishop Elizacoechea was carried in the same sedan chair that transported Father Campos from San Ignacio to Fronteras. His entourage, on horseback and escorted by Captain Anza and his soldiers from Fronteras, was at Banámichi on Friday, December 13, 1737, for the bishop to make his inspection there.[109] The party likely remained there through Saturday and Sunday, striking out over the mountains via Saracachi on Monday morning, with the bishop being carried in the sedan chair by loyal Pimas. Anza had sent soldiers northward to escort Father Keller of Suamca, and Father Rapicani of Guevavi, down to San Ignacio where the bishop's party would meet with them on Thursday. Supervising the carrying of the sedan chair, Anza rode his horse closely alongside, across the precipitous mountain range, affording himself closer contact and a more lengthy and involved discussion with a bishop than he had ever had previously. For Anza, a devout Catholic and Jesuit brother, it was the opportunity of a lifetime. There were other benefits as well.

Martín de Elizacoechea was born in Azpilkueta, Nafarroa in 1679, not twenty miles from where Juan Bautista de Anza was born and raised. Although born of a background similar to Anza's, he had pursued a very different career, being educated at the University of Alcalá in Spain. There he was awarded the degree of doctor y catedrático de artes. As a master educator he was appointed dean and chancellor of the University of Mexico. Before being appointed bishop of Durango, he had been bishop of Cuba and of Michoacán.[110] Although his impressive educational record and notoriety throughout Nueva España and the New World may have been intimidating to Don Juan at first, it must have been almost like a family reunion for the two men to be able to speak of things of home in their native tongue during the many miles and days of the inspection. The bishop's personal secretary and his confessor, Pedro de Echenique and Juan Ignacio de Arrasain, respectively, were also old-country Basques from the same region of Nafarroa as the bishop.[111] The party also met many of their countrymen along the way to the various communities and missions. To think that they would have been speaking Spanish is to defy logic.

*Martín Obispo de Durango* [signature]

The entourage arrived in Cucurpe on Monday night, and the next day the bishop interviewed Father Nicolás Perera and went over his mission books with him to make sure everything was in order. It is likely that soldiers had also been sent to escort Father José Xavier Molina from Dolores to Cucurpe to meet with the bishop. Father Molina had been at Dolores for only about a month, assisting the aging Father Velarde, who had just died on December 2, a couple of weeks before the bishop's arrival. However, he would have been able to bring the mission records from Dolores for Bishop Elizacoechea to inspect.

On Wednesday Captain Anza and his soldiers escorted the group over the mountains to Santa Magdalena where Father Gaspar Stiger, missionary at San Ignacio, and probably Fathers Keller and Rapicani were waiting to meet them. The expedition camped there that night, and early next morning Bishop Elizacoechea went over the Magdalena record books. Then everyone moved north to San Ignacio.

The bishop interviewed each of the missionaries there to meet him and inspected the church. Still plainly visible was a spot where the floor tile had been removed and replaced over a grave in front of the Gospel side of the main altar.[112] The reason that soldiers had been sent only as far north as Suamca and Guevavi to bring priests to meet with the bishop was because there was no missionary at San Xavier del Bac. Thirty-one-year-old José Javier, who had been in the Pimería Alta for only a few months and had been assigned briefly to San Xavier, had come sick to San Ignacio and had died there on October 25. Father Stiger had ensured that his body was provided a grave in the most honorable resting-place.

Once he had finished his interviews with three missionaries, Bishop Elizacoechea went over their record books with them and his secretary, Pedro de Echenique. Once each of the books of baptisms, marriages, and deaths were seen to have been kept properly, escribano Echenique wrote a note of approval in each one and the bishop signed with his rubric.¹¹³ What Echenique wrote in the baptismal registry of Santa María Suamca is indicative of them all:

> In the village mission of San Ignacio on the nineteenth day of the month of December, in 1737, the Most Illustrious Lord Doctor Don Martín de Elizacoechea, Bishop of Durango, Kingdom of Nueva Vizcaya, of the council of His Majesty etc., was presented this book with two others in which are registered the entries of baptisms, marriages, and burials of the natives of the villages of Santa Magdalena, Soamca, Ricibas, San Pedro, Santa Cruz, Quiburi, Obtuabo, Seugtubors, Scucbac, Baicat, Bapcomarric, San Xavier del Bac, Tucson, Upsan, Toasin, Coatac, Quitoabo, Santa Catalina—Martín Obispo de Durango (rubric)"¹¹⁴

*D Pedro de Echenique* (rubric)

What a thrill it must have been for each of the little villages on the bishop's route to have a visitor of such importance pass through their community, escorted by the well-known commander Juan Bautista de Anza. A special thrill, at least for the family of Juan de Villa, came when the bishop's entourage and all the soldiers stopped at the little town of San Ignacio for the night. Late that night Juan's wife, María Guadalupe German, gave birth to a healthy baby girl. Just one month previously Juan and María Guadalupe, who had once been the personal servants of Father Campos, had buried their little one-year-old daughter, María Loreto.¹¹⁵ That bitterness must have been allayed by the thought that this newest addition to their family, María Rosa, would be baptized the next day while the bishop was there.

Early the next morning, Friday, December 20, 1737, Fathers Stiger, Rapicani, and Keller, Bishop Elizacoechea and his entire entourage, Captain Anza and all of his soldiers, and practically all the townspeople were in attendance at the church for little María Rosa's baptism. There were old-country "Spaniards," Spanish criollos, mestizos of every mix and walk of life, and dozens of Pima Indians in the congregation. Juan Ignacio de Arrasain, the bishop's confessor, performed the baptism. Standing as godmother for the little girl was her aunt, Mariana German. Her godfather was none other than Sonora's famous and beloved Captain Juan Bautista de Anza.¹¹⁶ What a story the little girl would one day have to tell among her peers! How proud her parents must have been that day! How grand the feast must have been that everyone sat down to enjoy that afternoon, just five days before Christmas!

Pages from mission record books, or the books themselves, no longer exist to tell us what took place next on the bishop's tour of inspection. His party may have stayed at San Ignacio for the Christmas holidays, and Juan Bautista de Anza and his soldiers from Fronteras may have gone home. It is not known if the bishop went to inspect the missions in the Altar River valley in January, but it is likely. And if he did, Anza surely went with him. Just as assuredly, Captain Anza escorted him back over the mountain and down the San Miguel River to Pópulo, from where they crossed over another small mountain range to Ures. From there it is likely that Anza escorted Bishop Elizacoechea in his coach to the missions of the Pimería Baja. The only thing that is known for certain, however, is that they arrived in Álamos, Sonora exactly one month after the big day at San Ignacio.[117] The bishop examined the Álamos mission records the next day, Tuesday, January 21, 1738. Shortly thereafter, Captain Anza and Bishop Elizacoechea said their last farewells, never to see each other again. Anza rode home with his soldiers to Fronteras, and the bishop continued on his inspection tour to the south with an escort of soldiers from the Presidio of Sinaloa.

## The Royal Cédula

*Lo que passo ala R.$^1$ not.$^a$ de V.M. reputando este extraño acaecim.$^{to}$ no por desmerecedor de ponerse en su soberana intelig.$^a$—Juan Antonio Arzpô de Mexico (rúbrica)* . . . I bring this to the royal attention of Your Majesty, appreciating in this strange event that [Don Juan Bautista de Anza] is not an undeserving person to be brought to your kingly mindfulness—Juan Antonio [de Vizarrón y Eguiarreta], Archbishop of Mexico (rubric)[118]

Juan Bautista de Anza had actually once seen a royal cédula, or decree, dictated by Felipe V, king of Spain. But that had been nearly thirty years before, in faraway Hernani. He had been but a boy, and that now seemed like another life in a mystical world far removed from the reality of his present life at Fronteras. It had been handed down by the king to prevent the closure of the grain mills at Zeago and Errotaberri.[119] Since his father, Antonio de Anza, had petitioned to have the mills closed to prevent further financial losses for his client, the decree had actually been in opposition to Anza's position in the matter. Now, after all those years, another royal cédula was on its way from Spain to the New World, instructing a newly appointed viceroy, the duque de la Conquista, to thank Juan Bautista de Anza in King Felipe's royal name for his quick action in preventing a general uprising during the Agustín Aschuhuli affair. In it, the viceroy was instructed to investigate the occurrence and recommend a suitable reward for Captain Anza, if what the duque's predecessor, Viceroy Juan Antonio de Vizarrón y Eguiarreta, had reported was true. If, on the other hand, the report turned out to be fictitious or exaggerated, the new viceroy was to recommend a suitable punishment. The cédula, a translation of which follows, was sent to the duque de la Conquista while he was preparing to leave Spain for the New World:

The King

To the Duque de la Conquista, Marqués de Gracia; my governor, captain general of the Kingdom of Nueva España, and resident of the Real Audiencia of Mexico City:[120]

The Archbishop Viceroy,[121] your predecessor in these responsibilities, reported with testimony dated the tenth of June of the year just past, of the commotion caused by the two nations of Guaymas [Indians][122] of the Province of Sonora, and of the diabolical running insurrection of an Indian named Agustín Ascuhul, native of one of these nations, who claimed to have resurrected Montezuma. After containing this general disturbance, Don Juan Bautista de Anza, captain of the Royal Presidio of Fronteras in the Pimería Alta, apprehended this Indian aresibi, mayordomo or false prophet, and verified his guilt. Prefacing his actions by having the Holy Sacrament of repentance administered, he ordered him hung from a tall palm tree. Having seen the said report and testimony in my Council of the Indies, it seemed appropriate to send you a copy of it and other information, that you might be instructed in all that has happened in this case upon your arrival in Mexico. When you find that the success of Don Juan Bautista de Anza in pacifying the situation is certain, you will attend to expressing, in my Royal name, the gratitude that I have for his prudence and swift action in anticipation of the damages that could have occurred from a similar disturbance in terrifying the rest of the bordering provinces. I order and command (as I have done) that you report to me what you feel would be a suitable reward for the zeal that, in this instance, has been manifest in my royal service, with consideration of anything that might be feigned and worthy of punishment according to my will.

Written at Buen Retiro, July 13, 1739.

I, The King (rubric)[123]

It is not known whether the new viceroy received the cédula before he left Spain or after he arrived in the New World. He had a terrible experience on his journey to Nueva España, as his flotilla battled storms and other problems, including an attack from pirates. However, he did arrive in the New World and he did receive the cédula. He responded back to the king from Veracruz on July 10, 1740, before he arrived at his new post in Mexico City.[124] The dates of the various correspondence dealing with the Aschuhuli affair give an idea of just how difficult communication was between the frontier, Mexico City, and Spain. Captain Anza had wrapped up the entire matter on June 9 and written his report to Viceroy Vizarrón on June 25, 1737. Viceroy Vizarrón sent his report to the king almost a full year and one month later on July 10, 1738. King Felipe V signed the royal cédula exactly one year and three days later on July 13, 1739. The response from the duque de la Conquista lacked just three days of being written one full year after the cédula, on July 10, 1740.[125]

Unfortunately, Juan Bautista de Anza had died exactly two months and one day before the duque had written to the king informing him he would investigate the matter. Anza never knew the king had commended him. He was probably unaware that the royal commendation was even in the works. That was not why he was striving so hard in the service of the king, anyway. He did so out of belief and loyalty.

## Beyond Terrenate

*tengo dado q$^{to}$ V.E. en consulta de viente y cinco de Maio prox$^{mo}$ de la acaezido el dia nueve el propio mes de la lastimosa muerte q. dieron los yndios a D$^n$ Juan Baptista de Anza Cap$^n$ del R$^l$ Presidio de Fronteras, y el abanze q. el dia doze dio a los Apaches D$^n$ Jph Diaz del Carpio Cap$^n$ del de Janos en que murieron treze y ha preso catorce — Ju$^o$ Bapt$^{ta}$ de Belausaran* . . . I have given notice to Your Excellency in a report on the twenty-fifth of last May of the occurrence on the ninth of the same month of the sad death of Don Juan Bautista de Anza, captain of the Royal Presidio of Fronteras, caused by the Indians, and of the attack made on the Apaches on the twelfth by Don José Díaz del Carpio, captain of the Presidio of Janos in which thirteen died and fourteen were taken prisoner — Juan Bautista de Belauzaran [126]

For nearly fourteen years Captain Juan Bautista de Anza and his family had lived at Fronteras in the commander's quarters on the very point of the promontory where the presidio was located, overlooking the valley below. There had been little danger of a concerted attack by Apaches on the presidio itself. The family had lived there in relative security and safety. That was all to change, however, on a dismal Monday morning, May 9, 1740, as the captain and a few soldiers were returning from a tour of the missions on the upper Santa Cruz River. Somewhere beyond Santa Maria Suamca and the ranch at Terrenate, it appears that, for some unexplained reason, the soldiers fell behind their captain a few too many paces. Suddenly, in one violent moment before they could come to his aid, a small mounted band of Apaches appeared out of the brush with bow strings taut and arrows flying. The captain's helmet careened from his head and arrows shot at nearly point-blank range toppled him from his horse. In the few seconds it took his soldiers to gallop to the scene, the Apaches had scurried away with his horse and the captain lay dying on the ground.

A Jesuit visitador, vice-provincial Juan Antonio Baltasar, who never knew the captain and was certainly not there at the time of his death, published the only account we have of the incident fifteen years after the fact. He made his visit to Sonora four years after Anza's death, and then waited another eleven years to record it.[127] There are problems with the account, but here it is:

> It is now nearly fifteen years since the commander of the Presidio of Fronteras, Juan Bautista de Anza, an experienced and courageous man who brought fear to the barbarians, was overpowered because he disregarded the dangers. Upon leaving the mission of Father Ignacio Keller he was advised by that prudent Jesuit to go with caution, keeping the people of his company in tight formation, because it was fairly certain the enemy would be haunting his route. Very recent footprints that were, without a doubt, those of the barbarians lying in wait for the opportunity to fire their shot, had been discovered and [should have] encouraged Anza further to use extreme vigilance. The captain did use extreme caution while traveling through ridges and canyons where Apaches normally attacked. However, upon reaching open country, and judging all danger had been bypassed, he rode ahead a little. They assaulted him from behind some brush, knocked him to the ground, and in a few moments deprived him of the helmet covering his shoulder-length hair[128] to celebrate their triumph. His followers were unable to get there quickly enough to help him.[129]

The foregoing account makes it appear as though Anza had become reckless, possibly in his hurry to get home, and secondary sources have generally interpreted it that way it, adding to and embellishing what little fact is provided in the description of the incident. While any or all of the various interpretations may be correct, it should be borne in mind that the foregoing account was not written by an eyewitness, or even someone who knew the parties involved. It appears to be a regurgitation of an "I told you so" version by Father Keller. While Anza might have become reckless, there was no one on the frontier who knew the dangers from the Apaches better than he did. He had been fighting Apaches for many years before Father Keller even arrived in the New World. Although he and his soldier escort may have let down their guard in some way, it is also likely that a combination of coincidental events provided a perfect opportune moment for a small band of Apache warriors.

News of the disaster spread quickly across the northern frontier. Older vecinos everywhere, who had known and loved Anza since his arrival in the New World at the youthful age of nineteen, were in shock. The younger generation, who had come to know him as a protector and benefactor, was saddened by the news and worried about the future. Jesuit missionaries and their little flocks at the missions of the north went into mourning, for truly this man had been both a friend and promoter of the Company of Jesus and its cause, as well as a brother. Even Anza's detractors—and he had stirred up a number of them with his political strategies and decisions over the years, especially in the recent silver debacle—were shocked and saddened by his sudden demise. If there was happiness or rejoicing over this turn of events, it had to have been among the Apaches. Certainly Captain Anza had been a scourge to their raiding parties for many years. However, there was soon to be mourning among their people, also. News of Anza's death reached the next closest presidio, a hundred miles to the east at Janos, a couple of days later. On Thursday, May 12, Captain José Díaz del Carpio, a fellow Basque from Gamarra in Araba, Spain,[130] who had been the commander at Janos since the death of Anza's father-in-law in 1733, led a detachment of soldiers bent on retaliation. Riding hard out of Janos they tracked down and killed a party of thirteen Apache warriors, but there is nothing to indicate that the band that killed Anza was that big or even that any of this group might have participated in the killing. An ugly cycle of retaliatory killing that had been going on for years was perpetuated that spring day. A number of widows and children mourned lost husbands and fathers that fateful May.

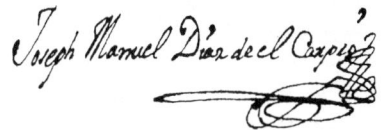

This was certainly the case back home at Fronteras. María Rosa, beloved by her family and neighbors, was left a young widow, probably in her early to middle forties. Both of her parents were dead and she had no immediate family nearby. There was extended family back in the San Buenaventura Valley of Chihuahua and she had three brothers living at Janos,[131] but her closest pariente was her aunt, María Nicolasa Gómez de Silva, living on the Santa Cruz River near the mission of Guevavi and its visita, Tumacácori. There in the valley of Guevavi, María Nicolasa and her husband, Manuel José de Sosa, suddenly found themselves in the employ of Anza's widow. Undoubtedly, the Sosas and many others of Rosa's neighbors did all they could to extend aid and comfort to the grieving widow. There was only so much they could do, however. She had a growing family of six children who needed care and nurturing, especially in this time of anguish. The ages of María Manuela and María Gertrudis are unknown, but the eldest son, Francisco Antonio, was only fifteen years old. The youngest, Juan Bautista, was not quite four. María Margarita was thirteen and Josefa Gregoria was only eight. Still, friends and compadres were there, desiring to help. Two compadres who stood in the best position to provide temporal aid were Agustín de Vildósola and Pedro Felipe de Anza. They had known and worked with each other for many years in the mining industry of northern Sonora and were the godfathers of Don Juan and Doña Rosa's two youngest children.

Born on August 28, 1700, Vildósola was a Basque from Billaro in Bizkaia, Spain[132] and had worked closely with Rosa's late husband for nearly twenty years — ever since the former had first arrived in the New World.[133] Like Anza, he owned mining interests at Basochuca and Tetuachi, and also across the valley to the west of Basochuca at the Real de Nuestra Señora de Rosalia del Oro.[134] At the time of Anza's death, Vildósola was the militia captain for all of Sonora, with the newly commissioned grade of sargento mayor. Although he most likely would have helped with the retaliatory expedition against the Apaches for the killing of Captain Anza, the great Yaqui rebellion was simultaneously erupting in the south and Vildósola abandoned his holdings in the north to take charge of the defense of Sonora.[135] However, by the time the late captain's family had left Fronteras, the viceroy, the duque de la Conquista, had appointed Don Agustín governor of Sonora, as a consequence of his swift and decisive actions against the Yaqui insurrection.[136] In his position as governor, it is certain that he did not forget the welfare of Don Juan and Rosa's youngest daughter, his goddaughter, Gregoria.

This was also the case with the godfather of the nearly four-year-old Juan Bautista de Anza, the second, youngest of the late captain's children. Pedro Felipe de Anza, first cousin of the senior Juan Bautista was born in Donostia, Gipuzkoa, Spain, on August 23, 1698.[137] He had first come to the New World while Captain Anza and his growing family were living at the Presidio of Janos. He lived with the family there, and when the elder Juan Bautista was appointed captain at Fronteras in 1726, he moved with them. He had managed the mining interests of Captain Anza for a number of years and would continue to do so for the captain's family for many years to come.

Upon the death of Don Juan, Pedro moved to Pitic, where Agustín de Vildósola was developing a large *hacienda de labor*, a ranch and farming operation. Don Pedro lived there for a number of years at the newly established Real Presidio de San Pedro de la Conquista and appears to have been in a partnership with Governor Vildósola.[138] Just how much help he was able to render Rosa's family and his young godson at this time is uncertain. In another twenty years, however, he would be living in Mexico City and in a partnership with the richest man in Mexico, fellow Basque José de Laborda. With mining interests in Zacatecas and Taxco, he would be in a position to help his godson finance an exploratory expedition to establish a route between Sonora and Alta California,[139] something that the senior Juan Bautista de Anza had requested permission to do just three years prior to his untimely death.

Where the body of Captain Anza was buried is a question that has yet to be answered. It is doubtful that the soldiers carried him back to Santa María Suamca for burial. The records kept at Suamca by Father Keller during that period seem to be complete. Had the captain's body been carried there, it is likely the burial would have been recorded. On the other hand, the records of Fronteras were not as meticulously kept, but the death of such a prominent individual and his burial there would likely have been recorded. No such document seems to exist. Considering the fact that the month of May can be very hot in the desert, it is likely that the soldiers would not have carried the body any great distance before conducting a burial service. If they were close to Terrenate, it seems logical that they would have dug the grave there, since there was undoubtedly a cemetery already on the site. On the other hand, if the distance to some point of Spanish civilization was too great, likely they buried the captain where he fell.

Regardless, the captain's final resting-place is in a lonely, unmarked grave somewhere at or in between the present-day villages of Santa Cruz[140] and Fronteras, Sonora. Although we will likely never know exactly where he is buried, Juan Bautista de Anza's outstanding accomplishments on one of the wildest, harshest, and least-tamed frontiers of the entire New World need not be forgotten. It has been said that Spain, especially in the New World, has not been kind to her heroes of the past. Although that may be true, much of the blame lies with those of us who have written its history in the New World. If we have failed to fully record that history, it is not because the Spanish escribanos of times past did not write it down for us—it is because we have failed to read what they wrote.

The documents that tell about the life of Juan Bautista de Anza are voluminous, and those are only the ones of which we are aware. More pertinent and exciting information will undoubtedly surface. In the meantime, the preceding chapters are a much-edited version of the information that we already have. Everyone who reads them will form his or her own opinion of who this man really was. However, in conclusion, the author, after living so closely with the dusty memories of this man for so long, would like to suggest how Juan Bautista de Anza might have wanted to be remembered by those of us living over 250 years later. Were he able to speak to us today, above all else he would probably say:

> I served my God the best I knew how and with all the energy I possessed.
> I served my King every bit as faithfully.
> I loved my family and provided for them the best I could.
> I was proud to be Basque.
> I was proud to be a Spanish citizen.
> I was proud to be a Jesuit brother for the short time the honor was bestowed upon me.
> I was proud to be a Spanish presidial cavalry officer and a justicia mayor.
> Although I fought many ugly battles, both with the sword and with the pen, and made many mistakes, I strove with every fiber in my being to be a peacemaker among all peoples, to the best of my understanding.
> I should like to be remembered as a peacemaker.

# Appendix

TABLE 1. *Muster Roll of the Janos Presidio, April 10, 1723*

| No | Name | Title | Roll | Arms | Horses | Mules |
|---|---|---|---|---|---|---|
|  | Captain Antonio Bezerra Nieto | Capitán | Present | — | — | — |
| 1 | Francisco Ign. Gomez Robledo | Teniente | Absent | Fully armed | 15 | 1 |
| 2 | Don Juan Bautista de Ansa | Alférez | Present | Fully armed | 15 | 1 |
| 3 | Diego Lainez | Sargento | Absent | Fully armed | 12 | 1 |
| 4 | Francisco Griego | Cavo de escuadra | Present | Fully armed | 12 | 1 |
| 5 | Juan Lopez de Ocanto | Cavo de guardia | Present | Fully armed | 10 | 1 |
| 6 | Don Josseph Gomez de Sylba | Alférez reformado | Present | Fully armed | 10 | 1 |
| 7 | Francisco Pacheco | Cavo de escuadra | Present | Fully armed | 10 | 1 |
| 8 | Christobal Fontes | Soldado | Present | Fully armed | 10 | 1 |
| 9 | Salbador Domingues | Soldado | Present | Fully armed | 10 | 1 |
| 10 | Antonio Luzero | Soldado | Present | Fully armed | 10 | 1 |
| 11 | Josseph Rodriguez | Soldado | Present | Fully armed | 10 | 1 |
| 12 | Gregorio Barela | Soldado | Present | Fully armed | 10 | 1 |
| 13 | Miguel Luzero | Soldado | Present | Fully armed | 10 | 1 |
| 14 | Christobal de Ibarra | Soldado | Absent | Fully armed | 10 | 1 |

(*continues*)

TABLE 1. Continued

| No | Name | Title | Roll | Arms | Horses | Mule |
|----|------|-------|------|------|--------|------|
| 18 | Manuel de la Peña | Soldado | Absent | Fully armed | 10 | 1 |
| 19 | Pedro Carbajal | Soldado | Absent | Fully armed | 10 | 1 |
| 20 | Blas de Medina | Soldado | Absent | Fully armed | 10 | 1 |
| 21 | Lucas Barba | Soldado | Absent | Fully armed | 10 | 1 |
| 22 | Josseph Espindola | Soldado | Absent | Fully armed | 10 | 1 |
| 23 | Cayettano Madrid | Soldado | Absent | Fully armed | 10 | 1 |
| 24 | Miguel Romero | Soldado | Absent | Fully armed | 10 | 1 |
| 25 | Thimotheo de Solis | Soldado | Absent | Fully armed | 10 | 1 |
| 26 | Nicolas Moreno | Soldado | Present | Fully armed | 10 | 1 |
| 27 | Juan Ruiz de Inojos | Soldado | Absent | Fully armed | 10 | 1 |
| 28 | Francisco Grijalba | Soldado | Present | Fully armed | 10 | 1 |
| 29 | Josseph Dominguez | Soldado | Absent | Fully armed | 10 | 1 |
| 30 | Salbador Mizquia | Soldado | Absent | Fully armed | 10 | 1 |
| 31 | Josseph Montaño | Soldado | Present | Fully armed | 10 | 1 |
| 32 | Josseph de Echaves | Soldado | Absent | Fully armed | 10 | 1 |
| 33 | Mathias Marquez | Soldado | Present | Fully armed | 10 | 1 |
| 34 | Marcial Gomez | Soldado | Present | Fully armed | 10 | 1 |
| 35 | Josseph Luxan | Soldado | Absent | Fully armed | 10 | 1 |
| 36 | Juan de Dios Barrios | Soldado | Present | Fully armed | 10 | 1 |

TABLE 1. *Continued*

| No | Name | Title | Roll | Arms | Horses | Mules |
|---|---|---|---|---|---|---|
| 37 | Juan Marquez Rodriguez | Soldado | Present | Fully armed | 10 | 1 |
| 38 | Pedro Xaramillo | Soldado | Present | Fully armed | 10 | 1 |
| 39 | Juan Marquez | Soldado | Present | Fully armed | 10 | 1 |
| 40 | Thomas Lopez | Soldado | Present | Fully armed | 10 | 1 |
| 41 | Agustin de Espindola | Soldado | Present | Fully armed | 10 | 1 |
| 42 | Juan Josseph de Albizu | Soldado | Absent | Fully armed | 10 | 1 |
| 43 | Josseph Madrid | Soldado | Present | Fully armed | 10 | 1 |
| 44 | Francisco Xavier Rodriguez | Soldado | Present | Fully armed | 10 | 1 |
| 45 | Francisco Xavier de la Parra | Soldado | Present | Fully armed | 10 | 1 |
| 46 | Dionisio Lainez | Soldado | Absent | Fully armed | 10 | 1 |
| 47 | Josseph Zambrano | Soldado | Present | Fully armed | 10 | 1 |
| 48 | Antonio Contreras | Soldado | Present | Fully armed | 10 | 1 |
| 49 | *Don Pedro Bezerra Nieto* | Soldado | Present | Fully armed | 10 | 1 |
| 50 | Juan Moreno | Clarinero | Present | Fully armed | 10 | 1 |
| | Total | | | | 514 | 50 |

AHP, Autos de Visitta echa al real Presidio de San Phelipe y Santiago de Janos por el Capitan Don Gregorio Alvarez Tuñon y Quiros, Visitador General de las Armas de estte Reino de la Nueva Vizcaya, 10 April 1723, ff. 377–390.

Absent = Absent in the service of His Majesty

The original spellings of names have been retained. Antonio Bezerra Nieto compiled this list for the inspection of his presidio. It is interesting that the only soldiers to whom he gave the title "Don" are members of his family, indicated in italic type.

TABLE 2. *Silver Impounded by Juan Bautista de Anza, 1736*

| Slab found by José Fermín de Almazán | Arrobas (@) | Libras (#) |
| --- | --- | --- |
| Liquefied, 2@ in pieces | 2 | — |
| Lorenzo Velasco | 8 | — |
| Lorenzo Velasco (42@ 18# in the rough, weighed in a tanate in various pieces, lost 1@ when liquefied) | 41 | 18 |
| Lorenzo Velasco | 23 | 17 |
| Given to Siraumea and Urrea by Almazán | 20 | 3 |
| Left from 12@ Urrea gave Siraumea (Siraumea spent 6@ and Urrea spent 1@ 19# leaving 4@ 6# ) | 4 | 6 |
| Granulated metal from smelting | 1 | 7 |
| Sum | 99 | 51 |
| Total | 101 | 1 |

| Arrobas (@) | Libras (#) | Onzas | Balls and Chunks of Other Persons | Arrobas (@) | Libras (#) | Onzas |
|---|---|---|---|---|---|---|
| — | — | — | Francisco López | 1.0 | 6.0 | — |
| — | — | — | Juan Chamorro | 1.0 | 5.0 | — |
| — | — | — | Juan Phelipe Martín | 4.0 | — | — |
| — | — | — | Andres Gonzales, Joseph Jimenez, and Luis de Villanueva | 4.0 | 14.0 | — |
| — | — | — | Pedro López | 10.0 | — | — |
| — | — | — | Santiago Ruiz de Ael, the notary (found by Indian, Dionisio) | 14.0 | 20.0 | — |
| 11.0 | 21.0 | 12.0 | Santiago Ruiz de Ael | — | — | — |
| 5.0 | — | — | Bernardo de Urrea | — | — | — |
| — | — | — | Juan Carlos López | 5.0 | 5.0 | — |
| 1.0 | 3.5 | — | Gregorio | — | — | — |
| — | 8.0 | — | Melchor Montalvo | — | — | — |
| — | 5.5 | — | Joseph Villegas | — | — | — |
| — | — | — | Nicolás Alfonso Ochoa—7@ 2# minus 8# tare of the tanate (this should leave 6@ 19#, but Anza calculated it at 6@ 17#) | 6.0 | 17.0 | — |
| — | — | — | Ignacio de los Reyes (paid to Santiago Ruiz de Ael as part of his total above in the left-hand column—7#) | — | — | — |

*(continues)*

|  | Silver Taken in Trade | | | Balls and Chunks of Other Persons | Silver Found/Purchased | | |
|---|---|---|---|---|---|---|---|
|  | Arrobas (@) | Libras (#) | Onzas | | Arrobas (@) | Libras (#) | Onzas |
|  | — | — | — | Joseph de Olvera bought from Almazán | — | 12.0 | 14.0 |
|  | — | — | — | Juan de Contreras—1@ 15# minus 2# tare of the talega | 1.0 | 13.0 | — |
|  | 2.0 | 15.0 | — | Bernardo de Urrea | — | 10.5 | — |
|  | — | — | — | Joseph de Usarraga | — | — | — |
|  | 1.0 | 9.5 | 3.0 | Agustín de Vildósola | — | — | — |
|  | — | 17.0 | 4.0 | Francisco Salmón | — | — | — |
|  | — | — | — | Pedro Camargo—11 marcos received from Villegas recorded above | — | — | — |
|  | — | 7.0 | — | Francisco Serrano | — | — | — |
| Sum | 20.0 | 86.5 | 19.0 | | 36.0 | 112.5 | 14.0 |
| Anza's calculation Total | 23.0 | 12.0 | 3.0 | | 40.0 | 14.0 | 6.0 |
| Actual calculation Total | 23.0 | 12.0 | 11.0 | | 40.0 | 15.0 | 6.0 |

Taken from AGN, Minería 160, leg. 1, ff. 93v–95v.

The left-hand column shows silver taken in trade; the right-hand column shows silver found or purchased by the owner.

At 25 libras per arroba and 16 onzas per libra, Anza miscalculated the left-hand column by 8 onzas and the right-hand column by one libra (taking into account the 2-libra error in Ochoa's silver), but he signed the total "salbo yerro"—"barring errors." The actual total of all the silver that was weighed and impounded was 164 arrobas, 39 libras, 1 onza. By modern calculation, that was 2 tons, 139 pounds, and 1 ounce of silver!

"Sum" totals the column; "total" converts libras to arrobas.

*Basques Involved in the Famous "Arizona" Silver Discovery*

1. Almazán, José Fermín de. Resident of Agua Caliente and one of the first prospectors on the site after the discovery of the silver. He discovered the largest *plancha*, which weighed more than a ton, while working for Lorenzo Velasco, who thus became the owner of the piece of silver.
2. Anza, Juan Bautista de. Born June 29, 1693, in Hernani, Gipuzkoa, he came to New Spain in 1712. His first recorded ownership of a mine in the New World was the San Antonio Mine at the Real de Minas de Nuestra Señora de Guadalupe de Aguaje, south of present-day Hermosillo, Sonora. He and other Basques later founded the Real de Minas de Nuestra Señora de Aránzazu de Tetuachi above the Sonora River.

3. Anza, Pedro Felipe de. Born August 23, 1698, in San Sebastián, Gipuzkoa, about four miles from where Juan Bautista de Anza was born in Hernani. Pedro Felipe was Juan Bautista's first cousin and lived with the family both at Janos, Chihuahua, and Fronteras, Sonora. He signed, as a witness, most of the documents that were written at Fronteras concerning the silver discovery. He was godfather of the junior Juan Bautista de Anza.
4. Aresti, Agustín de. One of two Mexico City lawyers appointed by Domingo de Guraya to represent Santiago Ruiz de Ael before the Real Audiencia in his effort to order Captain Anza to return the silver he had impounded.
5. Echagoyen, Juan de. A Mexican-born Basque and one of the three Jesuit missionaries who advised Anza on how he should proceed with the mysterious silver discovery. More than the other Jesuits who were consulted, Echagoyen tended to believe that the silver was not a hidden treasure, but a natural phenomenon.

6. Echevarri, Francisco Antonio. As *oidor* of the Real Acuerdo, he was called upon by Viceroy Vizarrón for advice on whether the silver was natural or a treasure.
7. Garduño, Francisco de. Witness to the statements and transactions of Luis de Mendivil concerning the silver taken in trade by him at San Antonio de Motepore. He later moved to the San Luis Valley.

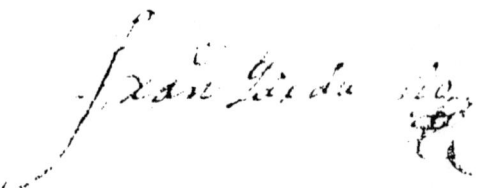

8. Garnica, Tomás de. *Arriero*, or mule packer, who had been freighting on the camino real between Chihuahua and Santa Fe, New Mexico, for a number of years. Captain Anza commissioned him to transport the 300-pound piece of silver from the discovery site at San Antonio de Padua to Chihuahua, from where another packer delivered it to Domingo de Gomendio in Mexico City.

9. Garrastegui, Francisco de. A criollo, or Mexican-born Basque, with roots in Arrasate, Gipuzkoa, who replaced Gabriel Prudhom Butrón y Mujica as alcalde mayor of Sonora and was in office at the time of the silver discovery. He opened up the borders of Sonora to Juan Bautista de Anza for further exploration beyond the boundaries and was then sued by José de Mesa and Francisco de Longoria, because they wanted to be commissioned to explore the territory to the north.
10. Gomendio Urrutia, Domingo de. Born in the village of Berriz, Bizkaia, he was *alcalde ordinario* of Mexico City and the receiver of the 300-pound chunk of silver that was chiseled from the ton-and-a-quarter piece discovered by José Fermín de Almazán. He established a 500-peso-per-year endowment for El Colegio de las Vizcaínas, a Basque college for girls in Mexico City, and was rector of the Basque Cofradia (Confraternity) de Aránzazu during the time of the 1736 silver discovery. A financier and broker, he was Juan Bautista de Anza's *aviador*, or supplier, for the Presidio of Fronteras and had been Antonio Bezerra Nieto's financier at the Janos presidio for many years prior to that.

]

11. Gorraez, José de. *Escribano mayor de gobernación y guerra* in Mexico City. He wrote much of what was recorded in Mexico City about the silver discovery. He, too, was a donor of a 100-peso- per-year endowment to El Colegio de las Vizcaínas.

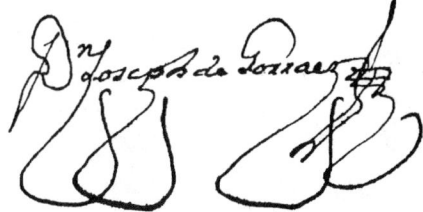

12. Gortazar, Blas de. As Agustín de Vildósola's accountant, he compiled a detailed list of all the silver that Vildósola had taken in trade at Tetuachi. From Gipuzkoa, his New World contact for immigration to Nueva España was probably Vildósola.

13. Guraya, Juan Domingo de. A resident of Mexico City to whom Santiago Ruiz de Ael gave full power of attorney to represent him before the Real Audiencia in Mexico City in his attempt to get the silver that Anza had impounded returned to him.

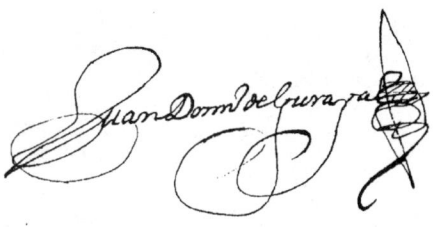

14. Leiva, José de. A Basque on his father's side of the family, Leiva was of mixed race. He lived in the San Luis Valley and was thus able to arrive on the discovery site early. He obtained some of the silver and traded it for supplies to Agustín de Vildósola in Tetuachi.
15. Longoria, Francisco de. One of the early prospectors on site after the silver discovery, he filed the first legal mining claim to a portion of the "hill of San Antonio de Pádua." A resident miner of Sonora, Longoria lived at San Ignacio, and later became the lieutenant governor of the province.

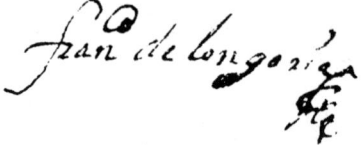

16. Mendivil, Luis de. Merchant and miner of San Antonio de Motepore who received some of the silver through trade.

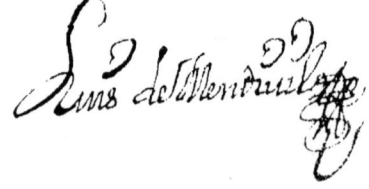

17. Mesa, José de. Resident of the Pimería Baja in central Sonora and one of the earliest prospectors to arrive on the scene from that far south. He had lost his family in an Apache raid. Seeking a commission to explore beyond the borders of Sonora, he sought to block Anza from receiving the same vice-regal appointment by claiming he was the first to discover the silver.
18. Miranda, Francisco Xavier de. Alguacil mayor del Santo Tribunal and Sonora militia captain. He was thirty-six years old at the time of the silver discovery and probably a younger brother of Antonio de Miranda, who, along with Juan Bautista de Anza and three other Basques, founded the *real de minas* at Tetuachi. Francisco was one of the mining experts whom Anza appointed to determine if the silver was natural or a treasure.

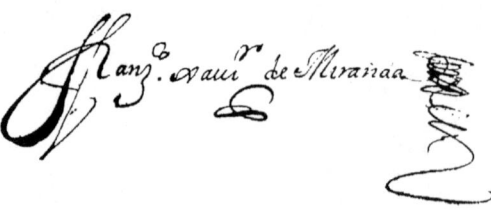

19. Morueta, Antonio Bautista de. A witness to many of the transactions and statements about the silver at the Real de Minas de San Antonio de Motepore.

20. Murrieta, Martín de. *Teniente* general of Sonora and Ostimuri from 1725 to 1727, he witnessed most of the statements made about the silver in the Real de Minas de San Antonio de Motepore.

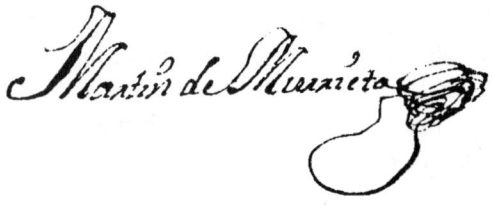

21. Ochoa, Nicolás Alfonso de. Illiterate resident of Agua Caliente and one of the first prospectors on the scene after the initial discovery. He found several fairly large pieces of the silver.
22. Olave, José de. Juan Bautista de Anza's deputy *justicia mayor* for the San Luis Valley and witness to all the proceedings at the time of the second examination of the discovery site by Anza and the mining authorities.

23. Osorio, José de. Resident of Agua Caliente and scribe who wrote most of the first letters signed by Bernardo de Urrea.

24. Prudhom Butrón y Mujica, Gabriel de. *Alcalde mayor* of Sonora from July 1727 until July 1735, he probably drew a draft map of Sonora in which

Arizona was shown, but it is unlikely that he had anything to do with the final map that speaks of the "Real de Arizonac."

25. Quiroz y Nerea, Nicolás. One of the prospectors living at Agua Caliente. He was one of the signers of the petition asking Anza to return everyone's silver that Longoria delivered to the captain as he was about to mount his horse to leave Arizona for San Antonio de Padua.
26. Segura, Claudio Antonio de. He was living in the San Luis Valley at least as early as 1733 and was a resident of Agua Caliente at the time of the silver discovery. He signed, with the other residents of Agua Caliente, the petition requesting Anza to lift the embargo.

27. Serrano, Francisco Perez. One of the earliest miners, and possibly one of the original Basque founders of the Real de Minas de Nuestra Señora de Aránzazu de Tetuachi. He was still living at Tetuachi and operating one of its mines at the time of the 1736 silver discovery. He was the father of Ana María Perez Serrano, the wife of Juan Bautista de Anza Jr.

28. Sesma, Juan de. Witness to the statements taken in Motepore about the exchange of the silver.

29. Urias, Pedro Regala de. Resident of Agua Caliente and signer of the petition that was given to Anza to return the silver as he was mounting his horse to ride up to the San Luis Valley.

30. Urrea, Bernardo de. Anza's deputy *justicia mayor* for the Agua Caliente district and resident of Arizona. One of the first people on the site after the discovery of the silver, and witness to practically everything that took place from then on. He was in charge of the guard placed over the area until after the second examination of the site by Anza and the mining experts.

31. Usarraga, José de. A militia sergeant in Sonora at the time of the Seri war of 1725, he rose to *alférez* under militia captain, Agustín de Vildósola, the rank that he held at the time of the 1736 discovery. He was one of the mining experts appointed by Anza in the summer of 1737.

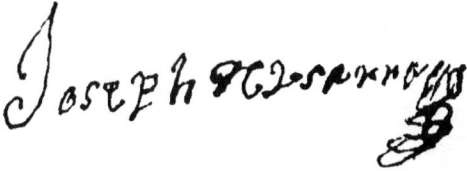

32. Usarraga, José Joaquín de. Son of José de Usarraga and evidently living in the vicinity of Agua Caliente at the time of the discovery, as he acted as assistant to Bernardo de Urrea in his duties as deputy justicia mayor. He was appointed alférez of the Presidio of Tubac by the junior Juan Bautista de Anza on February 20, 1761.

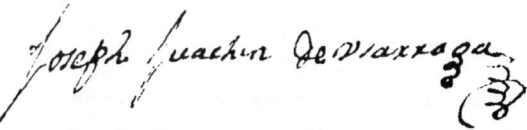

33. Veitia, José de. *Oidor* of the Real Acuerdo, which was called upon by Viceroy Vizarrón for advice on whether the silver was natural or treasure.
34. Velasco, Lorenzo de. Resident and rancher of Santa Ana whose hired man, José Fermín de Almazán, discovered the ton-and-a-quarter slab of silver.

Once the silver was returned to him, Velasco parlayed it into what was probably the largest ranching operation in Sonora at that time. He and his wife donated large sums of money to the church and were probably the main sources of revenue for the building of the churches at Magdalena and San Ignacio. Upon his death in 1750, Lorenzo was buried in the church at Magdalena. His widow, Sabina Moraga, who died in 1767, was buried beneath the Altar of the Virgin in the church at San Ignacio.

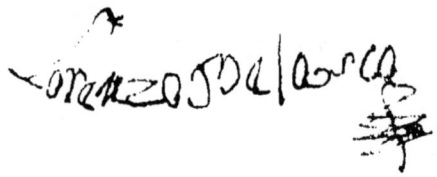

35. Vildósola, Agustín de. Born in Villaro, Bizkaia on August 28, 1700, he was living in Sonora at least as early as February 1722, where he quickly developed mining interests at San Juan Bautista, Nacosari, Basochuca, Guepavérachi, Santa Rosalia, and Tetuachi. He became militia captain (1728–1741) and the second governor of Sonora (1741–1748). He and Juan Bautista de Anza worked closely together until the latter's death on May 9, 1740. He was living at Tetuachi at the time of the silver discovery in the Pimería Alta in 1736.

36. Vizarrón, Juan Antonio de. Archbishop of Mexico and Viceroy of Nueva España from March 18, 1734, to August 17, 1740. He died in 1747. Though born in the Port of Santa María de Cádiz while his parents were en route to Nueva España, he had roots in Gipuzkoa in the same area of the Basque country as Juan Bautista de Anza and was a distant cousin of Anza's schoolteacher, Juan Bautista de Vizarrón. His protectorship of and 6,000-peso endowment to El Colegio de Vizcaínas is an indicator of his prominence in the Basque community of Mexico City and Nueva España.

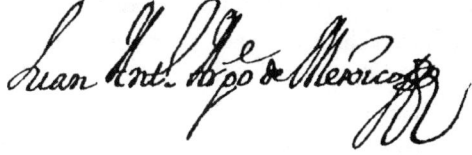

37. Zarasua, Juan José de. *Escribano real* in Mexico City and one of two lawyers appointed for Santiago Ruiz de Ael by Domingo de Guraya in the litigation to get his impounded silver back. Three others were very closely associated with the Basque community through marriage or work relationships, and may have been Basque or of Basque descent themselves.

38. Padilla, Andrés de. There are more "Spaniards" with the surname Padilla, since the name is widespread throughout Spain, but it is also not an uncommon name among Basques. It would not be surprising if Andrés, who was Juan Bautista de Anza's deputy *justicia mayor* for the district of Motepore, was Basque, since Anza's other known deputy *justicias* were. Whether he was Basque or not, he was allied with them, and especially Anza, as early as the 1720s at Tetuachi. His name is prevalent among those (mostly Basques) who were instrumental in getting Gregorio Álvarez Tuñón y Quirós ousted as captain of Fronteras and Anza instated in his place.

39. Romero, José. There were at least five Romero families living in the San Luis Valley in 1736. Ignacio, Nicolás, José, and Cristóbal probably all settled there with their father, Diego Romero, in the 1720s. José was Anza's *alférez* in the San Luis Valley and the only Romero whose signature shows up on the *planchas de plata* documents. He signed, as a witness, a number of the silver documents that Anza generated at San Antonio de Padua, Arizona and in the San Luis Valley. José Romero had a Basque wife, Josefa de Mondragon. His brother, Nicolás, also had a Basque wife, Higinia de Perea.

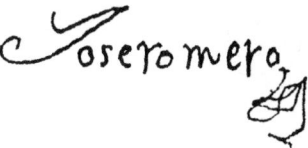

40. Sosa, Manuel José de. Juan Bautista de Anza's foreman on the Guevavi and San Mateo Ranches, his clerk, and his wife's uncle by marriage. He was married to Nicolasa Gómez de Silva. He traveled to Mexico City with all the documents and some silver samples and presented the entire package to Viceroy Vizarrón. Even though the name Sosa is generally considered to be Spanish, it is also a Basque name that means "grassland." His use of "de" in his surname may be an indicator that he was Basque. In the early 1720s he was involved with the Basques who were instrumental in the fight to have Gregorio Álvarez Tuñón y Quirós removed as captain of Fronteras and Juan Bautista de Anza installed in his place. Thus, he could have been Basque. If not, he certainly knew and understood the culture.

# Notes

PREFACE

1. Hubert Howe Bancroft, *History of Arizona and New Mexico, 1530–1888* (San Francisco: History Company, 1889).
2. Herbert Eugene Bolton, *Anza's California Expeditions*, 5 vols. (Berkeley: University of California Press, 1930).
3. Alfred Barnaby Thomas, *Forgotten Frontiers: A Study of the Spanish Indian Policy of Don Juan Bautista de Anza, Governor of New Mexico, 1777–1787* (Norman: University of Oklahoma Press, 1932).
4. Bolton, *Anza's California Expeditions*, vol. 1, *Outpost of Empire*, p. 43.
5. See, for example, Alberta Johnston Denis, *Spanish Alta California* (New York: Macmillan, 1927), p. 167; and, Fay Jackson Smith, *Captain of the Phantom Presidio: History of the Presidio of Fronteras, New Spain, 1686–1735, Including the Inspection by Brigadier Pedro de Rivera in 1726* (Spokane: Arthur H. Clark, 1993), pp. 33 n. 3, 136.
6. See, for example, Donald Rowland, "The Sonora Frontier of New Spain, 1735–1745," *New Spain and the Anglo-American West: Historical Contributions Presented to Herbert Eugene Bolton*, ed. George P. Hammond (Lancaster, Pa.: Lancaster Press, 1932), p. 150 n. 9; Rufus Kay Wyllys, *Arizona: The History of a Frontier State* (Phoenix: Hobson and Herr, 1950), p. 51; Paul M. Roca, *Paths of the Padres through Sonora* (Tucson: Arizona Pioneers Historical Society, 1970), p. 396; *The Old West: The Spanish West* (New York: Time-Life Books, 1973), p. 70; and Elizabeth A. H. John, *Storms Brewed in Other Men's Worlds: The Confrontation of Indians, Spanish, and French in the Southwest, 1540–1795* (Lincoln: University of Nebraska Press, 1975), p. 557. In her account, Dr. John even has the fictitious first Juan Bautista de Anza, as well as the second (actually the true first), both killed by Apaches in Sonora. In reality, the Anza of that first generation, Antonio de Anza, died of natural causes in Hernani, Gipuzkoa, Spain, having never set foot on the American continent. The maternal grandfather of the junior Juan Bautista de Anza, Antonio Bezerra Nieto, actually was a presidial captain, but in Chihuahua, not Sonora. He, too, died of natural causes. The only Anza family member, whether maternal or paternal, to be killed by Apaches was Juan Bautista de Anza, the father.
7. Julio César Montané Martí, *Juan Bautista de Anza: Diario del Primer Viaje a la California, 1774* (Hermosillo: Reprográfica, S.A., 1989), pp. 7, 9.
8. His paternal grandfather was Antonio de Anza and his maternal grandfather was Antonio Bezerra Nieto, both of whom are discussed extensively in the body of this work.

9. The difficulty in reading the archaic Spanish is often multiplied tenfold when the writer was Basque (or of some other ethnic background) and spoke broken Spanish, such as our subject, or if his education was limited. The handwriting is often poor or written on pages that are now rotting away with ink that has run and/or smeared. See, for example, eight small pages of Antonio María Bucareli y Ursua's personal handwriting in Donald T. Garate, "Anza's Return from Alta California: Anza Correspondence, 1776–1778," in *Antepasados*, vol. IX (San Leandro: Los Californianos, 1998), which took this author over eighty hours to translate and prepare for publication. This kind of difficulty has discouraged English-speaking scholars from examining primary documents closely or even consulting them.

10. As an example, many writers of the day spell our subjects' name "Ansa," as do most of their relatives still living in the Basque Country today. The elder Anza, however, spelled his name "Juan Bauptista de Anssa," and his son spelled it "Juan Baptista de Anza." In the massive documentation still in existence in archives in Spain it is found that the grandfather spelled his name "Antonio de Ansa" one-third of the time and "Antonio de Anssa" two-thirds of the time. In fact, on August 29, 1709 he spelled his surname both "Ansa" and "Anssa" one time each, and on June 17, 1710, he spelled his name "Ansa" twice and "Anssa" once. See Hernaniko Udalaren Artxiboa (hereinafter HUA), E-7-I-11-5, Informes de Antonio de Ansa, ff. 7v, 26v. With variations like this, who can say what is correct! Since Juan Bautista de Anza, the son, spelled his surname with a z, the spelling of the name has been standardized accordingly throughout this work. Modern spelling rules have also been applied to all other Spanish and Basque names and words. For example, "Bauptista" as spelled by the senior Anza, and "Baptista" as spelled by the junior Anza, have been standardized to the modern "Bautista."

11. Probably the most glaring of such inconsistencies has been the use, in the twentieth century, of the Spanish preposition "de" with the Basque surname "Anza." Certainly, Bancroft, Bolton, Thomas, and every other author who has used primary documentation in his or her research never used "de Anza" when referring to either Juan Bautista by his surname only. The Spanish "de," when used with a complete Basque name, creates a Spanish "title of nobility," to which all Basques were entitled by Spanish law. See Donald T. Garate and Maria de Lourdes Gortarez, *Anza: A Documentary Analysis of the Surname of Juan Bautista de Anza* (Tumacácori, Ariz.: National Park Service, 1993). No one in our subject's day, including the Anzas themselves, ever referred to them as "de Anza." See, for example, Garate, "References to 'Anza,'" presented at the third annual Anza World Conference held in Arizpe, Sonora, in which nearly five hundred examples are given of Anza contemporaries referring to them as "Anza," "Señor Anza," "Capitán Anza," "Gobernador Anza," and so on. In ten years of research and the examination of thousands of old Spanish documents, the author did find one instance in which a contemporary referred to the senior Anza as "Capitán de Anza." That lone contemporary, however, was Miguel Gerstner, a German Jesuit who spoke and wrote extremely broken Spanish and never knew the man to whom he referred. See Tumacácori National Historical Park Microfilm Collection (hereinafter TUMA), Guevavi Mission Register, Burial Entry for Rosa María Bezerra Nieto, roll 2, p. 61.

12. A number of authors have confused the two Anzas, associating the events of one with the generation of the other.

13. As an example, one tradition holds that the junior Juan Bautista de Anza was educated by the Jesuits in the College of San Pedro y San Pablo in Mexico City. See Montané Martí, *Juan Bautista de Anza*, p. 10. Another says that he was a Franciscan lay brother, educated at the College of the Holy Cross, also in Mexico City. See Roca, *Paths of the Padres*, p. 349. Yet another tradition states "that he was educated in the College of San Ildefonso in Mexico City and completed his studies in the military academy, graduating as a lieutenant of engineers." See J. N. Bowman and R. F. Heizer, *Anza and the Northwest Frontier of New Spain*, Southwest Museum Papers, no. 20 (Los Angeles: Southwest Museum, 1967), p. 32. No documentation has ever surfaced to substantiate any of these claims. In fact, the first two are unlikely and the third is spurious, as the body of this work will show.

14. For instance, while there are hundreds who could claim descendancy through the senior Juan Bautista de Anza, there are also those who claim to be descendants of the younger Juan Bautista. This is an interesting assertion in light of the fact that he personally swore that he and his wife were childless in his last will and testament, a document that she dutifully filed and recorded to obtain her widow's pension. See Archivo General de Indias (hereinafter AGI), Guadalajara, leg. 289, exp. 536, "Testamento de Juan Baptista de Anza," Santa Fe, New Mexico, 8 November 1780, f. 6v, clausula 1a. Among those who know he had no children, some claim that he adopted the two daughters of his older brother, Francisco, after the latter's death. Although he claimed to have loved them as if they were his own daughters, he never adopted his two nieces. The nieces did, however, continue to live in the same house with Anza, his wife, and their mother, as their family had done even when their father was living. And they and their descendants could and can claim the senior Juan Bautista de Anza as an ancestor. See Archivo General de la Nación (hereinafter AGN), Provincias Internas (hereinafter PI), leg. 250, Juan Baptista de Anza a Jacobo Ugarte y Loyola, 18 November 1786, ff. 413–414.

15. Among those authors who are extensively quoted by other scholars, Almada is the most notorious for not footnoting at all. I have used him as a starting point to go in search of possible pertinent material, yet I have found his work so full of errors in its detail that I would never consider using it as a reference without first finding primary documentation to back it up. Just as an example, he states that the senior Juan Bautista de Anza was born in Spain in 1694 and came to the northern regions of Nueva España at a very young age, establishing himself in the Real de Minas de Tetuachi. He says that the junior Anza was born in 1734 and that his father died in 1737. He further states that Anza in-law Gabriel Vildósola was the son of Sonora governor Agustín Vildósola, that he was a brother of José Antonio de Vildósola, and that he was born in Villares, Spain, a town that does not even exist (its true name is Villaro). With the possible exception of Anza having arrived at a very young age (he was nineteen), all of the foregoing statements are incorrect, as will be shown in the body of this work. See Francisco R. Almada, *Diccionario de Historia, Geografía, y Biografía Sonorenses* (Hermosillo: Gobierno del Estado, 1983), pp. 51, 52, 725, 726.

16. One of today's popular ideas holds that the junior Juan Bautista de Anza was not

the founder of San Francisco. It seems to stem, at least in part, from the desire of some well-meaning people to credit José Juachín Moraga with the founding. See, for example, Sandy Kimball, *Moraga's Pride: Rancho Laguna de los Palos Colorados* (Moraga: Moraga Historical Society, 1987), p. 22. The first clouding of the issue came in a twenty-page chapter entitled "The Anza Myth," in Bowman and Heizer, *Anza and the Northwest Frontier*, pp. 52–73. Weber relegated their essay to a single, short footnote, but appears to agree with them (see David J. Weber, *The Spanish Frontier in North America* [New Haven: Yale University Press, 1992], p. 451 n. 65). It is strange that Bowman and Heizer would spend so much time delving into the semantics of a single word when it took them only one day to misidentify the remains of some poor soul in Arizpe as that of Juan Bautista de Anza. Obviously, the word "founder" has to do with "setting a foundation for." Over the years thousands of people have participated in building the foundation of San Francisco. However, if there is any one person who can be said to have "set the foundation for" what is today San Francisco, it is Juan Bautista de Anza. As I have stated elsewhere, "According to *Webster's New World Dictionary, Third College Edition*, 'to found' is 'to begin to build or organize; to bring into being.' According to this definition, José Juachín Moraga was one of the founders of San Francisco, as was every recruit and all their families who helped build, organize, and bring it into being. By this definition even Fernando de Rivera y Moncada was a founder of San Francisco. However, if one person is to be designated as the leader; as the one who determined, in the first place, that it would be possible to found such a colony; as the one who organized the founding expedition and saw it safely to its destination over a year's time and 1,800 miles of extremely inhospitable country; recruited, trained, and commanded the other 'founders,' including Moraga; chose the site for the building that was to take place; and did more to bring San Francisco into being than all the others put together, it has to be said that Juan Bautista de Anza was the founder of San Francisco." See Garate, "Anza's Return from Alta California," p. 178.

17. Historians have made many "off the wall" statements about the Anzas, seemingly as filler for lack of accurate information. These are pure speculation, with no documentation of any kind, or even circumstantial evidence, to back them up. As one example, see Manuel Patricio Servin, "California's Hispanic Heritage: A View into the Spanish Myth," in *New Spain's Far Northern Frontier: Essays on Spain in the American West, 1540–1821*, ed. David J. Weber (Dallas: Southern Methodist University Press, 1979), p. 122, in which Servin states that Juan Bautista de Anza "was in all probability a mestizo." One must assume that the author is speaking of the mestizaje, or mixing of races, that occurred on this continent between the Spaniards and the Indians, and not that which occurred among the various races and cultural groups in Spain long before the so-called Spaniards came to the Americas. If that is the case, there is not one scrap of evidence to back the statement, and everything points to just the opposite. The junior Anza claimed he was "Español." All of his service records and the baptismal and death records of him and his brother and sisters say the same. The senior Juan Bautista de Anza was pureblooded Basque for many generations back, and though the Spanish ethnicity of his wife's people is unknown, the Bezerra Nietos and the Gómez de Silvas were longstanding Spanish families with no indication of intermarriage with Indians.

18. Of all the misinformation that I have seen or heard about the Anzas, my all-time favorite story came by way of a drunken Sonoran cowboy. He was a little man intently consuming a partial bottle of Bacanora, a notoriously strong Mexican "moonshine," during the festivities at the feast day of San Juan at Arizpe in 1996. We were waiting for the beginning of the annual *sacada de gallo*, an ancient Spanish event in which contestants try to pull a buried chicken, with only its head sticking up, out of the ground while galloping by on horseback. While we waited, he informed me that Juan Bautista de Anza was one of the greatest Sonorans who had ever lived. Then, with tears welling up in his eyes, he described how Pancho Villa and a band of revolutionaries had cornered him and murdered him in the church. His story might have been plausible had the junior Anza not died ninety years before Villa was born! "Anza is still buried up there," he informed me, "and you can go up and visit the grave at any time." In fact, "*Tenemos tiempo*—we have time. Let's go up there and I'll show you the grave right now. It is open and you can look down and see the remains," he told me. When I refused his offer to guide me in a viewing of the grave and to help him polish off his bottle of Bacanora, he lost interest in talking to me and wandered off without my having even gotten his name. He, at least, had an excuse for his misinformation.

19. Garate, "Juan de Oñate's Prueba de Caballero, 1625: A Look at His Ancestral Heritage," *Colonial Latin American Historical Review* 7, no. 2 (1998): 148.

20. As a side note, prior to 1990 the annual celebration had always been called "De Anza Days," but through its own research, the state park had come to the conclusion that his true surname was "Anza," even though park staff were still erroneously interpreting him as Juan Bautista de Anza III. Since then, that error has also been corrected.

21. The word "Anzaholic" was coined by Dr. Jack S. Williams at the fourth annual Anza World Conference held at Monte Vista, Colorado in 1999, to describe the author and others like him (probably including Dr. Williams himself) who have devoted an inordinate amount of time to the study of Juan Bautista de Anza.

22. My good friend, Maestro Julio César Montané Martí, once asked Dr. Officer if he thought I would have become interested in Juan Bautista de Anza had the illustrious captain not been Basque. I do not recall what Dr. Officer's exact answer was, but the true answer would have to be a resounding "Yes!" Because my job at Tumacácori National Historical Park required at least a certain amount of interest, and since both Anzas were such energetic and outstanding soldiers, politicians, and frontier leaders, I would have become interested in them at any rate. The fact that they were Basque, however, has been icing on the cake!

CHAPTER ONE. ANZA IN ANTIQUITY

1. From the Fuero of Nafarroa (ca. 1200), "Prólogo," reprinted in Ralph E. Giesey, *If Not, Not: The Oath of the Aragonese and the Legendary Laws of Sobrarbe* (Princeton, N.J.: Princeton University Press, 1968), p. 47. This and all other translations to English from the original Spanish throughout this work are the author's own unless otherwise specified.

2. Basque spelling rules of today are herein applied to the names of places, cities, provinces, and so on in the Basque Country, such as the Provinces of Araba, Bizkaia, Gipuzkoa, and Nafarroa, rather than the old Spanish spellings of Álava, Vizcaya, Guipuzcoa, and Navarra.

3. See Gorka Aulestia, *Basque-English Dictionary* (Reno: University of Nevada Press, 1989), pp. 10, 11, 13, 14, 33, 220, 296, 306; and Gorka Aulestia and Linda White, *English-Basque Dictionary* (Reno: University of Nevada Press, 1990), pp. 113, 116, 159, and 254. See also, Xabier Kintana and Joseba Tobar, *Euskal Hiztegi Modernoa: Euskara-Espainiera, Espainiera-Euskara* (Bilbo: Itabat Taldea, 1977), pp. 61, 70, 71, 639 and 713; José Antonio Montiano and José Ramón de Urquijo, *Diccionario de Bolsillo Ikas: Euskera-Castellano, Castellano-Euskera, con unas 10,000 palabras de las más usuales en los dialectos Vizcaíno y Guipuzcoano* (Bilbao: Academia Montiano, 1976), pp. 13, 14, and 208; and Luis María Mujica, *Hiztegi Orokor-Teknikoa: 2. Euskara-Gaztelera* (Bilbao: Ediciones Vascas Argitaletxea, 1977), pp. 78, 80, 394, and 563.

4. Disregarding the names beginning with the letters *I* and *G*, and taking into account variations in spelling and the addition of descriptive suffixes to the root word, those names include the following: Aincibero, Ainciburu, Ainciburo, Aincildegui, Aincille, Aincimburu, Aincica, Aincio, Aincioa, Ainciondo, Aincizar, Ainduroa, Aindurriaga, Aindurrinaga, Ainsa, Aintsuberro, Aintzuberro, Aintziburu, Aintzuburu, Ainza, Ainzildegui, Ainzillegui, Ainziondo, Ainzoain, Ainzua, Ainzuain, Ainzubieta, Ainzuriza, Anca, Ancarano, Ancarola, Ancaubidart, Ancesti, Ancharte, Ancho, Anchorena, Anchoriz, Anchubero, Anchustegui, Ancia, Anciar, Ancibar, Ancibay, Ancibure, Anciburu, Ancieta, Ancilla, Ancin, Anciola, Anciondo, Anciso, Ancizar, Ancisaraimburu, Ancizo, Ancizu, Anda, Andaberri, Andabuan, Andaburu, Andagoya, Andalabar, Andama, Andamendi, Andanza, Andaraz, Andareche, Andariaga, Andariate, Andartz, Andasgoiti, Andatzategui, Andaya, Andazarrate, Andeca, Andecabeitia, Andechaga, Andechategui, Andechea, Anderal, Anderas, Anderaz, Anderazo, Anderica, Anderexo, Andes, Ando, Andoaga, Andoagui, Andoain, Andoegui, Andoez, Andoin, Andoinche, Andoiz, Andola, Andollu, Andonaegui, Andonegui, Andonote, Andora, Andosilla, Andua, Anduaga, Anduarte, Anduberri, Andueza, Anduezarena, Anduezu, Anduintz, Anduitz, Anduitze, Aunduiza, Anduize, Anduizu, Andulain, Andurain, Anduralde, Andurandegui, Andurra, Andurralde, Andurriaga, Anduya, Anduyaga, Anduze, Anduzqueta, Anduzu, Ansa, Ansabal, Ansalaz, Ansati, Ansiama, Ansiarte, Ansiburu, Ansil, Ansilla, Anso, Ansoain, Ansoandia, Ansoin, Ansoalde, Ansoar, Ansoagegui, Ansoberro, Ansoborro, Ansodi, Ansoguerri, Ansola, Ansolaberri, Ansolaena, Ansolaras, Ansolarez, Ansolea, Ansoleaga, Ansoliaga, Anson, Ansonea, Ansonecoa, Ansonegui, Ansorena, Ansorregui, Ansotegui, Ansotemi, Ansoti, Ansoyan, Ansu, Ansua, Ansuaga, Ansuain, Ansuarena, Ansuategui, Ansuaz, Ansuberro, Ansueta, Ansurez, Ansuriza, Ansutegui, Anta, Antsoso, Anza, Anzalde, Anzarena, Anzati, Anzelle, Anzeta, Anzi, Anzil, Anzin, Anziola, Anziondo, Anziturbi, Anzizar, Anzizu, Anzo, Anzoain, Anzoategui, Anzoberro, Anzola, Anzolaberri, Anzorandia, Anzorena, Anzorregui, Anzu, Anzuaga, Anzuan, Anzuane, Anzuategui, Anzuas, Anzuay Anzue, Anzuela, Anzueta, Anzunategui, Anzuola, Anzurez, and Anzuriza. The foregoing list of 217 Basque surnames was compiled from Isaac Lopez-Mendizabal, *Etimologías de Apellidos Vascos* (Buenos Aires: Edi-

ciones Librería del Colegio, 1958), José A. Mugica, *Apellidos de Iberia* (Bilbao: Editorial EDILLI, S.A., 1968), and *Apellidos Vascos de Iberia* (Bilbao: Editorial EDILLI, S.A., 1968).

5. Ramón Ansa Zinkunegi, "Sobre el Origen del Patronímico Ansa" (paper presented at the second annual Anza World Conference, Arizpe, Sonora, 1997), p. 4. See also Lopez-Mendizabal, *Etimologías,* pp. 287 and 289, and Mugica, *Apellidos Vascos,* p. 137.

6. Lopez-Mendizabal, *Etimologias,* p. 254.

7. Ibid., pp. 258, 289, and 290.

8. The most burning question that the Ansas of Hernani and surrounding areas had, when I first told them the story of their illustrious *pariente* who led the expedition to San Francisco, California, was, "Why did he spell his name that way?" None of them spelled their name with a z, and they had never known anybody who did. Like the majority of Ansas throughout the world, they all spelled their name with an s.

9. Although there are hundreds of signatures of Juan Bautista de Anza in existence, there is only one known signature of his niece, executed on January 10, 1799, in Arizpe, Sonora. See NSAA, Información Matrimonial, f. 214v. See also University of Arizona (hereinafter AZU) Microfilm Collection, film 811, roll 11, Arizpe Parish Records, and Family History Library Microfilm Collection (hereinafter FHL), Salt Lake City, microfilm no. 1389122.

10. Rachel Bard, *Navarra: The Durable Kingdom* (Reno: University of Nevada Press, 1982), p. 10.

11. Romans 15:28, *The New American Bible* (New York: Catholic Book Publishing Co., 1970), p. 194. See also Romans 15:24.

12. Rachel Bard, "Aimery Picaud and the Basques: Selections from The Pilgrim's Guide to Santiago de Compostela," *Essays in Basque Social Anthropology and History,* ed. William A. Douglass (Reno: Basque Studies Program, 1989), p. 193.

13. William A. Douglass and Jon Bilbao, *Amerikanuak: Basques in the New World* (Reno: University of Nevada Press, 1975), p. 21.

14. Christianity probably did not become a universally accepted religion in the mountainous Basque country until sometime in the tenth century. See Bard, *Navarra,* p. 13.

15. Douglass and Bilbao, *Amerikanuak,* pp. 23 and 33.

16. The six tribes were Aquitanos, Vascones, Caristios, Autrigones, Vardulos, and Vacceos. Their territory took in much of southwestern France and northeastern Spain. See Mugica, *Apellidos Vascos,* two-page map between pages 128 and 129.

17. Douglass and Bilbao, *Amerikanuak,* pp. 24–38.

18. Ibid., p. 39.

19. Juan Carlos I, present-day king of Spain, is a fortieth great-grandson of this first king of Nafarroa, Iñigo Arista. See Gobierno de Navarra, "Genealogía de los Reyes de Navarra," *Diario de Navarra* (Pamplona: Sedes Reales de Navarra, 1993).

20. Juan José Menezo, *Reinos y Jefes de Estado desde el 712* (Madrid: Edita Histori Hispana, 1987), pp. 9–65. Other writers claim 1200 and no other previous time.

21. Rodney Gallop, *A Book of the Basques* (Reno: University of Nevada Press, 1970), p. 13.

22. Giesey, *If Not, Not,* p. 40.

23. The oldest son of Sancho el Mayor, García, was given the Kingdom of Nafarroa.

Fernando received the *condado* (county or province) of Castilla after his father made it a kingdom. Ramiro was awarded Aragón. See Gregorio de Balparda y de las Herrerías, *Historia Crítica de Vizcaya y de sus Fueros* (Bilbao: La Editorial Vizcaina, 1974), 1:451.

24. From "Distribución que Sancho el Mayor hizo entre sus hijos. Acto de fidelidad prestado por el infante don Ramiro en favor de su hermano don García." Reprinted in Balparda, *Historia Crítica* (Bilbao: La Editorial Vizcaina, 1974), 1:452 n. 83.

25. Alberto y Arturo García Carraffa, *Diccionario Heráldico y Genealógico de Apellidos Españoles y Americanos* (Madrid: Lithografía de Foruny, 1947), p. 9.

26. From the Fuero of Nafarroa (ca. 1200), "Prólogo," reprinted in Giesey, *If Not, Not*, p. 47. In the original document it is spelled "Ansso."

27. The ancient spelling was generally "Cize," and the pass was called "El Puerto Cisereo." Correct pronunciation and modern Basque spelling rules render it "Zitsa." Anza, as pointed out previously, was generally spelled "Ansa" anciently.

28. Giesey, *If Not, Not*, p. 40.

29. Douglass and Bilbao, *Amerikanuak*, pp. 40–41.

30. Menezo, *Reinos y Jefes*, pp. 23–25.

31. Giesey, *If Not, Not*, pp. 46 and 47.

32. From "Santi Jacobi Dominum, Guía del viaje a Santiago, Capítulo VII: De los nombres de la tierra y de las cualidades de las gentes que hay en el camino de Santiago," reprinted in part in Balparda, *Historia Crítica* (Bilbao: La Editorial Vizcaina, 1974), 2:158.

33. Who actually wrote the *Guía* is open to debate. Rachel Bard gives convincing evidence that it was probably Picaud. See Bard, "Aimery Picaud," p. 191. For our purposes, the author is irrelevant. Whoever he was, he was contemporary, and the document, with all its flaws, is relevant to twelfth-century Zisa and the Compostela pilgrimages.

34. From "Santi Jacobi Dominum," reprinted in Balparda, *Historia Crítica*, 2:158.

35. Many generations afterward, when this part of the world came under French rule, the name, of course, became St. Jean Pied de Port ("St. John at the Foot of the Pass"), as it is known today in the Province of Benafarroa, France. The Basques call it Donibane Garazi.

36. L'Office de Tourisme, *St. Jean Pied de Port: Ongi Etori* (St. Jean Pied de Port: Office de Tourisme, 1996) p. 5.

37. See García Carraffa, *Diccionario Heráldico*, and *El Solar Vasco Navarro* (San Sebastian: Librería Internacional, 1966). See also Lopez-Mendizabal, *Etimologías*.

38. Menezo, *Reinos y Jefes*, p. 21.

39. These low-cut shoes, tied on by long laces wrapped around the ankle and calf, are today made of either leather or rubber and are still worn extensively in the Basque Country for folklore celebrations.

40. From "Santi Jacobi Dominum," reprinted in Balparda, *Historia Crítica*, 2:158.

41. Bard, "Aimery Picaud," p. 212 n. 68.

42. Mugica, *Apellidos Vascos*, p. 78. See also Garate, "Basque Names, Nobility and Ethnicity on the Spanish Frontier," *Colonial Latin American Historical Review* 2, no. 1 (1993): 80–82.

43. Bard, *Navarra*, pp. 46–51.

44. Ibid., p. 7.

45. García Carraffa, *Enciclopedia Heráldica y Genealógica Hispano-Americana* (Madrid: Nueva Impr. Radio, 1952–1963), 48:7.
46. From "Santi Jacobi Dominum," reprinted in Balparda, *Historia Crítica*, 2:158.
47. Ibid.; see also Bard, "Aimery Picaud," p. 202; and Julen Lizundia Aramaio, project coordinator, *Euskal Herriko Atlasa: Geografia-Ekonomia-Historia-Artea* (Donostia: Erein, 1979), pp. 22 and 66.
48. Zisa, situated on the main road to Compostela, was an important pilgrim stop and became Christianized early on. At this time it was under the jurisdiction of the bishop of Bayonne. See Balparda, *Historia Crítica*, 1:253.
49. García Carraffa, *Diccionario Heráldico*, 48:7.
50. Ibid., 3:9.
51. See, for example, Gipuzkoako Artxibategi Orokorra (hereinafter GAO), Tolosa, SS212, exp. 2, Demanda de filiazion por Antonio de Ansa como padre y administrador de Don Juan Bauptista y Don Juan Phelipe sus hijos y ausentes en Yndias, 1718, f. 11v.
52. Balparda, *Historia Crítica*, 1:219.
53. Lizundia, *Euskal Herriko Atlasa*, p. 66.
54. Balparda, *Historia Crítica*, 1:386 and 2:75.
55. Today, after nearly nine hundred years, that house is still a famous *casa solar* in the town of Hernani.
56. The early records of Hernani were lost in 1512 when French armies sacked and burned the town. See Hernaniko Udalbatza, *Hernani 1996ko Gida* (Bilbao: DYCA, Hernaniko Udala, 1996), p. 4.
57. Ibid., p. 7.
58. F. Borja de Aguinagalde, *Gipuzkoako Leinuen Aztarna Bila* (XV–XIX) (Zarautz: Gipuzkoako Foru Aldundia, 1994), pp. 64–65.
59. The upper nobility were the "caballeros" or "ricos hombres," and lower nobility were the "infanzones." See Bard, *Navarra*, p. 44; Garate, "Basque Names," pp. 81–86; and Alberto Santana, *Baserria* (Donostia: Gipuzkoako Foru Aldundia, 1993), p. 10.
60. Balparda, *Historia Crítica*, 2:194, 270, 344–346.
61. See for example, GAO, Demanda de filiazion, f. 40; or HUA, A-1-1-7, Libro de Elecciones de los del Gobierno de la villa de Hernani, Septiembre 29 de 1695, ff. 55v–57v.
62. Dario de Areitio y Mendiolea, *El Fuero de Vizcaya* (Bilbao: Imprenta Provincial de Vizcaya, 1977), pp. 323–380.
63. Garate, "Basque Names," pp. 83–85.
64. Hernaniko Udalbatza, *Hernani 1996ko Gida*, p. 4.
65. García Carraffa, *El Solar Vasco Navarro*, 6:166–167.
66. Urbieta's story was also the source of inspiration for Victor Hugo's drama *Hernani*, written in 1829. Present-day Hernani has a street named "Victor Hugo" in his honor southwest of the old part of town.
67. HUA, E-4-I-1-1 to 20, Construcción y obras de la Iglesia.
68. Hernaniko Udalbatza, *Hernani 1996ko Gida*, pp. 4 and 6; and HUA, D-3-3-1 and 2, Edificios Públicos. Although it was also constructed in the sixteenth century, the town hall had to undergo extensive reconstruction after an enemy grenade exploded the munitions cache stored there on September 16, 1875, during the last of Spain's Carlist wars.

69. From personal conversation between the author and historian Luix Mari Zaldua, September 19, 1996, in the town plaza of Hernani.

70. Gallop, *Book of the Basques*, p. 184.

71. Santana, *Baserria*, p. 10.

72. Based on HUA, Elecciones, 1695, f. 56, in which forty-five eligible voters are listed. Considering the "one fireplace, one vote" rule, if those forty-five "fireplaces" had an average of six family members (father, mother, three children, and one grandparent), there would have been 270 people living in Hernani that year. In an interesting litigation between the village *concejo* and the *patrono* of the church in 1490, the concejo claimed there were 300 married couples living in the town, but the patrono showed that there were only 150. See HUA, E-4-II-1-1, Patronato, Personal, Regimen Interior.

73. GAO, Carta de pago de Juanes de Ansa, PT-15T-21, 1471, ff. 251–251v.

74. Garate, "Basque Names," p. 84.

75. See Elizbarrutiko Histori Artxiboa (hereafter EHA), Donostia, Libros de Bautizados, Cassados, y Finados de San Juan Bautista de Hernani empezando en el año 1584. See also FHL, microfilm nos. 1157187, 1157190, and 1157191.

76. GAO, Carta de pago, ff. 251–251v.

77. Carla Rahn Phillips and William D. Phillips Jr., *Spain's Golden Fleece: Wool Production and the Wool Trade from the Middle Ages to the Nineteenth Century* (Baltimore: Johns Hopkins University Press, 1997), pp. 42, 168, 183, 212–214, 234, and 280.

78. Douglass and Bilbao, *Amerikanuak*, pp. 49–50.

79. Hernaniko Udalbatza, *Hernani 1996ko Gida*, p. 4.

80. EHA, Libros de Bautizados, 1, 2, 3, and 4.

81. EHA, Segundo Libro de Matrimonios de San Juan Bautista de Hernani, f. 14.

82. GAO, Demanda de filiazion, "Arbol Genealógico," preceding p. 1.

83. Ibid., Testimonios dados por Ignacio Antonio de Leyzaur, Juan de Galardi, Joseph de Arratia, Nicolas de Zuaznavar, y Sebastian de Zubelza, ff. 10, 14v, 18v, 22v, and 26.

84. EHA, Primer Libro de Matrimonios de San Juan Bautista de Hernani, f. 60v.

85. María Joan de Aguirre, Catalina de Echeberria, Catalina de Aguirre, or Catalina de Aranburu. See EHA, Primer Libro de Bautizados de San Juan Bautista de Hernani, ff. 140v, 151v, 164v, 175v, 179, and 195v.

86. Ibid., f. 203.

87. Ibid., ff. 214, 227, and 234v; EHA, Segundo Libro de Bautizados, ff. 8v and 17.

88. From personal observances of the author in Hernani and other Basque communities of our day.

89. EHA, Segundo Libro de Matrimonios, f. 2; Segundo Libro de Bautizados, ff. 35v, 49, 66, 81, and 111v; and Libro Tercero de Bautizados, f. 1.

90. GAO, Demanda de filiazion, f. 1.

91. EHA, Segundo Libro de Matrimonios, f. 14.

92. From Hernaniko Udalbatza, *Hernani 1996ko Gida*, and personal observations of the author.

93. EHA, Segundo Libro de Bautizados, ff. 100, 111v, and 128; Libro Tercero de Bautizados, ff. 18v, 37v, and 49. See also GAO, Demanda de filiazion; and Gipuzkoako Pro-

tokoloen Artxibategi Historikoa (hereafter GPAH), Oñati, leg. III-1267, 1689, ff. 77–78; leg. III-1268, 1691, ff. 40–42; and leg. III-1352, 1737, ff. 20–24.

CHAPTER TWO. LIFE IN HERNANI

1. GPAH, leg. III-1267, Censso de 80 ducados por Antonio de Anssa y Don Agustin de Zavala, en favor de Juan de Galardi, 27 May 1689, f. 77v.
2. EHA, Libros de Bautizados de Hernani, 2, f. 63.
3. All information concerning the inventory and makeup of the Anza Botica, unless otherwise noted, comes from GPAH, leg. III-1352, Inventario de Vienes de Antonio de Ansa, 10 July 1737, ff. 20–24.
4. HUA, E-7-I-9-8, Demanda interpuesta por Antonio de Ansa contra Teresa de Portugal, unnumbered folios following f. 27v at the end of the pleito.
5. A *tortilla* in the Basque Country, as well as everywhere else in Spain, was and is an omelet, eaten with many meals.
6. EHA, Libros de Bautizados de Hernani, 3, ff. 106 and 115.
7. EHA, Libros de Matrimonios de Hernani, 2, f. 53v.
8. EHA, Libros de Bautizados de Hernani, 2, f. 100.
9. A "vellón" was the fleece, or the wool, from one sheep. The copper coin called a *ducado de vellón* took its name from the fact that in Roman times copper coins had a sheep stamped on them. It was the provincial coinage for the Kingdom of Castilla, including the Basque country. A ducado de vellón was worth nearly three *pesetas*, a dozen *reales*, and approximately 400 *maravedís*. See Real Academia Española, *Diccionario de Autoridades, Edición Facsímil del Diccionario de la Lengua Castellana de los años 1726–1737* (Madrid: Editorial Gredos, 1990), II:344 and III:436.
10. GPAH, Censso de 80 ducados, f. 77.
11. HUA, C-2-2-8, Libranza a favor de Sebastián de Ollo, clérigo, por enseñar a leer y escribir a los mozos, 1564, f. 15.
12. All information concerning Antonio's education and his establishment of a pharmacy are found in GPAH, leg. III-1267, Censso de 80 ducados, ff. 77–78v.
13. HUA, Antonio de Ansa contra Teresa de Portugal, f. 5v.
14. EHA, Libros de Finados de Hernani, 2, f. 49.
15. GAO, Demanda de filiazion: Testimonio de Nicolas de Sassoeta, f. 22v; and EHA, Libros de Bautizados de San Vicente de San Sebastián, 5, ff. 54, 75, 87v, 109v, 123v, 134, 142, and 160.
16. EHA, Libros de Bautizados de Hernani, 2, f. 63.
17. Ibid., ff. 28, 48v, 77, 94v. See also FHL, microfilm no. 0665425, Primero libro de bautizmos, ff. 3v, 5, 6, and other unnumbered folios.
18. EHA, Libros de Finados de Hernani, 2, f. 10v.
19. Ibid., f. 39; and GPAH, leg. III-1268, Contrata para el Casamiento de Antonio de Anssa y Lucia de Sassoetta en 3 de febrero 1691, ff. 40-40v.
20. EHA, Libros de Bautizados de Hernani, 2, ff. 100 and 108.

21. GPAH, Contrata para el Casamiento, ff. 40–42.

22. All preceding and subsequent information concerning this loan and its particulars and participants, except as otherwise noted, are found in GPAH, leg. III-1267, Censso de 80 ducados, ff. 77–78v.

23. HUA, Antonio de Ansa contra Teresa de Portugal, f. 5v.

24. May 27, 1689.

25. EHA, Libros de Bautizados de Hernani, 3, f. 106. He had also been vicar from April 26, 1688 to December 2, 1688. See ibid., ff. 84 and 88.

26. All references to the agreement as well as the story that necessitated its execution, except as otherwise noted, come from GPAH, leg. III-1270, Venta de Censo por los Hijos de Estevan de Çuaznavar, 3 de Henero de 1693, ff. 1–2v.

27. EHA, Libros de Bautizados de Hernani, 2, f. 119v.

28. Reading original documents archived in HUA, one quickly becomes aware that the Sasoetas and the Zuaznabars were two of the most influential families in Hernani.

29. See, for example, HUA, E-7-III-3-10, Autos instruídos contra Pedro de Berra por injuriar al Capitan Esteban de Zuaznabar.

30. EHA, Libros de Bautizados de Hernani, 3, f. 56.

31. Ibid., f. 69.

32. GPAH, Contrata para el Casamiento, ff. 40v–41. Beyond the money that was provided here, Lucia's dowry from her two brothers and her mother is an interesting list of items: a silver basin valued at forty reales, ten silver spoons valued at thirty-three reales, a house with all its various floors and rooms and kitchen garden on Kale Nagusia for the space of twelve years, two used beds with six bedcloths (five new, and one of which was of Rouen linen, the others of common linen), three new tablecloths (two of French linen and the other of common linen), eight pewter plates, a two-liter pitcher and another the size of one-liter pitcher, two wooden chests (one of which was new), one Rouen linen bed tapestry composed of five curtains and a top that was still in the chest and had never been washed, two pairs of Rouen linen undershorts, four common linen handkerchiefs (all new), four dresses, one silk shawl, and a camlet dress valued at a hundred reales of silver.

33. In 1699 the *curaduría*, or guardianship, was passed from the Anzas to Juan Bautista de Zuaznabar (possibly an uncle or cousin) for him to take his turn at caring for the boys. See HUA, E-7-I-9-5, Autos instruídos para determinar había de ser el titular de la curaduria de bienes de los menores Teodoro y Miguel Antonio de Zuaznavar, hijos del capitan don Esteban de Zuaznavar. He was still acting as Miguel Antonio's guardian in 1708. Teodoro had already turned twenty-five by then, the legal age of majority. See E-7-I-11-2, Pedimento de Miguel Antonio de Zuaznavar contra Juan de Zuaznavar, administrador de su persona y bienes.

34. Information concerning the weddings comes from EHA, Libros de Matrimonios de Hernani, 2, ff. 53–53v.

35. Information about their clothing comes from GPAH, Contrata para el Casamiento, f. 41v; GPAH, Inventario de Vienes, f. 22; and HUA, Antonio de Ansa contra Teresa de Portugal, f. 5v.

36. See HUA, Antonio de Ansa contra Teresa de Portugal, f. 6; and HUA, E-7-I-11-8,

Pleito pendiente entre Juana de Roteta, viuda de Juan Bautista de Araeta, de una parte, y Francisco Antonio de Beroiz, de la otra, sobre deudas contraidas por la primera en reparos efectuados en los molinos de Ceago, ff. 45v and 58–59v.

37. EHA, Libros de Bautizados de Hernani, 2, ff. 63, 73v, 79v, 85, 96, 100, 108, and 118.

38. GPAH, Contrata para el Casamiento, f. 41v.

39. HUA, E-7-I-5-9, Pleito entre doña Polonia de Aranguren y Arteaga, viuda del capitan don Alonso de Herenosu y doña Magdalena de Herenosu, 1670; and GPAH, leg. III-1321, Cavildo eclisiastico para concurso de los Vienes del Capitan Don Alonso de Ereñozu de 2797 y medio de vellon, 13 de Diciembre de 1706, ff. 199–201.

40. HUA, E-7-I-11-4, Demanda interpuesa por Antonio de Anssa curador de Francisco Antonio de Veroiz contra Maria de Lecumberri viuda de Nicolas de Lecuona, 1709, f. 49.

41. HUA, E-7-I-5-8, Demanda interpuesta por Juan de Zabala Garagarza, maestro carpintero, contra doña mariana de Herenosu, Viuda del Sargento Mayor don Miguel de Beroiz, en razon del pago de la construccion de una casa levantada por el primero, 1668.

42. HUA, Pleito entre Juana de roteta y Francisco Antonio de Veroiz, ff. 49v–50.

43. EHA, Libros de Finados de Hernani, 2, f. 69v.

44. HUA, Demanda contra Maria de Lecumberri, ff. 25–25v.

45. GPAH, Contrata para el Casamiento, ff. 40–42.

46. HUA, A-1-7, Libro de Elecciones de los del gobierno de la villa de Hernani desde 29 de septiembre desde 1676 hasta 29 de septiembre de 1732, ff. 57, 104, and 108; HUA, Antonio de Ansa contra Teresa de Portugal, f. 6; GAO, Demanda de filiazion: Relacion de los actos positivos, 18 de julio de 1718, ff. 30–30v; and GPAH, leg. III-1308, Carta de pago de 27627 Reales de plata a esta villa y su Thesorero en favor de Simón de Zelarain, 28 de Septiembre de 1699, f. 712.

47. See, for example, GPAH, leg. III-1305, Censo de 300 ducados de plata de situazion principal y 15 ducados de Vellon derrenda añal por Antonio de Ansa deudor principal, 22 de septiembre 1698; leg. III-1279, Traspasso a favor de Sebastián de Araeta, 19 de octubre de 1703; and leg. III-1342, Compromiso por Antonio de Ansa y otros, 22 de Junio de 1735 años.

48. See, for example, GPAH, leg. III-1307, Rendamiento de Cassa. Antonio de Ansa a favor de Ignacio de Atolegui por Maria Ignacia de Zavalegui, Abril 1702; leg. III-1310, Poder Por Antonio de Ansa Curador adlitem de Don Juachin Ignacio de Berastegui para Andres Garcia procurador de Valladolid, 30 de Abril de 1712; leg. III-1322, Curaduria adlitem discernida a Antonio de Anssa de Don francisco Antonio de Verois y sus hermanas ante justicia ordinaria de esta villa, 1 de Abril de 1707 años; and HUA, E-7-I-11-5, Pleito entre Antonio de Anssa curador de Francisco Antonio de Veroiz, de una parte, y Antonio de Amitesarobe, de la otra, en razon de los molinos de Zeago, 1709.

49. See, for example, GPAH, leg. III-1282, Una liquidazion de quantas entre Antonio de Anssa y Catalina de Urrizmendi, 30 de Maio de 1707; leg. III-1288, Benta Real para Estevan de Echeverria y su mujer, 17 de septiembre de 1714; and leg. III-1337, Compromiso por Antonio de Ansa, 15 de Septiembre de 1730 años.

50. GPAH, leg. III-1287, Obligazion para la provision de la grasa o azeite de Vallena, primero de septiembre de 1713, ff. 245–250v.

51. Gallop, *A Book of the Basques*, pp. 16–17.

52. Gernikako Batzar Etxea Artxiboa, Gernika (hereinafter GBEA), 2263, Genealogía de Don José Luis Torres, Vildosola, Luque, Anza: Compulsa de oficio honorifico, primero de enero de 1772, ff. 687–688.

53. GBEA, 1258, Manuel de Ibarrola, Sauto, Lopez de Echavarri, Andechaga: Eleccion de Alcalde en Don Manuel de Ybarrola, primero dia del mes de Henero de 1768, ff. 74–74v.

54. GBEA, 2263, Los juntados y congregados tocantes al servicio de ambas magestades Divina y Humana en esta Anteiglesia de Ceanuri, ff. 33–35.

55. All information concerning the election of 1695, except as otherwise noted, comes from HUA, A-1-7, Libro de Elecciones, ff. 55v–57v.

56. From a conversation between the author and Ramón Ansa of Andoain, Gipuzkoa and Victoriano and María Lizeaga Ansa of Hernani on May 22, 1997.

57. GPAH, Censo de 300 ducados, f. 62v.

58. A cántaro with matching bolillas, made of polished silver, was owned and prized by every major town and village in the Basque country. An excellent example may be seen at the Casa de Juntas Museum in Gernika, Bizkaia.

59. HUA, E-4-I-1-31, Comunicacion dirigida a los hijos de la villa residentes en Indias, 22 de Noviembre de 1721, f. 10.

60. HUA, Pleito entre Juana de roteta y Francisco Antonio de Veroiz: Testimonio de Nicolas de Sassoeta, 12 de Septiembre del año de 1709, f. 49v.

61. Resurrección María de Askue, *Euskaleriaren Yakintza* (Bilbao: Diputación de Bizkaya, 1948), p. 341. Had the child been a girl, the bell would have tolled twice.

62. EHA, Libros de Bautizados de Hernani, 3, f. 115.

63. Askue, *Euskaleriaren Yakintza*, pp. 183–184. Had the child been a girl, a cluster of flowers would have been attached to the basket handle.

64. Ibid., p. 184.

65. HUA, E-4-I-1-12, Compromiso entre el consejo y Juan de Ayerdi, maestre Cantero para construir la pila bautismal con arreglo a la traza, 1566.

66. EHA, Libros de Bautizados de Hernani, 3, f. 115.

67. The main fiesta in Hernani was, and still is, that of San Juan in honor of Saint John the Baptist. See Hernaniko Udalbatza, *Hernani 1996ko Gida*, p. 7.

68. It is also possible that young Juan Bautista's paternal grandfather, Juanes de Ansa, also had the middle name of "Bautista," although none of the known records of the day reflect it. However, the paternal grandfather was and often is one's namesake in the Basque culture.

69. The Basques of Zisa, and probably the surrounding villages of Gipuzkoa and Benafarroa, including Hernani, had three sayings that they applied to San Antonio: (1) *Gauza galdua edireiteko, har San Antonio ararteko*—To find a lost object, San Antonio is the favorite; (2) *Mirakulu nahi bada, San Antoniori egin galda*—If you want a miracle, ask it of San Antonio; and (3) *Eriak ditu sendatzen, izuriteak hedatzen*—he is apt to heal sickness, and scatter the plague. See Askue, *Euskaleriaren Yakintza*, p. 290. Which of these three things may have inspired Juan Bautista de Anza or his parents to take San Antonio de Padua as his patron, as well as when it might have happened, has gone unrecorded. The only thing known for certain is that San Antonio was chosen prior to 1718.

70. Askue, *Euskaleriaren Yakintza*, p. 184.

71. This information comes from personal experience gained by the author over many years of association with his own and other Basque families in both the New World and the Old.

72. EHA, Libros de Finados de Hernani, 2, f. 62v.

73. GPAH, Censso de 80 ducados, f. 78.

74. The ancient cleaning station was personally visited by the author and discussed with historian Luix Mari Zaldua on September 11, 1996. See also Hernaniko Udalbatza, *Hernani 1996ko Gida*, front cover.

75. EHA, Libros de Bautizados de Hernani, 3, ff. 109, 112, 115, 115v, 117, 118v, 122v, and 134.

76. HUA, D-1-1-1, Documentos relativos a la barbacana situada entre las calles Mayor y de Cardaberaz, 1685–1899.

77. HUA, D-3-1-1, Noticias relativas a la construccion de casas nuevas de Ayuntamiento, 1680–1826.

78. HUA, Construccion de casas nuevas, 1680–1702.

79. GPAH, Censso de 80 ducados, f. 78; and HUA, E-7-I-5-16, Diligencias practicadas entre el general Don Miguel de Oquendo, Domingo de Artusa, Domingo de Larrañaga y el capitán Don Francisco de Ayerdi ante los licenciados Sebastián de Burgoa y Antonio de Miner, abogados de la Chancilleria de Valladolid, 1674.

80. The present Karabel Bridge is made of stone, but it was not constructed until 1805, replacing the older wooden structure built in 1558. See HUA, D-5-1-2, Puente de Carabel, 1558–1890.

81. HUA, E-4-III-1-2, Documentos referentes al Convento de San Agustin de Hernani que fue la antigua iglesia parroquial, 1547–1574.

82. The ancient fort at Santa Barbara was personally visited by the author and discussed with historian Luix Mari Zaldua on September 11, 1996. See also Hernaniko Udalbatza, *Hernani 1996ko Gida*, p. 4.

83. Juan Bautista de Vizarrón was born on November 4, 1661, at the Solar de Estibariz on the outskirts of Ituren, Nafarroa, to Juan de Vizarrón and Gracia de Camioa. See Archivo Diocesano Pamplona (hereinafter ADP), Bautizados de Ituren, libro 2, f. 89v.

84. EHA, Libros de Matrimonios de Hernani, 2, f. 53v.

85. EHA, Libros de Bautizados de Hernani, 3, ff. 106, 107, 115, and 115v.

86. HUA, B-5-I-1-1, Escrituras de conduccion y otros documentos referentes a los maestros de la Villa, Don Juan Bautista de Vizarron, Don Bernardo de Vizarrón, Don Jose Agustin de Galardi, Don Ignacio Antonio de Ugalde y Don Juan Manuel de Larrarte, 1718–1813.

87. GPAH, Inventario de Vienes, f. 24.

88. Hernaniko Udalbatza, *Hernani 1996ko Gida*, p. 16.

89. The Spanish word for ball, *pelota*, is probably a corruption of the Basque word *pilota*. The game of Basque handball is world famous today and has been played at least since the Middle Ages. See Gallop, *A Book of the Basques*, pp. 230–250.

90. HUA, E-4-I-1-28, Documentos referentes a la conservacion y reparacion del reloj publico emplazado en la torre de la iglesia parroquial, 1628–1763.

91. HUA, E-4-I-1-1, Hoja suelta que corresponde a una copia de cierta licencia real concedida en el año 1540.

92. HUA, E-4-I-1-29, Dictamenes en razon de quien habia de sufragar los gastos originados por las reparaciones de los destrozos causados en dicho altar por la caída de un andamio que se habia alzado para la lucidura de los interiores de la iglesia, 1700–1725.

93. EHA, Libros de Finados de Hernani, 2, f. 8.

94. Juan Domingo de Larreta of Goizueta, Nafarroa, married María Estevan de Anza on November 7, 1728 in the San Juan Bautista parish of Hernani. See EHA, Libros de Matrimonios de Hernani, 3, f. 3v.

95. EHA, Libros de Bautizados de Hernani, 3, f. 127; and, Libros de Finados de Hernani, 2, f. 31v.

96. EHA, Libros de Bautizados de Hernani, 3, f. 141v.

97. EHA, f. 154.

98. See EHA, Libros de Bautizados de Hernani, 4, ff. 245–266v; and Libros de Bautizados, 5, ff. 18–147.

99. Information about María Estevan's children: Juan Antonio Estevan Raimundo, María Antonia Rita Juachina, María Teresa, and Josepha Manuela Saturnina de Larreta is found at EHA, Libros de Bautizados de Hernani, 4, ff. 145v, 158, 167, and 174v.

100. HUA, E-4-I-1-29, Una liquidazion de quentas, f. 129v.

101. HUA, Censso de 80 ducados, f. 78.

102. HUA, E-7-I-8-4, Demanda de don Jose de Sasoeta presbitero contra el Doctor Don Agustin de Zavala por los alimentos suministrados a su mujer Catalina de Sasoeta y sus tres hijos, 1695.

103. HUA, E-7-I-14-6, Pleito entre Francisco de Zavala, poder habiente de Jose Antonio de Zavala, de una parte, y Sebastián de Cardaveraz Egusquiza y Ana Maria de Cardaveraz, viuda del dr. don Agustin de Zavala, 1722.

104. EHA, Libros de Bautizados de Hernani, 3, f. 176; and 4, ff. 3 and 10.

105. EHA, Libros de Finados de Hernani, 2, f. 26v.

106. Santiago Urquijo, "Cuenta de la medicina en la villa de Hernani," unpublished thesis (Hernani: Udalaren Artxiboa, N.D.), II:397–398, 545.

107. HUA, Antonio de Ansa contra Teresa de Portugal, f. 5.

108. GPAH, Censo de 300 ducados, f. 162v.

109. Phillips and Phillips, *Spain's Golden Fleece*, pp. 214, 266, and 280.

110. All information concerning the trip to Endaia, except as otherwise noted, comes from HUA, Pleito entre Juana de roteta y Francisco Antonio de Veroiz: Testimonio de Nicolas de Sasoeta, ff. 48v–50v.

111. The word *lehengusutipi* means a "male second cousin."

112. EHA, Libros de Matrimonios de Hernani, 2, f. 65v.

113. HUA, Pleito entre Juana de roteta y Francisco Antonio de Veroiz: Testimonio de Ana Maria de Larramendi, f. 46v.

114. A *doblón de a dos* was a gold coin worth two *escudos*. There were also *doblones de a cuatro* and *doblones de a ocho*. See Real Academia Española, *Diccionario de Autoridades*, II:324.

115. GPAH, Contrata para el Casamiento, f. 41v.

116. Born on June 4, 1686, Francisco Antonio was seven years older than Anza. See EHA, Libros de Bautizados de Hernani, 3, f. 75.

117. From the song "Gazte Gaztetatikan" by José María Iparragirre. See Luis Iriondo, *Iparragirre: Zure Oroiz* (Bilbao: Eusko Jaurlaritza Kultura Saila, 1981), p. 21. English translation from the original Basque and setting into verse by the author.

118. HUA, E-7-I-4-5, Pleito entre Pedro de Echanove y Juan Perez de Albistur, 1652.

119. HUA, E-7-II-21-5, Pleito ejecutivo seguido contra Francisco de Cler y su esposa Josepha de Peña, arrendatarios de las ferrerias de Ereñozu, a pedimento de don Pedro Ignacio de Atorrasagasti, 1715.

120. HUA, E-7-I-4-14, Informacion recibida a instancia de Don Miguel de Oquendo, General de la Escuadra de Cantabria, 1662.

121. EHA, Libros de Bautizados de San Vicente de Donostia, 5, f. 54.

122. Ibid., ff. 75, 87v, 109v, 123v, 134, 142, and 160.

123. HUA, Pleito entre Juana de roteta y Francisco Antonio de Veroiz: Testimonio de Matheo de Aiarragarai, 12 de Septiembre del año de 1709, f. 42.

124. HUA, Informacion recibida a de Don Miguel de Oquendo.

125. HUA, Pleito entre Juana de roteta y Francisco Antonio de Veroiz: Testimonio de Matheo de Aiarragarai, ff. 40–42v.

126. HUA, E-7-I-11a-5, Demanda de Juan de Camino ferron de la ferreria de Fagollaga contra Ramos de Arbelaiz carbonero por falta de pago y por incumplimiento de contrato, 1712.

127. HUA, Demanda contra Maria de Lecumberri: Testimonio de Joseph de Ysasa, 2 de Junio de 1710, ff. 33–34v.

128. HUA, Testimonio de Joseph de Yribarren; Testimonio de Juan de Arrazaun, 2 de Junio de 1710, ff. 34v–37.

129. HUA, Pleito entre Juana de roteta y Francisco Antonio de Veroiz: Testimonio de Domingo de Zuaznavar, ff. 45–48v.

130. HUA, Antonio de Ansa contra Teresa de Portugal: Memoria de las deudas y obligaciones, f. 6.

131. HUA, E-7-III-2-10, Autos de dununciacion de cuatros sacas de lana instruidas por Joan Beltran de Portu, Alcalde de Sacas de esta Provincia, 1673.

132. HUA, Pleito entre Juana de roteta y Francisco Antonio de Veroiz: Testimonio de Juan de Zapian, f. 77.

133. EHA, Libros de Matrimonios de Hernani, 2, f. 19; Libros de Bautizados de Hernani, 2, f. 117v; and 3, ff. 3v, 14, 27v, 39v, 55, 74, and 108v.

134. HUA, E-7-III-2-11, Procedimiento seguido a instancia del sindico procurador del Concejo de Hernani contra Juan Bautista de Araeta y consortes por haber introducido sidras de fuera en contravencion de las ordenanzas, 1673.

135. HUA, Pleito entre Juana de roteta y Francisco Antonio de Veroiz: Testimonio de Nicolas de Sasoeta, f. 50.

136. All of the information concerning the difficulties and litigation concerning the Molinos de Zeago comes from HUA, Pleito entre Juana de roteta y Francisco Antonio de Veroiz, ff. 1–110v.

137. There had been six sisters, but little María Christina had recently died.

138. HUA, C-5-III-1-3, Testimonio del contrato convenido en 1418 entre el Concejo de la Villa de Hernani y Juan Martinez de Ayerdi por el que se determina la participacion y las obligaciones que a las dos partes contratantes correspondia en los molinos de Ceago y Errotaberria, 1418.
139. HUA, Demanda contra Maria de Lecumberri, ff. 35v–36v.
140. EHA, Libros de Finados de Hernani, 2, f. 62v.
141. Ibid., sec. f. 75.
142. Ibid., sec. 2, f. 6v.
143. Ibid., sec. 2, f. 20v.
144. GPAH, Curaduria adlitem, f. 29; and HUA, Pleito entre Antonio de Anssa y Antonio de Amitesarobe, ff. 11–12v.
145. HUA, Pleito entre Antonio de Anssa y Antonio de Amitesarobe: Auto de Prueva, f. 18.
146. María Josefa was Francisco de Beroiz and Margarita de Larramendi's oldest child.
147. HUA, Demanda contra Maria de Lecumberri, f. 18.
148. HUA, ff. 32v–33.
149. HUA, Pleito entre Antonio de Anssa y Antonio de Amitesarobe: Real probision, ff. 90–90v.
150. AGN, Historia, leg. 333, Carta de Juan Bauptista de Anssa al Reverentissimo Padre Provincial, abril 21 de 1736, f. 77, in which Anza writes that he has been in Nueva España for twenty-four years.
151. All information concerning Hernani's native sons who were living in "Indias" comes from HUA, Comunicacion dirigida a los hijos de la villa, ff. 1–16.
152. EHA, Libros de Bautizados de Hernani, 2, ff. 67 and 118v.
153. Ibid., 3, f. 19v.
154. Ibid., ff. 80 and 118v.
155. Ibid., ff. 74v and 112.
156. Ibid., ff. 96 and 109.
157. José Luz Ornelas, *La Conquista de Sinaloa: Colección de documentos para la historia de Sinaloa* (Culiacán: Escuela de Historia de la Universidad Autonoma de Sinaloa, 1991), p. 26.
158. FHL, microfilm no. 0665425, Culiacán Parish Records.

CHAPTER THREE. THE NEW WORLD

1. Figuratively speaking, Anza here refers to the Society of Jesus as his "mother."
2. Archivo Histórico Hacienda, Temporalidades (hereinafter AHH, Temp.), leg. 17, exp. 21, Juan Bauptista de Anssa al Muy Reverendo Padre Provincial Andres Nieto, Julio 28 de 1729, f. 63.
3. Except as otherwise noted, all information that follows concerning the Real de Minas de Nuestra Señora de Guadalupe de Aguaje was taken from Archivo de Hidalgo de Parral (hereinafter AHP), Auttos de Visitta hechos Por el capitán Don Antonio Be-

zerra Nieto en la provinzia de Sonora y ostimuri, Año de 1718, ff. 16–29. Also at AZU, microfilm 318, 1718A.

4. Robert C. West, *Sonora: Its Geographical Personality* (Austin: University of Texas Press, 1993), p. 50. The date of the establishment of Nuestra Señora de Guadalupe de Aguaje is uncertain. West sets it at "sometime before 1717." Juan Mateo Manje spoke of a number of mines that were established in 1700 and 1701, listing them by name. He also said there were "others." It is impossible to know if one of those "others" was Nuestra Señora de Guadalupe de Aguaje, but it is safe to assume that its establishment came somewhere between 1700 and 1717.

5. Present-day Hermosillo, Sonora.

6. AHP, Auttos de Visitta, f. 16.

7. Ibid., ff. 14v–15.

8. Ibid., ff. 14–14v.

9. Ibid., ff. 32–32v.

10. West, *Sonora*, p. 50.

11. Paul M. Roca, *Paths of the Padres through Sonora* (Tucson: Arizona Pioneers Historical Society, 1970), p. 169.

12. AHP, Auttos de Visitta, ff. 13v–14.

13. Francisco Xavier Mestanza was missionary to Cucurpe and its visitas of Tuape and Opodepe, all on the San Miguel River. See AHP, Pleito de Francisco Montes, alias el Pintor, Capitan General de la Pimeria Alta, contra Francisco Joatime, Ignacio Medeguear, Melchor Conusi, Francisco Tanauti, y Santiago, 26 Abril de 1718, f. 15v.

14. AHP, Auttos de Visitta, ff. 31v–32.

15. AHP, Pleito de Francisco Montes, f. 15v.

16. AHP, Auttos de Visitta, ff. 32v–33.

17. West, *Sonora*, p. 61.

18. Ibid., p. 66.

19. Of the Lower Pimas at San Francisco Xavier de Tucuaba in January 1718, Bezerra Nieto said, "They have been at war with the gentile Seri Indians and Fronterizos since antiquity, experiencing murders at their hands every day, and from whose villainy they have sought my aid." See AHP, Auttos de Visitta, f. 15. Concerning the Pimas at La Santisima Trinidad del Pitic, he stated, "They all told me that it is only from the gentile Seri Indians that they are plagued with injury and death and other damage, and no one else. Even though they told me, I already knew that the enmity between the said two tribes is ancient, but they are both friends of the Spaniards." See AHP, Auttos de Visitta, f. 15v.

20. Charles W. Polzer, S.J., and Thomas E. Sheridan, editors, *The Presidio and Militia on the Northern Frontier of New Spain: A Documentary History*, vol. 2, part 1, *The Californias and Sinaloa-Sonora, 1700–1765* (Tucson: University of Arizona Press, 1997), p. 279.

21. That this was the type of house used in Sonora, see AHH, Temp., leg. 278, exp. 20, Superior Decretto del Gorbernador Señor Don Juan de Guemes y Horcasitas, Real de Nuestra Señora del Rossario de Nacossari, 22 de Mayo de 1749, ff. 24–27v. See also

Thomas E. Sheridan, *Empire of Sand: The Seri Indians and the Struggle for Spanish Sonora, 1645–1803* (Tucson: University of Arizona Press, 1999), p. 188.

22. Francisco Xavier de Gamboa, *Commentaries on the Mining Ordinances of Spain: Dedicated to His Catholic Majesty, Charles III*, trans. from the original Spanish by Richard Heathfield (London: Longman, Rees, Orme, Brown and Green Publishers, 1830), II:332.

23. West, *Sonora*, p. 52.

24. The full terminology used in the Auttos de Visita was *hacienda de sacar plata por beneficio de fuego*, "establishment for extracting silver through the workings of fire."

25. Gamboa, *Commentaries on Mining Ordinances*, II:187–188. See also West, *Sonora*, pp. 51–52.

26. Gonzalez de Mercado was probably also Basque, but his name belies the fact.

27. The word *panino* was used to describe the appearance of the ground, the color and shade of the ore, and other signs showing the presence and extent of precious metal. See Gamboa, *Commentaries on Mining Ordinances*, II:328. Bezerra Nieto uses the term once in the Auttos de Visita on folio 19v to describe the condition of the ore from this particular mine. He spells it "pañino."

28. Donald T. Garate, "Vizcaínos, Jesuits, and Álvarez Tuñón: An Ethnic View of a Frontier Controversy," *Journal of the Society of Basque Studies in America* XVI (1996): 81.

29. Francisco de Aldamiz was born in Gautegiz de Arteaga on August 28, 1691, to Juan de Aldamiz and María Andres de Ocollo. See Bizkaiko Eleizaren Histori Artxibua (hereinafter BEHA), Libro tercero de bautizmos, f. 20.

30. Gamboa, *Commentaries on Mining Ordinances*, II:126.

31. See two similar versions of a diary of the junior Juan Bautista de Anza, both written in full in his hand: AGN, Provincias Internas (hereafter PI), leg. 47, Diario que formo oi 24 de febrero de 1768 años, f. 314; and, Biblioteca Nacional de México, Departmento de Manuscritos, Estampas e Iconografia (hereinafter BNM), núm. 255/93, año 1769, 02.24, Diario que formo oi 24 de Febro de 1768 años, f. 2v.

32. West, *Sonora*, p. 61.

33. Gamboa, *Commentaries on Mining Ordinances*, II:324.

34. Ibid., p. 321.

35. Ibid., p. 328.

36. Ibid., p. 331.

37. AHH, Temp., leg. 278, exp. 11, Respuesta a Varias calumnias, y Postulados, de la Cecular âsamblea de San Juan, f. 2.

38. West, *Sonora*, p. 51.

39. Gamboa, *Commentaries on Mining Ordinances*, II:330.

40. West, *Sonora*, p. 63.

41. See Garate, "Vizcaínos, Jesuits, and Álvarez Tuñón," in its entirety, but especially pp. 79–83.

42. Iñigo de Loyola, Francisco Javier, and other founders of the Jesuit order, or Company of Jesus, were Basque. Consequently, the Basques have always been a major support group of the Jesuits. One Basque historian has said, "Through the origin of its

founder [Ignacio de Loyola]—and many of its disciples—the Company of Jesus occupied an impeccable position in the heart of Basque society, which played an important roll in its historical development. During the last centuries, our people have been aroused by the fluctuating events of the Jesuits, remaining loyal to them through good and bad. In peace and in war, in work and in leisure, in triumph and calamity, in their homeland or in bitter exile, the Basques have always been wherever there were Jesuits." See Tomás Uribeetxebarria Maiztegi, *Jesusen Lagundia Bizkaian* (Bilbo: Bizkaiko Foru Artxibategiko Erakustarteoa, 1991), p. 17.

43. West, *Sonora*, pp. 64–65.
44. Gamboa, *Commentaries on Mining Ordinances*, II:98.
45. AHP, Auttos de Visitta, ff. 21v–22.
46. West, *Sonora*, pp. 56.
47. AHP, Auttos de Visitta, f. 49.
48. West, *Sonora*, p. 48.
49. José de Zubiate (whose actual name was José de Orio y Zubiate) may have been the first person to run cattle in Sonora. He was an old-country Basque, born on May 29, 1659, in Eskoriaza, Gipuzkoa. See EHA, Bautizmos de Eskoriaza, libro 2, f. 10v.
50. José de Aguirre was another old-country Basque born in Aranaz, Nafarroa on April 12, 1687. See ADP, Bautizmos de Aranaz, libro 2, f. 9. For his marriage to Pascuala Nicolasa de Zubiate, see AZU, film 811, roll 10, marriage presentations for the year 1711 in the real de minas de Nacosari.
51. Although married to a criolla of Basque descent, Gregorio Álvarez Tuñón had an avid aversion for the Basques. See Garate, "Vizcaínos, Jesuits, and Álvarez Tuñón," pp. 68–69. He was born in the Álvarez family home on Calle de las Zurradores in the San Andrés Parish of Valladolid, Spain in 1678. He was the eldest of twelve children born to Juan Álvarez Tuñón y Quirós and Andrea María Ruiz. See Archivo Diocesano de Valladolid, Bautismos de San Andres, libro 5, f. unnumbered, and 6, ff. 2v, 10v, 22, 42, 52, 68v, 86v, 116v, 129v, 148, and 162v.
52. Gamboa, *Commentaries on Mining Ordinances*, II:97–98.
53. AHP, Auttos de Visitta, f. 8.
54. Ibid., ff. 4, 5, and 6.
55. Almada claimed, and numerous other secondary sources have followed suit, that Bezerra Nieto began service at Janos in 1686. See Almada, *Diccionario*, p. 92. However, Captain Juan Fernández de la Fuente certified on July 20, 1688, that Antonio Bezerra Nieto had joined his company at Janos as a soldier to replace Francisco Leopoldo Vásquez, who had died on March 26, 1688 in combat. See University of Michigan (hereinafter MIU), Zacatecas Collection (hereinafter ZCCL), 1688: Fernandez de la Fuente Certificacion. That the spring of 1688 was the time of his entrance into military service is borne out in at least two statements that Bezerra Nieto himself made. On October 10, 1721, he wrote that he had been in the service "for more than thirty-three years." See AHH, Temp., leg. 17, exp. 80, Bezerra Nieto Informe del Real Presidio de San Phelipe y Santiago de Janos, f. 1. Almost two years later on June 20, 1723, he said that he had been in the service "for thirty-five years." Bezerra Nieto Informe del Real Presidio de San Phelipe y Santiago de Janos, AHH, leg. 278, exp. 36, f. 1.

56. See MIU, ZCCL, 1713: Juan Fernandez de la Fuente Certificacion, in which he certified that Antonio Bezerra Nieto presented a royal title dated April 8, 1713, naming Bezerra Nieto as the new presidial captain at Janos to take Fernández de la Fuente's place.

57. Donald T. Garate, "La Ganadería de Sonora en la inspección militar de 1718," in *Sonora: 400 Años de Ganadería* (Hermosillo: Sociedad Sonorense de Historia, A.C., 1996), pp. 52–55.

58. AHP, Auttos de Visitta, ff. 14, 15, and 15v.

59. Since Sonora was part of the larger jurisdiction of Nueva Vizcaya at this time, its highest governing official was its alcalde mayor. It was the governor of Nueva Vizcaya, Manuel San Juan de Santa Cruz, who ordered this general inspection of mines and ranches in Sonora, dated October 13, 1717, in the town of Parral, Chihuahua. See AHP, Auttos de Visitta, ff. 1–3v.

60. The crown collected a tax of 20 percent on all silver mined in all the colonies.

61. Mining Ordinance Number 37 stated: "For as much as it commonly happens, that there are persons who hold many mines that they have taken, discovered, purchased, or acquired in some other manner, and who do not work them or keep them in activity, either because it is not in their power, or because they are engaged in working others that they consider better, in consequence of which they neglect to sink or explore the former mines, or to raise the ores from them, although sometimes better than the ores raised from the mines prosecuted by them: and whereas the mines they omit to work as aforesaid, become filled with water, to the injury of other adjoining and surrounding mines, which are kept at work, and which become deeper than the former. Wherefore, to obviate these and other inconveniences that follow or might follow from not working the mines,—We ordain and command that all persons shall be obliged to keep their mines worked by at least four persons in each mine or *pertenencia* (claim), whether they be sole proprietors of such mines or hold them in partnership; for however that may be, the setting on such four persons in the whole extent of each mine shall be sufficient to show that such mines are kept at work; which four persons aforesaid are to employ themselves about the working of the mine in which they shall be set on, in raising water or ore, or in doing some other work for its improvement, either within or without the mine: under the penalty, if any mine whatsoever shall not be kept worked by such four persons as aforesaid, during the term of four months successively, that the person to whom it may belong shall, ipso facto, forfeit it, and that he shall, from that time forth, have no right to the mine, unless by making registry thereof anew, and going through the other proceedings, in conformity with these ordinances; such mine to be adjudged to any person who may denounce it as insufficiently worked, provided he go through the proceedings aforesaid. But if, for any reasonable impediment, such as war, mortality, or famine, occurring in the part or place within the jurisdiction of which the mine may be situated, or within twenty leagues around, it shall be impossible to keep it worked by such four persons: in these cases, the aforesaid term of four months shall not run. If, however, such impediments shall exist out of the jurisdiction within which such mines shall be situated, and beyond such twenty leagues around, they shall not be admitted as an excuse for not keeping the mine at work, according to and under the penalties contained in this our ordinance." See Gamboa, *Commentaries on Mining Ordinances*, II:75–76.

62. Anyone could denounce a mine, whereby he would give information that it had been insufficiently worked as per Mining Ordinance Number 37. After due process, if the charges were proven, the mine would be awarded to the denouncer. See ibid., p. 323.

63. Each municipality, or jurisdiction, had its own court, presided over by a *teniente del justicia mayor*, or "deputy to the chief justice." At this date, the deputy justice for Nuestra Señora de Guadalupe de Aguaje was Manuel de Acuña. See AHP, Auttos de Visitta, f. 28. His superior at this time, the justicia mayor for all of Sonora, to whom appeals were taken, was Manuel de Hugues San Martín of the Real de Minas de San Antonio de Motepore. See AHP, Pleito de Francisco Montes, f. 16.

64. This was most likely Sonora's first weapons legislation.

65. The original name for the Presidio of Fronteras.

66. Manuel de Acuña.

67. The militia review was supposed to have taken place on Monday, January 24, 1718. The record is silent as to whether it actually happened or not.

68. Manuel de Acuña.

69. AHP, Auttos de Visitta, ff. 25–26v.

70. AHH, leg. 278, exp. 11, Respuesta a varias calumnias, 1722, ff. 1v–2.

71. GAO, Demanda de filiazion: Demanda de Anttonio de Ansa, ff. 1v and 2v.

72. AHP, Cartas y documentos sobre la oposición de los vecinos de motepore, Provincia de Sonora, para reconocer como Justicia Mayor a Joaquin José de Rivera, por decir que era hijo de mulata: Carta de Gregorio Albarez Tuñon y quiroz al Señor Governador y Capitan General Don Manuel San Juan de Santa Cruz, Febrero 10 de 1720, f. 19. Also at AZU, film 318, 1720A.

73. Garate, "Vizcaínos, Jesuits, and Álvarez Tuñón," pp. 74–75.

74. Francisco Xavier de Barcelón was married to a Basque criolla, Francisca de Heredia, and lived at Nacozari prior to the silver discovery at Tetuachi. See Garate, "Vizcaínos, Jesuits, and Álvarez Tuñón," p. 68. He served as both a corporal and a sergeant in the compañía volante of Fronteras. See Burrus, S. J., *Kino and Manje: Explorers of Sonora and Arizona—Their Vision of the Future* (St. Louis: Jesuit Historical Institute, 1971), pp. 210, 344, and 372. The name was sometimes spelled "Barcelona." See Polzer and Sheridan, *The Presidio and Militia*, p. 283.

75. A person of the name of José de Goicoechea was, like Juan Bautista de Anza, born in Hernani, Gipuzkoa. If he is the same person as the miner, he was nineteen years Anza's senior, born March 9, 1674. See EHA, Libros de Bautizados de Hernani, 3, f. 15v. On the other hand, he could have been a brother or relative of Martin de Goicoechea, the owner of the Santo Domingo Mine living at Aigame during Bezerra Nieto's 1718 inspection. See AHP, Auttos de Visitta, f. 32v.

76. Although Antonio de Miranda's place of birth cannot definitely be identified as Hernani, he may be one of two people by that name recorded in the parish records there. See EHA, Libros de Bautizados de Hernani, 3, ff. 70 and 86. Regardless, the name "Miranda" is nearly ubiquitous in that region of Gipuzkoa, and there is a good chance that Antonio and Juan Bautista de Anza knew each other in the old country. There is also a good chance that Antonio was a brother of, or related in some other way, to Gregorio Álvarez Tuñón's and Rafael Pacheco Zeballos's wives, as they were both Mirandas. See

AZU, microfilm 811, roll 10, Libro de Bautismos de Nacosari empezando Octubre, 1775, unnumbered pages. The name is also seen as López de Miranda.

77. Evidently not realizing that "Ju°" was a universal abbreviation for "Juan," Smith rendered the name "Julio Domingo de Berroeta." Fully 50 percent of Basque males in this era were named "Juan." I have even seen a few named "Julian," but I have yet to see anybody named "Julio." Numerous other such errors in Fay Jackson Smith's *Captain of the Phantom Presidio* (such as confusing Governor Alday with Governor San Juan de Santa Cruz throughout, accepting as fact that Juachín José de Rivera was a mulato even though he effectively proved he was not, repeatedly confusing the offices of alcalde mayor and justicia mayor and who was serving in them, etc.) make it necessary to cross reference the work closely to distinguish between error and historical fact. Smith does appear to be following Donohue's lead in saying Rivera was appointed "alcalde mayor," when in actuality he was appointed "justicia mayor." See John Augustine Donohue, S.J., *After Kino: Jesuit Missions in Northwestern New Spain, 1711–1767* (St. Louis: Jesuit Historical Institute, 1969), p. 26. The surname Berroeta, of course, is Basque. Whether rendered "Berrueta" or "Berroeta," the name signifies an area of "wetland briar patch," and had its origins in Gipuzkoa and Nafarroa. See García Carraffa, *El Solar Vasco Navarro*, II:463. Juan Domingo owned a store at Bavicanora both prior to and after the silver discovery at Tetuachi. He and José de Goicoechea were *compañeros*, "close friends." See AHH, Temp., leg. 17, exp. 64, Juan Domingo de Berroeta al Muy Reverendo Padre Cristóbal de Cañas, Enero 27 de 1722, ff. 1–4.

78. He was still living at Tetuachi and operating one of its mines at the time of the 1736 Arizona silver discovery. He was the father of the junior Juan Bautista de Anza's wife, Ana María Pérez Serrano. See Donald T. Garate, "Who Named Arizona? The Basque Connection," *Journal of Arizona History* 40, no. 1 (1999).

79. Fay Jackson Smith erroneously sets Berroeta's place of residence as the mission of Baviácora. However, the letter from which she quotes is clearly signed at the real de minas of Bavicanora on January 27, 1722. See Smith, *Captain of the Phantom Presidio*, pp. 41–44; and AHH, Temp., leg. 17, exp. 64, Berroeta a Cañas, f. 4.

80. The original Aránzazu, high in the mountains southwest of Hernani and famous among the Basques, was and is visited yearly by tens of thousands of religious pilgrims. Even Iñigo de Loyola, founder of the Jesuits, is known to have gone to Aránzazu for spiritual enlightenment and guidance prior to one of his pilgrimages. See Juan Plazaola, *Rutas Ignacianas* (Loyola: Edita Euskojaurlaritza, 1991), pp. 41–42.

81. The exact date of Don Gregorio's appointment seems to be uncertain. Almada, *Diccionario*, p. 47, sets the date as 1708. Smith, *Captain of the Phantom Presidio*, p. 25, leaves it vaguely open between 1709 and 1711. Luis R. Gonzáles, *Etnología y Misión en la Pimería Alta, 1715–1740* (México: Universidad Nacional Autónoma de México, 1977), p. 127, sets 1706 as the date that Álvarez Tuñón became interim captain at Fronteras, with his appointment as capitán vitalicio coming "a little later."

82. Garate, "Vizcaínos, Jesuits, and Álvarez Tuñón, pp. 67–69.

83. Domingo Jironza Petriz de Cruzat was the first capitán vitalicio, appointed when the first captain, Francisco Ramirez de Salazar, died before taking command. Through political maneuvering, Jironza was replaced by a man named Jacinto Fuensaldaña. The

latter individual held the office until his death, at which time Martín de Ibarburu was appointed interim captain until Gregorio Álvarez Tuñón y Quirós could be permanently established in the position. See Smith, *Captain of the Phantom Presidio*, pp. 19–25 and 105.

84. Smith, *Captain of the Phantom Presidio*, p. 105.

85. The citizens were unsuccessful in their attempt to remove Fuensaldaña and were even charged with paying half of his court expenses in Mexico City. It is doubtful that any payment was made, and Fuensaldaña died, solving their problem of his mismanagement of the garrison. However, they soon learned they had fallen from the frying pan into the fire when Don Gregorio took over as its captain. See AGN, Cárceles y Presidios, Autos de Inspección 2, Demanda del Duque de Linares, ff. 23–26; and Smith, *Captain of the Phantom Presidio*, p. 25.

86. Juan Mateo Manje y Cabero was born in the Province of Aragón, Spain in the year 1670. He came to Nueva España in 1692 at the request of his uncle, Domingo Jironza Petriz de Cruzat, former governor of New Mexico, alcalde mayor of Sonora, and soon-to-be captain of the Presidio of Fronteras. Known for his exploratory expeditions with the famed Father Kino, he was already one of the old guard by the time of Juan Bautista de Anza's arrival in the New World. See Burrus, *Kino and Manje*, p. 47.

87. AHH, Temp., leg. 278, exp. 31, Señores Vezinos del Valle de Sonora y sus Contornos, febrero 9 de 1720, ff. 1–3.

88. Polzer and Sheridan, *The Presidio and Militia*, pp. 257–258 and 278–279.

89. Ibid., pp. 279–286.

90. AHP, Cartas y documentos: Carta del General Don Anttonio Bezerranieto al gobernador Don Manuel San Juan de Santa Cruz, Abril 12 de 1718 años, f. 187.

91. AHH, Temp., leg. 278, exp. 41, Informe de Joseph Maria Genobese, f. 4v. Tanateros were the absolute bottom rung of the social ladder, at least to an employer like Álvarez Tuñón. By associating the Basques with tanateros, he was in effect labeling them the "scum of the earth."

92. Álvarez Tuñón and Pacheco Zeballos were married to sisters, María Magdalena de Miranda and Michaela López de Miranda, respectively. See AZU, Libro de Bautismos de Nacosari, unnumbered pages.

93. Ibid., f. 25.

94. BNM, núm. 21/699, año 1722-02-08, Un discreto y Venerable Anciano a sus Compatriotas y Paisanos de la Provincia de Sonora, ff. 3–3v.

95. Donohue, *After Kino*, p. 21.

96. Thomas C. Barns, Thomas H. Naylor, and Charles W. Polzer, *Northern New Spain: A Research Guide* (Tucson: University of Arizona Press, 1981), p. 113.

97. San Juan de Santa Cruz was born at Sopuerta, Bizkaia. See Polzer and Sheridan, *The Presidio and Militia*, p. 291.

98. Martín de Alday was born in Eskoriaza, Gipuzkoa on October 3, 1657, to Martín de Alday and Catalina de Lamariano. José de Zubiate was born in the same village on May 29, 1659, to Baltazar de Orio and María de Çubiate. See EHA, Bautizmos de Eskoriaza, libro 2, ff. 7 and 10v.

99. Donohue states that "marriage had made him [Rivera] a relative of Tuñón." See

Donohue, *After Kino*, p. 26; and AHH, Temp., leg. 278, exp. 31, Señores Vezinos, f. 1v. The validity of that statement is uncertain because the letter from which Donohue quotes simply says that Rivera was a *paniaguado* of Álvarez Tuñón. A paniaguado is a close friend, often boarding with the person in question. Unless there is some other reference to this supposed relationship, it would be more accurate to say that Rivera was an "intimate friend" of Álvarez Tuñón than to call him a "pariente." In reality, the word "puppet" would probably most accurately describe him.

100. Barns, Naylor, and Polzer, *Northern New Spain*, p. 113.

101. AHP, Cartas y documentos: Capitan Don Rafael Pacheco Zevallos Nombramiento, Arizpe, 11 del mes de Marzo de 1718 años, f. 3.

102. His ethnic background is unknown, but the surname is more likely to be Spanish than Basque.

103. GAO, Demanda de filiazion: Testimonios y Auto, ff. 10–29 and 40v–41v.

104. AHP, Cartas y documentos: El Capitan Don Raphael Pacheco Zevallos, nombramiento de teniente de justicia mayor, ff. 3.

105. Ibid., f. 4.

106. AHP, Carta de Joachin Josepha de Ribera la Gobernador y Capitán General, Señor Don Manuel San Juan de Santa Cruz, febrero 4 de 1720, f. 15v.

107. Ibid.

108. In other words, Rivera had not proven to their satisfaction that he was not born of a mulata, that he was of legitimate birth, or that he had the requisite limpieza de sangre and noble bloodlines.

109. The decorum and propriety of the Spanish code of ethics is always to be marveled at. Here we have men whose animosity toward each other is obvious and yet they go around "kissing" each other's hands, or at least talking about it.

110. AHP, Cartas y documentos sobre la oposición: Carta de Anza, et al. a Don Joachin de Rivera, febrero 2 de 1720, f. 5.

111. AHP, Carta de Joachin Joseph de Ribera a Don Manuel San Juan de Santa Cruz, febrero 4 de 1720, f. 16.

112. Ibid., f. 16v.

113. AHP, Carta de Joachin Jose de Ribera al General Don Gregorio Albarez Tuñon y Quiros, febrero 6 de 1720, f. 17.

114. AHP, Alvarez Tuñon a San Juan de Santa Cruz, ff. 19–19v.

115. AHH, Temp., leg. 278, exp. 31, Señores Vezinos, ff. 1–3. Of all the people in Sonora who knew the kind of service that Don Gregorio was performing, those at the presidio at Fronteras should have known best. Of the twelve citizens who signed the letter, at least five were probably Basque—Miguel Antonio de Mondragon, Joseph Antonio de Salazar, Bernardo de Calbo, Juan de Arvizu, and Andres de Peralta.

116. In this instance we find a prominent "Spaniard" from Aragón allied with the Basques. His personal feelings about them as an ethnic group are unknown. Chances are, coming from Aragón, he had close ties to and associations with, and possibly even heritage in, the Basque country. The second name of his uncle, "Petriz de Cruzat" (Pedro of the Crusade), is an ancient Basque name from Nafarroa, given to one Don Guevara because of services rendered in the first crusade to the Holy Land. See García Carraffa, *El*

*Solar Vasco Navarro,* III:84–85. Regardless, Manje had a personal axe to grind and was obviously more than willing to stand on the side of whatever cause might bring Don Gregorio down. He and his uncle, Domingo Jironza Petriz de Cruzat, had been forced out of Fronteras by the political tactics of Don Gregorio and his uncle, Jacinto Fuensaldaña. Manje was not impressed by the way either of the latter two individuals had operated the presidio. See AHH, Temp., leg. 278, exp. 37, Juan Matheo Manje al Muy Reverendo Padre Visitador Joseph Maria Genovese, and Smith, *Captain of the Phantom Presidio,* pp. 23–24.

117. Donohue, *After Kino,* p. 26, and Smith, *Captain of the Phantom Presidio,* p. 33, both say that Manje went to Parral to present the case before the governor. However, Rivera in his February 6th informe to Álvarez Tuñón clearly states, "sale para Mexico Manje y para el Parral Alday"—"Manje left for Mexico and Alday for Parral." The confusion has come from the fact that there were two Aldays, the soon-to-be governor, Martín de Alday, living in Chihuahua and probably totally oblivious at this point to what was happening, and Pedro de Alday, operating a hacienda de sacar plata at Banámichi (see AHP, Auttos de Visitta, f. 37v) and deeply involved in the controversy. Both Pedro and Martín de Alday were Basque. Their blood relationship is unknown, but Pedro was possibly Martín's son or nephew.

118. This is Jamaica, Sonora, not the island of Jamaica.

119. AHP, Ribera a Albarez Tuñon, f. 18v.

120. Plural of *arcabuz,* or "harquebus," an early type of portable firearm, originally supported on a forked rest during firing. Although this type of firearm had long since been replaced by the lighter *miquelete,* developed in Nafarroa, the word *arcabuz* continued to be used, at least in Nueva España, into the mid-1700s. Only then does one start to see use of the word *escopeta,* or "musket."

121. AHH, Temp., leg. 278, exp. 11, Informe al Señor Gobernador y Capitan General de la Nueva Vizcaya, febrero 22, 1720, f. 17.

122. Agustín de Vildósola was born in Billaro, Bizkaia, Spain to José de Vildósola and Francisca de Aldecoa on August 28, 1700. See BEHA, Bautismos de San Bartolome de Villaro, f. 104v. See also Bizkaiko Foru Aldundia Artxiboa (hereinafter BFA), leg. 291, núm. 26, Informacion de Vizcainia de don Agustin de Vildosola y consortes, f. 53v.

123. Polzer and Sheridan, *The Presidio and Militia,* p. 385.

124. AHH, Temp., leg. 278, exp. 11, "Respuesta a Varias calumnias," ff. 1v and 25. The "Reply to Various False Charges" was written in response to charges leveled at the Jesuits by Gregorio Álvarez Tuñón y Quirós at a secret meeting held at San Juan Bautista. It has the handwriting of a *notario eclesiástico,* an "ecclesiastic scribe," who wrote much of the correspondence of the day—a man by the name of Manuel José de Sosa. Another document compiled by Sosa, written in response to Don Gregorio's charges and signed by seventeen men (at least thirteen of whom were known to be Basque), carries the date of February 20, 1722. See AHH, Temp., leg. 278, exp. 35, Carta al Exelentisimo Señor, ff. 1–2. If this particular document was not written on that date, it certainly was written sometime between the middle of January and then. The pages containing the "Respuesta" and other testimonials about the same subject have become mixed up in the legajo and require some sorting to maintain continuity in the flow of the text. This par-

ticular quotation starts on the off side of folio 1 and is continued on the front side of folio number 25.

125. Everything concerning the story of this Apache campaign, except as otherwise noted, comes from AHH, Temp., leg. 278, exp. 11, ff. 1–25v.

126. AHP, Investigacion del Alcalde Maior Miguel Albarez de la Bandera en el pueblo de Tuape, el 17 del mes de octubre del año 1720, ff. 476–477.

127. Sheridan, *Empire of Sand*, p. 59.

128. The original Spanish reads, "Dexase aqui entre renglones."

129. Roca, *Paths of the Padres*, pp. 154–155.

130. Ibid., p. 161.

131. Sheridan, *Empire of Sand*, pp. 36–97.

132. Smith, *Captain of the Phantom Presidio*, pp. 86–87.

133. The campaigns against the Apaches led by the Anzas finally came to an end with the death of the junior Juan Bautista de Anza on December 19, 1788. See AGN, PI, leg. 83, f. 46.

### CHAPTER FOUR. THE CAVALRY OF THE FRONTIER

1. From an *hoja de servicio* (service record) in the Municipal Archive of Parral, dated March 20, 1724, containing this and other *filiaciones* (physical descriptions) of soldiers, dated March 23, 1724, and provided to me by Dr. Sergio Becerra Kahuam through Carmen Boone de Aguilar.

2. Description of the Janos presidio comes from the color map of the same, drawn by José de Urrutia in 1766 and archived today in the British Library of London (hereinafter BLL), *Plano de San Felipe y Santiago de Janos*. A facsimile is also published in Max L. Moorhead, *The Presidio* (Norman: University of Oklahoma Press, 1975), pp. 134–135.

3. See MIU, ZCCL, 1713: Juan Fernandez de la Fuente Certificacion.

4. Francisco Almada, claims, among other seriously flawed statements about Bezerra Nieto, that he took part in the failed attempts at reconquering New Mexico under Domingo Jironza Petriz de Cruzat. See Almada, *Diccionario*, p. 92. This is doubtful because those attempts took place in 1681 and 1689. The 1681 date is doubtful because Bezerra Nieto himself claimed that he did not join the military until 1688. And the date of 1689 is also doubtful because he was listed as a soldier at Janos throughout that year. However, there may be some truth in the statement. In the fall of 1691, Bezerra Nieto was called by Nueva Vizcaya's governor, Juan Isidro de Pardiñas, to "carry out business in the service of the king." His records at Janos show a break in service between 1692 and 1698. His absence from Janos during those years could have allowed for him to go to New Mexico in 1692 with Martín de Alday and other Nueva Vizcaya soldiers during the successful reconquest of New Mexico by Diego de Vargas. This information was supplied to the author by historian Rick Hendricks of Las Cruces, New Mexico in a letter dated May 21, 1997. See also MIU, ZCCL, 1691, 1692, and 1697: Certificaciones.

5. GBEA, 1593, Genealogia de José Luis Torres, Vildosola, Luque, Anza, Guernica, 20 febrero 1793: Testimonio de Manuel Vasques, teniente gobernador y juez politico de

Sonora en el Real de Minas de Nuestra Señora de Rosario de Nacosari en 2 de mayo de 1753, f. 279.

6. Tomás Antonio was a bachiller and deputy priest at Janos during his father's tenure there and many years after his parents' death (see University of Texas, El Paso (hereinafter TXE), Microfilm Collection, Janos Baptisms and Deaths, unnumbered pages; also FHL, microfilm nos. 1156624 and 1156625). Felipe, at least in 1718, lived at San Juan Bautista de Sonora (see AHP, Auttos de Visitta, f. 5v). Pedro was a soldier at Janos for many years (see TXE, Janos Baptisms and Deaths, unnumbered pages; also FHL, microfilm nos. 1156624 and 1156625). Gaspar was married to Micaela Grijalva and lived at or in the vicinity of the Divisadero Ranch between Santa María Suamca and Guevavi in the 1740s (see TUMA, Mission Registers of Santa María Suamca, ff. 42, 44, and 47; and Los Santos Angeles de Guevavi, ff. 77 and 82). María Rosa lived on the Divisadero Ranch after the death of her husband, Juan Bautista de Anza (see AHH, Temp., leg. 278, Reconvension del Padre Visitador Duquesne al Governador de Sonora, 1747, f. 23).

7. TXE, Janos Baptisms and Deaths, unnumbered pages; also FHL, microfilm nos. 1156624 and 1156625.

8. Naylor and Polzer, *The Presidio and Militia*, 1:584.

9. AHH, Temp., leg. 278, exp. 11, Respuesta a Varias calumnias, written in February of 1722 says that Anza was the alférez at Janos at that time, and Nicolás de Oro said that Anza was a son-in-law of Bezerra Nieto in April of 1722. See AHH, Carta de Nicolas de Oro, f. 1.

10. Biblioteca y Museo de la Universidad de Sonora, Colección de Microfilmes, Testimonio de las diligencias seguidas a pedimento de los herederos de Don Manuel Esteban Tato ante el Gobernador Don Pedro Corbalan contra el Capitán don Josef Antonio de Vildosola. Microfilm roll 2, sec. no. 51/729. María de Anza, who was married in 1734 to José Antonio Romo de Vivar, and was the daughter of Captain Juan Bautista de Anza and María Valenzuela, was one of the heirs named in the litigation. She is most likely one of the known Marías—either María Gertrudis or María Manuela.

11. Carmen Pellat personal archive, Arizpe, Sonora, Marriage Presentation of José Antonio Romo de Vivar and María de Ansa, Fronteras, Sonora, ff. 6–12v. The original presentation, in which María de Ansa is said to be sixteen years of age, is dated March 19, 1734 in the Real de Minas de Nuestra Señora del Rosario de Nacozari. It is in the possession of Carmen Pellat of Arizpe, Sonora, Mexico. Although the author was not allowed to photograph it, he was given permission to copy it word for word, the transcript of which is in the Mission 2000 documents of Tumacácori National Historical Park. It clearly states that María was the daughter of Captain Juan Bautista de Anza and María Valenzuela. Whether the two had been "legitimately" married is unknown. The presentation does not say that Anza was a *viudo*, or "widower," but it likely would not have made such a statement since he was married to María Rosa Bezerra Nieto at the time of his daughter's marriage.

12. See baptismal record for Juan Joseph Antonio Tato at Basochuca on December 31, 1749, at AZU, film 811, roll 12, Bautismos de Nacosari, f. unnumbered. She and her brother-in-law, Gabriel de Vildósola, were his godparents.

13. She appears as a witness for a marriage at Guevavi on July 26, 1756 with Ignacio

Diaz del Carpio (see TUMA, Mission Register of Los Santos Angeles de Guevavi, f. 32). She and Diaz del Carpio were probably husband and wife, which has led to the misconception that José Manuel Diaz del Carpio was a brother of Anza's wife (see John L. Kessell, *Mission of Sorrows: Jesuit Guevavi and the Pimas, 1691–1767* (Tucson: University of Arizona Press, 1970), p. 157). María Gertrudis and her brother, Francisco de Anza, were witnesses at marriages that took place at Suamca on July 8, 1755 and December 25, 1756 (see TUMA, Mission Register of Santa María Suamca, ff. 19 and 100).

14. This comes from personal conversations with both Tom Chávez, director of the museum at the Palace of Governors in Santa Fe, and Dr. Charles Polzer, past director of the Documentary Relations of the Southwest in Tucson. Dr. Polzer has uncovered some bit of evidence in the archives of Spain that Juan Bautista de Anza was in Santa Fe but the author has not seen that documentation to corroborate or expand on it.

15. See TXE, Janos Baptisms and Deaths, unnumbered pages, in which Juan Bautista de Anza is recorded as godfather repeatedly at baptisms during those years. Since he is not recorded as a "proxy" godfather in any of the records, he had to have been present for each of them. Although this certainly would not preclude him having gone to Santa Fe, it, along with the fact that he was an officer at Janos, shows that he was not stationed at Santa Fe permanently for any amount of time.

16. All of the foregoing information was gleaned from TXE, Janos Baptisms and Deaths, unnumbered pages.

17. The first indication that Pedro Felipe de Anza was in the New World comes from a Janos baptismal record dated April 1, 1724, at which he and Josefa Pacheco were godparents. See TXE, Janos Baptisms and Deaths, unnumbered page, but the fourth one in sequence from the beginning of the book.

18. Everything concerning the soldiers who manned the Janos presidio, except as otherwise noted, comes from AHP, Auttos de Visitta echa al real Presidio de San Phelipe y santiago de Janos por El Capitan Don Gregorio Alvarez tuñon y Quiros Visitador General de la Armas de este Reino de la Nueva Vizcaya, Año 1723, ff. 1–12v.

19. The military campaign of 1695 against the Pima was conducted in reaction to the murder of Father Francisco Xavier Saeta at the Mission of Caborca in western Sonora. The expedition was made up of forces from four separate units in Sinaloa, Sonora, and Nueva Vizcaya. It left Janos on June 17 and arrived back there four months later on October 6, 1695, after having covered over a thousand miles in what is today southern Arizona, northern Sonora, and northwest Chihuahua. It was the largest combined military effort staged up to that time in all of northern Nueva España. See Naylor and Polzer, *The Presidio and Militia*, pp. 582–718.

20. Ibid., pp. 600–605.

21. BNM, núm. 21/699, Un discreto y Venerable Anciano, f. 8v. Although this document maligning Don Gregorio is unsigned, it carries the elaborate and totally distinct rubric of Martín de Ibarburu. Compare the rubric of Martín de Ibarburu that accompanies his signature at AHH, leg. 278, exp. 35, Carta al Exellentisimo Señor, f. 3v, with the two rubrics that appear here at ff. 1 and 15. There is no mistaking who wrote the letter. Gonzáles tried to make the case that the letter was possibly written by the "sarcastic pen" of Agustín Campos (see Gonzáles, *Etnología y Misión*, pp. 237–238). This is obvi-

ously not the case, however, for two reasons: (1) Campos's problems clearly revolved around other matters than Don Gregorio, and (2) this author has read, studied, and translated hundreds of passages of Campos's writings in the San Ignacio mission register in regard to the matter that will be taken up in chapter 5 of this work. The handwritings of Campos and "El Anciano" do not even resemble each other.

22. Smith, *Captain of the Phantom Presidio*, pp. 37–39.

23. Garate, "Vizcaínos, Jesuits, and Álvarez Tuñón," pp. 78–79.

24. AHH, Temp., leg. 17, exp. 64, Juan Domingo de Berroeta al Muy Reverendo Padre Cristobal de Cañas, enero 27 de 1722, f. 1.

25. Ibid., ff. 1–2v.

26. Ibid., f. 2.

27. AHH, leg. 17, exp. 43, Joseph de Goicoechea al mui Reverendo Padre Christtoval de Cañas, enero 28 de 1722, ff. 1v and 14.

28. Garate, "Vizcaínos, Jesuits, and Álvarez Tuñón," p. 81.

29. Most historians have assumed that El Anciano de la Soledad was some old-timer in the Real de Minas de la Soledad. Those who had done business with him, and certainly the Basque community, knew that El Anciano was none other than the old man who owned the mine called La Soledad at Aguaje, Martín de Ibarburu.

30. This refers to the fact that there was some animosity between Don Gregorio and Don Rafael prior to this meeting.

31. Jamaica was the hacienda where Don Gregorio maintained his residence, instead of Fronteras where he was supposed to live. In his Catholic zeal, one of the worst insults that Don Martín could throw at Don Gregorio was to call him a Protestant, thus the statement "Protestants in Jamaica." Ibarburu may also be making a comparison here to Don Gregorio's people at Jamaica, Sonora, and the English on the island of Jamaica, an insult with dual meaning!

32. BNM, núm. 21/699, Un discreto y Venerable Anciano, ff. 1–15v.

33. AHH, Temp., leg. 278, exp. 35, Carta al Exelentisimo Señor, ff. 1–2. See also Garate, "Vizcaínos, Jesuits, and Álvarez Tuñón," p. 83.

34. TUMA, Mission Register of Santa María Suamca, ff. 41, 45–47, 88, and 99, in which Nicolasa Gómez de Silva was recorded as mother, godmother, witness, and employer.

35. It is apparent that this letter was intended for Viceroy Zuñiga. The flowery writing alone indicates that. The next political level down from him was the governor of Nueva Vizcaya, the Basque Martín de Alday. As can be seen at the end of the letter, the majority, if not all, of those intended to sign this letter were Basque. Some of the old-timers knew Alday personally, and the others were associated with him through the Basque network that was prominent on the frontier. They would never have addressed him in this manner, as is obvious from other letters sent to him by the same individuals.

36. These were educated men, every one of them, as evidenced by their beautiful handwriting. Why, then, was their language "unskillful"? It was not because they were uneducated in writing skills, but rather that they spoke broken Spanish. With the exception of Juan Mateo Manje, all were Basque and spoke Spanish as a second language.

Unfortunately, Manje's ethnicity is unknown. What is known is that he came from Aragón, which anciently was part of the Kingdom of Nafarroa, and there were still many Basque speakers there in his day, especially along the border with Nafarroa. All that can be said is that he may have been a Basque speaker. Regardless, the majority of those targeted to sign this letter felt inadequate in their ability to speak the Spanish language.

37. Approximately seventy-five miles.

38. Jamaica was the name of Don Gregorio's hacienda, located on the Río Moctezuma southwest of present-day Cumpas, Sonora.

39. Juan Bautista de Escalante.

40. A cuera was a heavy leather vest worn as armor.

41. As part of the common courtesy of the day, all formal letters ended with "B.L.M." (besa la mano) or "B.L.P." (besa los pies), in which the writer closed by kissing the "hand" or "feet" of the person to whom the letter was written.

42. Juan Bautista de Anza, Pedro de Alday, Juan Mateo Manje, Antonio de Miranda, Juan Domingo de Berroeta, and others.

43. AHH, Temp., leg. 278, exp. 11, Carta al Mui Ilustre Señor, n.d., ff. 19–20.

44. Ibid., Respuesta a Varias calumnias, ff. 1–9v and 25–25v.

45. Ibid., Carta al Señor Gobernador y Capitan General del Reino de la Nueva Vizcaya, ff. 12–16.

46. Ibid., Los Vecinos, Mineros, Labradores, y Criadores de Ganados, Muladas y cavalladas de los Reales de Minas de Nacosari, Monte grande y Bacanuchi, ff. 21–22v. A note attached to this letter says it was signed by Juan de Arvisu, Juan Mateo Manje, Francisco Xavier Barcelón, Francisco Pacho, Cristóbal de León, Juan de León, Cristóbal de Ochoa, and Felipe del Valle.

47. Father Oro is most likely referring to the letter to Mui Ilustre Señor (AHH, leg. 278, exp. 11, ff. 19–20) and possibly the "Respuesta."

48. Father Oro here speaks of the Opata Indians.

49. AHH,, Temp., leg. 278, exp. 33, Carta de Nicolas de Oro al Padre Provincial Alexandro Romano, Abril 20 de 1722 años, f. 1.

50. Ibid., exp. 43, Nicolas de Oro a Mi Padre Provincial Alexandro Romero, Marzo 8 de 1722 años, ff. 2–2v.

51. Ibid., exp. 29, Informe de Don Anttonio Bezerra Nieto, ff. 1–2.

52. Ibid., Informe de Joseph Maria Genobese, ff. 1–18v.

53. See letters from Fathers Daniel Januske and Luis Xavier Velarde, Juan Mateo Manje, Juachín Ignacio de Ozaeta y Gallaistegui, Juan Manuel de Zelaya, Antonio de Miranda, Juan Miguel Mondragon y Velasco, etc., at AHH, Temp., leg. 278, exp. 11, 28, 37, 38, and 43; and Father Ignacio Arceo at AHH, leg. 58.

54. AHH, leg. 58, exp. 36, Informe del Capitan Don Anttonio Bezerra nietto, 20 dias del mes de Junio del año 1723, ff. 41–42v.

55. Anza first came to the New World in 1712. See AGN, Historia, leg. 333, Anssa al Padre Provincial, f. 77. He first came to Sonora two years later in 1715. See AGI, Guadalajara, leg. 135, f. 148.

56. AHH, Temp., leg. 17, exp. 25, Informe de General Don Andres de Rezabal en la mision del Espiritu Santo de Moris en doze de mayo de 1701, f. 19.

57. Ibid., Informe de Joseph Maria Genobese, f. 2.

58. The name Rezabal means "wide rivulet" in the Basque language.

59. The story of Don Gregorio's arrest and the brief description of his subsequent activities in Mexico City are taken from Smith, *Captain of the Phantom Presidio*, pp. 67–77.

60. AHP, Testimonio De los Auttos que se fulminaron Sobre y En razon de las Inobediencias que tubo el Capitan Don Gregorio Albarez Tuñon y Quiros y sus Soldados Contra el Señor Sargento Mayor de las Armas de Este Reyno Sus presidios y fronteras, Año de 1723, ff. 1–14v.

61. Campos first came to San Ignacio in 1693. See AGN, Historia, leg. 333, Respuesta a los 35 pliegos del consejo de ingenios (9 de febrero, 1736), f. 3v.

62. Barnes, Naylor, and Polzer, *Northern New Spain*, p. 119. See also Polzer and Sheridan, *The Presidio and Militia*, pp. 37 and 107.

63. FHL, microfilm no. 1224039, Pasajeros de Indias, ff. 272v–281.

64. Ibid., f. 276. Polzer and Sheridan, in *The Presidio and Militia*, pp. 37, say that Father Romano was a native of Naples. This agrees with the Pasajeros de Indias, which says that he was a "native of Patti in the Bishopric of Naples." The Pasajeros de Indias gives his age as twenty-eight in 1691.

65. FHL, microfilm no. 1224039, Pasajeros de Indias, f. 275v. Polzer and Sheridan, in *The Presidio and Militia*, pp. 107, say that Father Arjó was a native of Benasque, Huesca, Aragón, and that he was born in 1663. This slightly disagrees with the Pasajeros de Indias because Tarrazona is in Zaragosa, not Huesca, and the Pasajeros sets his age as twenty-four in 1691. Thus, according to that source he would have been born in 1667.

66. Most sources, including the Pasajeros de Indias, claim that Campos was a native of Sijena, Aragón. There are, however, some interesting questions about that claim that will be taken up in chapter 5.

67. TUMA, Libro de Bautismos de la Mision de San Ignacio, ff. 25–34. Also at Bancroft Library, Berkeley (hereinafter BLB), Alphonse Pinart Collection of the Pimería Alta.

68. TUMA, Libro de Bautismos de la Mision de San Ignacio, f. 34.

69. Ibid., f. 36.

70. To see that Lázaro Chihuahua was with Father Campos on the trip to Mexico City, see ibid., f. 36. For further information about him being the padre's coach driver, see ibid., ff. 20, 24, 39, 41, 44–47, and 52.

71. Ibid., f. 34.

72. AHP, Auttos de Visitta echa al real Presidio de San Phelipe y santiago de Janos, ff. 1–3.

73. AHP, Ordenes del General Don Martin de Alday, Reconquistador de la Provincia de la Nueva Mexico, Capitan Vitalizio del Real Presidio de Nuestra Señora de la Limpia Concepcion del Pasaxe, en quince dias del mes de Deziembre de 1722, ff. 1–1v.

74. AHP, Aceptacion y Obedecimiento, ff. 2–3.

75. All of the information about the inspection tour is taken from AHP, Autos de Visitta de los Presidios de Nueva Vizcaya.

76. Everything concerning the inspection at the Presidio of Janos comes from AHP, Autos de Visitta echa al real Presidio de San Phelipe y santiago de Janos, ff. 1–12v. The

details concerning procedure have been compiled from numerous sources concerning military inspections of the time.

77. This count of forty-eight is two short of the full complement of fifty soldiers that each presidio was supposed to have. The count could have been two under at this particular time for a variety of reasons (sickness, death, slow recruitment), or the scribe may have written down a wrong number under one of the categories.

78. Everything from this point to the end of the description of the inspection of the Fronteras presidio, except as otherwise noted, is taken from AHP, Testimonio de los Auttos, ff. 1–14v.

79. AHH, leg. 17, exp. 64, Berroeta a Cañas, f. 2v. See also Gonzáles, *Etnología y Misión*, p. 152; and Smith, *Captain of the Phantom Presidio*, p. 43.

80. Smith, *Captain of the Phantom Presidio*, p. 46.

81. It is not clear whether he maintained the home there or if Don Gregorio provided it for him. At any rate he referred to it as the "habitation for the accommodation of my person." See AHP, Testimonio de los Auttos, f. 1.

82. Thomas H. Naylor and Charles W. Polzer, compilers and editors, *Pedro de Rivera and the Military Regulations for Northern New Spain, 1724–1729: A Documentary History of His Frontier Inspection and the Reglamento de 1729* (Tucson: University of Arizona Press, 1988), p. 8.

83. Ibid., pp. 8 and 10.

84. GBEA, 1593, Testimonio de Manuel Vasques, f. 279.

85. Letters between Felipe Segesser, a Jesuit priest and close friend of Juan Bautista de Anza, and his brother in Switzerland can be shown to average about one year between posting and receiving a letter in return. See BLB, Segesser letters, in two rolls of microfilm.

86. "The town" wrote this letter. It was at "my [the town's] expense" that the portal was built. It was necessary for "me [the town] to appeal," after a "general meeting of my [the town's] residents," to "my [the town's] children" for donations to help with the needed repair work. And, the letter was written from "my town hall." Hernani's town government at this time was made up of Alcalde Miguel de Arrascue and Regidores Teodoro de Zuaznabar y Larramendi and Antonio de Anza. It was the ever-loyal escribano de número Antonio de Ayerdi who actually wrote and copied the letters to be sent to Hernani's native sons in the Americas.

87. HUA, Comunicacion dirigida a los hijos de la villa, ff. 1–2.

88. Ibid., f. 2.

89. Ibid., ff. 3–9.

90. This is a designation of Spanish citizenship, not ethnic and cultural heritage. Anyone who came from Spain, be they Castilian, Montañes, Basque, Aragonese, Catalonian, Gallego, and so on, was labeled "Spaniard" on all official documents.

91. TXE, Janos Baptisms, unnumbered page.

92. Ibid., unnumbered page.

93. AHP, leg. 1727, Carta de Anttonio Bezerra al Señor Gobernador y Capitan General Don Joseph Lopez de Carvajal, Diziembre 18 de 1726, ff. 1–1v. Also at AZU, film 318, 1727A, frames 210–211.

94. Naylor and Polzer, *The Presidio and Militia*, p. 487.

95. Naylor and Polzer, *Pedro de Rivera*, p. 274.

96. Except as otherwise noted, everything in the description of the Fronteras presidio comes from personal knowledge of the author obtained on numerous visits to the site, and from the Urrutia color map drawn in 1766. See BLL, *Plano Del Presidio de Fronteras*. A facsimile is also published in Moorhead, *The Presidio*, pp. 124–125.

97. Naylor and Polzer, *Pedro de Rivera*, p. 266.

98. Smith, *Captain of the Phantom Presidio*, p. 155.

99. See woodcut entitled *Fronteras, Sonora* in John Russell Bartlett, *Personal Narrative of Explorations and Incidents, 1850–1855* (Chicago: Rio Grande Press, 1965).

100. Pedro de Rivera, *Diario y Derrotero de lo Caminado, Visto y Observado en la Visita que hizo a los Presidios de la Nueva España Septentrional*, Archivo Historico Militar Mexicano Num. 2, (Mexico, D.F.: Taller Autográfico, 1946), p. 58. See also Smith, *Captain of the Phantom Presidio*, pp. 98–99; and Donohue, *After Kino*, pp. 50–51.

101. AHH, leg. 17, exp. 21, Carta de Nicolas de Oro, f. 1.

102. Rivera, *Diario y Derrotero*, p. 56.

103. Ibid., p. 107. See also Naylor and Polzer, *Pedro de Rivera*, p. 80.

104. Naylor and Polzer, *Pedro de Rivera*, p. 10.

105. Smith, *Captain of the Phantom Presidio*, p. 101.

106. Ibid., p. 103.

107. Ibid., pp. 106–107.

108. Rivera, *Diario y Derrotero*, p. 108. This particular translation comes from Naylor and Polzer, *Pedro de Rivera*, p. 82.

109. Smith, *Captain of the Phantom Presidio*, pp. 122–128.

110. Rivera here figured the cost of maintaining two soldiers at 431 pesos each for the seventeen years that Don Gregorio had been capitán vitalicio, and a fine in the total of 14,654 pesos was levied against him. As part of his commission to streamline and economize the presidios, the inspector general also cut the wages of the soldiers from 431 to 400 pesos annually. See Rivera, *Diario y Derrotero*, Tercer Estado, item 25.

111. The viceroy of Nueva España, Juan de Acuña, the marqués de Casafuerte.

112. Rivera, *Diario y Derrotero*, pp. 128–129. This particular translation comes from Naylor and Polzer, *Pedro de Rivera*, pp. 112–113.

113. Smith, *Captain of the Phantom Presidio*, p. 129.

114. Rivera, *Diario y Derrotero*, p. 58.

115. AHP, leg. 1727, Bezerra a Lopez de Carvajal, ff. 1–1v (also at AZU, film 318, 1727A, frames 210–211.

116. Nine months previous to María Margarita's birth date of June 29, 1727, it would be September 29, 1726. This would mean that Juan and Rosa's second child was conceived just a couple of weeks before he left to escort General Rivera to Fronteras. By this date Rosa was fully two months pregnant.

117. Charge No. 10: "He is charged with failing to hurry with his army to fight the Seri about a year ago, more or less, in the uprising in which they burned and killed twenty-two people of the mining camp of Opodepe. He failed to respond in spite of being called twice by the alcalde mayor of this province. He excused himself from going

with the frivolous pretext that the frontier was not under his command but under that of the Sinaloa presidio. At the news of the urgent necessity he should have hurried in fulfillment of his obligations to pacify the Indians, preventing the further hostile acts they committed." Quoted and translated in Smith, *Captain of the Phantom Presidio*, p. 124.

118. For an excellent description of and documentation concerning this uprising, see Sheridan, *Empire of Sand*, pp. 97–121.

119. Charge No. 9. See Smith, *Captain of the Phantom Presidio*, p. 124.

120. Item No. 13 of Rivera's regulations for Fronteras as quoted and translated in ibid., p. 199.

121. The three padres of the Pimería Alta in the early 1720s: Agustín de Campos, Luis María Gallardi, and Luis María Marciano.

122. AHP, Temp., leg. 17, exp. 34, Carta del Padre Agustín de Campos al Padre Rector Marcos de Somoza, San Ignacio, Agosto 1 de 1729, f. 8.

123. Juan Bautista de Anza al Brigadier Don Pedro Rivera, Junio 6 de 1728. See Naylor and Polzer, *Pedro de Rivera*, p. 155.

CHAPTER FIVE. APACHES, LIVESTOCK, POLITICS, AND JESUITS

1. AGI, Guadalajara, leg. 135, Carta de Juan Bautista de Anza al Señor Governador Manuel Bernal de Huidobro, Pueblo del glorioso San Miguel Arcangel de los Ures y Agosto 13 de 1735, f. 151. Translation is the author's. However, two different authors have very capably translated the entire letter from which this passage comes. See Rowland, "The Sonora Frontier," pp. 157–162; and Polzer and Sheridan, *The Presidio and Militia*, pp. 303–312. Future references to this particular Anza letter will follow the translation of Drs. Polzer and Sheridan, with notes used to point out some key differences between it and that of Dr. Rowland. Minor differences between the two, and the way I might have translated it, exist in nearly every sentence, pointing up the difficulties of translating eighteenth-century documents. For example, Dr. Rowland translates the above sentence as "From the said mountains they spy out the mules and horses which wander in the fields, and by night they gather and drive them off, and if any persons chance to travel through some of the narrow passes they sally out and kill them." (See Rowland, p. 160.) Drs. Polzer and Sheridan render it: "From these mountains they spy out horses, mules, and cattle roaming the countryside and at night they round them up and drive them away. And if they see any persons traveling through a narrow pass they come out to kill them." (See Polzer and Sheridan, p. 307.)

2. Between one-quarter and one-third of the area that the Presidio of Fronteras was expected to protect lay within the present-day state of Arizona. It was from here that the majority of Apache raids into Sonora were organized and executed.

3. Their name for themselves was Quechan, the name by which they are known today. See Jacobo Sedelmayr, S.J., *Before Rebellion: Letters and Reports of Jacobo Sedelmayr, S.J.* (Tucson: Arizona Historical Society, 1996), p. xxxi.

4. Known today as the Maricopa Indians. See ibid., including frontispiece map.

5. In the early days, the Jesuit missionaries, especially Father Campos, referred to the desert people as Papabi O'otam (plural), or Papab O'otam (singular). See TUMA or BLB microfilm of the San Ignacio baptismal registry. See also frontispiece map in Sedelmayr, *Before Rebellion*. That designation quickly evolved into "Papago," a name by which they were known for many generations. However, they have always called themselves O'odham and are known by that name today. The word *o'odham* in the native tongue means "people." The word *tohono* means "desert." Thus, the Papabi O'otam, or Papagos, of Anza's day were the ancestors of today's Tohono O'odham.

6. The Seri Indians of then, as today, called themselves Comcáac. Then, as now, they lived in the desert country along the eastern coast of the Gulf of California.

7. These two tribes, because of an evident willingness to cohabit with the Spaniards, so completely assimilated into the Spanish culture that they no longer exist as distinct tribes today.

8. Pimas, like the Papagos, are of the larger group known as O'odham. Whereas the Papagos call themselves Tohono O'odham, or desert people, the Pimas of today refer to themselves as Akimel O'odham, or river people.

9. Pimas, or O'odham, who lived on the upper Santa Cruz and San Pedro Rivers. In the junior Anza's day they were assimilated into the larger O'odham nation and do not exist as a tribe today.

10. This native group call themselves Yoeme. They originated in southern Sonora and, of course, Juan Bautista de Anza had been in contact with them from the time he first arrived in the province in 1715.

11. This particular Indian tribe called themselves Indeh. An Athapascan-speaking people, related to the Navajos, the Apaches were not indigenous to the area, but came down from the north—anthropologists tell us from as far north as Canada.

12. Polzer and Sheridan, *The Presidio and Militia*, p. 306.

13. Rowland, "The Sonora Frontier," statement of Don Juan Bautista de Anza, p. 159.

14. As this work progresses, the reader will see extensive evidence of the Apaches attacking at night during the full moon and of the presidial soldiers planning their campaigns around the full moon.

15. Polzer and Sheridan, *The Presidio and Militia*, p. 306. Rowland translates the last phrase as "the first to discover the track starts a smoke signal." His translation could very well be right because we know from other accounts that the Apaches used smoke to signal one another. However, in this instance, we will never know for sure because the word in question is smudged and totally illegible.

16. Thomas E. Sheridan, *Arizona: A History* (Tucson: University of Arizona Press, 1995), p. 28.

17. Edward H. Spicer, *Cycles of Conquest: The Impact of Spain, Mexico, and the United States on the Indians of the Southwest, 1533–1960* (Tucson: University of Arizona Press, 1962), pp. 229–236.

18. Polzer and Sheridan, *The Presidio and Militia*, pp. 306–307.

19. Rowland, "The Sonora Frontier," statement of Don Agustín de Vildósola, p. 151.

20. Polzer and Sheridan, *The Presidio and Militia*, p. 307.

21. Rowland, "The Sonora Frontier," Vildósola statement, pp. 155–156.

22. Polzer and Sheridan, *The Presidio and Militia*, p. 307.

23. Statistics from the San Ignacio Mission records show that over a ninety-one year period just under 1 percent of all deaths recorded resulted from murder (12 out of 1,268), and four of those deaths cannot be conclusively blamed on the Apaches. Present death statistics in the United States show a similar percentage of violent deaths caused by murder (approximately 1 percent). In comparison, automobile wrecks cause approximately 2 percent of all deaths in the United States in our day.

24. Polzer and Sheridan, *The Presidio and Militia*, p. 307.

25. Rowland, "The Sonora Frontier," Vildósola statement, p. 155.

26. Polzer and Sheridan, *The Presidio and Militia*, p. 305.

27. Ibid., p. 307.

28. Rowland, "The Sonora Frontier," Vildósola statement, p. 155.

29. Weber, *The Spanish Frontier in North America*, p. 233.

30. Polzer and Sheridan, *The Presidio and Militia*, pp. 305–306.

31. AZU, microfilm 811, roll 11, Informacion Matrimonial de la Jurisdiccion del Real de Nacosari, random unbound pages, folios unnumbered, but it is the eighty-ninth folio from the beginning of the roll. Although five sheets of this marriage presentation still exist, they are faded, worn, and torn, and none of them are dated. Other documents in this pile of loose pages range in time from 1704 to 1738. These particular pages are with some others that were written in 1734, and that is the probable date of these. Since this document is marriage information given prior to the wedding of Juan Núñez and María Rosa Samaniego, we can turn to the Suamca Mission register to corroborate the 1734 date. Juan and María Rosa first appear as husband and wife there on May 15, 1735, where they were godparents at the baptism of the son of one of Suamca's Pima officials. They were living at Guevavi at the time, and although there may have been earlier records, including their marriage documentation, all the entries in the Guevavi book prior to 1739 have been lost. Regardless, we know that they were married prior to May 15, 1735, probably sometime in 1734. Since Juan Núñez had worked on the Guevavi and San Mateo Ranches for more than two years prior to that, Juan Bautista de Anza had to have owned those two places at least since 1730 or 1731, and probably since the late 1720s.

32. Ibid.

33. See TUMA, Mission Register of Los Santos Angeles de Guevavi, ff. 2, 16, and 122; Mission Register of Santa María Suamca, ff. 11, 42, 92, and 116; and Mission Register of San Ignacio de Cabórica, ff. 98 and 150.

34. AZU, microfilm 811, roll 11, Informacion Matrimonial, unnumbered f. 89.

35. The assumption is that they were married at Guevavi. Their marriage record does not appear in the Santa María Suamca book of marriages, and the beginning pages of the Guevavi book have long since rotted away. The first surviving record of a marriage that occurred there is dated 1739. See TUMA, Mission Register of Los Santos Angeles de Guevavi, f. 9.

36. All of the events that took place at Guevavi, Suamca, and San Xavier between 1732 and 1734, except as otherwise noted, are found in John L. Kessell, *Mission of Sorrows: Jesuit Guevavi and the Pimas, 1691–1767* (Tucson: University of Arizona Press, 1970),

pp. 45–58. Information relative to the priests' places of birth and cultural background can be found in Roca, *Paths of the Padres*, pp. 359–360.

37. All information concerning the baptismal service at San Jago de Obtuavo comes from TUMA, Mission Register of Santa María Suamca, ff. 2–5.

38. TUMA, Mission Register of Santa María Suamca, Bautismo de Ignacio, chiquillo Apachito, f. 29.

39. Although the evidence is confusing as to whether or not these two villages were one and the same, this author has come to the conclusion that they were two distinct places in the minds of the people who lived there and the Jesuit missionaries who served them. This is because Father Keller on occasion used both names on the same page in the mission registers, which would seem to indicate that he moved from one site to the other, no matter how close they might have been, rather than that he was forgetting what he had called the mission from one entry, or day, to another. See, for example, TUMA, Mission Register of Santa María Suamca, f. 16, in which Father Keller was at Guevavi on July 9, 1736 to baptize María Rosa, the daughter of Juan Núñez and María Rosa Samaniego. After a one-week trip to Obtuavo, San Xavier del Bac, and Tucson, then back to Obtuavo in which nineteen baptisms were performed at those places, he was at Gusutaqui for a baptism on July 16. See also ibid., f. 20 in which he was at Gusutaqui on February 17, 1737. Fourteen baptisms later, he had been at San Xavier del Bac and Arivaca and was at Guevavi on March 24. It seems strange to think that he would call the village Gusutaqui one day and Guevavi a week or a month later. Furthermore, in 1737 when he was at San Xavier, he mentioned the fact that he had Francisco, the governor of Guevavi, with him. Francisco Cobesia (see next note) was governor of Guevavi from 1728 to 1741. Although no governor was recorded for Gusutaqui prior to 1738, it is known that its governor that year was a man named Felipe (see ibid., ff. 27 and 29). Both Guevavi and Gusutaqui are names that are seen regularly in numerous records of the late seventeenth and early eighteenth centuries, and some authors have concluded that they were the same village because they seem almost interchangeable. When the Spaniards first arrived they were evidently two villages, but after a number of years the name Gusutaqui disappears. Apparently it was absorbed into the Mission of Guevavi.

40. Francisco Cobesia was governor of Guevavi from at least 1728 to 1741. See TUMA, San Ignacio Mission Register, ff. 68; Suamca Mission Register, f. 20; and the Guevavi Mission Register, f. 10.

41. Translation by John L. Kessell. See Kessell, *Mission of Sorrows*, p. 49.

42. Ana Gertrudis and Luis Ignacio Sosa were baptized at Santa María Suamca on November 4, 1743 and June 4, 1746, respectively. See TUMA, Suamca Mission Register, ff. 41 and 45.

43. AZU, microfilm 811, roll 10, Real de Nuestra Señora del Rosario de Nacosari: Bautismos del Real Presidio de Santa Rosa de Corodéguachi, f. 33v.

44. Located where the Río Rico golf course is today.

45. One of three units that today make up Tumacácori National Historical Park.

46. AGI, Guadalajara, leg. 419, sec. 3m, p. 12, Testimonio de Ignacio Romero, Santa María Suamca, 14 de Octubre 1754, ff. 40–43. For a translation of the same, see Donald

T. Garate, *Pedro de la Cruz, Alias Chihuahua: Conspirator, Scapegoat, Victim* (Tumacácori: National Park Service, 1999), p. 10.

47. AHH, Temp., leg. 17, exp. 69, Breve resumen de los desastres, muertes, robos, y asolamientos acaezidos en la Provincia de Sonora, f. 1v, item 7. For a translation of the same, see Sheridan, *Empire of Sand*, p. 240. A number of factors come together to give a distinct appearance that Sicurisuta and Sicurisutac were two distinct places and that the names are derived from the Basque language. Although almost nothing is known of either site, their descriptions place Sicurisuta somewhere between Guevavi and Arivaca, whereas Sicurisutac was south of Guevavi and the San Luis Valley. When the placement of the two ranches is taken into consideration with their meaning in the Basque language, everything falls into place. *Siku* means "dry" and can be used to describe a rocky outcropping. *Erizut* means a "vertical finger." The letter *a* means "the," and the letter *c* (more properly *k*) pluralizes whatever it follows. Thus, *siku-erizut-a* is possibly "the upright rocky finger," which is a perfect description of Thumb Rock above Peña Blanca Lake northwest of Guevavi and present-day Nogales, Arizona. *Siku-erizut-ak*, on the other hand, would possiby mean "the upright rocky fingers," and is a marvelous description of the half-dozen or so jagged, vertical peaks of the present-day El Pinito Mountains southeast of Nogales, Sonora and above the southwest side of the San Luis Valley. It stands to reason that a ranch anywhere in the vicinity of either of these outstanding geological features would take the same name.

48. Pima County Records (hereinafter, PCR), Old Poston Record Book: Don Antonio Narbona, Capitan de la compania del Real Presidio de Fronteras y actual comandante del Tucson certificacion, p. 19.

49. Ibid., and TUMA, Mission Registers: Guevavi, ff. 2, 18, 51, 78, 79, 102, and 104; Suamca, ff. 21 and 33. Antonio Narbona received testimony for his certification from Manuel Vicente Sosa, who was the son of Juan Nicolás de Sosa and María del Carmen Bais. María del Carmen was the daughter of Juan Manuel Bais and María Josefa de Luque. She was born at Sópori in 1737 and was baptized at Guevavi while the first Captain Anza was still living. She grew up with the junior Juan Bautista de Anza, being just eight months younger than him. Her mother, María Josefa de Luque was still living on the Sópori Ranch as late as 1775, as evidenced by her participation with her grandson, Manuel Vicente de Sosa, as godparents for a baptism at Mission Tumacácori. See TUMA, Mission Register for Tumacácori, f. 18.

50. See, for example, University of Texas, Austin, W. B. Stephens Collection (hereinafter TXA, WBS), 1744, Entregas de las Misiones, ff. 377, 382, and 386, in which the Mission of Áti had 268 beef cattle and 628 sheep, Guevavi had 871 cattle and 1,270 sheep, and the Mission of Saric had some 100 cattle and 988 sheep for delivery in 1761.

51. Again, there are no clear records of workmen or their numbers on private ranches, but for examples of sabaneros who worked on the ranches and missions of the Pimería Alta, see TUMA, Mission Registers: Guevavi, ff. 49 and 54; San Ignacio baptisms, ff. 16, 20, and 50; Magdalena burials, f. 30; and Suamca burials, f. 41. The majority of sabaneros were Indian, but some were of Spanish or mestizo origin. Most herded sheep and/or goats, although *sabaneros de bueyes* (herders of oxen) were not uncommon. These were, however, distinct from the *boyeros* (ox drivers) who drove the oxen for

plowing or freighting. Sabaneros, who herded the above-mentioned animals to and from pasture, were also distinct from *vaqueros* (cowboys) and *caballeros* (horsemen), who herded the latter animals for the same purpose. Although the word *sabanero* is not one that is seen or heard in modern American Spanish, it is common in the ancient documents of northern Sonora.

52. A Nijora was a person from an unknown Indian tribe, usually brought to the area as a child slave by some tribe farther to the north and sold to the Spaniards who, in turn, often raised them as their own children.

53. TUMA, Mission Registers: Guevavi, Suamca, and Tumacácori.

54. AHH, Temp., leg. 17, exp. 21, Carta de Juan Bauptista de Anssa al Muy Reverendo Padre Provincial Andres Nieto, Real de San Antonio de Motepore y Julio 28 de 1729, f. 64v.

55. Smith, *Captain of the Phantom Presidio*, pp. 145–153.

56. AGN, Ramo de Tierras, Inventario y apreciso de los bienes pertenecientes al General Gregorio Álvarez Tuñón y Quirós, vol. 474, exp. 2, f. 5.

57. Ibid., p. 135.

58. Once again, we see evidence of a Basque's self-consciousness concerning his ability to write (or speak) the Castilian language. Juan Bautista de Anza's handwriting was anything but "coarse." Its flowing and easy-to-read style is simply beautiful. Like the other writers of the day, he almost never used punctuation. What punctuation he did use, however, generally makes more sense than the average. His sentence structure, grammar, and often choice of words, on the other hand, is atrocious, sometimes making it extremely difficult to grasp his meaning. It is obvious that he was thinking in Basque and translating his words into Spanish. For the student of his works, it is always a pleasure to find a letter signed by him but written by his scribe, associate, ranch foreman, relative by marriage, and dear friend Manuel José de Sosa. Manuel José was a trained escribano, and letters written by him, but bearing the signature of Juan Bautista de Anza, are generally much clearer in their meaning and are far easier to read and translate.

59. The choice of words here in the original Spanish is interesting—*de Palacio*—which literally means "from" or "of the palace." Unfortunately, Anza left us without the name of this person, or the names of the missionary padres of whom he speaks later in the letter.

60. Juan de Acuña, viceroy of Nueva España at the time.

61. Gabriel de Prudhom Butrón y Mujica.

62. Anza is probably referring to the alcalde mayor here, although he was also known to refer to himself on occasion as "este caballero."

63. The viceroy.

64. This gives a closer idea of the full amount of the "24,431 pesos plus court costs" that Don Gregorio was fined.

65. Anza here refers to Cristóbal de Cañas who was *visitador general* for the Province of Sonora at the time.

66. Unfortunately it is impossible to surmise who the Jesuit priest was who advised Anza to get advice from a "learned" person, or who it was in Parral that was deemed "learned."

67. This last sentence is an excellent example of the broken Spanish and confused sentence structure, grammar, punctuation, and word usage employed by Juan Bautista de Anza. The original Spanish reads, "me prevengo anticipandole alas cuerdas orejas de VR$^{ma}$ elsonido que puede causar contra mi credita: la impostura de algunos," which literally says, "I prepare myself anticipating it to the wise ears of your Reverence the noise that can cause against my credit the false charges of some."

68. Cristóbal de Cañas.

69. Spanish citizens recognized two majesties, God and King. The Divine Majesty, of course, was God.

70. AHH, Temp., leg. 17, exp. 21, Carta de Juan Bauptista de Anssa al Muy Reverendo Padre Provincial, ff. 63–65.

71. TXA, WBS, sec. 902, Carta de Nicolas de Perera al Padre Provincial, junio 25 de 1740, ff. 91–95. See also Sheridan, *Empire of Sand*, pp. 132 and 137.

72. Sheridan, *Empire of Sand*, pp. 97–122.

73. Polzer and Sheridan, *The Presidio and Militia*, p. 307.

74. AHH, Temp., leg. 278, exp. 34, Informe de Gabriel Prudhom Butron y Muxica, Real de Nuestra Señora de la Concepcion del Agua Caliente, Pimería alta en 4 de Marzo de 1735, ff. 1, 1v, 19, and 19v.

75. Sheridan, *Empire of Sand*, pp. 122–125.

76. Agustín de Campos.

77. Manuel Bernal de Huidobro.

78. Juan de Acuña, the marqués de Casafuerte.

79. Anza here refers to himself. There are at least three meanings to the word *caballero*, of which Juan Bautista de Anza only fits two. First, in the truest sense of the word, a caballero was someone who owned and rode a horse. Anza, of course, owned many. Secondly, *caballero* means "gentleman," and is the usage that Anza here employed to describe himself. Lastly, a caballero was a "knight." There were numerous orders of the *caballería*, or "knighthood." It was not an easy matter to obtain membership in any of the orders, and neither Juan Bautista de Anza ever belonged to any of them. A tradition has developed in Sonora in which the junior Anza is often referred to as the "Caballero de Anza," a term that was never used in his day, nor could it have been. That was a designation reserved strictly for the knights, and since he was never a knight, neither he nor any contemporary of his ever used such a designation.

80. Marcos de Somoza was rector at Cucurpe and father superior of the missions of the Pimería Alta.

81. The missionaries felt their supplies were too short that year to be able to feed and quarter troops.

82. El Día de Santiago, or the feast day of Saint James, was coming up on July 25, exactly two weeks from the date of this letter. This is evidently a petition for help to the saint.

83. AHH, Temp., leg. 17, exp. 21, Carta de Juan Bauptista de Anssa al Muy Reverendo Padre Visitador Nicolas de Oro, Motepore y Julio 11 de 1729, ff. 37–37v.

84. Polzer and Sheridan, *The Presidio and Militia*, p. 307.

85. In spite of all his many and illustrious titles, Gabriel de Prudhom Butron y Mu-

jica, Barón de Heyder, Gravushing, Goldakre went by his simple Basque name of Gabriel Mujica, as evidenced in a statement by his grandson Luis María Beldarrain. See AGN, PI, sec. 250, Peticion de Don Luis Maria Beldarrain al Exelentisimo Señor Don Bernardo Galvez, Alamos y Noviembre 25 de 1785, f. 334v. Both the names Butron and Mujica are Basque, but he must have also had Catalonian heritage through the surname Prudhom.

86. AHH, Temp., leg. 278, exp. 34, Informe de Prudhom Butron y Muxica, f. 19.

87. Sheridan, *Empire of Sand*, pp. 126–133.

88. Polzer and Sheridan, *The Presidio and Militia*, p. 307.

89. Rowland, "The Sonora Frontier," Vildósola statement, p. 152.

90. AGN, Historia, leg. 333, Juan Bauptista de Anssa al Reverentissimo Padre Joseph Barba, Abril 21 de 1736, ff. 79–79v.

91. Anza claimed that it was Jesuit Provincial Juan Antonio de Oviedo who bestowed the honor on him. Father Oviedo left office on November 4, 1729. See Barnes, Naylor, and Polzer, *Northern New Spain*, p. 119.

92. Peter Masten Dunne, S.J., *Black Robes in Lower California* (Berkeley: University of California Press, 1952), p. 178.

93. AGN, Historia, leg. 333, f. 77. Dunne, in his article on Anza and Campos, probably not knowing that Captain Anza was Basque and certainly not understanding that in Anza's day *vizcaino* meant "Basque," missed the point of what the captain was saying in his translation. He rendered "assi por la razon general de Vizcaino" as "because of what it has done for Nueva Vizcaya." See Peter Masten Dunne, S.J., "Captain Anza and the Case of Father Campos," *Mid America* XXIII (1941): 59.

94. Dunne, "Captain Anza and the Case of Father Campos," p. 59.

95. See ibid., p. 60. Eminent Southwest historian Dr. Charles Polzer has expressed this same opinion to the author. However, a review of the Pasajeros de Indias documents reveals that nearly every shipload of Jesuits that came to the New World had a few "brothers" with them. Whether the designation of these brothers was anything more or less than the station in which Anza found himself is beyond the scope of this work. However, it points to the fact that there were Jesuit brothers and that, regardless of concessions that might have been made, Anza at least felt that he had had this honor bestowed upon him.

96. AGN, Historia, leg. 333, f. 77.

97. Ibid., f. 78v.

98. Anza here speaks of Iñigo Loyola, founder of the Jesuit order and, by this time, already a canonized saint. Loyola was born and raised between the two villages of Azcoitia and Azpeitia in the Province of Gipuzkoa, a mere twenty miles from Anza's home in Hernani.

99. The Pima Nation.

100. AGN, Historia, leg. 333, Juan Bauptista de Anssa al Padre Provincial Joseph Barba, Imuris y Abril 21 de 1736, f. 79.

101. AGN, Historia, leg. 333, Joseph Agustin de Campos a Mi Padre Provincial Joseph Barba, Presidio y Mayo 8 del 1736, f. 25.

102. Juan Estanislao Nieto.

103. Father Campos was probably seventy years old at the time (see Pasajeros de Indias, FHL, microfilm no. 1224039, p. 278), although there is some conflicting evidence

that says he may have been sixty-six. Regardless, he had served as a missionary in the Pimería Alta for forty-three years. See AGN, Historia, leg. 333, Campos a Barba, Presidio, ff. 25–26.

104. Terrenate lies a mere eight miles south of the present-day Arizona-Sonora border.

105. See TUMA, Suamca Mission Register, ff. 10, 29, 70, and 118; and Guevavi Mission Register, ff. 19, 30, 58, 75, 81, 86, 88, 91, and 97.

106. James E. Officer, Mardith Schuetz-Miller, and Bernard Fontana, editors, *The Pimería Alta: Missions and More* (Tucson: Southwest Mission Research Center, 1996), p. 49; Naylor and Polzer, *The Presidio and Militia*, p. 492; Bolton, *The Spanish Borderlands*, p. 358 n. 2; Kessell, *Mission of Sorrows*, p. 51 n. 12; and Officer, *Hispanic Arizona*, p. 31.

107. Perea was a son-in-law of Francisco de Ibarra, founder of Nueva Vizcaya. Ibarra, of course, was from Durango, Bizkaia. The name "Perea" also has its origins in Bizkaia and Araba. Perea brought the first European settlers, including his son-in-law, Mungúia, to Sonora. He died at Banámichi, and his wife, María de Ibarra, had the body taken to Aconchi where it was buried in the church. Munguía Villela came to Sonora in 1737 with Perea and dedicated his career to ranching, establishing a headquarters at what became Suamca and is today the town of Santa Cruz, Sonora. See Hacinto Suárez, "Diccionario Biográfico Vasco-Mexicano" (Reno: Basque Studies Library, University of Nevada; unpublished manuscript, 5 volumes, n.d.), unnumbered pages. The name and house of nobility called Villela was established in the center of what became the town of Munguía, Bizkaia before the ancient village itself came into existence. Both names have their origins there, however. See García Carraffa, *El Solar Vasco Navarro*, VI:278–279, and Jaime de Kerexeta, *Fogueraciones de Bizkaia del Siglo XVIII* (Bilbao: Instituto Labayru-Bilbao Bizkaia Ku, TXA, 1992), pp. 198, 201, 426, and 431. The name "Romo" had its origins in Lekeitio, Bizkaia and seems to have spread to other parts of the Basque country from there. See Lopez-Mendizabal, *Etimologias de Appellidos Vascos*, p. 678; and García Carraffa, *El Solar Vasco Navarro*, V:365. There is evidence, however, that the Romos de Vivar of Sonora were originally from Eskaroz in Nafarroa. See note 10, chapter 4, this volume. One associate of José Romo de Vivar, whose signature appears on several documents with him, was the Basque Antonio de Gasteategui. See Naylor and Polzer, *The Presidio and Militia*, pp. 495, 304, and 305.

108. Burrus, *Kino and Manje: Explorers of Sonora and Arizona*, p. 336.

109. Sonora and Sinaloa had been broken off from Nueva Vizcaya in 1734 and established as a separate political unit. Manuel Bernal de Huidobro had been the governor of Sinaloa and now became the governor of both provinces. See Barnes, Naylor, and Polzer, *Northern New Spain*, p. 111.

110. Burrus, *Kino and Manje: Explorers of Sonora and Arizona*, p. 542. Here is more proof that the word *terrenate* is Basque. The official language of Spain was Castilian, or Spanish. Other languages of Spain, including Basque, Catalonian, and Gallego, were said to be *vulgar*, or common languages. They were *vulgarmente*, or commonly, spoken among pockets of Spanish citizenry of one of those ethnic backgrounds. The language

that was *vulgarmente* spoken at Terrenate, and in many other scattered communities throughout Sonora, was Basque.

111. Rowland, "The Sonora Frontier," pp. 151–164.

112. AGN, Historia, leg. 333, Joseph Agustin de Campos al Ilustre Señor, San Joseph de Himuri y noviembre 30 de 1735, f. 43–43v.

113. The conversation with Captain Anza is hypothetical. However, every statement made by Father Campos is taken directly from one of five letters written by him to his superiors on the subject of his removal from San Ignacio. In the ten days that it took for him to be physically carried from San Ignacio to Cuquiárachi, it is practically guaranteed that he spoke with Anza about his many afflictions. The captain was really the only person in the group in whom he could confide. The soldiers had their duties and could do nothing for him. The Pima Indians, who carried him, although sympathetic to his cause, were likewise in no position to help. Father Nieto, newly arrived from Mexico City (see Donohue, *After Kino*, p. 72), had originally been sent to take his place at San Ignacio, and knew nothing of the things about which the old padre spoke. That left only Anza, a "brother for the Mass," as Father Campos called him. If Father Campos was even partially as senile or mentally disturbed as some of the contemporaries of his day, or secondary sources of our day, have portrayed him, then he would have told Captain Anza everything that he later wrote to his superiors—over and over again. Since much of what he said is highly controversial and does not paint a pretty picture of some of his fellow Jesuits, every quotation is carefully noted so that anyone desiring to do so can carefully check my translations. This first quotation is taken from AGN, Historia, leg. 333, Joseph Agustin de Campos a Mi Padre Provincial Andres Garcia, Cuquiárachi y Agosto 13 de 1736, f. 80.

114. Ibid., f. 80v.

115. Ibid., Joseph Agustin de Campos a Mi Padre Provincial Joseph Barba, Cuquiárachi y Mayo 5 del 1736, f. 30.

116. Ibid., Campos a Garcia, f. 81v.

117. Ibid., Anssa a Barba, f. 77v.

118. Ibid., Nicolas de Perera a Mi amado Padre Visitador Luis Maria Marciano, San Ignacio y Marzo 8 año de 1736, f. 53v. Perera says Diego Romero's "son" was sent to Fronteras. Of Diego's known four sons, José, the militia lieutenant, logically would have been the one who went.

119. Ibid., Anssa a Barba, f. 77v.

120. Ibid., Perera a Marciano, San Ignacio, f. 54.

121. Among all the hundreds of pages of documentation about the place called "Arizona," this letter of Father Perera, written at one o'clock in the morning by a missionary stationed 150 miles away and unfamiliar with the area, after an extremely trying and fearful day, is the only known reference to Arizona being a "real." The actual real was Agua Caliente. Arizona, which was located only a stone's throw away, was a ranch owned by Bernardo Urrea. This is all taken up in detail in chapter 6.

122. AGN, Historia, leg. 333, Perera a Marciano, San Ignacio, ff. 52 and 53.

123. Ibid., Anssa a Barba, f. 77v.

124. Ibid., Perera a Marciano, San Ignacio, f. 52.

125. Ibid., f. 52v.

126. Ibid., f. 53.

127. Ibid., f. 54.

128. AGN, Historia, leg. 333, Nicolas de Perera a Mi amado Padre Visitador Luis Maria Marciano, Sasabac y Marzo 8 año de 1736, f. 55v.

129. Ibid., Perera a Marciano, San Ignacio, f. 54.

130. An extremely interesting perspective can be gained about the movement of people across the vastness of what we today call the Southwest by this unusual name. Many years after the Campos incident, on November 19, 1773, a lady by the name of Barbara de Neyra died and was buried at San Ignacio—a Ute Indian! She was married to a man who was probably a Pima Indian with the Basque name of Mariano Uribe. She must have been one of those Nijoras, captured in the north and brought to San Ignacio, where she was probably sold to Francisco de Neyra as a child. See TUMA, San Ignacio Burial Register, f. 158. In all the documentation on the Campos incident, Francisco de Neyra is only referred to as "Neyra." It is in TUMA, San Ignacio Baptismal Register, f. 96, where he is recorded as a godfather, that we learn his full name.

131. AGN, Historia, leg. 333, Perera a Marciano, San Ignacio, f. 55.

132. Ibid., Perera a Marciano, Sasabac, f. 56.

133. The reader is here referred to Dunne, "Captain Anza and the Case of Father Campos," for an interpretation of the incident strictly from the other padres' points of view.

134. AGN, Historia, leg. 333, Joseph Agustin de Campos a Mi Padre Visitador Luis Maria Marciano, San Joseph de Himuri y marzo 10 de 1736, ff. 20–20v.

135. Father Campos here speaks of Luisa Ignacia and María Guadalupe German, daughters of Francisco Xavier German and María Manuela García, married to Juan José Martín and Juan de Villa, respectively. See TUMA, San Ignacio Baptismal Register, ff. 41, 96, 97, 101, and 112. Martín and Villa were the two men Father Campos sent for the three priests' horses that Thursday morning after the near uprising, March 8, 1736.

136. She died in childbirth on July 4, 1731, and was buried by Father Campos in front of the door inside the chapel of Francisco Xavier in the church at Magdalena. See TUMA, San Ignacio Burial Register, f. 31. The new baby, Eugenio German, brother of Lucia Ignacia and María Guadalupe, was baptized by Father Campos two days later at San Ignacio. See TUMA, San Ignacio Baptismal Register, f. 78.

137. AGN, Historia, leg. 333, Juan Estanislao Nieto a Mi amado Padre Provincial Joseph Barba, San Joseph de Hymuris y Abril 23 de 1736, ff. 63v–64. See also Sheridan, *Empire of Sand*, p. 125. As a young man, Campos had been "strong of body and light skinned with dark hair and brown eyes." See Pasajeros de Indias, FHL, microfilm no. 1224039, p. 278.

138. AGN, Historia, leg. 333, Anssa a Barba, f. 77v.

139. Ibid., f. 78.

140. Ibid., Respuesta a los 35 pliegos del consejo de ingenios, San Ignacio, n.d., ff. 1v–5.

141. TXA, WBS, 1747, Joseph Toral a Mi Padre Provincial Joseph de Barva, Mision de Guepaca y Marzo 25 de 1736, f. 26. This statement points up the need for further research about Agustín Campos. He himself claimed to be a "paisano" of Bernal de Huidobro. See AGN, Historia, leg. 333, Campos al Ilustre Señor, f. 43v, where he signs the letter "Your Humble Chaplain and Affectionate Paisano." In these years, the word *paisano*, without exception, was someone from the same town or district. According to Sheridan, *Empire of Sand*, p. 124, Bernal de Huidobro was born in Burgos, which would guarantee that Campos was born there also. On page 24 of the same work we are told that Campos was born in Logroño. This seems to correct an earlier statement made by Polzer and Sheridan, *The Presidio and Militia*, p. 289, that says Campos was born in Sijena, Aragón. The Pasajeros de Indias, which is the only known original document that spells out where he was born, gives Sijena as his birthplace. See FHL, microfilm no. 1224039, p. 278.

142. AGN, Historia, leg. 333, Juan a Mi amado Padre Visitador Luis Maria Marciano, Babiacora y febrero 20, 1736, f. 68; Juan de Echagoien a Mi amado Padre Visitador Luis Maria Marciano, Babiacora y febrero 23, 1736, f. 69; Juan de Echagoien a Mi amado Padre Visitador Luis Maria Marciano, Babiacora y Marzo 10, 1736, f. 72; Juan a Mi amado Padre Visitador Luis Maria Marciano, Babiacora y Marzo 11 de 1736, f. 67; and Juan de Echagoien a Mi Padre Provincial Joseph Barba, Babiacora y Abril 8 de 1736, f. 62–62v.

143. Dunne, "Captain Anza and the Case of Father Campos," p. 54, claims that "Julio [sic] Echagoian" was Father Campos's companion at San Ignacio during the time of this incident and that his life was at risk. Other secondary sources have picked up on his statement and perpetuated the error. See Donohue, *After Kino*, p. 73. It is hard to imagine how Father Echagoyen could have been assisting Father Campos at San Ignacio when his letters clearly show that he was at his Mission of Baviácora, 120 miles away, during the entire time.

144. AGN, Historia, leg. 333, Christobal de Cañas a Mi Amado Padre Provincial Joseph Barba, Arizpe, i Abril 5 de 1736, f. 61. Dunne renders this statement, "what is certain is that Campos has gone from abyss to abyss so that he is enraged or crazy or completely out of himself." He then uses that statement for the basis of his interpretation that Campos's "mind was becoming clouded," that he had a "grave mental affliction" and eventually a "complete mental breakdown." See Dunne, "Captain Anza and the Case of Father Campos," pp. 47, 51, and 53. He says that Campos's letters were "stormy, bitter, and obscure," without quoting anything from them (p. 50). Finally, he claims that after Campos was taken to Fronteras, "For several months [he] addressed numerous amazing missives to his superiors and fellow missionaries. They were long, inconsistent, querulous, and even scandalous. At times his mental condition was such as to inspire great pity for one who had served the missions so heroically in early years" (p. 58). Other secondary sources have continued with this line of thinking. See Donohue, *After Kino*, pp. 72–73; and Roca, *Paths of the Padres*, p. 359. Unfortunately, it is beyond the scope of this work to delve into the details of such matters. Suffice it to say that Campos's letters were anything but "obscure," as can be seen from the quotations from them in this chapter. The

"numerous amazing missives" that Campos wrote after he was removed from San Ignacio amounted to four letters: the first to José de Arjó, Cuquiárachi, May 4, 1736; the second to José Barba, started in Cuquiárachi on May 5 and finished at Fronteras on May 8, 1736 because "the multitude and seriousness of my infirmities, along with the atrocious injuries that Father Visitor Marciano has heaped upon me, and other troubles associated with his claims, has my head in such pain that I cannot sit to write everything at one time;" the third to Andres García, Cuquiárachi, August 13, 1736; and the final to José Sánchez, Cuquiárachi, August 13, 1736. (See AGN, Historia, leg. 333.) Campos was sick and debilitated, as evidenced by his terribly shaky handwriting at the end. He also could possibly be accused of being "absentminded," brought about by old age and its accompanying senility. His letters are "querulous," or complaining, and he was definitely "enraged," but whatever his faults, his mental capacity was crystal clear and his letters are easily understandable, very concise, and to the point (probably even more so than Perera's or Toral's). To protect the Jesuit mission system by labeling Campos mentally deficient, or even saying that he was assimilated into the Pima culture, is to sidestep the true issues of personality conflict, morality and integrity, corruption within the system, greed for power, and possibly even conspiracy.

145. TXA, WBS, 1747, Toral a Barva, f. 26.

146. AGN, Historia, leg. 333, Joseph Agustin de Campos a Mi Padre Visitador Luis Maria Marciano, San Ignacio Nuestro Padre y febrero 22 de 1736, f. 45. Campos on numerous occasions said that statements he was accused of making could not be found in his original writings, and this complaint deserves further investigation. None of the letters in existence today, including the "Respuesta a la junta de ingenios" that served to condemn Campos, are his originals. All claim to be copies, and were made under the direction of Marciano.

147. AGN, Historia, leg. 333, Anssa a Barba, f. 78v.

148. Ibid., Joseph Toral a Mi amado Padre Visitador Luis Maria Marciano, Hymuris y Abril 23, 1736, f. 48.

149. Ibid., Anssa a Barba, ff. 78–78v.

150. TXA, WBS, 1747, Toral a Barva, f. 30.

151. The story from this point until Anza and Campos leave San Ignacio bound for Fronteras, except as otherwise noted, comes from AGN, Historia, leg. 333, Joseph Toral a Mi amado Padre Visitador Luis Maria Marciano, San Joseph de Himuris y Abril 23 de 1736, ff. 48–51v.

152. Most likely José Romero.

153. AGN, Historia, leg. 333, Anssa a Barba, ff. 78v–79.

154. Marciano's original plan for Campos could have been considered nothing but imprisonment, until he could be transferred to the Jesuit college in Chihuahua. He was to be kept in a room at Cucurpe without being able to communicate with anyone, he was to have no writing materials, and was to be kept under constant surveillance. See AGN, Historia, leg. 333, Luis Maria Marciano a los Padres Velarde, Perera, Campos, Keller, Rojas, and Gallardi, Santa Rosalia del Pescadero y Febrero 27 de 1736, ff. 7v–9v. See also Dunne, "Captain Anza and the Case of Father Campos," pp. 51–52.

155. AGN, Historia, leg. 333, Anssa a Barba, f. 79.

156. Ibid., ff. 77–79v. Anza actually misdated this letter. It should have been dated April 23, 1736. When it is read in conjunction with the letters written by Fathers Toral, Nieto, and Keller on April 23, it becomes obvious that the captain already knew too many things that had happened after April 21. He can be forgiven for getting the wrong date considering all the stress and lack of sleep he had been subjected to over the course of the preceding several weeks, and especially because he was "writing it at night in an inconvenient place" and was "nearly blind" from the lack of light. (See f. 79v.) See also Nieto a Barba, ff. 63–64, Keller a Barba, f. 65; and Toral a Mariano, ff. 48–51v.

157. Ibid., Toral a Mariano, f. 51. This comes from a final note of April 24, 1736, written personally by Toral at the bottom of the letter that his scribe compiled the evening before.

158. Father Keller was thirty-three years old at the time, less than half of Father Campos's age. Some of Father Keller's contemporaries would accuse him of drinking too much in later years.

159. AGN, Historia, leg. 333, Joseph Agustin de Campos a Mi Padre Joseph Arjo, Cuquiárachi y Mayo 4 de 1736, f. 34v.

160. Father Toral claimed that he had been called on the carpet to answer charges concerning some uncomplimentary letters he had written to then Father Visitor José María Genovese. See TXA, WBS, 1747, Toral a Barva, f. 31.

161. José de Echevarria, a Basque and visitor general of the northern missions, was born in Donostia in 1688, just a few miles from where Anza was born and raised. See Polzer and Sheridan, *The Presidio and Militia*, p. 103; and Barnes, Naylor, and Polzer, *Northern New Spain*, p. 120.

162. AGN, Historia, leg. 333, Campos a Barba, Cuquiárachi, ff. 29v–30.

163. Ibid., Campos a Arjo, f. 33.

164. Ibid., Joseph Agustin de Campos a Mi Padre Rector Luis Maria Gallardi, San Joseph de Himuri y noviembre 20 de 1735, f. 40v.

165. As early as 1701, Father Juan María Salvatierra referred to Campos as "the great master of all the languages of this nation." See Burrus, *Kino and Manje*, p. 598. Antonio Bezerra Nieto said of him in 1718, "He is very fluent in their [the Pimas'] language and also capable in Spanish, making him very popular and highly esteemed in their nation." See AHP, Informe de General Don Anttonio Bezerranieto, Basochuca en 26 del mes de abril de 1718, f. 2. It is interesting that Bezerra Nieto would say Campos was "capable in Spanish" if he was a Spaniard and Spanish was his first language. If he had to learn Spanish as a second language, one wonders what his first language was. It is uncertain where he was born and raised, but the three possibilities of Burgos, Logroño, and Sijena, all of which border the Basque country, suggest that his first language might have been Basque. The name Campos was very common in the Basque region in antiquity, even though it is not of Basque origin. See García Carraffa, *El Solar Vasco Navarro*, III:21.

166. AGN, Historia, leg. 333, Campos a Arjo, f. 34.

167. Ibid., 33v.

168. Ibid., Campos a Barba, Cuquiárachi, f. 29.
169. Ibid., Campos a Arjo, f. 33v.
170. Ibid., Campos a Barba, Cuquiárachi, f. 29.
171. Ibid., Campos a Arjo, ff. 34–34v. See also Gonzáles, *Etnología y Misión*, p. 244, where thirty-three lines of Father Campos's letter to Father Arjo are transcribed and published in Spanish. Of the four letters that Father Campos wrote after leaving San Ignacio, contained on fifteen sheets of paper (folios) and constituting thirty pages of writing, these few lines concerning Father Velarde are the only ones that have ever been published or even commented on objectively prior to this work. There are 832 lines of writing contained in the four letters, which means that after Señor Gonzáles's thirty-three lines and the hundred or so that are quoted herein are discounted, there are still well over 600 lines of writing that have never been published. And that is just from those four letters. There are at least fifty more letters by various authors, including Campos, about his removal from San Ignacio that have never been transcribed, translated, or published. Some of them have been commented on, but to say this subject has ever been looked at thoroughly would be a gross overstatement. It is true that Campos's last four letters, because of his extremely shaky hand, are difficult to decipher. Even Señor Gonzáles had to rely on Carmen Camacho, a paleographer with the Archivo General de la Nación, to tell him what the thirty lines he published said.
172. AGN, Historia, leg. 333, Campos a Garcia, f. 81v.
173. Ibid., Campos a Arjo, f. 36.
174. TXE, Janos Deaths, unnumbered pages; also FHL, microfilm no. 1156624.
175. GBEA, 1593, Testimonio de Manuel Vasques, ff. 278–279.
176. Captain Anza had built the presidio chapel just a few years previously.
177. GBEA, 1593, Certificacion de la partida de bautizmo de Josefa Gregoria Juaquina de Anssa hallada en el primero libro de Bauptismos de Cuquiárachi a fojas ochenta y tres a la buelta, f. 761.
178. EHA, Libros de Finados de Hernani, 2, f. 86v.
179. Ibid., f. 90.
180. GPAH, leg. III-1352, Inventario de Vienes de Antonio de Ansa, ff. 20–24.
181. It is not unusual for people to think they were born in a town where the family lived when they were young, or that was better known for whatever reason (capital of the jurisdiction, greater population, seat of an important facility such as a presidio, etc.).
182. Father Rojas here refers to the priest assigned to the presidio, Pedro Verdugo del Castillo. Rojas himself was the priest at the Mission of Cuquiárachi at this time.
183. AGI, Guadalajara, leg. 169, exp. 536, num. 436, partida 4, Expediente promovido por Doña Ana Maria Perez Serrano viuda del Coronel Don Juan Bautista de Anza, sobre que se le declare la Pension que le corresponde en el Monte pio Militar: Certificacion de la partida de bautizmo de Juan Bautista de Ansa hallada en el primero libro de Bauptismos de Cuquiárachi a fojas noventa y seis buelta, f. 5.
184. Carmen Boone de Aguilar, "First Cesarean Operation in Alta California, New Spain's First?" (paper presented at the Fifteenth Annual Conference of the California Mission Studies Association, San Juan Capistrano, Calif., February 14, 1998), pp. 1–3.
185. AGN, Historia, leg. 333, Joseph Agustin de Campos al Muy Reverendo Padre Pro-

vincial Andres Garcia, Agosto 13 de 1736, ff. 80–80v. This is actually one of two letters that Father Campos wrote from Cuquiárachi that day. The other one was written to Father Visitor José Sánchez and is included in the same legajo.

186. The secondary literature has generally confused the date and place of Father Campos's death. Donahue, *After Kino,* p. 80, says that he died in Fronteras. Roca, *Paths of the Padres,* p. 359, says that he died in Chihuahua. Polzer and Sheridan, *The Presidio and Militia,* p. 289, say that he died in Chihuahua. Sheridan, *Empire of Sand,* p. 123, citing Dunne, says that he died en route to the Jesuit college in Chihuahua. While this last statement could possibly be true, there is nothing in the primary literature to indicate that Father Campos ever left Fronteras for anything other than brief visits to Cuquiárachi and Baseraca. Even Dunne, "Captain Anza and the Case of Father Campos," p. 58, says that "due to Campos's mental condition the plan of sending him to Chihuahua, three hundred miles southeast, seems to have been dropped." Although documentation of a final decision by Father Visitor Marciano, or his superior, has never been found, the following quotation from Father Toral's report to the father visitor in response to Anza's request that Father Campos be allowed to go home with him to Fronteras is the final word on the matter for the present: "I could not make that decision, Your Reverence. Only you can do that. I told him [Anza], however, that I would ask that this favor be granted Father [Campos], which I am now asking of Your Reverence, for the love of God. (See AGN, Historia, leg. 333, Toral a Marciano, f. 49v.)

It is obvious that the request to send Father Campos to Fronteras was granted, at least temporarily, because documentation shows that he lived there until at least August 13, 1736. There is nothing in the primary records to indicate that decision was ever rescinded or altered. Thus, the fact that Father Campos was at Baseraca is no more indication that he was on his way to Chihuahua than the fact that his being at Cuquiárachi shows that he was on his way back to San Ignacio. In reality, the old priest was probably sent to both places to provide some small amount of help at those missions, some degree of self-esteem to the old man, and a short reprieve for those taking care of him at Fronteras.

187. AGN, Jesuitas, leg. I, exp. 8, Carta de Nicolas de Oro al Muy Reverendo Padre Rector Joseph Maria Genovese, Julio 26 de 1737, f. 1.

CHAPTER SIX. THE FINAL YEARS

1. AGN, Minería 160, leg. 1, Observación de plata por Juan Bauptista de Anssa, ff. 29–29v. Nearly everything in this section comes from AGN, Minería 160. There are two legajos that contain most of the original papers that deal with the story told in this section. Legajo number one is entitled "Autos sobre el descubrimiento de las Platas blancas y con Metal, que sean hallado en volas, Planchas sueltas sin Beta ni Vena en la Pimeria alta de la Provincia de Sonora." Legajo number two is "Autos nuebamente echos Sobre el descubrimiento de San Anttonio de Padua en la Pimeria Alta de orden del Exelentisimo Arzobispo Virrey Governador y Capitan General destos Reynos de la nueba España pro el Capitan Vittalicio Don Juan Bauptista de Anssa Justicia mayor de la Provin-

cia de Sonora." Copies of most of the documents contained in these two legajos are also located in AGI, Guadalajara, leg. 185, although a couple of the original writings are located in the latter archive. The late Vivian Fisher, retired Special Collections librarian from the Bancroft Library in Berkeley, translated all the documents in AGI, Guadalajara, leg. 185. She also was the first to locate the original documents in AGN, Minería 160 in 1996. This story relies heavily upon those original documents. The author has also relied heavily upon the scholarship of Mrs. Fisher for this section, and credit is given where her translations are quoted. Secondary sources concerning the subject are extremely limited, and none of them have had the benefit of the original documents, with the exception of an article written by this author. The only article dedicated solely to the story of the discovery of the Planchas de Plata is Patricia Roche Herring, "The Silver of El Real de Arizonac," *Arizona and the West: A Quarterly Journal of History* 20 (1978): 245–258. Where this last article lacked the benefit of the original documents, the reader will find numerous discrepancies between it and what is printed herein. Unfortunately, both a larger, book-size version of Ms. Herring's writings on the subject entitled "The Romance of the Silver of Arizona" and Mrs. Fisher's translations of the Planchas de Plata documents have yet to be published. William A. Douglass, Director of Basque Studies at the University of Nevada, first convincingly showed that "Arizona" is a Basque name/word in his article "On the Naming of Arizona," *Names* 27, no. 4 (December 1979): 217–234. This author, using the original documents from Minería 160, attempted to expand that argument. See Donald T. Garate, "Who Named Arizona? The Basque Connection," *Journal of Arizona History* 40, no. 1 (1999): 53–82. For those wishing further information or verification, the original documents concerning this marvelous silver discovery, located in Minería 160, are easily obtainable on microfilm through the Archivo General de la Nación in Mexico City.

2. Bishop of Durango.

3. Two of the three areas were probably Agua Caliente and Oquitoa. The third area may have been Guevavi or the Santa Rita Mountains south of Tucson. Both Agua Caliente and Oquitoa had established *realitos*, or small registered mining camps, before the time of this letter. Prospecting and some mining were known to have taken place at Guevavi and Santa Rita fifteen years later, and may have been pursued there at this time also.

4. Juan de Acuña, the marqués de Casafuerte.

5. One arroba was approximately twenty-five pounds; so this piece of silver weighed about a ton and a quarter.

6. One vara was approximately three feet; so the silver was from nine to eighteen inches below the surface.

7. Juan Antonio de Vizarrón y Eguiarreta, archbishop of Mexico and viceroy of Nueva España from March 18, 1734, to August 17, 1740, was born at the port of Santa María in the city of Cádiz, to Pablo de Vizarrón and Ana de Eguiarreta. Although born at Ituren, Nafarroa, the same town as Juan Bautista de Vizarrón, Juan Bautista de Anza's schoolteacher in Hernani, Pablo went to Cádiz as a government official. He made his first trip to New Spain, leaving his wife and family behind, in July of 1670. See FHL, microfilm no. 1224038, Pasajeros de Indias, 1661–1695, unnumbered pages. It was after his

return from the New World that Juan Antonio was born. The future archbishop and viceroy received his education at the College of San Clemente in Rome. He was elected archbishop in 1730 and took office on January 19, 1732. He was always an avid supporter of the Basque College in Mexico City. See Suárez, "Diccionario Biográfico Vasco-Mexicano," unnumbered pages.

8. Manuel José de Sosa.

9. AGI, Guadalajara, leg. 185, Juan Bauptista de Anssa al Muy Ilustrisimo Señor Don Benito Crespo del Orden de Santiago, Presidio de Santa Rosa de Corodéguachi, enero 7 de 1737, ff. 8–9. The late Edgar Bledsoe of Green Valley, Arizona provided this translation of Anza's letter.

10. Spelled "Arizona," "Arisona," and "Arissona" in the original documents. These three variations in its spelling appear in dozens of documents and in far too many instances to calculate an exact number. In one instance, in the title of a map that has been shown to be spurious (see Garate, "Who Named Arizona?" pp. 64–66), it was spelled "Arizonac." It was evidently easier to read the map title than the dozens of documents pertaining to the subject of the silver discovery. Therefore, secondary sources almost universally have imagined a "real de minas" called "Arizonac," for which there is not one scrap of evidence beyond the title of the bogus map. Even the body of the map lists a "ranchería" called "Arizona."

11. L. Boyd Finch, "William Claude Jones: The Rogue Who Named Arizona," *Journal of Arizona History* 31, no. 4 (winter 1990): 410–411.

12. AHH, Temp., leg. 278, exp. 34, Informe de Gabriel Prudhom, ff. 1, 1v, 19, and 19v. The full title of this report which was signed by Gabriel Prudhom Butrón y Mujica at Nuestra Señora de la Limpia Concepción del Agua Caliente on March 4, 1735 reads "El Capitan de Caballeria Don Gabriel Prudhom Heyder Butron y Muxica, Baron d' Heyder Gravushing Goldakre, Alcalde mayor por el Rey nuestro Señor (que Dios guarde) y Capitan de Guerra de esta Provincia de la Nueva Andaluzia de San Juan Bapttista de Sonora, sus costas y Fronteras, etc." The title of the so-called Prudhom map quotes this heading almost to the word, but substitutes "Arizona" for "Agua Caliente." The descriptive note written on the map also clearly quotes from this document. Even though this report says on folio 1 that Señor Prudhom had served "nearly eight years in administering the government of this province" (he still had from March to July complete his eight-year term), the map claims that he had already served eight years, with a purported date of 1733. The report is clearly signed with Señor Prudhom's elaborate, gaudy signature and rubric. The map is not signed by him, even though it claims to be. For further information on this subject, see Garate, "Who Named Arizona?" pp. 64–66.

13. TUMA, Guevavi Mission Register, ff. 28, 29, and 47.

14. TUMA, Libro de Bautismos de San Ignacio, ff. 16, 17, 36, 66, 76, 97, 99, 101, and 102; Enterrados de San Ignacio, ff. 80, 105, and 130; Magdalena Mission Register, ff. 29, 30, 34, 39, and 58.

15. Garate, "Who Named Arizona?" p. 62.

16. AGN, Minería 160, leg. 1, Notificacion del autto de arriba, Noviembre 22 de 1736, f. 21.

17. Many Yaqui names end in *mea*. It can mean "warrior," "slayer," or "pertaining

to." The root word *sirau* means "flower." Thus, his Yaqui name was "pertaining to flowers" and may be translated something like "Flower Warrior." It is spelled at least three different ways in the original documents—"Siraumea," "Sirumea," and "Siruamea." The spelling "Siraumea" was chosen because it occurs most often.

18. AGN, Minería 160, leg. 1, Autos de Vista de las Peticiones Passen todos, 8 de Henero de 1737, f. 91v.

19. Everything in the story of the silver discovery from this point to when Juan Bautista de Anza was notified of it, except as otherwise noted, comes from AGN, Minería 160, leg. 1, Declaracion de dicho Antonio, primero descubridor, ante Juan Bauptista de Anssa, ff. 15v–17; Resolucion de habiendo visto la plancha grande, ff. 17–17v; Declaracion de Santiago Ruiz de Ael ante Bernardo de Urrea, f. 23v (the foregoing three references are all dated November 21, 1736); Declaracion de Bernardo de Urrea ante Juan Bauptista de Anssa, 23 del mes de Noviembre de 1736, ff. 25v–26; Declaracion del asumpto del Notario del Santo Ofizio Don Santiago Ruiz de Ael ante Juan Bauptista de Anssa, ff. 34v–35; Declaracion sobre el mismo asumpto del Indio Antonio por Bernardo de Urrea, ff. 35v–36 (these last two declarations are dated December 1, 1736).

20. TUMA, Libro de Bautismos de San Ignacio, ff. 33 and 102; Enterrados de San Ignacio, f. 41; Magdalena Mission Register, f. 33.

21. AGN Minería 160, leg. 1, Peticion de Don Santiago Ruiz de Ael Notario del Santo Oficio, Enero 3 de 1737, f. 79.

22. TUMA, Libro de Bautismos de San Ignacio, ff. 9, 10, 37–39, and 99.

23. Ibid., ff. 30, 31, 36–38, 46, 47, 52, 111, and 112.

24. A *marco* is eight *onzas* (ounces), or one-half *libra* (pound). It must have been a large bill that over sixty-five pounds of silver would not fully liquidate.

25. Both of these men were from that area originally and returned there after the silver strike. See Sheridan, *Empire of Sand*, pp. 99 and 101, and FHL, microfilm nos. 1909863 and 1909868, Mission Records of San Miguel de Horcasitas.

26. See Douglass, "On the Naming of Arizona." Also, Garate, "Who Named Arizona?" Although non-Basque speakers over the years have wrestled with the word in an attempt to find something similar in the Pima language, the best they have come up with is something vaguely similar in *ali-shondag*. There is no such stretching of the imagination with the Basque word. There is also no evidence that there was ever a Pima ranchería in that area and much evidence to show that the Pima never inhabited the area. In Anza's day, the indigenous people told him they never went there because of the Apache threat. Some one hundred years later, when Alphonse Pinart was compiling his vocabulary of the Pima language, the local natives told him their name for that area was not *arizona*, but *ta ak'á*, meaning "where the mountain range ends," an excellent description of the site (see Alphonse Louise Pinart Collection, Mexican Manuscripts 487, folder 1, page 28, at the Bancroft Library, University of California, Berkeley). Bernardo de Urrea, who was a criollo Basque born in Culiacán, Sinaloa, is the first person on record that lived there. He owned the Arizona ranch at the time of the silver discovery and he still owned it in 1751 at the time of the Pima rebellion. It is entirely plausible that he built his spacious ranch house under one of many large oak trees that did, and still do,

grow there. Lastly, the Pima theory comes up completely short when one considers that there are three villages in Brazil, a river and village in Honduras, and a town in the San Luis Province of Argentina all named "Arizona." Although the Pima never visited those countries, the Basques were a large percentage of the population in the settlement of those areas during Spanish colonial times.

27. AGN, Minería 160, leg. 1, Informe de Juan Bauptista de Anssa al Ilustrisimo y Exelentisimo Señor Doctor Don Juan Anttonio de Vizaron, Henero 13 de 1737, f. 102v.

28. Everything from this point in the story until Captain Anza left San Antonio de Padua and arrived at Arizona, except as otherwise noted, comes from AGN, Minería 160, leg. 1, Informes de Juan Bauptista de Anssa, Noviembre 15, 16, y 18 de 1736, ff. 1–2v, and 6v; Cartas de Christoval de Cañas, Joseph Toral, y Juan de Echagoien al Capitán y Justicia Mayor Don Juan Bauptista de Anssa, Noviembre 15 y 17 de 1736, ff. 3–12v; Informes, diligencias, y decretos de Juan Bauptista de Anssa en el puesto del descrubrimiento, Noviembre 21 hasta Noviembre 24 de 1736, ff. 13–21v, 25–29, and 93v–95v; and Informes y diligencias de Bernardo de Urea del Agua Caliente y Arizona, Noviembre 21 hasta 23 de 1736, ff. 23–25. All direct quotes are separately noted.

29. AGN, Minería 160, leg. 1, Reverendo Padre Juan de Echagoien a Don Juan Bauptista de Anssa, 10 de Diziembre de 1736, f. 51v.

30. Ibid., Toral a Anssa, f. 9v. The original Spanish says "un indizuelo tontillo de Tubutama."

31. Ibid., Echagoien a Anssa, f. 19. Translation by Vivian Fisher.

32. Anza here speaks of the three missionaries being assigned to Suamca, Guevavi, and San Xavier. See "Guevavi to Sópori," in chapter 5 of this volume.

33. AGN, Minería 160, leg. 1, Dictamen y Paracer que da el Juez de estos auttos por los motibos que se beran, Henero 8 de 1737, ff. 92v–93.

34. Ibid., Don Juan de Zarazua en nombre de Don Santiago Ruis de Ael, Junio 3 de 1737, f. 129v.

35. Ibid., Decreto de Juan Bauptista de Anssa, Capitan Vitalicio del Real Pressidio de Santa Rossa de Corodeguachi y Justicia Mayor de esta provincia de Sonora por Su Majestad, 20 del mes de Noviembre de 1736, ff. 22–23. Translation by Vivian Fisher.

36. Ibid., Resolucion de habiendo visto la plancha grande, 21 del mes de Noviembre de 1736, f. 17.

37. Ibid., Demostracion de una vola que allo Joseph de Meza, 21 del mes de Noviembre de 1736, ff. 17v–18.

38. Ibid., Juan Bauptista de Anssa a los reverendos padres, visitador Joseph Toral, Juan de Echagoian, y Christoval de Cañas, Noviembre 22 de 1736, ff. 40–42v.

39. Ibid., Que se dize ttesoro este descubrimiento, qual valor y porcion puede hacer Su Majestad, Noviembre 22 de 1736, f. 20v.

40. Ibid., Decreto del Capitan Don Juan Bautista de Anza, Noviembre 22 de 1736, f. 20v.

41. Ibid., Cuentta y Razon de los Platas, Pimería Alta, N.D., f. 93v.

42. Everything from this point in the story until Captain Anza left Arizona and arrived at Santa Barbara, except as otherwise noted, comes from AGN, Minería 160, leg. 1,

Diligencias de la examinacion de las plattas, Noviembre 28 de 1736, ff. 29–31; Declaraciones de Don Santiago Ruiz de Ael, Antonio de Siraumea, y Francisco Lopez, Deciembre 1 de 1736, ff. 34v–36; Peticion de Don Santiago Ruiz de Ael y Decreto de Juan Bauptista de Anssa, Deciembre 1 de 1736, ff. 55–56; Nobramiento de Francisco Xavier de Miranda y Manuel Monrroy, Noviembre 28 de 1736, ff. 31–34; Decreto de Juan Bauptista de Anssa y Declaracion de Bernardo de Urrea, el dia 3 de Deciembre de 1736, ff. 56–57; Peticion de Francisco de Longoria y Reconocimiento de Juan Bauptista de Anssa, Deciembre 3 de 1736, ff. 86–87; Nombramiento de Andres de Padilla y declaraciones de Miranda y Padilla, Deciembre 3 de 1736, ff. 37v–38v y 39v; and Junta para cortarla plancha grande, Deciembre 3 de 1736, f. 39. All direct quotes are separately noted.

43. TUMA, Libro de Bautismos de San Ignacio, f. 93.

44. AGN Minería 160, leg. 1, Informe de Juan Bauptista de Anssa, dia 5 de Deciembre de 1736, 25v.

45. The petition was signed by Juan Phelipe Mirtin [sic], Joseph Ximines, Andrés Gonzales, Juan Antonio de Ribera, Joseph Cavallero, Nicolas Quiros y Neria, Juan Lorenzo García, Pedro Regala de Urias, Nicolas Alfonso de Ochoa, Juan Contreras, Melchor Monsalbo, Juan Joseph Martínez, Claudio Antonio Segura, Nicolas Martin, and Francisco de Longoria.

46. The next episode in the story of the silver, from the time Anza left San Antonio de Padua for the San Luis Valley, until his departure from the latter for Fronteras, except as otherwise noted, comes from AGN, Minería 160, leg. 1, Cartas de Toral, Echagoyen, y Cañas, Diciembre 9, 10, y 11 de 1736, ff. 42v–44; Escritos de Juan Bauptista de Anssa, Diciembre 5, 6, 13, 14, 15 y 20 de 1736, ff. 45–47, 48–50v, 53–54, 58v–60, 62v, 64v–65, and 66–67v; Declaracion de Nicolas Alfonso de Ochoa, 15 dias del mes de Diciembre de 1736, ff. 58–58v; Peticion de Francisco Longoria, Diciembre 16 de 1736, ff. 61–62; Escritos de Bernardo de Urrea, Diciembre 17, 18, y 20 de 1736, ff. 60–60v, 63, 64–64v, 68–69, 75, and 77v; Peticion de Francisco Perez Serrano, Diciembre 17 de 1736, ff. 75–77v. All direct quotes are separately noted.

47. AGN, Minería 160, leg. 1, Peticion y registra del sitio i donde las hallaron bolas y planchas, 16 dias del mes de Diciembre de 1736, f. 61v.

48. Ibid., Autto para que me returngo al Presidio de mi cargo, 20 del mes de Diciembre de 1736, f. 65.

49. The remainder of the story of the silver discovery at San Antonio de Padua up to the time that Manuel José de Sosa left for Mexico City, except as otherwise noted, comes from AGN, Minería 160, leg. 1, Informes del teniente Don Andres de Padilla, 24 del mes de Diziembre y Henero 3 de 1736, ff. 69–70, 80–81, and 84v–85; Declaracion y cuenta de Don Agustin de Vildosola, Diciembre 29 de 1736, ff. 70–71v; Declaracion de Francisco Salmon de Palazuelos, Diciembre 31 de 1736, ff. 71v–72v; Declaracion de Pedro Camargo, Henero 2 de 1737, ff. 72v–73; Declaraciones de Don Santiago Ruiz de Ael, Henero 2 y 3 de 1737, ff. 73–73v and 78–80; Declaracion de Luis de Mendivil, Henero 2 de 1737; Declaracion de los comerciantes mercaderes de este Real de San Antonio de Motepore de esta Provincia de Sonora, Henero 3 de 1737, ff. 81–82v; Declaracion y peticion de Antonio Siraumea, Henero 3 de 1737, ff. 84–84v; Declaracion de Don Bernardo de Urrea, Henero 8 de 1737, ff. 88–89v; and Declaraciones, ordenes, autos, y decretos de

Juan Bauptista de Anssa, Henero 8 de 1737, ff. 89v–103v. Direct quotations are noted separately.

50. AGN, Minería 160, leg. 1, Declaracion y cuenta de Vildosola, f. 71.

51. Ibid., Peticion de Don Francisco Perez Serrano, 17 dias del mes de Diziembre de 1736, f. 75.

52. Ibid., Declaracion de los comerciantes mercaderes, f. 81v.

53. Ibid., Declaracion de Ruiz de Ael, Henero 3, f. 78v.

54. Ibid., Auttos de Vistta de la peticiones presentadas, 8 dias de Henero de 1737, f. 90v.

55. Ibid., f. 91v.

56. Ibid., Dictamen de Juan Bauptista de Anssa, Henero 8 de 1737, f. 92v.

57. Ibid.

58. Ibid., Decreto de Juan Bauptista de Anssa, 10 dias del mes de Henero de 1737, f. 96.

59. Ibid., Cuenta de Manuel Joseph de Sossa, N.D., f. 123.

60. Ibid., Auto de Juan Bauptista de Anssa Justicia Mayor de esta Provincia, 26 de Henero de 1737, f. 125.

61. AGN, Reales Cédulas, vol. 59, f. 215.

62. Also spelled *aresivi, arisivi,* and *arisibi.*

63. Probably José Romero.

64. Father Segesser, of course, had become ill while serving at Guevavi (see chapter 5) after the death of Father Grazhoffer, and was removed to Fronteras. After his convalescence in the care of Anza's wife, Rosa Bezerra Nieto, he was assigned by his superiors to Mission San Francisco de Borja de Tecoripa in south central Sonora in the Pimería Baja.

65. Francisco de Aldamiz was still mining at Aguaje and was Anza's deputy justicia mayor for that district.

66. Reed mats. This word comes from the Aztec *tlapechtli,* which is a species of cane. Its most common corruption, still used in Sonora today, is *tapesco,* but it can be seen as *tapescle, tapextle, tapezcle, tapezte,* and other ways. In Anza's day in Sonora it was used to describe two things: (1) a woven reed and twig mat on which people slept, or (2) a small wooden platform used in the mines for working upward in the back of a shaft or as a landing place that made the ladders more secure and provided a place for the tanateros to catch their breath. Undoubtedly, Anza here refers to woven reed sleeping mats. It is interesting to note that he was fully accustomed to this Indian word, but Viceroy Vizarrón, in his report to the king, felt it necessary to qualify what the word meant. He said the old and sick were carried on *Hapeztles ô Zarzos*—zarzos, of course, being reeds. See AGN, Reales Cédulas, vol. 59, Juan Antonio de Vizarrón y Eguiarreta Arzobispo de Mexico al Rey, f. 215v.

67. Gulf of California.

68. Approximately 350 miles.

69. Saturday, June 1, 1737.

70. Viceroy Vizarrón's account of the Aschuhuli incident, which obviously takes its substance from this letter, also says that he was hung from a tall palm tree. See AGN, Reales Cédulas, vol. 59, Vizarrón al Rey, f. 215. Father Segesser, on the other hand, said

that Aschuhuli was shot with an escopeta and the body was then hung from the tree. See Theodore E. Treutlein, "The Relation of Phelipp Segesser: The Pimas and Other Indians," *Mid-America* XXVII (July 1945). There is supporting evidence for either type of execution.

71. Anza spelled the name "Aschuhuli." Most other writers of the day spelled it "Asuchul," or "Ascuhul." Since it is Anza's story, his spelling has been adopted herein.

72. Sunday, June 9, 1737.

73. Native sorcerers, or shamans.

74. AGN, Reales Cédulas, vol. 59, Juan Bauptista de Anssa al Virrey Juan Antonio Vizarrón y Eguiarreta, ff. 216–219v. A transcript of this letter was supplied to the author by Vivian Fisher. Translation by the author and Edgar Bledsoe.

75. AGN, Minería 160, leg. 1, Autorización de recompensa, Junio 3 de 1737, f. 124.

76. Ibid., Juan Bauptista de Anssa al Ilustrisimo y Exelentisimo Señor Don Juan Antonio de Vizarron, f. 103v.

77. Everything contained in this section, except as otherwise noted is taken from AGI, Guadalajara, leg. 185, Capitan Don Juan Bautista de Anssa al Señor Virrey Don Juan Antonio de Vizarron y Eguiarreta, Henero 14, 1737, ff. 1–9.

78. Garrastegui had evidently been appointed alcalde mayor after Gabriel Prudhom Butrón y Mujica at the end of July 1735. Since Sonora had now been granted its own governor, separate from Nueva Vizcaya, there was no further need for an alcalde mayor, so Garrastegui's term seems to have lasted only about two years. In fact, the office may have been terminated as an indirect result of the lawsuit brought by José de Mesa and others against Garrastegui over granting Anza the right to explore the regions between Sonora and the Colorado River.

79. Mythical cities of gold and vast wealth.

80. AGI, Guadalajara, leg. 185, Anssa al virrey, ff. 5–6. Translation by Vivian Fisher.

81. All of the information concerning the court suit filed by Mesa comes from ibid., Informe del Licenciado Melgarejo, 29 Agosto de 1737, ff. 103v–113v. Direct quotations are noted separately.

82. Ibid., f. 105v. Translation by Vivian Fisher.

83. Ibid., f. 106.

84. Ibid., f. 113v. Translation by Vivian Fisher.

85. AGN, Minería 160, leg. 2, Auto de Don Juan Antonio de Vizarron y Eguiarreta, Arsobispo de Mexico, del consejo de Su Majestad Virrey governador y capitan general de esta nueba España y Presidente de el Real Azienda de ella, etc., 8 de Junio de 1737, f. 4.

86. Everything concerning the final disposal of the San Antonio silver, except as otherwise noted, comes from ibid., Auto de Vizarron, ff. 1–5v; Obedizimiento, Autorizaziones, Nombramientos, Declaraciones, Auttos, y Decretos de Juan Bauptista de Anza, desde Julio 19 hasta Octubre 6 de 1737, ff. 1–20v. All direct quotations are noted separately.

87. AGN, Minería 160, leg. 1, Cuenta de Manuel Joseph de Sossa, N.D., ff. 123–124; and Autorización de recompensa, Junio 3 de 1737, f. 124. The dates of Sosa's ride and his stay in Mexico City were calculated backward from Viceroy Vizarrón's authorization to pay Sosa's bill for services rendered. The authorization was dated Monday, June 3. Al-

though Sosa's bill is not dated, we can assume that he presented it to the viceroy either on Saturday, June 1, or Friday, May 31. Sosa claimed that he had been in Mexico City at that time for three months and six days. Counting backward three months and six days from the first of June gives an arrival date in Mexico of February 22. Then, counting backward the twenty-six days Sosa claimed to have been on the road corroborates his departure date from Tetuachi on January 28.

88. The Pony Express was not implemented until April 3, 1860, and operated for only a year and a half. It was set up to change horses about every ten miles and riders every seventy-five. Had the Pony Express been running the planchas de plata documents to Mexico, they would have delivered them faster than Sosa. However, they would have changed horses 130 times and riders 18 times. Sosa probably changed horses fewer than 50 times and made the entire run by himself!

89. Everything relative to the fiscal's report is taken from AGN, Minería 160, leg. 1, Fiscal de Su Majestad Ambrosio Melgarejo al virrey Señor Don Juan Antonio de Vizaron y Eguiarreta, Marzo 23 de 1737, ff. 104–114v. Direct quotations are noted separately.

90. Ibid., ff. 110v–111.

91. Ibid., f. 112v.

92. AGN, Minería 160, leg. 2, Decreto de Juan Bauptista de Anssa, 14 de Agosto de 1737, f. 12v.

93. Silver mines were measured to "form a parallelogram of 160 varas in length and 80 in width, in the discoverer's, and 120 and 60 in an ordinary mine." See Gamboa, *Commentaries on the Mining Ordinances of Spain*, p. 327.

94. Saric, Sonora.

95. AGN, PI, 23, Diario de la Expedicion que practico por tierra el año de 1774, el Capitan Don Juan Baptista de Ansa desde Sonora a los nuevos Establecimeientos de Californias, ff. 247–247v. This diary entry for January 13, 1774 is translated in Bolton, *Anza's California Expeditions*, 2:7. It was not used here, however, because even Bolton fell into the trap of the so-called Prudhom map and translated the place-name as "Arizonac." The document cited in this note, from which he translated his works, distinctly spells it "Arizona," as do all other documents relative to the event, with the exception of the map.

96. "The Hill of the Balls."

97. A quintal was equal to one hundred pounds; so the author here exaggerates (doubles) the weight of the slab of silver found by Almazán, or else he is quoting the approximate weight of everything that was impouned.

98. The original Spanish word used by the author in this instance is *adarme*, which was one-sixteenth of an ounce.

99. AHH, Temp., leg. 17, exp. 69, Breve resumen de los desastres, ff. 1v–2, item 10. Translation by Edgar Bledsoe. This same statement with a slight variation in translation can be found in Sheridan, *Empire of Sand*, p. 241.

100. FHL, microfilm no. 0719840, Libro de Matrimonios de Banámichi, unnumbered folio.

101. Barns, Naylor, and Polzer, *Northern New Spain*, p. 115.

102. Burrus, *Kino and Manje*, pp. 526 and 546.

103. Barns, Naylor, and Polzer, *Northern New Spain*, p. 115.

104. Donohue, *After Kino*, p. 17.
105. Ibid., p. 61.
106. Burrus, *Kino and Manje*, p. 546.
107. Donohue, *After Kino*, p. 82.
108. Burrus, *Kino and Manje*, p. 546.
109. FHL, microfilm no. 0719840, Libro de Matrimonios de Banámichi, unnumbered folio.
110. Suárez, "Diccionario Biográfico Vasco-Mexicano," unnumbered pages.
111. García Carraffa, *El Solar Vasco Navarro*, III:170–171.
112. The left side of the altar as one faces it from the nave.
113. The only book that does not contain Bishop Elizacoechea's rubric is the Guevavi register. The first several pages of the book that would have contained it have long ago fallen away and been lost. See TUMA, Libro de Enterrados de Santa Magdalena, f. 28; Libro de Bautismos de San Ignacio, ff. 95–96; Libro de Finados de San Ignacio, f. 41; Libro de Bautismos de del Pueblo de Santa María Suamca, f. 26; and Libro de Enterrados de Santa María Suamca, f. 80.
114. Ibid., Bautismos de Santa Maria Suamca, f. 26.
115. Ibid., Enterrados de San Ignacio, f. 41.
116. Ibid., Bautismos de San Ignacio, f. 96.
117. FHL, microfilm no. 0666999, Mission Records of Alamos, Sonora.
118. AGN, Reales Cédulas, vol. 59, Vizarrón al Rey 10 de Julio de 1738, f. 215v.
119. See chapter 2, section titled "Invitation to Wanderlust," this volume.
120. Pedro de Castro Figueroa y Salazar, recently appointed viceroy of New Spain, traveling from Spain to Mexico City to assume his duties.
121. Juan Antonio de Vizarrón y Eguiarreta.
122. The report, of course, listed the two nations as the Guaymas and Pimas Bajos.
123. AGN, Reales Cédulas, vol. 59, Cédula del Rey Felipe V, Julio 13 de 1739, ff. 221–221v.
124. Details of the voyage, arrival, and subsequent letters and activities of Duque de la Conquista in Nueva España come from AGI, Audiencia de México, 1256.
125. As an interesting aside, the duque de la Conquista finally arrived in Mexico City on August 17, 1740, and died a year later on August 22, 1741.
126. AGI, Guadalajara, leg. 88, Juan Bautista de Belauzaran al Virrey, f. 564.
127. Donohue, *After Kino*, p. 107.
128. Ibid., p. 86, says, "Apaches suddenly jumped out from behind bushes on the trail. They hurled Anza from his horse. Brief seconds later they pulled the helmet from his head. And, triumphant over their great enemy, the Apaches had fled before help reached the fallen Captain." Kessell, *Mission of Sorrows*, p. 69 interprets this passage as, "Hidden by the chaparral, the Apaches lay in ambush. Without warning they were upon him. Before his men got to him, the valiant officer was slain. In an instant the hostiles had claimed their trophy—the crown of Anza's scalp." The discrepancy in the translation stems from the original Spanish: "le despojaron el casco de su cabellera" (see next note). Without resurrecting Father Baltasar and asking him what he meant by that passage, or finding another account that might shed some light on it, we will never know for certain

what he meant to say. *Despojar* can mean to "despoil, strip, or undress." *Casco* can indicate "skull, cranium, or helmet." The most common usage of *cabellera*, especially in that era, was "shoulder-length hair," which was a normal style for the time. See Real Academia Española, *Diccionario de Autoridades*. Of the many definitions of *casco*, none of them has anything to do with scalps or hats. It is highly doubtful that the Apaches had begun to take scalps at that time. See Thomas E. Mails, *The People Called Apache* (New York: BDD Illustrated Books, 1993), p. 310. It was a practice that they seem to have adopted from the Mexican culture many years after Anza's death. On the other hand, as far as we know, presidial soldiers were not using helmets during that period, but rather the flat-topped felt hat—which probably led Kessell to look for some other translation. This points up the problems involved in using as a source a person who only visited the area, and that four years after Anza's death, and then waited another eleven years before writing and publishing the story.

129. Juan Antonio Baltasar, S.J., *Apostólicos Afanes de la Compañía de Jesús en la América Septentrional* (Barcelona: Pablo Nadal, 1754; México, D.F.: Alvarez y Alvarez de la Cadena, 1944), bk. III, pp. 426–427. The original Spanish reads: "habrá como quince años, que el último, que lo fué del presidio de Fronteras, Juan Bautista de Anza, hombre práctico y valeroso, y que se había hecho temer de los bárbaros, quedó oprimido por no considerar su riesgo; porque al salir de la misión del padre Ignacio Keller, le previno aquel prudente jesuita que fuese con cuidado y con la gente de su compañía bien unida, por ser casi cierto que la saldrían los enemigos en su camino, añadiéndole aún para más estimularle a una cuidadosa vigilancia, que se habían reconocido pisadas muy recientes, que sin duda eran los bárbaros, que espiaban la coyuntura para hacer su tiro: lo practicó y cumplió el capitán en su viaje mientras anduvo entre seranías encajonadas en donde solían acometer los apaches; mas al hallarse ya en campo abierto, juzgando haver evitado todo el peligro, se adelantó un poco, y detrás de los matorrales le asaltaron, le derribaron, y en pocos instantes le despojaron el casco de su cabellera para celebrar el triunfo, sin que los de su comitiva pudiesen llegar a sazón de ayudarle."

130. FHL, microfilm no. 0162555, Libro de casamientos de Parral, Chihuahua, Marriage record of Joseph Díaz del Carpio and María Manuela de Alguinigo, August 11, 1723.

131. TXE, Bautismos y finados de Janos.

132. BEHA, Libro de Bautismos de San Bartolome de Villaro, f. 104v. See also, BFA, leg. 291, núm. 26, Informacion de Vizcainia de Don Agustin de Vildosola y consortes, f. 53v.

133. Donald T. Garate, "Vildósola'tarrak: A Sonoran Political, Military, and Ethnic Legacy," in *Los Vascos en las Regiones de México, Siglos XVI–XX*, vol. II, coordinadora Amaya Garritz (México: Universidad Nacional Autónoma de México, Ministerio de Cultura del Gobierno Vasco, Instituto Vasco-Mexicano de Desarrollo 1996), pp. 27–29.

134. NSAA, Bautismos, casamientos, y fallecimientos por el distrito de Basochuca. See also AZU, microfilm no. 811, roll 10.

135. Luis Navarro Garcia, *La Sublevación Yaqui* (Sevilla: Escuela de Estudios Hispano-Americanos, 1958), p. 96.

136. Edward H. Spicer, *The Yaquis: A Cultural History* (Tucson: University of Arizona Press, 1980), p. 48.

137. EHA, Libro de Bautizados de San Vicente de San Sebastian, 5, f. 54.

138. AGI, Guadalajara, leg. 188, Pedro Phelipe de Ansa al Señor Don Agustin de Vildosola, Henero treinta de 1749, ff. 307–308.

139. Donald T. Garate, "Basque Ethnic Connections and the Expeditions of Juan Bautista de Anza to Alta California," *Colonial Latin American Historical Review* 4, no. 1 (1995): 79 and 89.

140. The little Mexican town of Santa Cruz, Sonora, is built very close to or upon the site of the ancient Santa María Suamca.

# Glossary

(b = Basque; i = Indian; s = Spanish)

*abarkas* (b) Traditional Basque shoes.
*aberatsak* (b) Upper nobility.
*abogado* (s) Attorney.
*acequia* (s) Irrigation ditch, generally leading from the river to the fields.
*acuerdo* (s) A tribunal assembled in the form of a court.
*adarga* (s) An oval-shaped, rawhide shield carried by Spanish frontier cavalry soldiers.
*adelantado* (s) One commissioned by the king to explore beyond and advance the boundaries of the kingdom.
*ademador* (s) The worker who constructed the shoring inside the mine shaft.
*ademe* (s) A timber used for shoring inside a mine shaft.
Agerregi (b) Name of a baserri owned by Catalina de Sasoeta.
*aguaje* (s) A running spring.
*aita* (b) Father.
*aitona* (b) Grandfather.
*alcalde* (s) Mayor.
*alcalde de sacas* (s) Wool superintendent.
*alcalde mayor* (s) Political chief over a jurisdiction in Nueva España who served under the governor of a larger jurisdiction; lieutenant governor.
*alférez* (s) Second lieutenant.
*alguacil* (s) Constable; punished petty crime.
*alguacil mayor* (s) Chief constable.
*alta* (s) Upper, high.
*ama* (b) Mother.
*amona* (b) Grandmother.
*andi* (b) Big.
*antepara* (b, s) Canal leading from the acequia to the flour mill.
*Apachería* (s) Land of the Apaches.
*apez* (b) Priest.
*arcabuz* (s) Harquebus; an early type of portable firearm.
*aresibi* (i) An Indian prophet.
*armas* (s) Arms; weaponry.
*arrastre* (b) From *arri auste* (rock breaking); a mule-powered device, similar in principle to an animal–powered flour mill, used in crushing ore to prepare it for the smelters.
*arriero* (s) A mule packer or muleteer.
*arroba* (s) Approximately twenty-five pounds; one-quarter fanega.
*arroyo* (s) A streambed cut down into the earth, forming a small canyon; usually a dry wash in the Sonoran and Chihuahuan Deserts.
*asistencia* (s) A military officer's personal staff.
*asto* (pl. *astoak*) (b) Donkey.
*audiencia* (s) Court; group of law officers assembled for judicial inquiry.
*aviador* (s) Merchandise supplier.
*ayuntamiento* (s) Town hall (Basque *udaletxe*).
*bachiller* (s) Bachelor; one holding the lowest academic degree in the sciences, before *ingeniero* and *doctor*.

*baja* (s) Low, lower.
*barra* (s) An iron bar; crowbar; one of twelve or twenty-four shares into which a mining claim could be divided.
*barretero* (s) A working miner whose tools in trade were the wedge, pick, and crowbar *(barra)*.
*baserri* (b) Farmstead.
*baserriak* (b) More than one farm or farmstead.
*baserritarra* (pl. *baserritarrak*) (b) Farmer.
*bastón* (s) A walking cane that, when carried by its owner, was proof of his political or military rank.
*bidezidor* (b) Footpath.
*bizcocho* (s) Hardtack cakes; actually comes from the Italian *biscotto*.
*boca* (s) Literally "mouth"; opening of the main vertical mine shaft leading to the horizontal shafts below.
*bola* (s) Ball.
*bolilla* (s) Thimble-like object with matching lid, which was used in town elections to hold the name of a nominee.
*bosque* (s) Woods; in the desert it is usually a patch of trees along a river drainage.
*botas* (s) Leather leggings that protected the feet and legs from brush and cactus when one was mounted on horseback.
*botica* (s) Pharmacy; drugstore.
*boticario* (s) Pharmacist; druggist.
*boyero* (s) Ox driver.
*caballada* (s) The main horse herd; horse herd used for relaying as the ones being ridden got tired and/or sore-footed.
*cabecera* (s) Spanish mission headquarters; mission where the priest lived.
*cabo* (s) Corporal.
*cajón* (s) Canyon; generally a box canyon.

*camino* (s) Road or trail.
*camino real* (s) Literally "royal road"; an official government road.
*campaña* (s) A military campaign.
*cántaro* (s) Silver drumlike object about eight inches in diameter, rotated by a small crank. Used in town elections to mix the bolillas.
*cantero* (s) Stone cutter.
*capitán* (s) Captain.
*capitán de mar y guerra* (s) Captain of sea and war.
*capitán vitalicio* (s) Lifetime captain.
*carbonero* (s) Collier; charcoal maker.
*cargador* (s) Freighter.
*carpintero* (s) Carpenter.
*carreta* (s) A heavy, two-wheeled, wooden cart.
*casa solar* (s) House of nobility; ancestral home.
*castellano* (s) Spanish language.
*cédula* (s) Decree or order, sometimes called a *provisión*.
*cerro* (s) Mountain; hill; range of mountains; high ground.
*clarinero* (s) Trumpeter.
*comadre* (s) Midwife; the term by which the mother of a child referred to the child's godmother and vice versa.
*compadre* (s) The term by which the father of a child referred to the child's godfather and vice versa, or in the plural, the term by which parents referred to the godparents and vice versa.
*compañero* (s) Companion, or close friend.
*compañía* (s) A military company.
Compañía de Jesús (s) Company of Jesus; Jesuits.
*compañía volante* (s) Flying company; a company of soldiers without a permanent home base.
*condado* (s) County or province.
*convento* (s) All the buildings associated

with the church, living quarters, classrooms, and workshops, generally built around a garden and fountain, in a Spanish colonial mission; monastery.

*correo* (s) The mail service.

*corriendo la posta* (s) Riding relay, in which horses were changed at least once a day wherever there was a "post" or "relay" station.

*coyote* (s) Wild dog; a person born of a mestizo father and an Indian mother.

*crestón* (s) Either the crest of a helmet or an outcropping of a vein of ore; Los Crestones is the name of twin mountain peaks east of Arizpe, Sonora.

*criollo* (s) A person born on the American continent of Old World parents.

*cuartal* (s) Approximately twenty-five pounds; one-quarter fanega.

*cuenta* (s) Account.

*cuera* (s) A heavy leather vest worn as armor.

*curador* (s) Guardian.

*doblón* (s) A Spanish gold coin worth two, four, or eight *escudos,* depending on weight.

Donostia (b) Basque name of the city Spanish–speakers know as San Sebastián, in Gipuzkoa.

*ducado* (s) Large-denomination silver or copper coin.

*ducado de vellón* (s) A copper ducado.

*edaritegi* (pl. *edaritegiak*) (b) Tavern; bar.

*entrada* (s) A penetration into unknown territory.

*escalera* (s) Literally, a staircase, but in the mines of Sonora it was a pole, twenty to thirty feet long with notches cut into it for steps, whereby the workers descended into and ascended out of a vertical mine shaft.

*escopeta* (s) Musket.

*escribano* (s) Scribe, a well-paid government official.

*escribano de número* (escribano númeral) (s) Notary public.

Escuadra de Cantábria (s) Squadron (Fleet) of Cantábria.

*escudo* (s) Spanish gold coin.

*español* (fem. *española*) (s) Spaniard.

*espuelas* (s) Spurs.

*establecimientos de paz* (s) Peace establishments, or peace camps, developed in an attempt to get the Apaches to leave their warring way of life.

*estado* (s) A measurement said to be the "height of a man"; between five and six feet.

*estolda* (b) Drainage ditch leading from the mill to the acequia.

*etxe* (b) House.

*etxeko jaun* (b) Head of the house; father of the family.

Euskal Herria (b) The Basque country.

Euskara (b) The Basque language.

*expósito* (s) An abandoned infant, usually left on the doorstep of the church or someone's home.

*fanega* (s) Approximately 100 pounds.

*ferrería* (s) Iron foundry.

*folio* (s) A sheet of paper, usually with writing on both sides, the front side having a number and the backside having the same number with the designation *vuelta* (v) indicating the reverse side.

*frontón* (b) Handball (pilota) court.

*fuero(s)* (s) Charter(s); canon of regional laws (Basque *foru/forua*).

*gachupín* (s) A person living in New Spain (Nueva España) who was born in Old Spain.

*galeón* (s) Galleon; a sailing vessel, usually armed.

*galera* (s) A heavy, wooden, four-wheeled, freight wagon.

*garbileku* (b) Cleaning station (Span. *lavadero*).

*gela* (b) Room.
*generales* (s) General questions of a personal nature asked in most court cases and interrogatories.
*gente de razón* (s) Literally "people of reason"; generally people of Spanish descent, often landowners, but always a cut above the peasantry.
*gobernador* (s) Governor; a Spanish head of state at the province level in Nueva España; indigenous governor or overseer of mission affairs.
*gomesillos* (s) Young boys who guide the blind (properly *gomecillos*).
*guardaminas* (s) Superintendent of mines.
*guardamontes* (s) Forest ranger.
*guía* (s) Guide.
*hacienda de labor* (s) Generally a large cattle ranch in Sonora, but in other parts of Mexico it was similar to a southern U.S. plantation.
*hacienda de sacar plata* (s) Silver smelter.
*hechicero* (s) Native shaman; medicine man; sorcerer.
*hemen* (b) Here.
*herrero* (s) Blacksmith.
*hidalgo; hijo dalgo* (s) Literally "son of something"; person of the lesser nobility; landowner.
*hidalguía* (s) The lesser nobility.
Indias (s) Indies; (lowercase) female Indians.
*indio* (s) Male Indian.
*informe* (s) A written report.
*irakasle* (b) Schoolteacher.
*izeba* (b) Aunt.
*jauna* (b) Literally "the Lord," it is more closely translated as "Mr." or "Sir" (Span. *señor*).
*juez* (s) Judge.
*juez ordinario* (s) Ordinary judge.
Jupe (s) Comanche Indian tribe.
*justicia* (s) Judge or justice.

*justicia mayor* (s) Chief justice.
*kale* (b) Street.
*kardaberaz* (b) Thistle; popular surname in Hernani, Gipuzkoa.
*ladino* (s) An Indian, Negro, or other person of non-Spanish descent fluent in the Spanish language.
*legajo* (s) A bundle of historical papers, usually either tied together, or bound into a book, with string and archived.
*legua* (s) League; approximately 2.5 miles.
*lehengusutipi* (b) A male second cousin.
*lejos* (s) Far.
*libra* (s) Pound; two marcos or sixteen onzas.
*licenciado* (s) Licentiate; one who has obtained the degree of licentiate in a Spanish university.
*limpieza de sangre* (s) Cleanliness of blood line, generally meaning no Jewish, Moorish, or Indian ancestry.
*lobo* (s) The offspring of a black, mestizo, or mulato male and an Indian female.
*macana* (i) Pima war club.
*mador* (s) Foreman.
*madrileño* (s) A person from Madrid.
*maestro* (s) Master; schoolteacher.
*maisu* (b) Schoolteacher.
*makila* (b) Walking stick.
*maravedí* (s) Small-denomination Spanish coin, usually called a *txanpon* in Basque.
*marco* (s) One-half libra (pound) or eight onzas (ounces).
*matlazahuatl* (i) Typhus.
*mayor* (s) Chief; major; older to.
*mayorazgo* (s) Family estate.
*mayordomo* (s) Overseer; superintendent.
*mescal* (i) An intoxicating liquor made from the agave plant.
*mestizaje* (s) Mixing of races through intermarriage.

*mestizo* (s) A person of mixed European and Indian parentage.

*miquelete* (b) Spelled *mikelete* in Basque; a type of flintlock musket developed in Nafarroa and used extensively throughout Spain and the New World; named after the Pyrenees mountain troopers who were called "mikeleteak."

*molinero* (s) Miller.

*molino* (s) Flour mill.

*monten sus caballos* (s) Cavalry command to "mount your horses."

*mulato* (s) A person born of one "Spanish" (white) parent and one "African" (black) parent.

*nagusi* (b) Main.

*naiz* (b) I am.

Nijora (i) An Indian of an unknown tribe.

*notario eclesiástico* (s) Ecclesiastic scribe.

Nueva España (s) New Spain; today, Mexico.

*oidor* (s) One of the judges of the Audiencia.

*onza* (s) Ounce.

Opatería (s) Land of the Opata Indians.

*orza* (b) Weir or diversion box set at the point where the antepara leaves the acequia.

*osaba* (b) Uncle.

*paisano* (s) Although in today's usage the word means "countryman," in Anza's day it meant somebody who was from the same town or valley as another person.

*pariente* (s) A person who is a blood relative.

*partido* (s) A percentage of the ore, beyond the daily *tequio*, extracted from a mine by a barretero; a party of soldiers.

*picacho* (s) A sharp-pointed mountain peak, usually at a distance from other mountains of equal height; a peaked butte.

*pie* (s) Foot.

*pila* (s) Font (baptismal).

*pilota* (b) Basque handball (probably a corruption of the Spanish word *pelota*, meaning "ball").

Pimería (s) Land of the Pima Indians.

Pimería Alta (s) Land of the Upper Pima Indians.

Pimería Baja (s) Land of the Lower Pima Indians.

*plancha* (s) Slab or chunk.

*planchas de plata* (s) Slabs of silver.

*plata* (s) Silver.

*platero* (s) Silversmith.

*plaza* (s) Town square.

*pliego* (s) Packet, or pouch, of letters traveling together.

*presidio* (s) A community composed of a garrison of soldiers and their wives and families, as well as all other vecinos attracted to the settlement for protection or business purposes. Some presidios were fortified; others were not.

*prieto* (s) Black, or of a very dark color.

*prueba de nobleza* (s) Proof of nobility.

*puerto* (s) Gate, door, or passageway.

*rabanero* (s) Herdsman, usually of sheep and/or goats.

*ramada* (s) An arbor with upright poles and a thatched roof.

*ranchería* (s) An Indian farming village.

*rancho* (s) Ranch.

*real* (s) Royal or associated with the king; middle-denomination Spanish coin; shortened form of *real de minas*.

Real Acuerdo (s) A cabinet of legal advisers.

*real cédula* (s) A royal decree.

Real Chancillería (s) Supreme Court; in Valladolid it was for all northern Spaniards.

*real de minas* (s) Literally "royal mining camp," in which mining claims were regulated by Spanish law and the king received 20 percent of all precious metals extracted from the mines. More often than not, in their early stages reales de minas were lawless frontier boomtowns.

*Real Hacienda* (s) Royal Exchequer.

*realito* (s) Little mining camp.

*recua* (s) A pack or mule train used for carrying supplies.

*regidor* (s) Town councilman or alderman.

*repartimiento* (s) A system whereby 4 percent of the mission Indians could be worked in the mines at a minimum wage for two weeks.

*rúbrica* (s) Rubric; a squiggly symbol drawn after a person's signature that was as unique to that person as the signature itself; it could be used with any combination of first name and/or surname signatures, or it could be written by itself, similar to initialing a document in modern times.

*rueda* (s) Mill wheel.

*sagardoa* (b) The apple cider.

*sagarrak* (b) Apples.

*san* (s) Saint.

*sargento mayor* (s) Sergeant major.

*Santiago* (s) Saint James.

*Santo Tribunal* (s) Holy Office of the Inquisition.

*señor* (s) Literally "Lord," it is more closely translated as "Mr." or "Sir" (Basque *jauna*).

*sindico procurador general* (s) Attorney general.

*suge* (b) Snake; Spanish *víbora* or *culebra*.

*tanate* (i) Basket made of rawhide or agave strips; used for carrying ore from the mines to the arrastres.

*tanatero* (s) A person who carried the ore from the mine to the arrastre; his was the hardest and most poorly paid job; tanateros were generally Indian, African, or mixed bloods.

*tapisque* (i) Spanish corruption of a Nahuatl term, it referred to an Indian who worked in the mines under the repartimiento system.

*'tar* (pl. *'tarrak*) (b) Pertaining to a person of whatever class the suffix follows; denotes clan, kin, family, or origin.

*teniente* (s) Lieutenant in the army; deputy in the political world.

*tequio* (i) The daily amount of ore required to be extracted from a mine during working hours by a barretero.

*tesorero* (s) Treasurer.

*tesoro* (s) Treasure.

*tienda* (s) Store; tent used by soldiers.

*título* (s) Title.

*título de merced* (s) Land grant; literally "title of mercy."

*tlatole* (i) A Nahuatl word describing a conference or meeting in which advice or council is given.

*topil* (s) Native mission peace officer who served under the indigenous gobernador or alcalde; he imprisoned those who committed major crimes and conducted tapisques to and from the mines.

*tortilla* (s) An omelette in Spain; flat, pliable wheat or corn bread in Mexico.

*txakolin* (b) A bitter Basque wine.

*txakura* (b) Dog.

*txanpon* (b) Coin.

*txanponzorro* (b) Coin purse.

*txapela* (b) The hat, beret.

*udaletxe* (b) Town hall (Span. *ayuntamiento*).

*upelak* (b) Wooden casks.

*vaquero* (s) Cowboy.

*vara* (s) A measurement of approximately one yard, or three feet.

*vecino* (s) Any resident or citizen of a community.
*veedor* (s) Administrator; inspector.
*víbora* (s) Snake (Basque *suge*).
*viejo* (s) Old.
*visita* (s) A Spanish mission community without a resident priest.
*vizcainía* (s) Basque language, origin, or condition, as referred to by Spaniards anciently; today the term *vasquence* is used; *Euskara* in Basque.
*vizcaíno* (s) Used by Spaniards prior to the nineteenth century to refer to a Basque person.
*volante* (s) Flying; used to describe a military company without a permanent home base.
*xacal* (i) Nahuatl word used by the Spanish to describe the huts placed over vertical mine openings.
*zato* (b) Goatskin wine bag; the hide is tanned with the hair on, and the side of the skin with the hair is placed on the inside of the bag.
Zeago (b) Name of a flour mill owned by Francisco Antonio de Beroiz.

VERBS NO LONGER IN USE

*arcabucear* (s) To shoot someone or something with an arcabuz, or musket.
*rubricar* (s) To sign something with just one's rubric, leaving off the person's name.
*tlatolearse* (i, s) To hold a conference or discuss matters.

# Bibliography

ARCHIVES AND COLLECTIONS CITED

| | |
|---|---|
| ADP | Archivo Diocesano Pamplona (Parish Records of Nafarroa) |
| ADV | Archivo Diocesano de Valladolid (Parish Records of Valladolid) |
| AGI | Archivo General de Indias, Sevilla |
| AGN, PI | Archivo General de la Nación, Provincias Internas, Ciudad de México |
| AHH | Archivo Histórico Hacienda, Ciudad de México |
| AHP | Archivo de Hidalgo de Parral |
| AZU | University of Arizona, Tucson, Microfilm Collection |
| BEHA | Bizkaiko Eleizaren Histori Artxibua, Derio (Parish Records of Bizkaia) |
| BFA | Bizkaiko Foru Aldundia Artxiboa, Bilbao (Provincial Records of Bizkaia) |
| BLB | The Bancroft Library, Berkeley |
| BLL | British Library, London |
| BNM | Biblioteca Nacional de México (Franciscan Archives) |
| DRSW | Documentary Relations of the Southwest Microfilm Collection, Tucson |
| EHA | Elizbarrutiko Histori Artxiboa, Donostia (Parish Records of Gipuzkoa) |
| FHL | Family History Library Microfilm Collection, Salt Lake City |
| GAO | Gipuzkoako Artxibategi Orokorra, Tolosa (Provincial Records of Gipuzkoa) |
| GBEA | Gernikako Batzar Etxea Artxiboa, Gernika (Governmental Records of Bizkaia) |
| GPAH | Gipuzkoako Protokoloen Artxibategi Historikoa, Oñati (Notarial Records of Gipuzkoa) |
| HUA | Hernaniko Udalaren Artxiboa (Hernani Civil Records) |
| MIU | University of Michigan, Ann Arbor, Zacatecas Collection |
| NSAA | Nuestra Señor de la Asunción de Arizpe (Sonora) Mission Records |
| PCR | Pima County Records, Tucson |
| SCRC | Spanish Colonial Research Center Microfilm Collection, Albuquerque |
| SMH | San Miguel de Horcasitas (Sonora) Parish Records |
| TUMA | Tumacácori National Historical Park Microfilm Collection |
| TXA, WBS | University of Texas, Austin, W. B. Stephens Collection |
| TXE | University of Texas, El Paso, Microfilm Collection |

BOOKS, JOURNALS, AND MISCELLANEOUS WORKS

Aguinagalde, F. Borja de. *Gipuzkoako Leinuen Aztarna Bila*, XV–XIX. Zarautz: Gipuzkoako Foru Aldundia, 1994.

Almada, Francisco R. *Diccionario de Historia, Geografía, y Biografía Sonorenses*. Hermosillo: Gobierno del Estado, 1983.

Amador Carrandi, Florencio. *Catálogo de Genealogias Redactado y Compuesto por su Archivo*. Gernika: Archivo de la Casa de Juntas, 1958.

Ansa, Ramón. "Sobre el Origen del Patronimico 'Ansa.'" Paper presented at the second annual Anza World Conference, Arizpe, Sonora, 1997.

Areitio y Mendiolea, Dario de. *El Fuero de Vizcaya*. Bilbao: Imprenta Provincial de Vizcaya, 1977.

Askue, Resurrección María de. *Euskaleriaren Yakintza*. Bilbao: Diputación de Bizkaya, 1948.

Aulestia, Gorka. *Basque-English Dictionary*. Reno: University of Nevada Press, 1989.

Aulestia, Gorka, and Linda White. *English-Basque Dictionary*. Reno: University of Nevada Press, 1990.

Balparda y de las Herrerías, Gregorio de. *Historia Crítica de Vizcaya y de sus Fueros*. Tomos I y II. Bilbao: La Editorial Vizcaina, 1974.

Baltasar, Juan Antonio, S.J. *Apostólicos Afanes de la Compañía de Jesús en su Provincia de México*. Book III. México, D.F.: Alvarez y Alvarez de la Cadena, 1944. First published in Barcelona by Pablo Nadal in 1754.

Bancroft, Hubert Howe. *History of Arizona and New Mexico, 1530–1888*. San Francisco: History Company, 1889.

———. *History of the North Mexican States and Texas*. Vol. II, 1801–1889. San Francisco: History Company, 1889.

Bard, Rachel. "Aimery Picaud and the Basques: Selections from 'The Pilgrim's Guide to Santiago de Compostela.'" In *Essays in Basque Social Anthropology and History*, edited by William A. Douglass. Reno: Basque Studies Program, 1989.

———. *Navarra: The Durable Kingdom*. Reno: University of Nevada Press, 1982.

Barns, Thomas C., Thomas H. Naylor, and Charles W. Polzer. *Northern New Spain: A Research Guide*. Tucson: University of Arizona Press, 1981.

Bartlett, John Russell. *Personal Narrative of Explorations and Incidents, 1850–1855*. Chicago: Rio Grande Press, 1965.

Bolton, Herbert Eugene. *Anza's California Expeditions*. Vols. 1–5. Berkeley: University of California Press, 1930.

———. *Bolton and the Spanish Borderlands*. Edited and with an introduction by John Francis Bannon. Norman: University of Oklahoma Press, 1968.

———. *Rim of Christendom: A Biography of Eusebio Francisco Kino, Pacific Coast Pioneer*. New York: Macmillan, 1936.

———. *The Spanish Borderlands*. New Haven, Conn.: Yale University Press, 1921.

Boone de Aguilar, Carmen. "First Cesarean Operation in Alta California, New Spain's First?" Paper presented at the fifteenth annual conference of the California Mission Studies Association, San Juan Capistrano, Calif., February 1998.

Bowman, J. N., and R. F. Heizer. *Anza and the Northwest Frontier of New Spain*. Southwest Museum Papers, no. 20. Los Angeles: Southwest Museum, 1967.

Burrus, Ernest J., S. J. *Kino and Manje: Explorers of Sonora and Arizona — Their Vision of the Future*. St. Louis: Jesuit Historical Institute, 1971.

Catholic Biblical Association of America. *The New American Bible*. New York: Catholic Book Publishing, 1970.

Denis, Alberta Johnston. *Spanish Alta California*. New York: Macmillan, 1927.

Donohue, John Augustine, S.J. *After Kino: Jesuit Missions in Northwestern New Spain, 1711–1767*. St. Louis: Jesuit Historical Institute, 1969.

Douglass, William A. "Factors in the Formation of the New-World Basque Emigrant Diaspora." In *Essays in Basque Social Anthropology and History*, edited by William A. Douglass. Reno: Basque Studies Program, 1989.

———. "On the Naming of Arizona." *Names* 27, no. 4 (1979): 217–234.

Douglass, William A., and Jon Bilbao. *Amerikanuak: Basques in the New World*. Reno: University of Nevada Press, 1975.

Dunne, Peter Masten, S.J. *Black Robes in Lower California*. Berkeley: University of California Press, 1952.

———. "Captain Anza and the Case of Father Campos." *Mid-America* XXIII (1941): 45–59.

Elstob, Winston. Epilogue to *El Viaje De Juan Bautista de Anza Y La Fundación De San Francisco, 1775–1776*, edited by Helen Shropshire. N.p.: California Heritage Guides, [1976].

Finch, L. Boyd. "William Claude Jones: The Rogue Who Named Arizona." *Journal of Arizona History* 31, no. 4 (1990): 405–424.

Gallop, Rodney. *A Book of the Basques*. Reno: University of Nevada Press, 1970.

Gamboa, Francisco Xavier de. *Commentaries on the Mining Ordinances of Spain: Dedicated to His Catholic Majesty, Charles III*. Translated from the original Spanish by Richard Heathfield. Vols. I and II. London: Longman, Rees, Orme, Brown, and Green, 1830.

Garate, Donald T. *Anssa of Ernani: A Collection of Documents Establishing the Birthplace, Birth Date, and Parentage of Juan Bautista de Anza, Captain of La Caballería de las Fronteras Garrisoned at the Royal Presidio of Santa Rosa de Corodéguachi*. Tumacácori, Ariz.: National Park Service, 1992.

———. "Anza's Return from Alta California: Anza Correspondence, 1776–1778." In *Antepasados*, vol. IX. San Leandro: Los Californianos, 1998.

———. "Basque Ethnic Connections and the Expeditions of Juan Bautista de Anza to Alta California." *Colonial Latin American Historical Review* 4, no. 1 (1995): 71–93.

———. "Basque Names, Nobility and Ethnicity on the Spanish Frontier." *Colonial Latin American Historical Review* 2, no. 1 (1993): 77–104.

———. "La Ganadería de Sonora en la inspección militar de 1718." In *Sonora: 400 Años de Ganadería*. Hermosillo: Sociedad Sonorense de Historia, A.C., 1996.

———. "Juan de Oñate's Prueba de Caballero, 1625: A Look at His Ancestral Heritage." *Colonial Latin American Historical Review* 7, no. 2 (1998): 129–173.

———. *Pedro de la Cruz, Alias Chihuahua: Conspirator, Scapegoat, Victim*. Tumacácori, Ariz.: National Park Service, 1999.

———. "References to 'Anza.'" Paper presented at the third annual Anza World Conference, Arizpe, Sonora, Mexico, 1997.

———. "Vildósola'tarrak: A Sonoran Political, Military, and Ethnic Legacy." In *Los Vascos en las Regiones de México, Siglos XVI–XX*, vol. II, coordinadora Amaya Garritz. México: Universidad Nacional Autónoma de México, Ministerio de Cultura del Gobierno Vasco, Instituto Vasco-Mexican de Desarrollo, 1996.

———. "Vizcaínos, Jesuits, and Álvarez Tuñón: An Ethnic View of a Frontier Controversy." *Journal of the Society of Basque Studies in America* XVI (1996): 17–39.

———. "Who Named Arizona? The Basque Connection." *Journal of Arizona History* 40, no. 1 (1999): 35–57.

Garate, Donald T., and Maria de Lourdes Gortarez. *Anza: A Documentary Analysis of the Surname of Juan Bautista de Anza*. Tumacácori, Ariz.: National Park Service, 1993.

García Carraffa, Alberto y Arturo. *Diccionario Heraldico y Genealógico de Apellidos Españoles y Americanos*. Madrid: Lithografía de Foruny.

———. *Enciclopedia Heráldica*. Madrid: Nueva Impr. Radio, 1952–1963.

———. *El Solar Vasco Navarro*. San Sebastian: Librería Internacional, 1966.

Giesey, Ralph E. *If Not, Not: The Oath of the Aragonese and the Legendary Laws of Sobrarbe*. Princeton, N.J.: Princeton University Press, 1968.

Gobierno de Navarra. "Genealogía de los Reyes de Navarra." In *Diario de Navarra*. Pamplona: Sedes Reales de Navarra, 1993.

Gonzáles, Luis R. *Etnología y Misión en la Pimería Alta, 1715–1740: Informes y Relaciones Misioneras de Luis Xavier Velarde, Giuseppe María Genovese, Daniel Januske, José Agustín de Campos, y Cristóbal de Cañas*. México: Universidad Nacional Autónoma de México, 1977.

Hernaniko Udalbatza. *Hernani 1996ko Gida*. Bilbao: DYCA, Hernaniko Udala, 1996.

Herring, Patricia Roche. "The Silver of El Real de Arizonac." *Arizona and the West* 20 (1978): 245–257.

Iriondo, Luis. *Iparragirre: Zure Oroiz*. Bilbao: Eusko Jaurlaritza Kultura Saila, 1981.

John, Elizabeth A. H. *Storms Brewed in Other Men's Worlds: The Confrontation of Indians, Spanish, and French in the Southwest, 1540–1795*. Lincoln: University of Nebraska Press, 1975.

Kerexeta, Jaime de. *Fogueraciones de Bizkaia del Siglo XVIII*. Bilbao: Instituto Labayru-Bilbao Bizkaia Kutxa, 1992.

Kessell, John L. *Friars, Soldiers, and Reformers: Hispanic Arizona and the Sonora Mission Frontier, 1767–1856*. Tucson: University of Arizona Press, 1976.

———. *Mission of Sorrows: Jesuit Guevavi and the Pimas, 1691–1767*. Tucson: University of Arizona Press, 1970.

Kimball, Sandy. *Moraga's Pride: Rancho Laguna de los Palos Colorados*. Moraga: Moraga Historical Society, 1987.

Kintana, Xabier eta Joseba Tobar. *Euskal Hiztegi Modernoa: Euskara-Espainiera, Espainiera-Euskara.* Bilbo: Itabat Taldea, 1977.
Lafarga Lozano, Adolfo. *Hidalguias y Genealogias de las Encartaciones de Vizcaya.* Bilbao: Talleres Gráficos ARTE, 1967.
Lizundia Aramaio, Julen, koordinaketa orokorra. *Euskal Herriko Atlasa: Geografia-Ekonomia-Historia-Artea.* Donostia: Erein, 1979.
Lopez-Mendizabal, Isaac. *Etimologías de Apellidos Vascos.* Buenos Aires: Ediciones Librería del Colegio, 1958.
Mails, Thomas E. *The People Called Apache.* New York: BDD Illustrated Books, 1993.
Menezo, Juan José. *Reinos y Jefes de Estado desde el 712.* Madrid: Edita Histori Hispana, 1987.
Montané Martí, Julio Cesar. *Juan Bautista de Anza: Diario del Primer Viaje a la California, 1774.* Hermosillo: Reprográfica, S.A., 1989.

———. "Juan Bautista de Anza según Fray Pedro Font." Paper presented at the first annual Anza World Conference, Arizpe, Sonora, 1996.
Montiano, José Antonio y José Ramón de Urquijo. *Diccionario de Bolsillo "Ikas": Euskera-Castellano, Castellano-Euskera, con unas 10,000 palabras de las más usuales en los dialectos vizcaíno y Guipuzcoano.* Bilbao: Academia Montiano, 1976.
Moorhead, Max L. *The Presidio.* Norman: University of Oklahoma Press, 1975.
Mugica, José A. *Apellidos de Iberia.* Bilbao: Editorial EDILLI, S.A., 1968.

———. *Apellidos Vascos de Iberia.* Bilbao: Editorial EDILLI, S.A., 1968.
Mujica, Luis María. *Hiztegi Orokor-Teknikoa: 2. Euskara-Gaztelera.* Bilbao: Ediciones Vascas Argitaletxea, 1977.
Navarro García, Luis. *La Sublevación Yaqui.* Sevilla: Escuela de Estudios Hispano-Americanos, 1958.
Naylor, Thomas H., and Charles W. Polzer, *Pedro de Rivera and the Military Regulations for Northern New Spain, 1724–1729: A Documentary History of His Frontier Inspection and the Reglamento de 1729.* Tucson: University of Arizona Press, 1988.

———, compilers and editors. *The Presidio and Militia on the Northern Frontier of New Spain: A Documentary History.* Vol. 1, 1570–1700. Tucson: University of Arizona Press, 1968.
L'Office de Tourisme. *St. Jean Pied de Port: Ongi Ettori.* St. Jean Pied de Port: Office de Tourisme, 1996.
Officer, James E. *Hispanic Arizona, 1536–1856.* Tucson: University of Arizona Press, 1987.
Officer, James E., Mardith Schuetz-Miller, and Bernard Fontana, eds. *The Pimería Alta: Missions and More.* Tucson: Southwest Mission Research Center, 1996.
Ornelas, José Luz. *La Conquista de Sinaloa: Colección de documentos para la historia de Sinaloa.* Culiacán: Escuela de Historia de la Universidad Autonoma de Sinaloa, 1991.
Phillips, Carla Rahn, and William D. Phillips Jr. *Spain's Golden Fleece: Wool Production and the Wool Trade from the Middle Ages to the Nineteenth Century.* Baltimore: Johns Hopkins University Press, 1997.
Plazaola, Juan. *Rutas Ignacianas.* Loyola: Edita Euskojaurlaritza, 1991.

Polzer, Charles W., S.J., and Thomas E. Sheridan, eds. *The Presidio and Militia on the Northern Frontier of New Spain: A Documentary History*. Vol. 2, part 1, *The Californias and Sinaloa-Sonora, 1700–1765*. Tucson: University of Arizona Press, 1997.

Real Academia Española. *Diccionario de Autoridades, Edición Facsímil del Diccionario de la Lengua Castellana de los años 1726–1737*. Madrid: Editorial Gredos, 1990.

Rivera, Pedro de. *Diario y Derrotero de lo Caminado, Visto y Observado en la Visita que hizo a los Presidios de la Nueva España Septentrional*. Archivo Historico Militar Mexicano Núm. 2. México, D.F.: Taller Autográfico, 1946.

Roca, Paul M. *Paths of the Padres through Sonora*. Tucson: Arizona Pioneers Historical Society, 1969.

Rowland, Donald. "The Sonora Frontier of New Spain, 1735–1745." In *New Spain and the Anglo-American West: Historical Contributions Presented to Herbert Eugene Bolton*, edited by George P. Hammond, pp. 10–18. Lancaster, Pa.: Lancaster Press, 1932.

Santana, Alberto. *Baserria*. Donostia: Gipuzkoako Foru Aldundia, 1993.

Sedelmayr, Jacobo, S.J. *Before Rebellion: Letters and Reports of Jacobo Sedelmayr, S.J.* Translated by Daniel S. Matson with an introduction and annotations by Bernard L. Fontana. Tucson: Arizona Historical Society, 1996.

Sheridan, Thomas E. *Arizona: A History*. Tucson: University of Arizona Press, 1995.

———. *Empire of Sand: The Seri Indians and the Struggle for Spanish Sonora, 1645–1803*. Tucson: University of Arizona Press, 1999.

Smith, Fay Jackson. *Captain of the Phantom Presidio: History of the Presidio of Fronteras, New Spain, 1686–1735 (Including the Inspection by Brigadier Pedro de Rivera in 1726)*. Spokane: Arthur H. Clark, 1993.

Spicer, Edward H. *Cycles of Conquest: The Impact of Spain, Mexico, and the United States on the Indians of the Southwest, 1533–1960*. Tucson: University of Arizona Press, 1962.

———. *The Yaquis: A Cultural History*. Tucson: University of Arizona Press, 1980.

Suárez, Hacinto. *Diccionario Biográfico Vasco-Mexicano*. Unpublished manuscript, 5 volumes. Reno: Basque Studies Library, University of Nevada, n.d.

Treutlein, Theodore E. "The Relation of Phelipp Segesser: The Pimas and Other Indians." *Mid-America* XXVII (July 1945): 139–187; (October 1945): 257–260.

Uribeetxebarria Maiztegi, Tomás. *Jesusen Lagundia Bizkaian*. Bilbo: Bizkaiko Foru Artxibategiko Erakustarteoa, 1991.

Urquijo, Santiago. *Cuenta de la medicina en la villa de Hernani*. Unpublished thesis, vol. II. Hernani: Udalaren Artxiboa, n.d.

Weber, David J. *The Spanish Frontier in North America*. New Haven, Conn.: Yale University Press, 1992.

West, Robert C. *Sonora: Its Geographical Personality*. Austin: University of Texas Press, 1993.

Wyllys, Rufus Kay. *Arizona: The History of a Frontier State*. Phoenix: Hobson and Herr, 1950.

# Index

*abarcas*, 8, 234n. 39
*acequia*, 47
Aconchi (Sonora, Nueva España), 71, 76, 80, 166, 167
Acosta, Juan de, 150
Acuña, Juan de, 102, 110, 111, 121, 129, 157, 267n. 60, 278n. 4
Acuña, Manuel de, 58, 61, 65, 66, 249nn. 63, 66, 68
*adarga*, 118
*adelantado*, 191
*ademadores*, 61
Africa, 46
Africans, 56, 60, 75, 162
agave liquor. See *mescal*
Agerregi (farm), 23, 40
Agua Caliente (*real de minas*), 140, 157–78, 196, 217, 221–23
Aguaje, Nuestra Señora de Guadalupe de (*real de minas*), xix, 54–69, 71, 72, 73, 84, 86, 140, 186, 245n. 4
Aguirre, José de, 62, 74; personal information, 247n. 50
Aguirre, Lorenzo de, 31
Agur Jaunak (Basque song), xviii
Aiarragaray, Mateo de, 45, 46
Aigame, Nuestra Señora de la Purificación del (*real de minas*), 55
Ainsa: mountains in Spain, 1, 5–6; village, 6
Álamos (Sonora, Nueva España), 54, 59, 200, 203
Albizu, Juan José de, 213
Alcalá, España, 200

*alcalde*, 29, 30, 31
*alcalde de sacas*, 46
*alcalde mayor*, 67, 74, 76, 77, 80, 138, 159, 191, 221, 250n. 77, 284n. 78
*alcalde ordinario*, 218
Aldamiz, Francisco de, 59, 60, 65, 66, 184, 186, 283n. 65; birth information, 246n. 29
Aldamiz, Manuel de, 89
Alday, José Romualdo de, 97
Alday, Martín de, 74, 92, 96, 97, 253n. 117, 254n. 4; birth information, 251n. 92
Alday, Pedro de, 74, 77, 78, 92, 253n. 117
Alfonso V (king of Aragón), 10
Alfonso X (king of León y Castilla), 11
*alguacil mayor*, 63, 65, 195, 220
Almazán, José Fermín de, 160–62, 171, 173, 175, 194, 195, 197, 214, 216, 217, 218, 223
Altar River Valley, 203
Álvarez de la Bandera, Miguel, 76, 80
Álvarez Tuñón y Quirós, Gregorio, 62, 70, 73–79, 80, 86–103, 107, 108, 110, 111, 112, 113, 114, 127–29, 131, 135, 175, 225, 226, 251n. 85, 253n. 116; appointment as captain of Fronteras, 250n. 81; personal information, 247n. 51, 251n. 92; signature, 87
Álvarez, Vicente, 95
Álvarez y Zubialdea, Bentura de, 98
Alzega, Agustina de, 16, 17
Alzega, Juan Martinez de, 30
Amasola, José de, 64

Amasorrain, Miguel de, 105
American Southwest, xiii, xvii, xxi
Amitesarobe, Antonio de, 48, 49, 51
Amitesarobe, Santiago de, 22
Amitesarobe, Sebastián de, 26, 27
Andoain (Gipuzkoa, España), 10, 41
Andrés (Pima captain), 185
Ansorena, Domingo de, 50
*anteparas*, 48
Antonia de los Santos (slave), 84
Anza, Antonio de (father), xv, 18, 19–34, 38–40, 42, 46, 47, 49, 51, 69, 70, 82, 104, 106, 153, 156, 203, 227nn. 6, 8; 228n. 10, 239nn. 47–49; family tree, 33; signature, 25
Anza: botica, 19, 20, 21, 41, 46, 153; Castle, 9, 10; Days (annual Tubac celebration), xvii, 231n. 20; etymology of the name, 5–7, 228n. 10, 232n. 4, 233n. 8; Expedition to California, xv; family, xv, xviii, xxi, 4–16, 32, 35, 39, 40, 70, 104, 107, 156, 227n. 6; meaning of the name, 1–3; National Historic Trail, xvii; Solar, wife of Juan Bautista, 10; World Conference, xvii, xviii, xix, 228n. 11. *See also* Bezerra Nieto, María Rosa
Anza, Clara de (aunt), 18, 21, 32, 39
Anza, Felipe de (great-uncle), 17
Anza, Felipe de (uncle), 18, 21, 22, 34, 52
Anza, Francisca de (aunt), 18
Anza, Francisco Antonio de (son), 106, 113, 207, 229n. 14; baptismal record, 106
Anza, Gerónimo de (Aragonese Cortes attendant), 10
Anza, Gregoria. *See* Anza, Josefa Gregoria Juaquina de
Anza, Ignacio de (great-uncle 1), 17
Anza, Ignacio de (great-uncle 2), 17
Anza, José de (brother), 39, 40
Anza, José de (great-uncle), 17
Anza, Josefa de (aunt), 18, 32, 39
Anza, Josefa de (great-aunt), 17

Anza, Josefa Gregoria Juaquina de (daughter), xvii, 152, 153, 154, 207, 208; baptismal record, 152
Anza, Juan Bautista de (son), xiii–xviii, 2, 3, 13, 29, 80, 81, 116, 122, 127, 128, 151, 153, 155, 174, 193, 198, 207, 208, 222, 223, 228n. 10, 229nn. 13–16, 230n. 17, 231n. 18, 285n. 95; baptismal record, 153–54; death information, 254n. 133; not a caballero, 268n. 79; statement about Arizona silver, 198
Anza, Juan Felipe de (brother), 39, 40, 45, 69, 153; family tree, 33; signature, 39
Anza, Juanes de (fifteenth-century Hernani businessman), 14, 15
Anza, Juanes de (grandfather), 16–18, 21, 240n. 68; family tree, 33; marriage record, 16
Anza, Juanes de (great-granduncle), 17
Anza, María de (aunt), 18
Anza, María Estevan de (sister), 20, 23, 30, 32, 35, 38, 40, 69, 153; children, 242n. 99; family tree, 33; marriage information, 242n. 94; signature, 38
Anza, María Gertrudis de (daughter), 84, 103, 113, 207, 255–56n. 13
Anza, María Manuela de (daughter), 84, 103, 113, 207, 255nn. 10, 11
Anza, María Margarita de (daughter), 106, 107, 154, 207; baptismal record, 107
Anza, María Nicolasa de (cousin), 45
Anza, María Rosa de (granddaughter), 2, 233n. 9
Anza, Martín de (custodian of the king's armory), 10
Anza, Martín de (great-grandfather), 16, 17; family tree, 33
Anza, Miguel (custodian of the king's armory), 10
Anza, Nicolás (brother), 39, 40, 153
Anza, Pedro Felipe de (cousin; business manager; son's godfather), xv, 45, 52,

84, 154, 155, 181–83, 207, 208, 217, 256n. 17; signature, 85
Apache frontier, 37, 83
Apache Indians. See *Indios*
Apache peace settlements. See *establecimientos de paz*
Apachería, 117
Aquibisani, Eusebio, 123, 124
Araba, España, 5, 10, 42, 207
Arabs. See Moors
Araeta, Josefa de, 22
Araeta, Juan Bautista de, 27, 44, 45, 46, 47, 48, 49, 51
Araeta, Juan de, 16, 17
Araeta, Sebastián de, 31
Aragón, España, 5, 6, 7, 10
Aránzazu (Basque shrine in Spain), 71, 72, 250n. 80
*Aránzazu, Cofradia de*, 218
Aránzazu, Nuestra Señora de (*real de minas*). See Tetuachi
Arbelaiz, Ramón de, 46
*arcabuz*, 79, 91, 253n. 120
Arcarazo, Diego de, 76
Arceo, Ignacio, 111
*aresibi* (Indian prophet), 184, 185, 188, 204, 283n. 62
Aresti, Agustín de, 217
Argentina, 52
Arista, Iñigo (king of Nafarroa), 5
Arivaca (Sonora, Nueva España — present-day Arizona), 125, 126
Arizona: meaning of the name, 164, 280n. 26; present-day state, xiii, xviii, xix, xxi, 81, 108, 124, 125; ranch owned by Bernardo de Urrea, xiii, 140, 157–78, 196, 198, 222, 225, 271n. 121; silver discovery near, 131, 157, 198; so-called Prudhom map of, 159, 279nn. 10, 12; spelling of, 279n. 10
Arizonac (imaginary real de), 222, 279nn. 10, 12; 285n. 95
Arizpe (Sonora, Nueva España), xiv, xxi, 70, 72, 75, 80, 138, 140, 144, 164, 166, 183; cathedral, xxi
Arjó, José de, 95, 259n. 65
Arrasain, Estevan de, 44
Arrasain, Juan de, 46, 50
Arrasain, Juan Ignacio de, 201
Arrasate (Gipuzkoa, España), 218
*arrastre*, 58, 60, 61
Arratia, José de, 75
*arriero*, 61, 126, 177, 178, 218
Arriola, Miguel de, 61, 65
*arroba*, 157, 158, 170, 171, 194, 198, 214–16, 278n. 5
Artaxcos, Miguel de, 50
Artozqui, Simón de, 16
Arvizu, Juan de, 252n. 115
Aschuhuli, Agustín, 183–88, 203, 204, 283n. 70, 284n. 71; age, 188
ash trees, 2
Astigarraga (Gipuzkoa, España), 43
Asturias, España, 5
Atabaliba (Indian chief), 167
Atí, mission livestock, 266n. 50
Ati (Pima ranchería), 126
Austria, 122
*aviador*, 162, 218
Ayala Valley, 29
Ayerdi, Antonio de, 20, 21, 22, 23, 25, 30, 31
Ayerdi, Juan de, 34
Azpilkueta (Nafarroa, España), 200

Bacadéguachi (Sonora, Nueva España), 92, 93
Bacanuchi (Sonora, Nueva España), 60, 71, 164, 165
Bacanuchi River, 164, 165
Bacarica (Pima ranchería), 126
Bacoachi (Sonora, Nueva España), 71, 80
Bacuacucan (Pima ranchería), 126
Baicat (Pima ranchería), 202
Bais, Juan Manuel, 125
Ballesteros, Manuel, 75
Baltasar, Juan Antonio, 205

Baltzategui, Rodrigo de, 72
Banámichi (Sonora, Nueva España), 71, 76, 80, 144, 145, 166, 198, 200
Bancroft, Hubert Howe, xv
Bañuelos, Diego, 89
Bapcomarric (Pima ranchería), 202
bar men. See *barretero*
Barba, José (IHS), 136, 140, 148
Barba, Lucas, 212
Barcaiztegui, Josefa de, 22, 32, 39; family tree, 33
Barcelón, Francisco Xavier de, 72, 74, 77; personal information, 249n. 74
Barela, Gregorio, 211
Barrera, Ignacio Díaz de, 199
*barretero*, 59, 60, 160
Barrios, Cristóbal, 123
Barrios, Diego de (corporal), 111
Barrios, Juan de Dios, 63, 212
Bartolillo (Yaqui Indian), 161
Baseraca (Sonora, Nueva España), 101, 102, 156
*baserritarrak*, 13, 14, 41, 46, 47, 48
Basochuca (Sonora, Nueva España), 60, 62, 71, 84, 164, 207, 224
Basque: alliance of Sonora, 79, 134; dances, 13; elections, 29–31; names, 1; spelling rules, 232n. 2. See also Euskal Herria (country); Euskara (language); *sagardoa* (cider); *txakolin* (bitter wine); *txanponak* (coinage); *txapela* (beret); Vizcaínos
Basterrola (farm), 47, 49, 50
Baviácora (Sonora, Nueva España), 71, 80, 144, 166
Bavicanora (Sonora, Nueva España), 71, 87, 88
Bay of Biscay, 2; "British Ocean," 7
beech trees, 2
Belauzaran, Juan Bautista de, 205
Belen (Sonora, Nueva España), 185, 187
Benafarroa, Francia, xviii
Beroiz, Ana María de, 49
Beroiz, Francisco, 27, 44, 47, 48, 49
Beroiz, Francisco Antonio de, 43, 44, 46, 47, 49, 50, 75; birth information, 243n. 116
Beroiz, Gertrudis de, 49
Beroiz, María Josefa de, 49
Beroiz, Miguel de, 27, 44, 48
Beroiz children, 48, 49, 50
*Beroiz mayorazgo*, 48, 49
Beroqui (farm), 47
Berriz (Bizkaia, España), 218
Berroeta, Juan Domingo de, 72, 77, 87, 88, 89, 92; personal information, 250n. 77
Berrotaran, José de, 98
Berryessa, Manuel de, 110
Bezerra Nieto, Antonio, xv, xix, 61–69, 73, 82, 83, 84, 85, 86, 89, 93, 94, 96, 97, 99, 100, 103, 104, 106, 107, 109, 110, 113, 120, 151–53, 211, 213, 218, 227n. 8; burial record, 151; personal information, 227n. 6, 247n. 55, 248n. 56, 254n. 4; signature, 82; statement about Seris and Pimas Bajos, 245n. 19
Bezerra Nieto family, 156, 230n. 17, 255n. 6
Bezerra Nieto, Felipe, 63, 65, 66, 83; personal information, 255n. 6
Bezerra Nieto, Gaspar, 83; personal information, 255n. 6
Bezerra Nieto, María Rosa (Anza's wife), 83, 85, 95, 106, 107, 113, 136, 152–55, 207, 208, 261n. 116, 283n. 64; personal information, 255n. 6
Bezerra Nieto, Pedro, 83, 86, 213; personal information, 255n. 6
Bezerra Nieto, Tomás Antonio, 83, 106, 107, 151; personal information, 255n.6
*bidezidor*, 8, 43
Bilbao, Jon, 5
Billaro (Bizkaia, España), 207, 224
*bizcocho*, 81
Bizkaia, España, 1, 5, 138, 207
blackberry, 2

# Index

*bolilla*, 31, 240n. 58
Boltana (Huesca, España), 6
Bolton, Herbert Eugene, xv
Borrote brothers, 105
*botas*, 100
*boticario*, 19, 20, 21, 22, 28, 46, 153
*boyero*, 126
Buen Retiro, España, 204
Bula, Elena de, 16–18, 20, 22, 32, 39, 40; family tree, 33
Burgos, España, 10
Buti, Juan de, 31, 43, 44

Caballero, José, 161, 163, 164, 179, 282n. 45
*Caballeros de Santiago*, 12, 157
Cabullona Valley, 107, 108
Cádiz, España, 47, 52, 75, 95, 153, 224
Cajón de Jiósari, xviii
Calabazas Mission, 125
Calbo, Bernardo de, 252n. 115
California, 182, 189, 190, 193, 208; route to, 182
California Gold Rush, 62
Californianos, xviii
Camargo, Pedro, 180, 216; criticism of Anza, 180
*camino real*, 36, 41, 197
Campo, José de, 65
Campos, José Agustín de (IHS), 55, 56, 95, 96, 114, 124, 133, 136–51, 154–56, 159, 189, 262n. 121, 271n. 113; arrival at San Ignacio, 259n. 61; death and last days, 156, 277n. 186; language mastery, 275n. 165; mental and physical condition, 273–74n. 144; ordered imprisonment of, 274n. 154; personal information, 259nn. 61, 66; 269–70n. 103, 273n. 141; physical description, 143, 272n. 137; signature, 137; statement concerning conspiracy against, 274n. 146
Cananea (Sonora, Nueva España), 138
Cañas, Cristóbal de (IHS), 80, 87, 88, 124, 129, 130, 144, 166, 167, 267n. 65, 268n. 68
*canoas*, 134
Cantabria, España, 5
*cántaro*, 31, 240n. 58
*canteros*, 48
*capitán vitalicio*, 64, 73, 97, 128, 175
Carbajal, Pedro, 212
*carbonero*, 46, 61
*cardón* (cactus), 57
*cargador*, 126, 197
Carlist Wars, 12
Carlos I (king of Spain; Holy Roman Emperor Charles V), 12
*carpinteros*, 48
*carreta*, 46, 91
Casas Grandes (Nueva Vizcaya, Nueva España), 67, 83, 84
castellano (Spanish language), 38, 43, 62, 201, 257–58n. 36, 267n. 58, 270n. 110
Castilla, España, 5, 7, 10, 11, 28
Cataluña, España, 5
Catharina (wife of Julian de Ortega), 84
Catholicism, 4, 56, 64, 90, 91, 127, 154, 188
Cerro El Aguaje, 58
Cerro Prieto, xix, 54
Cerrogordo (Nueva Vizcaya, Nueva España), 97
Chamorro, Juan, 161, 162, 171, 178, 179, 215
Chamorro, Luisa, 161
charcoal, 15, 41, 57, 58, 61
Charlemagne, 6, 9
Charles V (Holy Roman Emperor). *See* Carlos I
chestnut trees, 2
chief justice. *See justicia mayor*
Chihuahua (city of Nueva Vizcaya, Nueva España), 197, 200, 218
Chihuahua, Lázaro, 96, 141, 145, 146
Chihuahua (province of Nueva Vizcaya, Nueva España), xiii, xix, 71, 74, 82, 83, 92, 105

Chinapa (Sonora, Nueva España), 71, 80, 165–68
Chiricahuas. *See* Sierra de Chiricahua
*cholla* (cactus), 57, 71
Coahuila (province of Nueva Vizcaya, Nueva España), 97, 99
Coatac (Pima ranchería), 202
Cobesia, Francisco, 124, 265n. 40
Cocóspera Mission, 148, 150
coinage: *doblones de* dos, 44, 242n. 114; *ducados de vellon*, 21, 23, 24, 25, 30, 237n. 9, 239n. 47; *escudos*, 105; *maravedís*, 34; *pesos*, 68, 99, 112, 181, 182, 218, 219, 224, 261n. 110, 267n. 64; *reales de plata*, 24, 25, 51; *txanponak*, 34, 42
*Colegio de las Vizcaínas*, 218, 219, 224
Colorado (state), xv
Colorado River, 189, 191
Comacavitcam (Pima ranchería), 126
Comanche Indians. *See Indios*
*Compañía de Jesús* (Company of Jesus). *See* Jesuits
*compañía volante de campaña* (flying campaign company), 56, 85, 90, 95, 97, 98, 99, 107
Company of Jesus. *See* Jesuits
Compostela. *See* Santiago de Compostela
Conchos (Nueva Vizcaya, Nueva España), 98
Contreras, Antonio, 85, 213
Contreras, Juan, 160, 216, 282n. 45
Corella, Francisco Felix, 97
Corodéguachi. *See* Fronteras
Corodéguachi (spring), 107, 109
Coronado. *See* Vásquez de Coronado, Francisco
*corriendo la posta*, 183
Cortés Monroy, Manuel, 158, 174, 177, 178
Council of the Indies, 204
Council of Trent, 14, 16, 27

councilman. *See regidor*
cousin. *See lehengusutipi*
cowboy. *See vaquero*
*coyote* (caste), 56, 186
creosote bush, 57
Crespo y Monroy, Benito (bishop of Durango), 124, 126, 157, 158, 181, 199, 200; signature, 199
*criollo* (born in America), xv, 202
Cruz, Tomás de la, 63
*cuartales*, 48
Cuba, 201
Cuchusuamea, Dionisio, 161, 163
Cucurpe (Sonora, Nueva España), 55, 140–47, 163, 180, 201, 245n. 13
*cuera*, 91, 100, 110, 118, 258n. 40
Culiacán (Sinaloa, Nueva España), xiii, 52, 54, 180
Cuquiárachi (Sonora, Nueva España), 71, 101, 108, 109, 110, 111, 112, 148, 151–56
*curador(a)*, 28, 48, 49
*Curso Moral*, 166
*Curso Salmantino*, 166

Delgado, Miguel, 190
deputy justice. *See teniente de justicia mayor*
desert broom, 71
*Día de San Juan*, 34, 107, 155, 185, 240n. 67
*Día de San Miguel*, 29, 31
*Día de Santiago*, 134, 268n. 82
*Diana* (written works of), 166
Díaz del Carpio, José, 205, 207; signature, 207
Dionisio (Indian), 162, 163
Divisadero Ranch, 122
*doblones de dos*. *See* coinage
Dolores (Sonora, Nueva España), 146, 149, 150, 201
Dolores Mission, 55
Dominguez, Ignacio, 171

Dominguez, Joseph, 212
Dominguez, Manuel, 74
Dominguez, Salvador, 211
Don Gregorio. *See* Álvarez Tuñon y Quirós, Gregorio
Don Martín. *See* Ibarburu, Martín de
Don Pelayo (king of Asturias), 5
Don Raphael. *See* Pacheco Zeballos, Raphael
Doña Gregoria. *See* Gómez de Silva, Gregoria Catalina
Donostia, Gipuzkoa, España (San Sebastián), 11, 15, 18, 21, 22, 26, 27, 28, 34, 41, 42, 45, 46, 53, 208
Douglass, William A., 5
*ducados de vellon. See* coinage
Duque de la Conquista, 203–4, 208
Durán, Juan Antonio, 81, 100
Durango, Nueva España, 82, 96, 101, 124, 158, 181, 182, 198, 199, 200

Ebro River, 2
Echagoyen, Juan de, 144, 166–68, 176, 217, 273n. 143; signature, 217
Echavarri, Francisco Antonio, 218
Echave y Barrutia, Juan Bauptista García de, 89
Echaves, Joseph de, 212
Echenique, Pedro de, 198–99, 201, 202; note written in Suamca mission register, 202; signature, 202
Echevarria, José de (Father Visitor), 149, 190, 275n. 161
Echeveste, Blasio de, 45, 46
*edaritegi(ak)*, 23, 27
Egino, Asencio de, 52
Egino, José de, 26, 35, 44
Egino, Miguel Antonio de, 52
*El Anciano de la Soledad. See* Ibarburu, Martín de
El Andalus, España, 5
El Paso del Norte (present-day Texas), 82, 109, 117
elderberry, 2, 57

Elejabeitia (Bizkaia, España), 29
Elgorriaga, Gracia de, 16, 17; family tree, 33
Elizacoechea, Martín de (bishop of Durango), 198, 200–203; signature, 201
Elizondo, Martín de, 138
Endaia. *See* Hendaia
England, 46
Ereñozu, Alonso de, 16, 27
Ereñozu, Mariana de, 27, 44, 48, 49
Ereñozu iron works. See *ferrerías de Ereñozu*
Errotaburu (farm), 47
Escalante, Francisco Xavier, 165–66, 168, 175–77
Escalante, Juan Bautista de, 81, 102
*escalera*, 59, 60
*escribano*, 110, 163, 172, 175, 177, 178, 183, 190, 195, 196, 201, 209
*escribano eclesiastico*, 89, 145
*escribano mayor de gobernación y guerra*, 219
*escribano (público) de número*, 14, 20, 23, 30, 31, 48, 69, 70, 75, 125
*escribano real*, 225
*Escritos de Santo Tomás*, 166
Escuadra de Cantábria, 46, 47
*escudos. See* coinage
España (Spain), xiv, xviii, 1, 3, 12, 30, 36, 42, 46, 103, 104, 108, 115, 153, 155, 203, 204, 207, 208
Espinal, Francisco, 97
Espindola, Agustín de, 213
Espindola, Joseph, 212
*espuelas*, 100
*establecimientos de paz*, 120
*estados*, 59
*etxeko jaunak*, 6
Eudeve Indians. See *Indios*
Europe, xix, 4, 37, 42
Europeans, xiii, 117
Euskal Herria (Basque Country), 1–3, 5, 7, 12, 29, 42, 46, 57, 115, 224

Euskara (Basque language), xiv, xvi, 1, 4, 8, 201, 267n. 58, 270n. 110
*expósito*, 75, 76

*fanegas*, 48
Felipe V (king of Spain), 51, 102, 104, 124, 203, 204
Fernandez, Gregorio, 75
Fernando (king of Spain), 11
*ferrerías de Ereñozu*, 27, 45, 46, 48
*ferrerías de Urruzuno*, 48
Figueroa family, 124
flying campaign company. See *compañía volante de campaña*
Fontes, Cristóbal, 85, 98, 211
Francia (France), 1, 7, 10, 12, 26, 31, 32, 36, 42–44, 46, 89
Francis I (king of France), 12
Franks, 4, 6
Fronteras (Sonora, Nueva España—Corodéguachi presidio), xix, xxi, 56, 68, 71, 72, 73, 78, 80, 81, 86, 89, 97, 101, 102, 106, 107, 108, 109, 110, 112, 113, 114, 115–21, 124, 125, 127, 128, 132, 136, 139, 147, 151–56, 158, 164, 166, 169, 176, 177, 180, 182, 183, 184, 188, 189, 193, 195, 197, 200, 203, 204, 205, 207, 208, 209, 217, 225; presidial captains, 250–51n. 83; presidio boundaries, 262n. 2
Fuensaldaña, Jacinto, 73, 250n. 83, 251n. 85, 253n. 116
*fueros*, 5, 29, 49

*gachupín* (European born), xv,
Gadsden Purchase, 158
Galardi, Juan de, 16, 21, 22, 23, 30, 75
Galicia, España, 5, 10
Gallardi, Luis María, 95, 114, 262n. 121
Gallardo, María Ana, 174
Gallo (Nueva Vizcaya, Nueva España), 97
Gamarra (Araba, España), 207
Gamboa, Francisco Xavier de, 62
Garazi Valley, 7

*garbileku*. See Hernani, Leoka garbileku
García, Juan Lorenzo, 160, 282n. 45
García, María Manuela, 143, 272nn. 135, 136
García, Ramos, 150
García Ramirez IV (king of Nafarroa), 11
Garduño, Francisco de, 218; signature 218
Garnica, Tomás de, 197, 218; signature 218
Garrastegui, Francisco de, 189–92, 218, 284n. 78
Gascones (ancient Basque tribe), 4
Gasteiz, Araba, España (Vitoria), 42
Gate to Hell. See Hernani, Ifernura Atea
Gautegiz de Arteaga (Bizkaia, España), 59
Genovese, José María (Jesuit visitor), 73, 89, 92, 93
German, Francisco Xavier, 272n. 135
German, Luis Ignacia, 272n. 135
German, María Guadalupe, 202, 272n. 135
German, Mariana, 202
German, Xavier, 143
Germany, 89
Gernika (Bizkaia, España), 29
Gernika, Tree of, 29
gila monster, 57
Gila River, 115, 189, 191
Gipuzkoa, España, 1, 5, 10, 11, 13, 15, 27, 46, 69, 72, 74, 82, 121, 178, 208, 224
Goicoechea, José de, 72, 77, 87, 88, 89, 249n. 75
Goicoechea, Josefa de, 26, 44
Goicoechea, Martín de, 89
Gomendio Urrutia, Domingo de, 197, 218; signature, 219
*gomesillo*, 148
Gómez, Marcial, 212
Gómez de Silva family, 230n. 17
Gómez de Silva, Gregoria Catalina, 82, 83, 86, 103, 104, 151, 152; burial record, 103
Gómez de Silva, José, 83, 86, 99, 211

Gómez de Silva, Nicolasa, 83, 89, 125, 207, 226, 257n. 34
Gómez de Silva, Pedro, 83
Gómez Robledo, Francisco Ignacio, 85, 86, 211
Gómez Robledo, Juan Ignacio, 99, 100
Gomiziaga, Miguel de, 64
Gonzales, Andrés, 215, 282n. 45
Gonzales de la Cueva, Diego, 194
Gonzalez de Mercado, Juan, 59, 65, 66
Gorraez, José de, 219; signature, 219
Gortazar, Blas de, 178–79, 219; signature, 219
Goths, 4, 6
Gran Quivira, 191
Gran Teguayo, 191
Granillo, Antonia, 107
Grazhoffer, Juan Bautista (IHS), 122, 126, 127
Great Plains, xiv
Gregorio, 215
Gregory XIII, Pope, 26
Griego, Francisco, 98, 211
Grijalva family, 124
Grijalva, Francisco, 85, 212
Guadalajara, Nueva España, 74, 75, 189, 191
*guardamontes*, 31
Guaymas (Sonora, Nueva España), 183, 185, 187
Guaymas Indians. See *Indios*
Guepavérachi (Sonora, Nueva España), 164, 224
Guevavi (Sonora, Nueva España), 121–27, 160, 168, 178, 195, 200, 201, 265n. 39; mission, 122, 123, 125, 126, 127, 157, 158, 168, 199, 207, 266n. 50; ranch, xiii, xix, 121, 122, 124, 125, 127, 145, 168, 226
*Guía del viaje a Santiago*, 7
Gulf of California (South Sea), xix, 55, 115, 128, 132, 185, 190
Guraya, Juan Domingo de, 217, 219, 225; signature, 219

Gusutaqui (Pima ranchería), 123, 265n. 39
Gutzutag. *See* Gusutaqui

*hacienda de labor* (farm or ranch), 84, 208
*hacienda de sacar plata*, 58, 61, 64, 66, 246n. 24
handball. See *pilota*
handball court. See *pilota leku*
hard tack. See *bizcocho*
*hechicero*, 188
Hendaia (Lapurdi, Francia), 10, 31, 32, 42–44, 45
Herauso, Francisco de, 21, 22, 30, 52
Herauso, Ignacio de, 52
Herauso, Mariana de, 23, 35
Herauso, Sebastián de, 35
Herauso, Sebastián Manuel de, 52
Hermosillo (Sonora, Mexico), 245n. 5
Hernani (Gipuzkoa, España), xiii, xvii, xviii, 7, 11, 12, 13, 14–53, 54, 69, 70, 75, 82, 103, 104, 105, 106, 108, 153, 217, 227n. 6, 235nn. 56, 66; Congreso General, 30; fiesta, 240n. 67; fort, 35, 36; fuero, 11; gela andi; 22, 30; Ifernura Atea, 13; Kale Kardaberaz, 12, 13, 17, 19, 22, 23, 27, 42; Kale Nagusia, 12, 13, 16, 17, 19, 21, 32, 41, 42, 44; Karabel Bridge, 37, 42, 241n. 80; Leoka garbileku, 18, 35, 41, 241n. 74; letter to native sons, 260n. 86; map, 36; Plaza Nagusia, 12, 16, 27, 34, 35, 38; Sala principal, xviii; San Agustín convento, 37; San Juan Bautista parish, xvii, 12, 16, 17, 21, 23, 25, 26, 32, 36, 38, 39, 40, 105; Santa Barbara fort, 37, 241n. 82; *udaletxe*, xvii, 12, 21, 22, 23, 29, 35, 50, 69, 235n. 68
*herrero*, 126
*hidalguía* (*hijos dalgo*), 11, 12, 69, 70, 235n. 59
Holy Roman Empire, 12
Huepac (Sonora, Nueva España), 71, 80

Huesca, España, 4
Huguenots, 89
Hugues San Martín, Baltazar, 97
Hugues San Martín, Manuel de, 77
Huidobro, Manuel Bernal de, 116, 132, 133, 134, 139, 144, 270n. 109; birthplace, 273n. 141

Ibarburu, Martín de (El Anciano de la Soledad), 59, 60, 64, 66, 73, 86, 88, 89, 251n. 83, 256n. 21, 257nn. 29, 31
Ibarra, Cristóbal de, 211
Iberian Peninsula, 3, 4
IHS. *See* Jesuits
Ímuris (Sonora, Nueva España), 125, 141, 143, 146, 147, 148
Indians. See *Indios*
*Indias* (Indies), 51
*Indios* (Indians), 56, 60, 68, 77, 142, 154, 162, 172, 179, 186, 266n. 51; Apache, xiv, xix, 51, 56, 73, 78, 79–81, 83, 84, 91, 96, 99, 103, 108, 113, 114, 115–21, 122, 126, 132, 136, 137, 190, 192, 196, 205, 206, 207, 220, 227n. 6, 254n. 133, 263nn. 11, 14; 286n. 128; Cocomaric O'opa, 115, 262n. 4; Eudeve, 116, 263n. 7; Guaymas, 55, 56, 115, 183, 185, 186, 204, 286n. 122; Janos, 83, 84, 99; Jocome, 83; Nijora, 126, 267n. 52, 272n. 130; O'opa, 115; Opata, 55, 56, 70, 71, 72, 80, 108, 113, 114, 116, 119, 121, 125, 126, 141, 146, 150, 156, 185, 263n. 7; Papago (Papabi O'otam), 115, 263n. 5; Pima (O'odham), 56, 96, 113, 114, 116, 119, 122, 123, 124, 125, 126, 127, 133, 137, 138, 140, 141, 142, 143, 146, 147, 164, 185, 190, 191, 196, 200, 202, 263n. 8; Pimas Altos (Piatos), 55, 116, 150; Pimas Bajos (Sibubapas), 55, 56, 116, 150, 183, 245n. 19, 286n. 122; Seri, xix, 56, 114, 115, 128, 132–35, 150, 185, 190, 192, 223, 245n. 19, 261n. 117, 263n. 5; Sobaípuri, 116, 123,
263n. 9; Suma, 83, 84; Ute, 272n. 130; Yaqui (Yoeme), 56, 59, 60, 72, 116, 125, 126, 134–35, 160, 161, 162, 164, 167, 171, 174, 180, 181, 192, 194, 197, 263n. 10, 279–80n. 17; Yuma, 115, 262n. 3
inhabitants. See *vecinos*
Inojos, Juan Ruiz de, 212
Inquisition, Holy Office of the (Santo Tribunal), 162, 163, 180, 195
Iparragire, José de, 47
*irakasle*, 38
Ireland, 56
Iribarren, José de, 46, 50
Irigoien, Josefa de, 26, 27, 28, 32, 34, 42
iron industry in Gipuzkoa, 15
*ironwood*, 57
irrigation ditch. See *acequia*
Irun (Gipuzkoa, España), 7, 10, 26, 43, 70
Iruñea, Nafarroa, España (Pamplona), 6, 10, 15, 24, 42
Isabel (Queen of Spain), 11
Isasa, José de, 46, 50
Isasa, Josefa de, 27
Ituren (Nafarroa, España), 37
Izagirre, Andres de, 31

Jaca (Aragón, España), 6
Jamaica (Sonora, Nueva España), 73, 78, 94, 102, 110, 257n. 31, 258n. 38
James (the apostle), 3, 4, 10
Janos (Nueva Vizcaya, Nueva España), 63, 64, 69, 83, 84, 85, 89, 95, 96, 98, 103, 104, 105, 107, 110, 114, 120, 152, 154, 200, 217; presidio, 64, 66, 79, 80, 82–86, 94, 96, 98–100, 108, 109, 113, 121, 152, 200, 205, 208, 211–13
Janos Indians. See *Indios*
Janos River, 83
Javier, Francisco, 246n. 42
Javier, José, 201
Jesuit Order. *See* Jesuits

Jesuits (Company of Jesus), 54, 55, 60, 64, 73, 74, 86, 87, 88, 89, 91, 92, 93, 95, 125, 127–31, 132, 133, 135–36, 137, 141, 143, 144, 147, 151, 152, 156, 166, 168, 176, 191, 198, 199, 200, 205, 206, 217; brothers, 269n. 95; support from the Basques, 246n. 42
Jimenez, Joseph, 215, 282n. 45
Jocome Indians. See *Indios*
John the Baptist, 34, 155
Jones, William Claude, 158
Juan, *El Sordo*, 48, 51
Juan II (king of Aragón), 10
Juana María (Pima girl), 123
*juez ordinario*, 28
juniper, 71
*justicia mayor*, xiii, 74, 76, 79, 157, 158, 164, 169, 172, 179, 180, 181, 189, 250n. 77
*Justicia y Ley*, 166

Kale Kardaberaz. *See* Hernani
Kale Nagusia. *See* Hernani
Karabel Bridge. *See* Hernani
Kardaberaz, Ana María de, 41
Kardaberaz, Sebastián de, 50
Karrantza (Bizkaia, España), 138
Keller, Ignacio Xavier (IHS), 122, 123, 140, 141, 143, 146–49, 200–202, 206, 208; personal information, 275n. 158
Kino, Eusebio Francisco (IHS), 122, 189, 190
Knights of Santiago. See *Caballeros de Santiago*

La California Mine, 59, 66
*la cuesta de las bolas*. See *planchas y bolas de plata*
La Poza Creek, 58
La Púrica, 71
*La Recopilación de Indias*, 166, 172
La Soledad Mine, 59, 66
Laborda, José de, 208
*ladino*, 63

Laines, Diego, 63, 86, 99, 100, 211
Laines, Dionisio, 213
land grants. See *títulos de merced*
Land of the Upper Pimas. *See* Pimería Alta
Larramendi, Agustín de, 16, 17
Larramendi, Ana María de, 24, 34, 44
Larramendi, Francisco de, 47
Larramendi, Margarita de, 27, 44, 47, 48, 49
Larreta, Juan Domingo de, 40, 153; children, 242n. 99; marriage information, 242n. 94
Lassa, Francisco Antonio de, 87, 88
laurel, 2
Leal, Antonio, 80
Lecumberri, María de, 49, 50, 51
Lecuna, Nicolás de (father), 49, 50, 51
Lecuna, Nicolás de (son), 51, 105
Lecuona, Martín de, 23
leggings (precursors to *chaps*). See *botas*
*lehengusutipi*, 43, 46, 75
Leiva, José de, 170, 220
Leizaola, Juan Bautista de, 98
Leizaur, Ignacio Antonio de, 75
Leizaur, Jose de, 23
Leoka Spring, 18
Leon, Cristóbal de, 80, 89
León, España, 5, 11
Leon, Juan de, 89
lesser nobility. See *hidalguía*
*libra*, 170, 214–16, 280n. 24
*limpieza de sangre*, 75, 77, 78
Lizarraga, Juan de, 36
Llanos de Terrenate, 138
Llavero, Francisco, 151
*lobo* (caste), 56, 179
Logroño, España, 10
Longoria, Francisco de, 160, 175, 177, 191, 192, 218, 220, 222, 282n. 45; mining claim at San Antonio, 177; petition to block Anza, 191; signature, 220

López, Francisco, 162, 170–71, 215
López, Juan Carlos, 170, 215
López, Pedro, 215
López, Tomás, 213
López de Lazcano, García, 10
López de Sequeiros, Nicolás, 162–64
López de Zequeiros, Pedro, 170
Los Ángeles (Sonora, Nueva España), 162, 191
Los Crestones, 71, 138
Los Santos Reyes Magos de Cucurpe. *See* Cucurpe
Louis XII (king of France), 12
Loyola, Iñigo (IHS), 246n. 42, 250n. 80, 269n. 98
Lubelza, Miguel de, 27
Lubelza, Sebastian de, 75
Lucerne, Switzerland, 122
Lugo, Cardinal (written works of), 166
Lujan, Joseph, 212
Luque, Antonia de, 138
Luque, María Josefa de, 125, 138, 266n. 49
Lutherans, 89
Luzero, Antonio, 211
Luzero, Miguel, 211

*macana*, 141
Madraz y Velasco, Juan Miguel, 89
Madrid, Cayetano, 212
Madrid, España, 12, 44, 46, 49
Madrid, Joseph, 213
*maestro molinero*, 47, 48, 51
Magdalena (Sonora, Nueva España), 145, 201; church, 224
*maisu*, 37
*makila*, 26
Maldonado, Juan Antonio, 77
Mamturss (Pima ranchería), 126
Manchón Moreno, Juan, 197
Manje, Juan Mateo, 73, 78, 82, 94, 110, 138, 190, 252–53n. 116; personal information, 251n. 86
*manzanita*, 71

Mapimí (Nueva Vizcaya, Nueva España), 98
*maravedís*. *See* coinage
Marciano, Luis María (IHS), 95, 139–150, 262n. 121, 274nn. 146, 154; signature, 140
*marco*, 162, 216, 280n. 24
Marqués, Juan, 213
Marqués, Matias, 212
Marqués de Casafuerte. *See* Acuña, Juan de
Marqués de Manziera. *See* Medina Dávila, Andrés de
Marqués de Valero. *See* Zuñiga, Baltazar de
Martín, Juan Felipe, 160, 215, 282n. 45
Martín, Juan José, 142, 272n. 135, 282n. 45
Martín, Nicolás, 282n. 45
Martínez, Miguel, 180
Mátape (Sonora, Nueva España), 96
Matidero (Aragón, España), 6
*matlazahuatl*, 199
*mayorazgo*, 48, 49
*mayordomo*, 28, 183, 185, 204
Medina, Blas de, 212
Medina Dávila, Andrés de, 190
Mediterranean Sea, 46
Melgarejo, Ambrosio, 192, 194, 197; calls Anza incompetent, 197; statement about Mesa, 192; statement about too many laws, 194
Mendiguren, Miguel de, 63, 69; signature, 69
Mendivil, Luis de, 180, 218, 220; criticism of Anza, 180; signature, 220
Mendo, Padre (written works of), 166
Merino sheep, 15
Mesa, José de, 162, 163, 171, 191, 192, 218, 220; and claims to have discovered the Arizona Silver, 192; petition to block Anza, 191
*mescal*, 148–49
mesquite, 57, 71, 99

# Index

Mestanza, Francisco Xavier, 55, 245n. 13
*mestizaje*, 126, 230n. 17
*mestizo* (caste), 56, 68, 84, 120, 162, 171, 172, 186, 202, 230n. 17, 266n. 51
Mexico (modern country), xiv, xvi, xviii
Mexico City, 51, 52, 58, 62, 71, 75, 78, 79, 83, 87, 91, 92, 93, 94, 95, 96, 97, 100, 101, 102, 103, 105, 109, 110, 111, 128, 133, 134, 139, 140, 148, 149, 158, 164, 167, 173–81, 183, 189, 191, 192, 193, 197, 198, 199, 201, 204, 208, 217, 218, 219, 224, 225, 226
Michoacán, Nueva España, 201
Milan, Italy, 12
Miner, Antonio de, 23, 36, 46, 49, 51
Miner, Nicolás de, 52
Miner, San Juan de, 30, 31
Miner, Sebastian de, 31, 35, 52, 105
mine-shoring constructor. See *ademadores*
mining in Sonora, 54–69, 70–72, 77, 90, 131, 194, 285n. 93; ordinance number thirty-seven, 67, 245n. 4, 248n. 61, 249n. 62, 278n. 3
Miranda, Antonio de, 72, 77, 89, 91, 220, 249n. 76
Miranda, Francisco Xavier de, 97, 102, 174, 175, 195–97, 220; signature, 220
Miranda, José de, 153
Miranda, Martín de, 24
Mizquia, Salvador, 212
Moctezuma River, 73
Mohammed (prophet), 188
Molina, José Xavier, 201
molinos de Errotaberri, 47, 51, 203
molinos de Zeago, 38, 47, 49, 51, 203
Mondragon, Josefa, 225
Mondragon, Miguel Antonio, 252n. 115
Monroy, Manuel. See Cortés Monroy, Manuel
Montalvo, Melchor, 215, 282n. 45
Montaño, Joseph, 212
Montezuma, legend of, 167, 184–88
Moors, 4, 5, 6, 7

Moraga, Diego, 54
Moraga, Francisco Xavier, 195; signature, 195
Moraga, Sabina, 161, 173, 224
Moraga, Xavier, 123
Moraga, Xavier (son of Ramos García), 150
Moravia, 122
Moreno, Juan, 99, 100, 213
Moreno, Nicolás, 212
Morueta, Antonio Bautista de, 221; signature, 221
Motepore (Sonora, Nueva España), 76, 78, 128, 130, 134, 162, 164, 175, 176, 180, 189, 218, 220, 221, 222, 225
*mulato(a)* (caste), 56, 68, 75, 78, 84, 122
mule packer. See *arriero*
mule train. See *recua*
Munguía Villela, Juan, 138
Muñoz, María, 106
Murrieta, Martín de, 221; signature, 221

Nacozari (Sonora, Nueva España), 60, 61, 62, 71, 92, 108, 152, 224
Nafarroa, España, 1, 26; fuero of, 5, 6, 8, 42, 47; kingdom of, 5, 7, 8, 10
Nájera, España, 10
Negro (race), 68, 161
New Mexico. See Nuevo México
New Spain. See Nueva España
New Vizcaya. See Nueva Vizcaya
New World, xiii, xvi, 4, 9, 13, 36, 54, 104, 121, 123, 136, 201, 203, 206, 207, 208, 209, 219
Neyra, Barbara de, 272n. 130
Neyra, Francisco de, 142, 272n. 130
Nicolás (Negro ladino crier), 62, 63, 64, 67
Nieto, Andres (IHS), 128, 130, 137, 140, 141, 143, 147, 148
*nopal* (prickly pear cactus), 71
North Sea. See Pacific Ocean

notary public. See *escribano (público) de número*
Nuestra Señora de Aránzazu de Tetuachi. See Tetuachi
Nuestra Señora de la Bien Aparecida Mine, 59
Nuestra Señora de los Dolores de Cósari. See Dolores
Nuestra Señora de Rosalia del Oro (*real de minas*), 71, 207
Nuestra Señora del Rosario de Nacozari. See Nacozari
Nueva España (Spain), xiii, xix, 51, 52, 54, 55, 89, 99, 102, 104, 109, 182, 194, 201, 204, 219, 224, 225
Nueva Vizcaya, xiii, 63, 74, 76, 92, 95, 97, 105, 106, 182, 198, 202, 248n. 59
Nuevo México, xv, 13, 102, 182
Nuñez, Antonio, 55
Nuñez, Blas, 55
Nuñez, José, 121, 195–97
Núñez, Juan, 121, 122; marriage information, 264nn. 31, 35

oak trees, 2, 57, 71
*Obras del Doctor Torresilla*, 166
Obtuavo (Pima ranchería) 123, 126, 202
Ocampo, Antonio de, 170, 180
Ocampo, Ignacio de, 60, 65, 66
Ocanto, Juan López de, 98, 211
Ochoa, Nicolás Alfonso de, 160, 173, 174–78, 196, 215, 221, 282n. 45
*ocotillo* (cactus), 71, 99
Officer, Jim, vii, xvii, xxi
Ogillurreta, Miguel de, 70, 75
Oiartzun (Gipuzkoa, España), 10, 43
*oidor*, 218, 223
Oiza, Antonia de, 45
Olacho, Cristóbal, 89
Olave, José de, 195, 221; signature, 221
Olazabal, Francisco de, 14
Ollo, Alonso de, 30

Olloquiegui, Dorotea de, 27, 28
Olvera, Joseph de, 216
Oñate, Juan de, 190
Oñati (Gipzukoa, España), 72
one fire, one vote. See suffrage
*onza*, 215, 216, 280n. 24
O'opa Indians. See *Indios*
Opata Indians. See *Indios*
Opatería, 199
Opodepe (Sonora, Nueva España), 176, 245n. 13
Oquitoa, Realito de, 167
Orcolaga, José de, 35
Orcolaga, Nicolás de, 27, 28
ore carrier. See *tanatero*
organ pipe cactus, 57, 71
Oro, Nicolas de (IHS), 93, 133, 156, 255n. 9; signature, 93
Ortega, Julian de, 84
*orza*, 48
Osorio, José de, 160, 162, 173, 221; signature, 221
Ostimuri, Nueva España, 185, 221
Oviedo, Juan Antonio de, 135, 269n. 91
Ozaeta Gallaistegui, Juachín Ignacio de, 89

Pacheco, Francisco, 98, 211
Pacheco Zeballos, Francisco, 80
Pacheco Zeballos, Raphael, 74, 75, 76, 80, 87, 88; marriage information, 251n. 92
Pacific Ocean (North Sea), 191
pack string. See *recua*
Padilla, Andres Sánchez de, 77, 175, 176, 178–81, 195–97, 225; signature, 225
Páez y Guzmán, Francisco, 76–78
*paloverde*, 57
Pamplona (Nafarroa, España). See Iruñea
*paniaguado*, 251–52n. 99
*panino*, 59, 193, 246n. 27
Papabi O'otam Indians. See *Indios*
Papago Indians. See *Indios*
Parra, Francisco Xavier de la, 213

Parral (Nueva Vizcaya, Nueva España), 58, 61, 71, 78, 92, 94, 96, 97
Parras (Nueva Vizcaya, Nueva España), 97
*partido*, 59
Pasaje (Nueva Vizcaya, Nueva España), 97
Patti, Italy, 95
Paul (the apostle), 3, 4
Pavia, Italy, 12
peace settlements. See *establecimientos de paz*
Peña, Baltazar de la, 89
Peña, Manuel de la, 212
Peralta, Andrés de, 252n. 115
Perea, Hijinia, 225
Perea, Pedro, 138, 270n. 107
Perera, Nicolás de (IHS), 132, 133, 140–51, 180, 201
Pérez Serrano, Ana María, 222
Pérez Serrano, Francisco, 72, 162, 176, 177, 179, 216, 222, 250n. 78; accuses Anza of injustice, 179; signature, 222
*pesos*. See coinage
Petriz de Cruzat, Domingo Jironza, 250n. 83, 251n. 86, 252–53n. 116, 254n. 4
pharmacist. See *boticario*
Picado Pacheco, Domingo, 101
Picaud, Amery, 7–9
*pilota*, 38, 241n. 89
*pilota leku*, 36, 38
Pima Indians. See *Indios*
Pimas Altos. See *Indios*
Pimas Bajos. See *Indios*
Pima uprising, 85
Pimería Alta, 55, 102, 108, 114, 121, 124, 127, 133, 143, 148, 149, 155, 157, 158, 165–69, 178, 182, 184, 185, 188, 192–94, 199, 200, 201, 204, 224
Pimería Baja, 183, 184, 191, 193, 203, 220
pine trees, 2, 57, 71
Pitic (Sonora, Nueva España), 55, 208
Piticai (Pima ranchería), 126

Plains of Terrenate. See Llanos de Terrenate
Planchas de Plata Canyon, 159
*planchas y bolas de plata*, 164, 169, 177, 193, 198
*platero*, 174
Ponce, José, 97
Ponce de León, Francisco Xavier, 103, 106, 107
Pony Express, 193, 285n. 88
poplar trees, 2
Pópulo (Sonora, Nueva España), 132, 133, 134, 140, 150, 162, 203
Portu, Juan Beltran de, 46
Portugal, 115
prickly pear cactus. See *nopal*
proof of nobility. See *prueba de nobleza*
Protestants, 89
Prudhom Butrón y Mujica, Gabriel, 129, 134, 139, 159, 218, 221–22, 267n. 61, 268–69n. 85; signature, 222
Prudhom map. See Arizona, so-called Prudhom map of
Prudhom report, 159
*prueba de nobleza*, 75
Puebla, Nueva España. See Puebla de los Ángeles
Puebla de los Ángeles, Nueva España, 199
Pyrenees Mountains, 2, 5, 6, 10, 15

Querétaro, 105
Quiburi (Pima ranchería), 202
Quino (Pima ranchería), 122
*quintal*, 198, 285n. 97
Quiros y Nerea, Nicolas, 160, 222, 282n. 45
Quitoabo (Pima ranchería), 202

Ramírez, Juan Antonio, 165–66, 168, 175
Ramírez, Juan José, 110
Ramiro I (king of Aragón), 5
Rapicani, Alejandro (IHS), 200–202
rattlesnake, 57

Raum (Pima ranchería), 126
*Real Acuerdo*, 194, 195, 198, 218, 223
*Real Audiencia*, 62, 170, 191, 192, 204, 217, 219
*real cédula* (royal decree), xiv, 51, 203–5
Real Chancillería, 36, 46, 49
*real de minas* (royal mining camp), 54, 60, 61, 63, 68, 70, 71, 76, 121, 150, 162, 164, 196, 220
*reales de plata*. See coinage
Recarte, Pedro de, 46
*recua* (pack train), 58, 71
*regidor*, 28, 29, 30, 31, 75
Remedios (Sonora, Nueva España), 146, 147, 148; mission, 146
*repartimiento* system, 60
*respuesta a varias calumnias*, 92, 93, 253n. 124, 255n. 9
Rezabal, Andrés de, 94, 96, 259n. 58
Ricibas (Pima ranchería), 202
Río Frio, Francisco de, 76
Rivera, Juachín José de, 74–79, 94, 251–52n. 99
Rivera, Juan Antonio de, 160, 282n. 45
Rivera, Pedro de, 109, 110, 111, 112, 113; signature, 111
Rivera, Teresa de, 76
Rodríguez, Antonio, 84
Rodríguez, Francisco Xavier, 85, 213
Rodríguez, Jorge, 65
Rodríguez, Joseph, 211
Rodríguez, Juan Marqués, 85, 212
Rojas, Carlos de (IHS), 151, 152, 154, 155; signature, 152
Romano, Alejandro, 92, 93, 95, 96, 259n. 64
Romano, Francisco Pedro, 151
Romans, 3, 4, 7, 15
Romero, Cristóbal, 124, 225
Romero, Diego, 124, 140, 158, 175, 225
Romero, Ignacio, 124, 225
Romero, José, 123, 124, 139, 140, 162, 168, 175, 176, 178, 184, 225, 283n. 63; signature, 225

Romero, Miguel, 212
Romero, Nicolás, 124, 225
Romero family, 178, 225
Romo de Vivar, José, 138, 270n. 107
Roncesvalles (Nafarroa, España), 6; battle of, 6
Roteta, Josefa de, 47, 49, 50
Rowland, Donald, 116
Royal Council of Castilla, 198
royal decree. See *real cédula*
royal mining camp. See *real de minas*
Royal Silver Bank, 194, 195
*ruedas*, 48
Ruiz, María Nicolasa, 121
Ruiz Calderón, José, 76
Ruiz de Ael, Santiago, 162–64, 169, 171, 174, 180, 181, 196, 215, 217, 219, 225; criticism of Anza, 180; signature 163; takes pity on Siraumea, 180–81

*sabanero*, 125, 126, 266n. 51
*sacada de gallo*, 231n. 18
Saeta, Francisco Xavier (IHS), 256n. 19
Sagade, Joseph, 77
*sagardoa*, 42
Saint James, Order of. See *Caballeros de Santiago*
Salazar, Francisco Ramirez de, 250n. 83
Salazar, Joseph Antonio de, 252n. 115
Salazar, Manuel Vicente, 125
Salmón, Francisco, 65, 179–80, 216
Salvador (Indian), 179
Samaniego, María Rosa, 122; marriage information, 264nn. 31, 35
Samaniego, Pablo, 122
Sambrano, Ignacio, 195, 196
Sambrano, José, 84, 213
San Agustín. See Hernani, San Agustín convento
San Andres de la Cananea. See Cananea
San Antonio de Casas Grandes. See Casas Grandes
San Antonio de Motepore. See Motepore

San Antonio de Padua, 34, 59, 240n. 69; site of *planchas de plata* silver discovery, 169–71, 173–80, 182, 183, 189, 192, 193–98, 218, 220, 221, 222, 225
San Antonio Mine (Aldamiz), 59, 66
San Antonio Mine (Anza), 59, 61, 66
San Antonio Pass, 168
San Bartolomé (Nueva Vizcaya, Nueva España), 97, 98
San Buenaventura Valley (Nueva Vizcaya, Nueva España), 83, 103, 104, 207
Sanchez, Nicolás, 111
Sánchez de Santa Ana, Francisco, 110
Sancho el Mayor (king of Nafarroa), 11, 233n. 23
Sancho Garcés III (king of Nafarroa), 5
San Felipe y Santiago de Janos. *See* Janos, presidio
San Felipe y Santiago de Sinaloa. *See* Sinaloa Presidio
San Francisco, California, 230n. 16
San Francisco de Conchos. *See* Conchos
San Francisco Xavier de Tucuaba, 54
San Ibañes, Joseph, 75
San Ignacio (Sonora, Nueva España), 55, 95, 96, 114, 124, 133, 139–49, 151, 152, 155, 159, 160, 161, 174, 175, 200–203, 220; church, 224; mission records, 264n. 23
San Ignacio de Cabórica. *See* San Ignacio (Sonora, Nueva España)
San Ignacio de Cuquiárachi. *See* Cuquiárachi
San Jago (Pima Indian), 123
San Jago de Obtuavo. *See* Obtuavo
San José de Basochuca. *See* Basochuca
San Juan, Fiesta de. *See Día de San Juan*
San Juan Bautista, 62, 65, 86, 87, 101, 224; capital of Sonora, 61, 65; citizens' meeting, 87; *real de minas*, 61, 65, 121; secret meeting, 87, 88, 89

San Juan de Santa Cruz, Manuel, 74, 75, 76, 78
San Lázaro (Sonora, Nueva España), 138, 178
San Luis de Bacadéguachi. *See* Bacadéguachi
San Luis Valley, 121, 122, 123, 124, 125, 126, 138, 139, 140, 158–60, 162, 168, 175, 176, 179, 195, 196, 199, 218, 220–23, 225
San Mateo (ranch), xiii, 121, 122, 125, 225
San Miguel, Fiesta de. *See Día de San Miguel*
San Miguel de Bacoachi. *See* Bacoachi
San Miguel de Ures. *See* Ures
San Miguel River, 54, 55, 191, 203
San Pedro (Pima ranchería), 202
San Pedro de Gallo. *See* Gallo
San Pedro de la Conquista Presidio (Pitic), 208
San Pedro River, 115, 122, 138
San Salvador de Leire (Nafarroa, España), 11
San Sebastián (Gipuzkoa, España). *See* Donostia
Santa Ana (Sonora, Nueva España), 161, 173, 223
Santa Barbara del Cajón, 71
Santa Barbara Ranch, 124, 158, 162, 164, 168, 176–78, 195
Santa Catalina (Pima ranchería), 202
Santa Cruz (Pima ranchería), 202
Santa Cruz (present-day town in Sonora), 209, 288n. 140
Santa Cruz River, 115, 122, 124–26, 168, 183, 199, 205, 207
Santa Fe, Nuevo México, 84, 109, 117, 197, 218
Santa Magdalena (Pima ranchería), 202. *See also* Magdalena, Sonora
Santa Magdalena River Valley, 55
Santa María (Church of Zeanuri), 29
Santa María de Parras. *See* Parras

Santa María Suamca. *See* Suamca
Santa Rosa de Corodéguachi. *See* Fronteras
Santa Rosalia del Oro, 71, 224
Santiago de Compostela, 4, 7, 9, 10, 11, 15
Santiago de Mapimí. *See* Mapimí
Santo Tribunal. *See* Inquisition, Holy Office of the
Santos, Antonia de los, 84
Santos de San Pedro, Juan Grande (bishop of Pamplona), 24
Santos Reyes Magos, los. *See* Cucurpe
San Vicente Mine, 59
San Xavier del Bac Mission, 122, 126–27, 199, 201, 202
Saracachi (Sonora, Nueva España), 71, 200
Saraube, 29
Saric (Sonora, Nueva España), 196; mission livestock, 266n. 50
Sarmiento, José de, 97
Sasabac (Pima ranchería), 142, 160
Sasoeta, Alonso de, 52
Sasoeta, Catalina de, 22, 23, 40, 41
Sasoeta, Domingo de, 22, 23, 24, 25, 32, 34
Sasoeta, Francisca de, 22, 52
Sasoeta, Juanes de (brother of Lucia de Sasoeta), 22
Sasoeta, Juanes de (father of Lucia de Sasoeta), 22; family tree, 33
Sasoeta, Lucia de (wife of Antonio de Anza), 19, 21–28, 32, 34, 37, 40, 42, 44, 52, 53, 106, 153; dowry, 238n. 32; family tree, 33
Sasoeta, María Josefa de, 22, 52
Sasoeta, Nicolás de, 22, 27, 28, 31, 32, 42–44, 45, 50
Sasoeta family, 22, 24, 52, 238n. 28
scorpions, 57, 58
Scucbac (Pima ranchería), 202
sedan chair, 147, 148, 200

Segesser von Brunneg, Felipe, 122, 126, 127, 184, 187, 283n. 64; signature, 122
Segovia, España, 26
Segura, Claudio Antonio, 160, 222, 282n. 45; signature, 222
Segura (Gipuzkoa, España), 11
*senita* (cactus), 57
Señora de la Límpia Concepción del Pasaje. *See* Pasaje
Seri: expedition, 132–35; 1725 war, 223
Seri Indians. See *Indios*
Sesma, Juan de, 222; signature, 222
Seug Bag (Pima ranchería), 126
Seug Tuburss (Pima ranchería), 126, 202
Seven Cities (of Cíbola), 191
Sevilla, España, 30, 40
shield. See *adarga*
Sicurisuta (ranch), xiii, xix, 125, 266n. 47
Sicurisutac (ranch), 125, 266n. 47
Sierra, Rosa de, 65
Sierra de Chiricahua, xix, 81, 108, 115, 117
Sierra del Carmen, 71
Sierra Espuelas, 108, 138
Sierra Huachuca, 138
Sierra Madre, 59, 61, 94, 108, 138
Sierra San Antonio, 71
Sierra Santa Teresa, 58
silver smelter. See *hacienda de sacar plata*
Sinaloa Presidio, 94, 112, 113, 190, 203
Sinaloa Province, xiii, xix, 52, 96, 132, 133, 134, 182, 185, 270n. 109
*sindico procurador*, 22, 29, 30, 31, 70
Sinoquipe (Sonora, Nueva España), 71, 80, 179
Siraumea, Antonio, 160–65, 167, 168, 171, 174, 177, 180, 181, 192, 194, 197, 214, 279–80n. 17
Sobaipuri Indians. See *Indios*
Sobrarbe, España, 1, 5–6
Soledad, mining camp, 140

Solis, Timoteo, 212
Somoza, Marcos de, 133, 268n. 80
Sonoita Creek, 125
Sonoitac Mission, 123, 126
Sonora, Nueva España, xiv, xviii, xix, 13, 54, 59, 60, 61, 62, 63, 65, 67, 70, 73, 74, 75, 77, 79, 80, 81, 82, 83, 85, 86, 87, 88, 89, 92, 93, 94, 95, 96, 97, 99, 100, 101, 103, 107, 108, 112, 113, 114, 116, 121, 127, 132, 134, 136, 139, 144, 152, 156, 158, 161, 162, 163, 167, 169, 173, 175, 179, 180, 189–95, 199, 200, 202, 204, 208, 218, 220, 221, 223, 224, 248n. 59, 270n. 109
Sonoran Desert, 57, 58, 108
Sonora River, xiv, 55, 62, 70, 71, 72, 164, 166, 176, 183, 200
Sonora secret meeting, 89, 92
Sópori (Sonora, Nueva España—present-day Arizona), 126; ranch, xiii, 125–27, 138
Soroa, Feliciana de, 24
Soroa, Francisco de, 23
Soroa, Ignacio de, 46
Sosa, Ana Gertrudis, 125, 265n. 42
Sosa, Luis Ignacio, 125, 265n. 42
Sosa, Manuel José de, xvi, 79, 80, 89, 92, 121, 125, 168–72, 175–78, 181–83, 189, 190, 192, 193–97, 207, 226, 267n. 58; fast ride to Mexico, 284–85nn. 87–88; "relative" of Anza, 158, 279n. 8; signature, 226
South Sea. *See* Gulf of California
Spain. *See* España
Spaniards (Spanish), xv, xvi, 36, 55, 63, 64, 68, 73, 77, 79, 84, 106, 114, 117, 118, 119, 120, 123, 124, 126, 132, 141, 145, 146, 150, 153, 158, 159, 162, 172, 184, 186, 187, 192, 199, 202, 209, 225, 245n. 19, 260n. 90, 266n. 51
Spanish Civil War, 12
Spanish language. *See* castellano
Spibah (Pima ranchería), 126

Stiger, Gaspar, 148, 180, 201, 202
Stonssutag (Pima ranchería), 126
Suamca, 122, 123, 127, 138, 140, 148–49, 160, 168, 199–202, 205, 208, 288n. 140
suffrage, 30
Suma Indians. *See Indios*

*tanate*, 60, 173, 214
*tanatero*, 60, 74, 160, 251n. 91
*tapestles*, 184, 283n. 66
*tapisques*, 60, 73, 87
Tápiz, Pedro (bishop of Durango), 199
Tarahumara (province), 182
Tarazona (Aragón, España), 26, 95
Taupari (Pima ranchería), 126
Taxco (Nueva España), 208
Tecoripa (Sonora, Nueva España), 150, 184, 188
*teniente de justicia mayor*, 58, 68, 75, 163, 164, 175, 176, 184, 195, 221, 223, 225, 249n. 63
Tepoca (Sonora, Nueva España), 141
*tequio*, 59
Terrenate, presidio, 139
Terrenate Ranch, 123, 138, 139, 148, 149, 164, 168, 205, 209, 270nn. 104, 110
Tetuachi (Sonora, Nueva España), xix, 70–74, 76–79, 84, 104, 138, 142, 167, 170, 175, 176, 178, 179, 183, 193, 207, 219, 220, 222, 224
Teuricachi (Sonora, Nueva España), 110
Texas, 102
Thomas, Alfred Barnaby, xv
Tiburón Island, xix, 128, 132, 134; expedition to, 128, 132–35, 136
*títulos de merced*, 124
*tlatol*, 66, 141, 184
Toacuquita (Pima ranchería), 125, 126
Toamuqui (Pima ranchería), 126
Toasin (Pima ranchería), 202
Tolosa (Gipuzkoa, España), 11, 29, 41
Tonacbi (Pima ranchería), 126

*topil*, 60
Toral, José (IHS), 144–49, 156, 166, 167, 198–99; petition on Padre Campos's behalf, 277n. 186; signature, 145
Torres, José de, 50, 51
Torres, Juan de, 105
town hall. *See* Hernani, *udaletxe*
Tubac (Sonora, Nueva España—present-day Arizona), xvii, 122, 126; Presidio, 223
Tubutama (Sonora, Nueva España), 133, 141, 167
Tucson (Pima ranchería), 202
Tuhto (Pima ranchería), 126
Tumacácori Mission, xvii, 126, 207
Tumacácori National Historical Park, xvii
Tupssi (Pima ranchería), 126
Tutumac (Pima ranchería), 126
Tutup (Pima ranchería), 126
Tuvante, Domingo, 123
*txakolin*, 42, 43
*txanponak*. *See* coinage
*txapela*, 23, 26
typhoid. See *matlazahuatl*

Ugalde, Domingo de, 30, 31
Ugalde, José de, 48, 50
Unbas (Pima ranchería), 126
United States, xiv, xvi, xviii, xxi, 158
*upelak*, 48
Upsan (Pima ranchería), 202
Urbieta, Juan de, 12, 36, 51, 235n. 66
Ures (Sonora, Nueva España), 55, 143, 144, 145, 147, 150, 200, 203
Urias, Pedro Regala de, 160, 223, 282n. 45; signature, 223
Urnieta (Gipuzkoa, España), 10
Urrea, Bernardo de, 157–60, 162–65, 169, 170, 173–78, 181, 182, 197, 214, 215, 216, 221, 223; house at Arizona, 169; signature, 223
Urrea, Bernardo Gaspar de, 174
Urruzuno Iron Foundry. See *ferrerías de Urruzuno*

Urumea River, 11, 12, 47
Urumea Valley, 27
Usarraga, José de, 162, 195, 196, 216, 223; signature, 223
Usarraga, José Joaquín de, 160, 162, 223; signature, 223
Usurbil (Gipuzkoa, España), 17, 45

Vaicat (Pima ranchería), 126
Valenzuela, María, 83, 84, 103; wife of Juan Bautista de Anza, 255nn. 10, 11
Valladolid, España, 36, 46, 49
Valladolid, Nueva España, 105
Valladolid High Court. *See* Real Chancillería
*vaquero*, 61, 125, 126, 267n. 51
*vara*, 59, 158, 197, 278n. 6
Vascones (ancient Basque tribe), 4
Vásques, Manuel, 152
Vásquez de Coronado, Francisco, 190
Vásquez Sotuyo, Francisco, 65
*vecinos*, 96, 100, 109, 110, 112, 113, 116, 117, 140, 179, 183, 185
*veedor de cuentas*, 31
Veitia, José de, 223
Velarde, Luis Xavier de (IHS), 55, 147, 149, 150, 201
Velasco, Lorenzo de, 161, 173, 214, 217, 223–24; signature, 224
Vera Cruz, Nueva España, 52, 75, 204
Verdugo, Lázaro de, 180
Verdugo del Castillo, Pedro, 121, 152, 154, 276n. 182
Vidal y Alvaro, Don Antonio, 76
Vildósola, Agustín de, 79, 89, 117, 119, 120, 134, 139, 152, 167, 178–79, 185, 207, 208, 216, 219, 220, 223, 224, 229n. 15; birth information, 253n. 122; commendation of Anza, 179; signature, 224
Vildósola, Gabriel Antonio de, 229n. 15
Vildósola, José Antonio de, 229n. 15
Vildósola Estate, xviii
Vildósola family, xviii

Villa, Juan de, 142, 202, 272n. 135
Villa, María Loreto, 202
Villa, María Rosa, 202
Villa, Pancho, 231n. 18
Villanueva, Luis de, 215
Villegas, Joseph, 215
Vitoria (Araba, España). *See* Gasteiz
Vizarrón, Jacinto Ignacio, 35, 38
Vizarrón, Juan Bautista de, 37–39, 43, 70, 224, 241n. 83
Vizarrón, María Bautista de, 38
Vizarrón y Eguiarreta, Juan Antonio de, 182–84, 189, 193, 195, 197, 203, 204, 218, 223, 224, 226, 286n. 121; personal information, 278n. 7; signature, 225
Vizcaínos (Basques), 3, 4, 7–9, 25, 34, 35, 58, 60, 64, 65, 69, 72–79, 87, 88, 89, 92, 96, 97, 102, 134, 136, 138, 160, 162, 164, 178, 179, 180, 189, 190, 192, 195, 197, 198, 201, 207, 217–26, 269n. 93; support for Jesuits, 246n. 42, 252n. 115, 257nn. 35, 36
Vizcaya. *See* Bizkaia
voting ball. *See* bolilla

washing place. *See* Hernani, Leoka garbileku
weaponry, 118
Wifredo I (king of Cataluña), 5
willows, 99
witch doctor. *See* hechicero
wool trade, in Gipuzkoa, 15

xacal, 58, 59
Xaramillo, Pedro, 213
Ximenez, José, 160

Yaqui Indians. *See* Indios
Yaqui rebellion, 208
Ytasi, Joseph, 123
yucca, 71
Yuma Indians. *See* Indios

Zabala, Agustín de, 21, 22, 23, 28, 30, 35, 40, 41, 47; signature, 28
Zabala, Ana María de, 32
Zacatecas, Nueva España, 99, 208
Zaragoza, España, 5
Zarasua, Juan José de, 225; signature, 225
*zato*, 42
Zeago Grain Mills. *See* Molinos de Zeago
Zeanuri (Bizkaia, España), 29
Zelaya, Juan Manuel de, 89
Zisa (Benafarroa, Francia), xvii, 6, 7, 8, 9, 10, 235n. 48
Zuaznabar, Domingo de, 16, 26, 46
Zuaznabar, Estevan de (capitán), 24, 44
Zuaznabar, Ignacio Antonio de, 52, 105
Zuaznabar, José de, 35, 52, 105
Zuaznabar, Juan Bautista de, 23, 25
Zuaznabar, Juan Francisco de, 50
Zuaznabar, Manuel de, 35
Zuaznabar, Mariana de, 37
Zuaznabar, Miguel Antonio de, 24, 25, 32, 35; *curaduría*, 238n. 33
Zuaznabar, Nicolás de, 75
Zuaznabar, Teodoro de, 24, 25, 32, 34, 35, 44, 104; *curaduría*, 238n. 33
Zuaznabar family, 24, 52, 238n. 28
Zubiate, Ignacio de, 98
Zubiate, José de, 62, 74, 98; personal information, 247n. 49, 251n. 98; signature, 74
Zuñiga, Baltazar de (viceroy), 90, 92, 94

## Juan Bautista de Anza